Your visual blueprint for
programming on the .NET platform

by Jeff Cogswell

Visual

From

maranGraphics®

&

Hungry Minds™

Best–Selling Books • Digital Downloads • e-Books • Answer Networks • e-Newsletters • Branded Web Sites • e-Learning

New York, NY • Cleveland, OH • Indianapolis, IN

Visual C++® .NET: Your visual blueprint for programming on the .NET platform

Published by
Hungry Minds, Inc.
909 Third Avenue
New York, NY 10022

Copyright © 2002 Hungry Minds, Inc.

Certain designs, text, illustrations copyright © 1992–2002 maranGraphics, Inc., used with maranGraphics' permission. All rights reserved. No part of this book, including interior design, cover design, and icons, may be reproduced or transmitted in any form, by any means (electronic, photocopying, recording, or otherwise) without the prior written permission of the publisher.

maranGraphics, Inc.
5755 Coopers Avenue
Mississauga, Ontario, Canada
L4Z 1R9

Library of Congress Control Number: 2001097476

ISBN: 0-7645-3644-3

Printed in the United States of America

10 9 8 7 6 5 4 3 2 1

1V/QZ/QU/QS/IN

Distributed in the United States by Hungry Minds, Inc.

Distributed by CDG Books Canada Inc. for Canada; by Transworld Publishers Limited in the United Kingdom; by IDG Norge Books for Norway; by IDG Sweden Books for Sweden; by IDG Books Australia Publishing Corporation Pty. Ltd. for Australia and New Zealand; by TransQuest Publishers Pte Ltd. for Singapore, Malaysia, Thailand, Indonesia, and Hong Kong; by Gotop Information Inc. for Taiwan; by ICG Muse, Inc. for Japan; by Intersoft for South Africa; by Eyrolles for France; by International Thomson Publishing for Germany, Austria and Switzerland; by Distribuidora Cuspide for Argentina; by LR International for Brazil; by Galileo Libros for Chile; by Ediciones ZETA S.C.R. Ltda. for Peru; by WS Computer Publishing Corporation, Inc., for the Philippines; by Contemporanea de Ediciones for Venezuela; by Express Computer Distributors for the Caribbean and West Indies; by Micronesia Media Distributor, Inc. for Micronesia; by Chips Computadoras S.A. de C.V. for Mexico; by Editorial Norma de Panama S.A. for Panama; by American Bookshops for Finland.

For U.S. corporate orders, please call maranGraphics at 800-469-6616 or fax 905-890-9434.

For general information on Hungry Minds' products and services please contact our Customer Care Department within the U.S. at 800-762-2974, outside the U.S. at 317-572-3993 or fax 317-572-4002.

For sales inquiries and reseller information, including discounts, premium and bulk quantity sales, and foreign-language translations, please contact our Customer Care Department at 800-434-3422, fax 317-572-4002, or write to Hungry Minds, Inc., Attn: Customer Care Department, 10475 Crosspoint Boulevard, Indianapolis, IN 46256.

For information on licensing foreign or domestic rights, please contact our Sub-Rights Customer Care Department at 212-884-5000.

For information on using Hungry Minds' products and services in the classroom or for ordering examination copies, please contact our Educational Sales Department at 800-434-2086 or fax 317-572-4005.

For press review copies, author interviews, or other publicity information, please contact our Public Relations department at 317-572-3168 or fax 317-572-4168.

For authorization to photocopy items for corporate, personal, or educational use, please contact Copyright Clearance Center, 222 Rosewood Drive, Danvers, MA 01923, or fax 978-750-4470.

Screen shots displayed in this book are based on pre-released software and are subject to change.

Trademark Acknowledgments

Permissions

maranGraphics

Certain text and illustrations by maranGraphics, Inc., used with maranGraphics' permission.

 is a trademark of Hungry Minds, Inc.

U.S. Corporate Sales	U.S. Trade Sales
Contact maranGraphics at (800) 469-6616 or fax (905) 890-9434.	Contact Hungry Minds at (800) 434-3422 or (317) 572-4002.

Visual C++® .NET

*Your visual blueprint for
programming on the .NET platform*

maranGraphics is a family-run business located near Toronto, Canada.

At **maranGraphics**, we believe in producing great computer books — one book at a time.

maranGraphics has been producing high-technology products for over 25 years, which enables us to offer the computer book community a unique communication process.

Our computer books use an integrated communication process, which is very different from the approach used in other computer books. Each spread is, in essence, a flow chart — the text and screen shots are totally incorporated into the layout of the spread. Introductory text and helpful tips complete the learning experience.

maranGraphics' approach encourages the left and right sides of the brain to work together — resulting in faster orientation and greater memory retention.

Above all, we are very proud of the handcrafted nature of our books. Our carefully-chosen writers are experts in their fields, and spend countless hours researching and organizing the content for each topic. Our artists

rebuild every screen shot to provide the best clarity possible, making our screen shots the most precise and easiest to read in the industry. We strive for perfection, and believe that the time spent handcrafting each element results in the best computer books money can buy.

Thank you for purchasing this book. We hope you enjoy it!

Sincerely,

Robert Maran

President

maranGraphics

Rob@maran.com

www.maran.com

www.hungryminds.com/visual

CREDITS

Acquisitions, Editorial, and Media Development

Special Contributor
Paul Watters

Project Editor
Jade L. Williams

Acquisitions Editor
Jen Dorsey

Product Development Supervisor
Lindsay Sandman

Development Editor
Kathleen McFadden

Copy Editor
Jill Mazurczyk

Technical Editor
Namir Shammas

Editorial Manager
Rev Mengle

Permissions Editor
Carmen Krikorian

Media Development Specialist
Megan Decraene

Editorial Assistant
Amanda Foxworth

Production

Book Design
maranGraphics®

Production Coordinator
Maridee Ennis

Layout
Melanie DesJardins
LeAndra Johnson
Kristin McMullan

Screen Artists
Mark Harris
Jill A. Proll

Cover Illustration
David E. Gregory

Proofreader
Laura Bowman

Quality Control
John Bitter

Indexer
TECHBOOKS Production Services

Special Help
Microsoft Corporation
Richard Graves

ACKNOWLEDGMENTS

Wiley Technology Publishing Group: Richard Swadley, Vice President & Executive Group Publisher; Bob Ipsen, Vice President & Executive Publisher; Joseph Wikert, Vice President & Publisher; Barry Pruett, Vice President & Publisher; Mary Bednarek, Editorial Director; Andy Cummings, Editorial Director

Wiley Production for Branded Press: Debbie Stailey, Production Director

TABLE OF CONTENTS

Visual C++ .NET:
Your visual blueprint for
programming on the .NET platform

TABLE OF CONTENTS

Visual C++ .NET:
Your visual blueprint for
programming on the .NET platform

TABLE OF CONTENTS

13) MANAGING FILES WITH .NET

14) MAKING A GUI WITH .NET

15) PROGRAMMING WITH .NET DIALOG BOXES

Visual C++ .NET:
Your visual blueprint for
programming on the .NET platform

16) ADDING .NET EVENT HANDLING

17) USING C++ MANAGED EXTENSIONS

18) C++ QUICK REFERENCE

APPENDIX

INDEX

HOW TO USE THIS BOOK

Visual C++ .NET: Your visual blueprint for programming on the .NET platform uses simple, straightforward examples to teach you how to create powerful and dynamic programs. The coding style and examples found in this book are used for instructional purposes. After you are comfortable working with C++ .NET, you can use the coding styles and methods that suit your needs.

To get the most out of this book, you should read each chapter in order, from beginning to end. Each chapter introduces new ideas and builds on the knowledge learned in previous chapters. After you become familiar with C++ .NET, this book can be used as an informative desktop reference.

Who This Book Is For

If you are interested in writing programs for the new Microsoft C++ programming language, *Visual C++ .NET: Your visual blueprint for programming on the .NET platform* is the book for you. This book will take you through the basics of using the Visual Studio Integrated Development Environment (IDE) software and familiarize you with the essentials of C++ programming. The book even covers advanced topics including .NET files, .NET GUI development, and Managed Extensions.

No prior experience with programming is required, but familiarity with the Microsoft Windows operating system installed on your computer is an asset.

Experience with programming languages is also an asset, but even if you have no programming experience, you can use this book to learn the essentials you need to program on the .NET platform using C++.

What You Need To Use This Book

To perform the tasks in this book, you need a computer with Microsoft Windows NT 4.0 or 2000 installed as well as Microsoft Visual Studio .NET. You do not require any special development tools since all the tools are contained within Visual Studio .NET. However, you do need a Web browser such as Microsoft Internet Explorer.

The Conventions In This Book

A number of typographic and layout styles have been used throughout *Visual C++ .NET: Your visual blueprint for programming on the .NET platform* to distinguish different types of information.

Courier Font

Indicates the use of C++ code such as keywords, variables, and functions.

Bold

Indicates information that must be typed by you.

Italics

Indicates a new term being introduced.

Apply It

An Apply It section usually contains a segment of code that takes the lesson you just learned one step further. Apply It sections offer inside information and pointers that can be used to enhance the functionality of your code.

Extra

An Extra section provides additional information about the task you just accomplished. Extra sections often contain interesting tips and useful tricks to make working with C++ easier and more efficient.

The Organization Of This Book

Visual C++ .NET: Your visual blueprint for programming on the .NET platform contains 17 chapters and an appendix. The first chapter, Getting Started with Visual C++ .Net, introduces you to C++, how to start Visual Studio.NET and open a new C++ project, and how you can run the C++ applications that you create.

Chapter 2, Working with C++ Basics, shows you how to use data types such as integers and strings. This chapter also shows you how to create functions that can help you organize your programs.

Chapter 3, Controlling Program Flow, introduces you to the essentials of loops in C++, where you can write lines of code that will run several times until a certain condition is satisfied.

The fourth chapter, Programming with Structures, gets you started with programming more complex data that is more sophisticated than simple numbers and strings.

Visual C++ .NET:
Your visual blueprint for
programming on the .NET platform

Chapters 5, Converting Data Types, shows you how you can easily convert one type of data, such as a number, into another, such as a formatted dollar amount with a currency symbol, thousand separators, and exactly two decimal places.

Chapter 6, Understanding Pointers, teaches you how the data you create is stored in a certain place in memory. When you know the location in memory, you can easily share data with other parts of your program quickly and efficiently.

Chapter 7, Programming with Classes, introduces you to the fundamental building block of object-oriented programming, the class. A class is simply a model consisting of data such as numbers and strings, along with abilities called member functions. Using classes you will learn how you can easily model complex data that includes behaviors.

Chapter 8, Programming with Inheritance, describes how you can take one class and expand on its data and methods to create a new, more specialized class. This new class is said to inherit the data and methods from the original class.

Chapter 9, Debugging Your Program, walks you through the process of debugging a program, and shows you how easy yet powerful this process is. You will see how you can trace through a program line by line and look at the data and see how it changes.

Chapter 10, Programming with .NET Strings, teaches you the new way that .NET handles strings. Strings are simply sequences of letters and numbers, and the .NET framework includes several handy tools that make your string processing easy.

Chapter 11, Programming with .NET Arrays, shows you how you can group together sets of similar data into a sequence called an array, and how this simplifies the storage and processing of similar data. You will also see how you can work with the members of the array individually and share them with other portions of your program.

Chapter 12, Handling Errors with .NET Exceptions, introduces you to the methods for dealing with unexpected situations called exceptions, and how you can be assured that your program will handle these situations properly, without the program crashing.

Chapter 13, Managing Files with .NET, shows you how you can use files to easily store your data onto the hard drive and later read it back in. There are several ways of storing data, and you will learn the different methods.

Chapter 14, Making A GUI with .NET, teaches you how your program can easily open a window, put controls such as buttons and listboxes on the window, and use the window to interact with the user of your program.

Chapter 15, Programming with .NET Dialog Boxes, shows you how you can make use of the standard dialog boxes that Windows provides you with, such as the standard File Open dialog or the standard Font dialog. Using these dialog boxes will save you the time of writing them yourself, and will give your program a standard look and feel.

Chapter 16, Adding .NET Event Handling, introduces you to the concepts of responding to various events such as when the user of your program clicks a button or types text into a textbox control.

Chapter 17, Using C++ Managed Extensions, teaches you about the new features of C++ found in the .NET environment that make C++ programming for Windows easier yet more powerful.

The final chapter contains a C++ quick reference to the various .NET programming features. After you are familiar with the contents of this book, you can use the C++ references to obtain at-a-glance information for some of the most commonly used C++ statements and .NET framework classes.

What Is On The CD-ROM

The CD-ROM disc included in this book contains the sample code from each of the two-page lessons. This saves you from having to type the code and helps you quickly get started creating C++ code. The CD-ROM disc also contains several shareware and evaluation versions of programs that can be used to work with *Visual C++ .NET: Your visual blueprint for programming on the .NET platform*. An e-version of the book and all the URLs mentioned in the book are also available on the disc.

INTRODUCTION TO VISUAL C++ .NET

Visual Studio .NET is the latest Microsoft application development environment and is a huge departure from previous versions of Visual Studio. While the addition of the .NET suffix provides a hint to the changes Microsoft has made to its premiere development tool, it only scratches the surface. Visual Studio .NET enables the programmer to create conventional console and Windows applications, as well as complete Enterprise Web solutions, which are corporate commercial-oriented Web applications.

.NET FRAMEWORK

The .NET suffix comes from the fact that Visual Studio .NET and all its languages are based upon or have full access to the new *.NET Framework*, which is a huge collection of libraries that encapsulates virtually all the functions and objects you need to create full-featured applications for your desktop, or for enterprise applications for the Web.

Besides its comprehensiveness, the .NET Framework provides unified methods for accomplishing most programming tasks with any of the Visual Studio languages. That is, with the exception of minor syntax differences, you accomplish .NET Framework programming tasks the same way in all Visual Studio languages.

The word comprehensive truly describes the .NET Framework, which boasts classes for doing everything from opening a file to displaying a window. The number of classes featured in the framework are almost uncountable and provide support for graphical objects such as buttons, check boxes, text boxes, scroll bars, labels, and menus, just to name a few.

More sophisticated graphical user interface (GUI) components such as dialog boxes, message boxes, TreeView controls, ListView controls, and windows are also included. Further, the .NET Framework features classes for more mundane programming tasks such as file management, error handling, drawing, imaging, threads, and so on.

VISUAL STUDIO LANGUAGES

The complete Visual Studio .NET includes myriad tools for application development, not the least of which are the three main programming languages Visual C# .NET, Visual Basic .NET, and, the language this book covers, Visual C++ .NET. C# is a brand new language that combines the Visual Basic visual tools with the power of C++ programming. For all intents and purposes, Visual Basic .NET, too, is a new language, which only vaguely resembles the previous versions of VB.

VISUAL STUDIO IDE

The Visual Studio integrated development environment (IDE) has undergone extensive changes. Although Visual Studio veterans should be able to find their way around with little effort, Microsoft has focused and streamlined the entire IDE. For example, the IDE now represents all open documents with graphical tabs. To switch to an open document, you need only click the appropriate tab.

Another example of streamlining is how the Microsoft Developers Network (MSDN) documentation and help is fully integrated into the IDE. Not only does the new help system display help topics in its own tabbed page in the IDE, but it also provides what Microsoft calls dynamic help. With dynamic help, the IDE watches what you are doing and automatically displays a list of related help topics.

For example, place the text cursor on a .NET Framework class name in your code, and Visual Studio automatically displays a list of links to related help topics. Moreover, when you are writing your application code, Visual Studio keeps an eye on you, marking syntax errors even as you type. As you learn to use Visual Studio, you will discover many other new conveniences.

HOW VISUAL C++ .NET FITS IN

Of the languages included with Visual Studio .NET, Visual C++ .NET is the least changed from the previous version. There are a couple of reasons for this. Whereas Visual Basic and Visual C# are Microsoft languages that they can define and enhance as they please, the C++ language must adhere to a strict set of guidelines in order to remain true to the ANSI specification. Moreover, unlike Visual Basic .NET and Visual C# .NET, Visual C++ .NET was not designed with .NET Framework managed applications in mind.

A *managed application* is a .NET Framework program that uses such features as automatic garbage collection, which relieves the programmer from having to remember to release allocated memory and resources. Although Visual C++ .NET can request the services for managed applications by specifying options in the code, the language itself does not automatically support managed development. To put it simply, in Visual Basic .NET and Visual C# .NET, managed development is the default. With Visual C++ .NET, managed development is tacked on after the fact.

In this book, you use the Visual C++ Managed Extensions for C++ development, which enables you to take advantage of the features of managed program development.

CREATE A VISUAL C++ .NET SOLUTION

Creating a solution is the first step towards starting a new Visual C++ .NET program. When you create a solution, you create a hierarchy for your projects and files that enables you to better organize everything needed to build an application. Specifically, a *solution* is a container that holds projects, whereas *projects* are containers that hold the files required to build one element of a solution.

Visual Studio creates a solution automatically when you create a new project, if there is not a solution open already, because every project must be contained in a solution. That is, you can create a solution that contains no projects, but you can never create a project that is not contained in a solution.

Some applications may require only a single project in their solutions. Others may require several. For example, you may need to develop an application that is divided into a

main executable file and several DLLs. The main executable file and each DLL can be projects within a single solution. In this case, you would create a single solution and add several projects to the solution.

A project, on the other hand, holds the files required to build one component of the application. For example, the project for the main executable module contains all the source-code files and resources needed to build that component, whereas the DLL projects contain all the files and resources needed to build each DLL.

There are two ways you can create a project. The first is through the File ⇨ New ⇨ Project menu item, which creates a new project with its own solution, and the other is through the File ⇨ Add Project ⇨ New Project menu, which creates a new project inside the existing solution.

CREATE A VISUAL C++ .NET SOLUTION

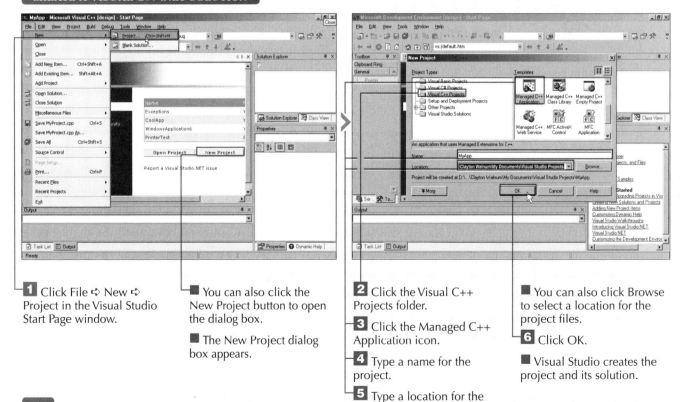

1 Click File ⇨ New ⇨ Project in the Visual Studio Start Page window.

■ You can also click the New Project button to open the dialog box.

■ The New Project dialog box appears.

2 Click the Visual C++ Projects folder.

3 Click the Managed C++ Application icon.

4 Type a name for the project.

5 Type a location for the project files.

■ You can also click Browse to select a location for the project files.

6 Click OK.

■ Visual Studio creates the project and its solution.

OPEN A VISUAL C++ .NET SOLUTION

Because very few programs can be written in one sitting, Visual Studio, like most other applications that enable you to edit documents, provides a way to open previously saved files. Opening a solution does more than prepare your source-code files for additional editing. The open process also reloads all the settings, options, and preferences that are associated with the solution, which enables you to pick up exactly where you left off the last time you saved the solution.

You do not need to load an entire solution if all you want to do is review a particular file. Visual Studio provides open commands for everything from a single file to a complete solution. You can even open projects from the Web. File

types that Visual Studio can open into its editing environment include source code files for several languages, script files, text files, resource files, XML files, and more.

However, if you open a single file source code file, you will not be able to compile it, since compiling requires an entire project, which, in turn, requires a solution.

Although this section describes how to open an entire Visual C++ .NET solution, opening single files follows a very similar procedure, except that you click the Miscellaneous Files command from the File menu rather than the Open Solution command.

OPEN A VISUAL C++ .NET SOLUTION

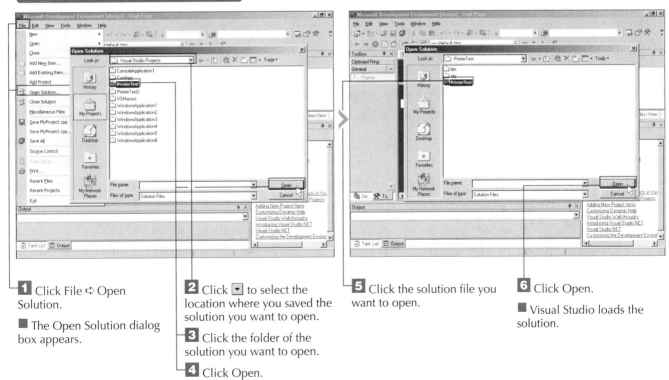

1 Click File ⇨ Open Solution.

■ The Open Solution dialog box appears.

2 Click ▾ to select the location where you saved the solution you want to open.

3 Click the folder of the solution you want to open.

4 Click Open.

5 Click the solution file you want to open.

6 Click Open.

■ Visual Studio loads the solution.

ENTER VISUAL C++ .NET SOURCE CODE

To write a C++ application, you must enter C++ code into a source-code file. When you create a solution for a Managed C++ Application, Visual Studio generates the files you need to get started with the new project, including a small skeleton program that you edit to create the main source code file.

The starting file that Visual Studio generates for you contains a complete, albeit simple, program that you can run immediately. However, the program simply displays *Hello World* in a DOS window and then terminates. By replacing the starting code provided by Visual Studio, you can create any type of application you like.

You can access the file you need to edit from the Solution Explorer window. The file has the name you assigned to the project, followed by the .cpp file name extension. Of course, the extension stands for C Plus Plus and identifies the file as C++ source code.

The .NET environment provides several features to help you when you are typing in your source code. Most of these features are found in the Edit menu, and include standard features such as Find and Replace. There is also an Advanced Features menu under the Edit menu that provides features such as Format Selection, which automatically formats the text with proper indentations. There is also in this menu an Increase Indent item and a Decrease Indent item that will move an entire block of selected text either to the right or to the left.

ENTER VISUAL C++ .NET SOURCE CODE

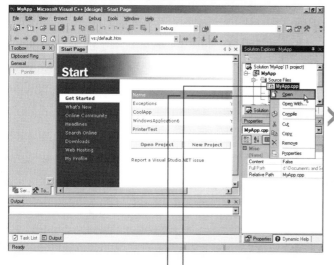

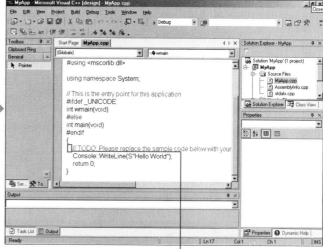

1 Start a Visual C++ project.

Note: See pages 4 and 5 for information on creating or opening an existing project.

2 Right-click the main source-code file.

3 Click Open.

■ The file appears in the code window.

4 Position the text cursor at the beginning of the TODO line.

Extra

The Visual Studio editor can be configured to look and act any way you want it to. If you click the Options command from the Tools menu, the Options dialog box appears, in which you can find the Text Editor options. Using these options, you can customize various editor settings, such as whether to use tabs or spaces or disable auto indenting. In the Environment settings, you can even select the font and text color you want to use with the editor.

You can easily see an outline version of your code using the outlining features of Visual Studio.NET. If you have a source code file open, you can click Edit ➪ Outlining ➪ Collapse to Definitions to see only the headers of the various items inside the code file. Each header will then have a plus icon next to it much like the folders in Windows Explorer. You can click the plus (+) icon to expand the entry and see the entire code under it.

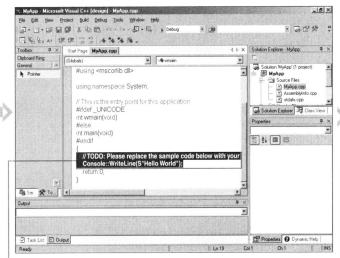

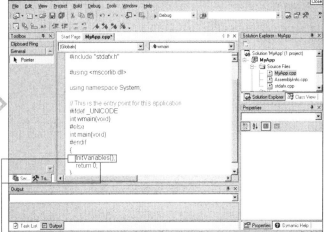

5 Press and hold the Shift key while pressing the down arrow twice to highlight two lines of code.

6 Press Delete.

■ Visual Studio removes the selected lines from the code.

7 Press Enter to start a new line.

8 Position the text cursor on the new line, press four spaces, and type your source code.

9 When you are finished typing code, save the solution.

Note: See page 8 for more information on saving a project.

SAVE A VISUAL C++ .NET FILE

Saving your solution files ensures that your work gets stored safely to disk. This may seem like an obvious statement, but creating and running programs is not like typing a document in Word or adjusting a spreadsheet in Excel. C++ programs, when they come across programming errors, have the power to lock up your computer. If you have not saved your files before attempting to run a program, and the program hangs, you lose all changes since your last save.

This cannot be stressed enough: Always save your files before testing changes to a program. Doing this not only saves the source code, but also saves the solution, including

modifications to project settings, options, and preferences. To save the file you are currently working on, click File ⇨ Save. The word Save on the menu will be followed by the name of the file you are currently editing. If you want to save it with a new filename, click File ⇨ Save As. Saving an entire solution is as easy as clicking File and then Save All.

If you want to be really safe, click the Options command from the Tools menu, which displays the Options dialog box. Then, in the Projects and Solutions settings, click the Save Changes to Open Documents option. Now Visual Studio automatically saves your work whenever you attempt to build or run a project.

SAVE A VISUAL C++ .NET FILE

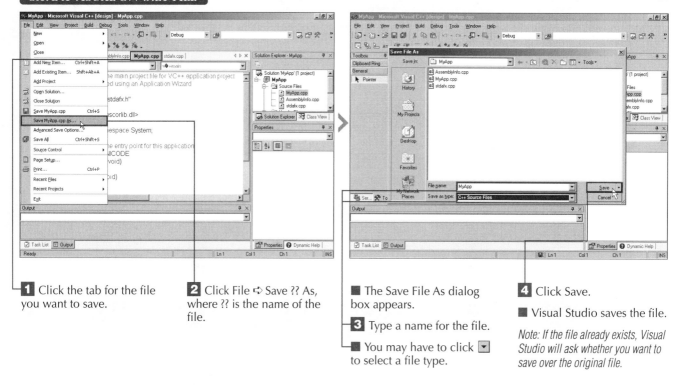

1 Click the tab for the file you want to save.

2 Click File ⇨ Save ?? As, where ?? is the name of the file.

■ The Save File As dialog box appears.

3 Type a name for the file.

■ You may have to click ▾ to select a file type.

4 Click Save.

■ Visual Studio saves the file.

Note: If the file already exists, Visual Studio will ask whether you want to save over the original file.

COMPILE A VISUAL C++ .NET FILE

When you compile a file in a project, Visual Studio takes the source-code file and converts it to an intermediate type of file called *object code*. If you have a project with multiple source code files, each source code file gets converted to its own object code file. The object code files in your project are the ones that the Visual C++ linker puts together to create the final executable file.

Normally, you compile and link your project in one step, creating the final executable. This process is called building the application. However, compiling a single file without performing a complete build is useful in that it enables you to find syntax errors in your code more quickly, without having to wait for the other files to compile and link.

When Visual C++ compiles a file, it reads though the source code line by line to ensure that every statement follows the syntax of the language. The compiler also looks for problems such as undefined variables and functions, paths of execution that cannot be reached, mismatched data types, and so on.

The compiler also looks for compiler directives, which are special directions to the compiler, as well as replaces constants and macros with the values that should appear in the code. For example, if your program defines a constant named PI that is equal to 3.14, the compiler replaces all occurrences of PI in the source code with the value 3.14.

COMPILE A VISUAL C++ .NET FILE

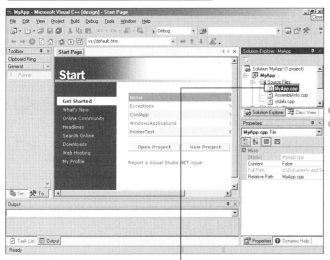

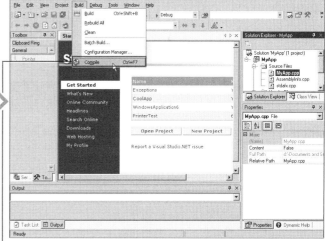

1 Start a Visual C++ project.

Note: See pages 4 and 5 for information on creating or opening an existing project.

2 Click the file you want to compile.

■ Visual Studio highlights the filename.

3 Click Build ⇨ Compile.

■ Visual Studio compiles the file, displaying its progress as it goes.

BUILD A VISUAL C++ .NET SOLUTION

When you build a solution, you create the final executable file for the application. The build process involves not only compiling all files in the project that need compiling, but also linking all of the resulting object code files together along with the libraries upon which the application code depends. After you build a solution, you can run your application outside of the Visual Studio environment just like any other application.

Visual Studio uses a *smart* build process that compiles only those files that have been changed. Note that such changes may not have been done directly to a file, but rather to a file on which another file depends. For example, if you make changes to a header file, all source code files that use the header file must be recompiled. Visual Studio keeps track of such changes and dependencies so that you get the quickest build time possible.

Visual Studio supports two types of builds: Debug and Release. A Debug build adds information to the resultant files that enables you to perform debugging tasks such a program traces and watching variables. Because the Debug version of the files are larger than they need to be, when your application is complete, you should do a Release build, which creates the final executable file for your application.

You can tell Visual Studio to build all the projects within the open solution, or you can tell it to build only the current project, called the startup project. Both items are available under the Build menu. To specify which project is the startup project, right-click the project in the Solution Explorer, and click Set as Startup Project.

BUILD A VISUAL C++ .NET SOLUTION

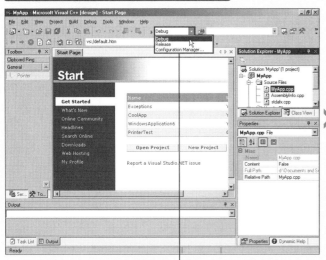

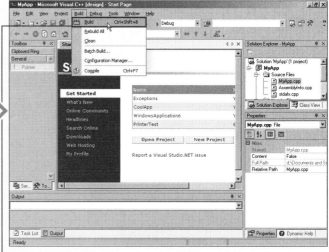

1 Start a Visual C++ project.

Note: See pages 4 and 5 for information on creating or opening an existing project.

2 Click ▼ to select the Debug or Release configuration.

■ Choose the Release configuration if you want to build the final, distributable version of the solution.

3 Click Build ➪ Build.

■ Visual Studio builds the solution, displaying its progress as it goes.

ADD A FILE TO A VISUAL C++ .NET PROJECT

The Visual Studio Add New Item command enables you to add additional files to the bare-bones project Visual Studio generated for you. For example, you may need to add a new source code file to your project in order to organize a group of related functions into its own file, or you may want to add a resource file that contains icons and bitmaps for your application.

Visual Studio enables you to add to a project just about any type of file you need, including source code files, text files, resource files, style sheets, header files, Web pages, and more. You can choose to create a new item and add it to the project, or you can add an existing item to your project.

After you have added an item to a project, it becomes a part of the entire solution. Visual Studio tracks any changes you make to the file and, if necessary, includes the file when compiling and linking the solution. All you have to do is provide content for the new item.

You can either add an existing file, or you can add a new file, which means Visual Studio will create a brand new file for you. To have Visual Studio create a new file for you, click File ⇨ File and click the type of file you want to create. To add an existing file, click File ⇨ Add Existing Item, and locate the file you want to add.

ADD A FILE TO A VISUAL C++ .NET PROJECT

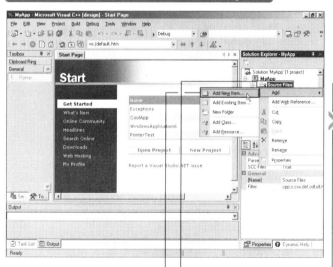

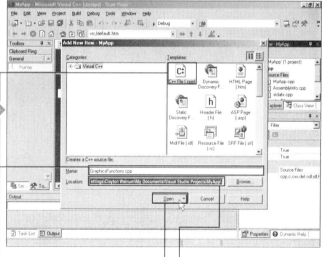

1 Start a Visual C++ project.

Note: See pages 4 and 5 for information on creating or opening an existing project.

2 Right-click the folder where you want to add the new item.

3 Click Add ⇨ Add New Item in the pop-up menu.

■ The Add New Item dialog box appears.

4 Click the type of item you want to add.

5 Type a name for the item.

6 Type the location where the item should be stored.

7 Click Open.

■ Visual Studio adds the item to the selected folder.

INTRODUCTION TO DATA TYPES

Data types and how computers store information is essential knowledge for any programmer. If you have programmed before, you already know that the smallest piece of information a computer can store is a *bit*, which can be set to 0 or 1. However, a single bit, because it can store only two values, is rarely suitable for storing

program data. For this reason, programming languages like C++ group bits together into larger storage areas, the smallest of which is an eight-bit value called a *byte*. Still, no matter what type of information a program deals with, it can always be broken down into a series of bits.

COMPUTER MATH

To better understand the way computers use bits to store information, you need to know about the binary, or base 2, number system. All your life you have been using what is known as the base 10 number system, which includes the digits 0 to 9.

Counting from 0 to 9 is a simple process, but when you get to one more than 9, you run out of digits. To solve this problem, you start over again at 0, but preface the 0 with a 1 to indicate that you now have reached the digit limit once, which means you need to add 1 x 10 to your 0 for a total value of 10.

Now, counting from 10 to 19 is a simple process, but when you get to 19, you run out of digits yet again. To fix this problem, you go back to 0, but add 1 to your count of 10s, giving you 20. This process continues until you get to 99, at which point you run out of digits for both your count of 10s and your count of 1s. To solve the problem, you replace both 9s with 0s, but preface both 0s with a 1, indicating that you have reached ten 10s one time, for a total value of 100.

The base 2 number system works exactly the same way, except there are only two digits, 0 and 1. So, when you count in base 2, you start with 0 then go to 1. At this point, you run out of digits. You solve the problem the same way you do in base 10, by starting over at 0 and prefacing that 0 with a 1 to indicate that you have reached the digit limit once. This gives you the base 2 number 10, which in base 10 is equivalent to 2.

The thing to notice is that, as you go from left to right, each digit in a number is the number base raised to a power one higher than the digit before. That is, in the base 10 system, the right-most digit is equivalent to 10^0 (or 1), the next digit is equivalent to 10^1 (or 10), the next is 10^2 (or 100), and so on. Similarly, in the base 2 number system, the right-most digit is equivalent to 2^0 (or 1), the next digit is equivalent to 2^1 (or 2), the next is 2^2 (or 4), and so on.

BYTES

In most programming environments, a byte is eight bits, and it represents an eight-digit binary number. Using your computer math, you can determine that a byte holds 256 different values, which are 0 to 255 for unsigned values and -128 to 127 for signed values.

Usually, even a byte is too small to hold the types of values a computer program needs to manipulate. A program can use bytes to store character information,

as long as that information conforms to the eight-bit ASCII codes defined for characters. A program can also use bytes to access memory-based data, such as the pixels of a 256-color bitmap. However, these days many programs use Unicode characters, which require multiple bytes to define a single character, and most bitmaps require multiple bytes, up to four, to define a single pixel.

INTEGERS

The next size up from a byte in C++ is a *short integer*, which comprises two bytes or 16 bits. Previously, Windows programming tools considered the 16-bit integer to be a full integer, rather than a short integer. Today, however, programmers use 32-bit programming tools to program in Windows 32-bit operating system, which demotes a 16-bit integer to a short integer. Short integers can hold 65,536 different values, in a range from 0 to 65,535 for unsigned values or -32,768 to 32,767 for signed values.

A full C++ integer is a 32-bit data type, which means it can hold values into the billions. In most cases where a program needs to manipulate positive or negative values, you use the integer data type.

Your programs can also use *long integers*, which are comprised of 64 bits or eight bytes. Wherever you need truly immense integer values, the long integer is the perfect choice.

All integer values can be *signed* or *unsigned*. The default is signed, which means that the integer can represent both positive and negative numbers. By using the unsigned keyword, you can exclude negative integers and enjoy a larger range of positive integers.

FLOATING POINT

An integer cannot represent every numerical value you need when writing a program. Sometimes, you have values that are not even integers. That is, you often need to manipulate numbers with decimal portions, such as 14534.874. For these types of values, you use the C++ *floating-point* data types, of which there are two: *float* and *double*.

The difference between the float and double data types is the number of bits they use to represent a value. The float data type uses 32 bits, and the double uses 64 bits. Because of the extra storage, a double can more accurately represent floating-point values with more decimal places. Still, the float data type works fine with returns and line feeds.

CHARACTERS

Traditionally, programs used the char data type, which is comprised of eight bits, to represent character information, including letters, numbers, punctuation, and special characters such as carriage returns and line feeds. In the international computing environment of today, the conventional 8-bit char data type is too small to represent the many characters used in some languages. For that reason, programmers often use the wide character data type, wchar_t, which can represent up to 65,565 different characters.

BOOLEAN

A Boolean value represents the logical outcome true or false. Although a single bit should be enough to represent a Boolean value, most programming languages, including C++, deal poorly with single bits. For that reason, a C++ Boolean value is comprised of eight bits.

POINTERS

Pointers are a special type of data that programs use to represent addresses in memory. Technically, a computer stores a pointer in memory as a long integer. However, programs rarely refer to pointers as long integers. Instead, programs use the pointer operator, which is an asterisk, to define and refer to pointers.

CREATE A CONSTANT

When you write a C++ program, good programming practice dictates that you replace numerical literals, which are values like 3 or 26.56, with English-like symbols. These symbols that represent values are called constants. Doing this makes your programs easier to read and maintain. For example, it is much easier to understand `sector = row * NUMOFCOLUMNS + column` than `sector = row * 10 + column`.

Even professional programmers tend to under use constants and pay for it later when they try to maintain code that they wrote weeks or months before. Even worse, someone who did not write the original code may be called upon to

perform maintenance, who has no idea what all the numbers in the program calculations mean.

Another advantage of constants is that they make it easy to change frequently used values in a program. Suppose, for example, you have used a literal value for the width of an image throughout a program. If you have to change the size of the image, you must find every occurrence of the width in the program and change it accordingly. With a constant, you need to change only one value — the definition of the constant — and the compiler automatically replaces all occurrences of the constant with the new value.

CREATE A CONSTANT

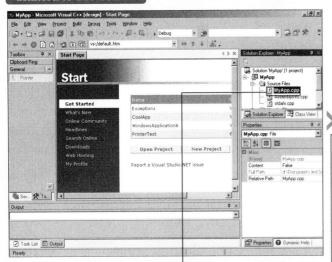

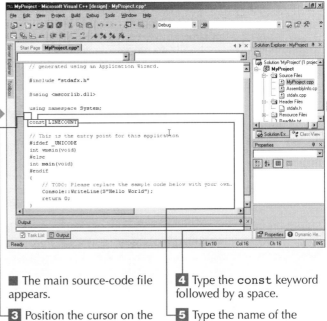

1 Click File ➪ New ➪ Project to create a new Managed C++ project.

Note: See page 4 for more information on creating a new project.

2 Open the main source-code file.

■ The main source-code file appears.

3 Position the cursor on the blank line following `using namespace System` and press Enter to start a new line.

4 Type the `const` keyword followed by a space.

5 Type the name of the constant, using all uppercase letters, followed by a space.

Apply It

You may wonder how constants are different from variables. Variables get their values when you run the program in which they are defined. That is, they get their values after the program is compiled. Constants, on the other hand, instruct the compiler to replace all occurrences of a constant with the value assigned to the constant. That is, as the compiler reads in your source code, it looks for references to constants and replaces them, before the source code is turned into executable code. This means that the final compiled program contains no references to constants, but rather only the values that the constants represent.

Just like variables, constants can have different data types. The default data type is int, so if you want to assign an integer to a constant, you need do nothing extra. However, if you want to assign some other type of value to a constant, you must include the data type between the const keyword and the name of your constant.

TYPE THIS:

```
#include "stdafx.h"

#using <mscorlib.dll>

using namespace System;

const double PI = 3.14;

int main(void)
{
    Console::WriteLine(PI);
    return 0;
}
```

RESULT:

```
3.14
```
Press any key to continue

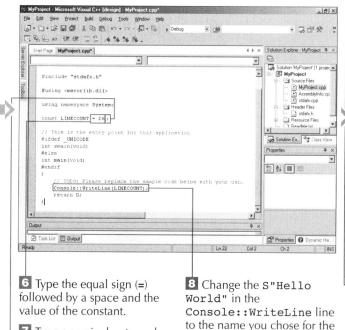

6 Type the equal sign (=) followed by a space and the value of the constant.

7 Type a semicolon to end the line and press Enter.

8 Change the `S"Hello World"` in the `Console::WriteLine` line to the name you chose for the constant.

9 Click Build ➪ Compile to compile and run your program.

Note: See page 9 for more information on compiling a program.

■ The value you assigned to the constant appears on the screen.

CREATE AN ENUMERATION

When you have a number of related constants, you can simplify the process of defining them by using an enumeration. An *enumeration* is simply a list of constants with related values. For example, you might want to define a set of constants that represent the days of the week, with SUNDAY being 0 and SATURDAY being 6. To do this with regular constants you need to define each constant separately, providing a value for each. But with an enumeration, you can let the compiler assign the values. All you have to do is supply the names of the constants.

Defining an enumeration is a simple matter of listing the names of the constants in the order of value. The compiler then assigns each constant in the list with a value, starting at 0 and incrementing the value for each constant in the list. That is, the second constant gets a value of 1, the third a value of 2, and so on.

After you have your enumeration defined, you can use each of the constant symbols in exactly the same way you use any other constant. The only difference is the way you have defined them.

CREATE AN ENUMERATION

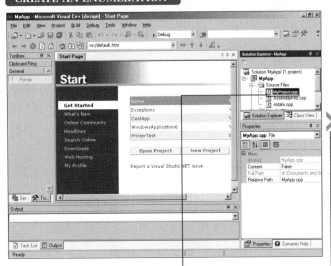

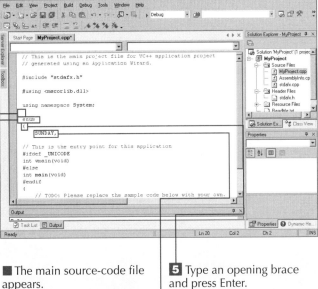

1 Click File ➪ New ➪ Project to create a new Managed C++ project.

Note: See page 4 for more information on creating a new project.

2 Open the main source-code file.

■ The main source-code file appears.

3 Position the cursor on the blank line following using namespace System and press Enter to start a new line.

4 Type the enum keyword and press Enter.

5 Type an opening brace and press Enter.

6 Type the name of the first constant, followed by a comma, and then press Enter.

Apply It

You can assign values to your enumeration other than the defaults. To do this, follow one or more of the constant names with an equals sign and a value. The compiler then assigns that value to the constant and continues assigning values to the remaining constants starting with the new value.

TYPE THIS:

```
#include "stdafx.h"
#using <mscorlib.dll>
using namespace System;
enum { ONE = 1, TWO, THREE, FIVE = 5, SIX };
int main(void) {
    Console::WriteLine(ONE);
    Console::WriteLine(TWO);
    Console::WriteLine(THREE);
    Console::WriteLine(FIVE);
    Console::WriteLine(SIX);
    return 0;
}
```

RESULT:

```
1
2
3
5
6
```

Press any key to continue

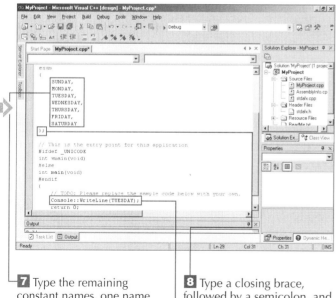

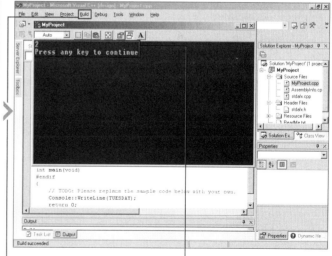

7 Type the remaining constant names, one name per line, followed by a comma, and then press Enter.

Note: Do not follow the last constant with a comma. Press Enter only.

8 Type a closing brace, followed by a semicolon, and then press Enter.

9 Change the S"Hello World" in the Console::WriteLine line to the one of the names you chose for a constant.

10 Click Build ➪ Compile to compile and run your program.

Note: See page 9 for more information on compiling a program.

■ The value you assigned to the constant appears on the screen.

CREATE A VARIABLE

You can stores values and numbers and other information in memory using variables. A *variable* is simply a word that has a value stored along with it. When you declare variables, you set up locations in memory where your program can store the many values it needs to perform its task. Internally, a computer refers to areas of memory by a numerical address, which is difficult for humans to work with. Defining a variable enables you to assign an easy-to-remember name to a memory location. The better the variable names you choose, the easier it is for you — or anyone else, for that matter — to understand what the program does.

After you have created a variable, you can store or retrieve values from the memory address associated with the

variable simply by referring to the variable name. When you store a value in a variable, you are assigning the variable. The type of values you can store in a variable, and the amount of computer memory used to store the variable, depends upon the data type of the variable. For more information on data types, please refer to this chapter's introduction.

To define a variable, you supply the data type and name of the variable. Then your program, with no additional help from you, can assign the variable to the appropriate amount of memory, as well as link the variable name to the address at which the program can find this memory.

CREATE A VARIABLE

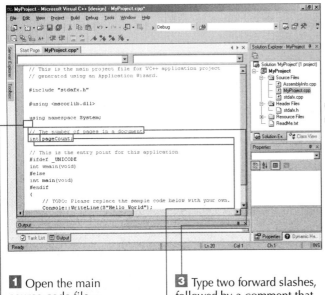

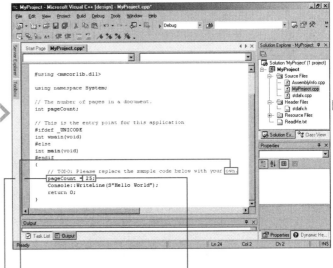

1 Open the main source-code file.

2 Position the cursor on the blank line following using namespace System and press Enter to start a new line.

3 Type two forward slashes, followed by a comment that describes the variable, and then press Enter.

4 Type a data type for the variable followed by a space.

5 Type a name for the variable, followed by a semicolon to end the line.

6 Position the cursor at the end of the TODO comment in the main() function and press Enter to start a new line.

7 Type the name you assigned to the variable, followed by a space, an equal sign, and another space.

8 Type an appropriate value for the variable followed by a semicolon to end the line.

Note: The type of value you provide for the variable depends upon the data type of the variable.

Extra

You can combine a variable definition and assignment into a single statement. Just follow the variable name with an equal sign, the value to which to set the variable, and a semicolon. For example, the line `int value1 = 75;` both declares `value1` to be an integer and assigns it a starting value of 75.

While variable names can be almost anything you want them to be, there are a few rules to think about. First, a variable name must start with an alphabetic character or an underscore. Other characters may be alphabetic, numeric, or an underscore. Second, identifiers must be spelled differently than language keywords. Finally, C++ variable names are case sensitive. For example, the variable name `CurrentDate` is different from `currentDate`.

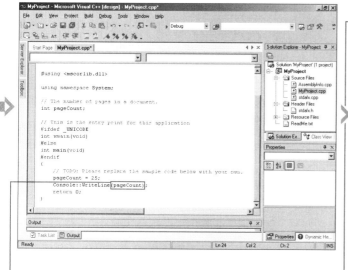

■9 Change the `S"Hello World"` in the `Console::WriteLine` line to the name you chose for the variable.

■10 Click Build ➪ Compile to compile and run your program.

Note: See page 9 for more information on compiling a program.

■ The value you assigned to the variable appears on the screen.

PERFORM SIMPLE MATH

The C++ language includes mathematical operators that you can use to perform simple calculations such as addition, subtraction, multiplication, and division. You can use these operators to perform calculations with variables and literal values. You can, for example, add two variables and place the result into another variable. Or, you can add a literal value to a variable and assign the result to another variable.

The operators defined for use in these calculations are the plus sign (+) for addition, the minus sign (-) for subtraction, the asterisk (*) for multiplication, and the forward slash (/) for division.

The most common way to perform these types of calculations is with *infix notation*, which is when you place the operator between the values involved in the calculation. This is the type of calculation you have used since grammar

school, so it is easy to use and understand in computer programs.

When you write a calculation in infix notation, you must assign the result of the calculation to what is called an *lvalue*, which is a symbol that can be placed on the left side of a calculation. The lvalue is a variable into which the program stores the result of the calculation.

When performing mathematical operations in programs, you must remain mindful of the data types involved in the calculation. Otherwise, you may not get the result you expect. For example, if you divide the integer 35 by the integer 10, you do not get 3.5, even if you assign the result of the calculation to a floating-point variable. When you divide integers, you get an integer result. To get the result 3.5 in this calculation, you must make at least one of the values in the calculation a floating-point type.

PERFORM SIMPLE MATH

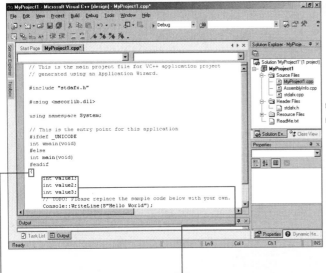

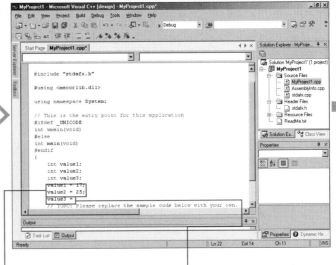

1 Open the main source-code file.

2 Position the cursor after the opening brace in the `main()` function and then press Enter to start a new line.

3 Declare three integer variables on different lines at the cursor location.

Note: See page 18 for more information on creating a variable.

4 After the variable declarations, assign a value to the first two variables you declared in step 3 and press Enter.

5 Type the name you chose for the third variable, followed by a space, an equal sign, and another space.

Apply It

You can also perform simple addition and subtraction on variables using prefix or postfix notation. C++ defines two special operators for this type of calculation, the increment operator (++) and the decrement operator (--). When you place the decrement or increment operator before a variable name, the program adds or subtracts from the variable first, before the program uses the variable in any further calculations. When you place the decrement or increment operator after a variable name, the program adds or subtracts from the variable after calculations in the expression are complete.

TYPE THIS:

```
#include "stdafx.h"
#using <mscorlib.dll>
using namespace System;
int main(void) {
    int value1 = 10;
    int value2 = 10;
    int value3;
    // This evaluates to 11 * 10 because value1
    // gets incremented before the multiplication.
    value3 = ++value1 * 10;
    Console::WriteLine(value3);
    Console::WriteLine(value1);
    // This evaluates to 10 * 10 because value2
    // gets incremented after the multiplication.
    value3 = value2++ * 10;
    Console::WriteLine(value3);
    Console::WriteLine(value2);
    return 0;
}
```

RESULT:

```
110
11
100
11
```

> **Press any key to continue**

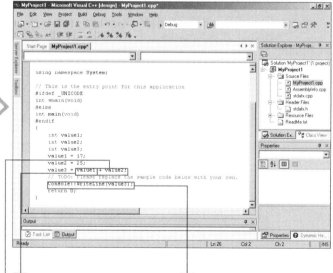

■ **6** Type the name of the first variable you declared followed by a space.

■ **7** Type the addition operator (+), followed by a space, the name of the second variable you declared, and a semicolon to end the line.

■ **8** Change the S"Hello World" in the Console::WriteLine line to the name of the third variable.

■ **9** Click Build ➪ Compile to compile and run your program.

Note: See page 9 for more information on compiling a program.

■ The value you assigned to the third variable, which is the sum of the first and second variables, appears on the screen.

BRANCH BASED ON A COMPARISON

By comparing the values of data in a program, you can make decisions about what the program should do. C++ provides program constructs that enable you to jump to different parts of a program depending on the results of a comparison. For example, if a user chooses an item in a menu, your program can jump to the part of the program that handles that menu command.

This kind of decision making works thanks to the *Boolean expression*, which is a calculation that always evaluates to true or false. You might say in your program, if menuChoice == 3 then jump to the menuItem3() function. In this case, menuChoice == 3 is the Boolean expression. Either menuChoice == 3 — which yields a true result — or it does not — which yields a false result. Besides the equal comparison operator (==), C++ also provides a not-equal operator (!=).

C++ provides the if statement for evaluating Boolean expressions. To write an if statement, you follow the if keyword with the Boolean expression you want to evaluate. After the Boolean expression, you write the code to be performed if the expression is true. If the Boolean expression is false, this code is skipped and program execution continues with the program line after the if statement.

Be very careful not to confuse the assignment operator (=) with the comparison equal operator (==). If you mix them up, your if statements will give you unexpected results. In fact, every if statement that uses an assignment operator instead of a comparison operator, such as the expression (value1 = 10), evaluates to true. This is because C++ assigns the value of 10 to value1, rather than comparing it with 10. This is one of those things that drives new C++ programmers crazy.

BRANCH BASED ON A COMPARISON

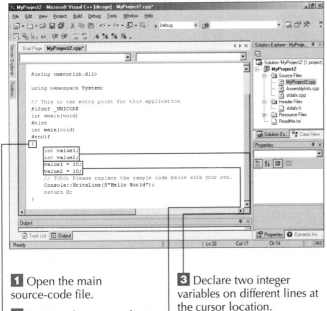

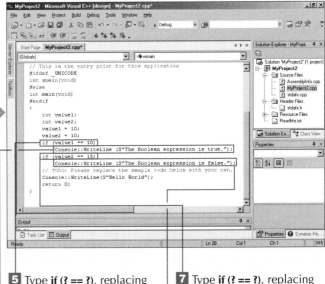

■1 Open the main source-code file.

■2 Position the cursor after the opening brace in the main() function and press Enter to start a new line.

■3 Declare two integer variables on different lines at the cursor location.

Note: See page 18 for more information on creating a variable.

■4 After the variable declarations, assign a value to each variable you declared in step 3 and press Enter.

■5 Type if (? == ?), replacing the question marks with the first variable and its assigned value, and press Enter.

■6 Type Console::WriteLine (S"The Boolean expression is true."); and press Enter.

■7 Type if (? == ?), replacing the question marks with the second variable and a value other than the assigned value, and press Enter.

■8 Type Console::WriteLine (S"The Boolean expression is false."); and press Enter.

Apply It

You can use an `if` statement to choose between two different outcomes by using an `else` clause. When you use an `else` clause, your program executes the statement associated with the `if` statement when the Boolean expression is true. However, in the case where the Boolean expression is false, the program executes the `else` portion of the statement.

```
#include "stdafx.h"
#using <mscorlib.dll>
using namespace System;
int main(void)
{
    int value1 = 10;
    int value2 = 20;
    int value3 = 30;

    if (value1 == 15)
        Console::WriteLine(S"value1 == 15.");
    else if (value1 == 27)
        Console::WriteLine(S"value1 == 27.");
    else if (value1 == 45)
        Console::WriteLine(S"value1 == 45.");
    else
        Console::WriteLine(S"value1 is not 15, 27, or 45.");
    return 0;
}
```

RESULT:

```
value1 is not 15, 27, or 45.
```

Press any key to continue

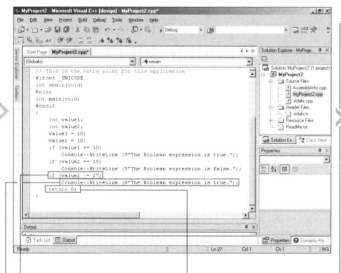

■9 Type **if (? != ?)**, replacing the question marks with the second variable and any appropriate value other than the assigned value, and press Enter.

■10 Type **Console::WriteLine (S"The Boolean expression is true.");**.

■11 Delete all other lines from the `main()` function, except the `return` statement.

■12 Click Build ➪ Compile to compile and run your program.

Note: See page 9 for more information on compiling a program.

■ The program displays the results of the three comparisons. Because the second comparison is false, the program does not execute the second `Console::WriteLine` statement.

MAKE MORE COMPLICATED COMPARISONS

C++ defines two logical operators that enable you to do comparisons between multiple Boolean expressions. You might, for example, want to branch to a specific part of your program if two Boolean expressions both evaluate to true. The logical operators enable you to perform this kind of comparison, as well as much more complicated ones.

The first of the logical operators is &&, which performs a logical AND. A logical AND compares two Boolean expressions and returns true if both expressions are true. The second logical operator is ||, which performs a logical OR. A logical OR compares two Boolean expressions and returns true if any of the expressions are true.

Creating a complex Boolean expression comprised of several smaller Boolean expressions and logical operators can become a tricky process if you are not careful. Such statements can be hard to read. Therefore, you would be wise to use plenty of parentheses to group expressions in a way that makes them easier to read and ensures that the comparisons are performed as you expect them to be.

To create a complex Boolean expression in this way, you surround basic Boolean expressions with parentheses and combine the basic expressions into larger expressions by joining them with the && or || operators.

MAKE MORE COMPLICATED COMPARISONS

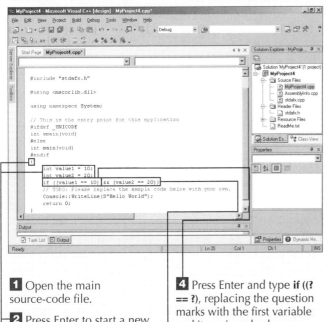

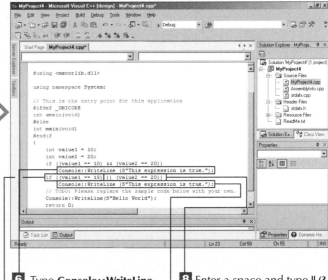

1 Open the main source-code file.

2 Press Enter to start a new line after the opening brace in the `main()` function.

3 Define two integer variables with starting values.

4 Press Enter and type **if ((? == ?),** replacing the question marks with the first variable and its assigned value.

5 Enter a space and type **&& (? == ?)),** replacing the question marks with the second variable and its assigned value, and press Enter.

6 Type **Console::WriteLine (S"This expression is true.");** and press Enter.

7 Press Enter and type **if ((? == ?),** replacing the question marks with the first variable and a value other than its assigned value.

8 Enter a space and type **|| (? == ?)),** replacing the question marks with the second variable and its assigned value, and press Enter.

9 Type **Console::WriteLine (S"This expression is true.");** and press Enter.

Apply It

Complex Boolean expressions can get as complicated as you need them to be, using various combinations of the `&&` and `||` operators. When you start constructing these types of Boolean expressions, you see how important using parentheses can be. Some expressions can be so long that they would be difficult to untangle without the formatting help you get from parentheses. Also, the parentheses ensure that the program evaluates the expressions the way you want them to be evaluated, because parentheses can change which expressions the program evaluates first.

TYPE THIS:

```cpp
#include "stdafx.h"
#using <mscorlib.dll>
using namespace System;
int main(void) {
    int value1 = 10;
    int value2 = 20;
    int value3 = 30;
    if (((value1 == 10) && (value2 == 20)) || (value3 == 25))
        Console::WriteLine (S"This expression is true.");
    if ((value1 == 10) && ((value2 == 20)) || (value3 == 25))
        Console::WriteLine (S"This expression is true.");
    return 0;
}
```

RESULT:

```
This expression is true.
This expression is true.
```

Press any key to continue

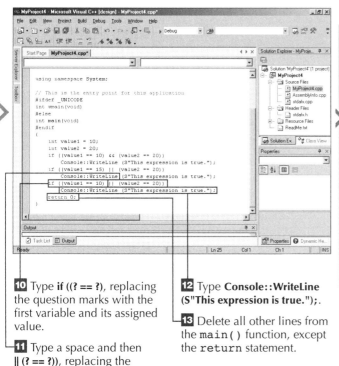

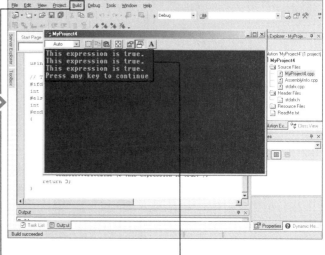

10 Type **if ((? == ?)**, replacing the question marks with the first variable and its assigned value.

11 Type a space and then **|| (? == ?))**, replacing the question marks with the second variable and its assigned value, and press Enter.

12 Type **Console::WriteLine (S"This expression is true.");**.

13 Delete all other lines from the `main()` function, except the `return` statement.

14 Click Build ⇨ Compile to compile and run your program.

Note: See page 9 for more information on compiling a program.

■ The program displays the results of the three comparisons.

CALL A FUNCTION

By calling functions, you can take advantage of the C++ and .NET libraries, which enable you to do everything from print a line on the screen to manage files. You can also call your own functions, allowing you to break your programs down into logical steps and more easily manageable chunks of code.

When you call a function, you are actually telling your program to branch to another part of computer memory, perform whatever instructions it finds there, and return to the line after the function call. Thanks to function names, which are not unlike variable names, your program can assign memory addresses to easy-to-understand alphabetic symbols. Usually, function names describe what a function does. For example, a function named abs() returns the absolute value of a given number.

To call a function, you type the name of the function, followed by the required arguments in parentheses.

Arguments are values that the function needs in order to do its work. You must supply these values when you call the function. Usually, you will also supply a variable into which the function can return the result of its processing. You do this by prefacing the function call with the name of the variable and the assignment operator (=).

Call to library functions are usually prefaced by a name followed by double colons. For example, in the call to Console::WriteLine, Console is the name of the namespace that contains the WriteLine function. In fact, the Console namespace is itself inside another namespace named System. However, you do not have to specify the System namespace in the Console::WriteLine call because of the line using namespace System near the top of the program. Without that line, the call to WriteLine would have to look like this: System::Console::WriteLine.

CALL A FUNCTION

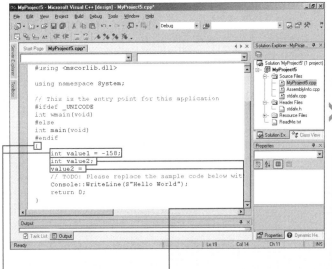

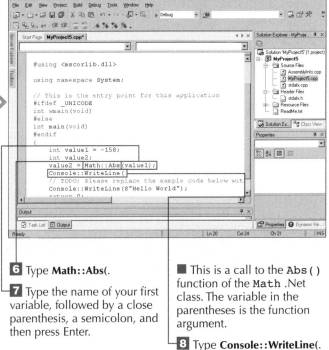

1 Open the main source-code file.

2 Press Enter after the opening brace in the main() function.

3 Define an integer variable with a starting value less than 0.

Note: See page 18 for more information on creating a variable.

4 Declare another integer variable without a starting value, and press Enter.

5 Type the second variable you declared, followed by a space, an equal sign, and another space.

6 Type **Math::Abs(**.

7 Type the name of your first variable, followed by a close parenthesis, a semicolon, and then press Enter.

8 Type **Console::WriteLine(**.

■ This is a call to the Abs() function of the Math .Net class. The variable in the parentheses is the function argument.

Apply It

Often, you need to supply various types of arguments to a function call. Virtually any type of data a program can work with can be used as an argument to a function call. Moreover, these arguments can be both literal values, as in the number 35, or variable names. When you look up a function in a reference, you can find out the number of arguments needed by the function, as well as the required data types of the arguments.

TYPE THIS:

```
#include "stdafx.h"
#using <mscorlib.dll>
using namespace System;
void TestFunction(int val1, int val2, String* val3) {
    System::Console::Write("val1 = ");
    System::Console::WriteLine(val1);
    System::Console::Write("val2 = ");
    System::Console::WriteLine(val2);
    System::Console::Write("val3 = ");
    System::Console::WriteLine(val3);
}
int main(void) {
    int value = 25;
    System::Console::WriteLine(S"Hello World");
    return 0;
}
```

RESULT:

```
val1 = 25
val2 = 356
val3 = This is a test.
```

Press any key to continue

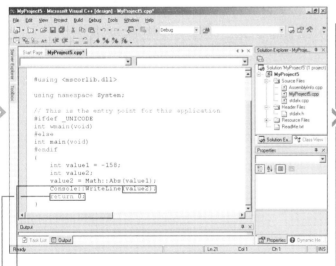

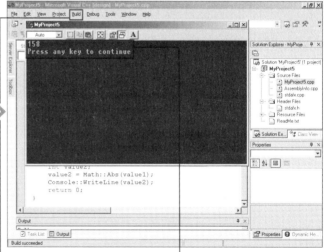

9 Type the name of your second variable, followed by a close parenthesis and a semicolon.

10 Delete all other lines from the main() function, except the return statement.

■ This is a call to the WriteLine() function of the Console .Net class. The variable in the parentheses is the function argument required by WriteLine(). In this example, the argument is the value you want to display.

11 Click Compile ➪ Build to compile and run your program.

Note: See page 9 for more information on compiling a program.

■ The program displays the absolute value of the first variable you defined.

12 Return to the main source-code file.

CONTINUED ▶

CALL A FUNCTION (CONTINUED)

Functions enable you to break your programs down into easily manageable chunks of code, as well as shorten programs by substituting a single chunk of code for tasks the program needs to perform several times. After you have written a function, and are sure that it works correctly, you can forget the details of how the function performs its task and just think of it as another command.

For example, to load a data file in C++ requires several lines of program code. You can hide all these file-loading details in a function named LoadDataFile(). Then, when you need to load the program data file, you simply call the function, rather than rewriting all the code necessary to load the file.

When you write a function, keep in mind that it should not do too much. The function should perform a single task and then return to the calling program line. The name of the function should describe what the function does, and the function should not do more than its name implies.

Functions also require a data type for their return value, as well as a list of arguments that the function needs to perform its task. The number of arguments required depends on how you write the function. The arguments listed for a function are called *parameters*.

CALL A FUNCTION (CONTINUED)

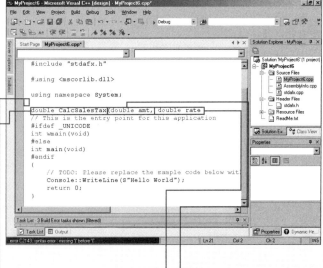

■ Position the cursor on the blank line following **using namespace System** and press Enter to start a new line.

■ Type a return data type for the function, a space, the name of the function, and an open parenthesis.

■ Type a data type for the first parameter, followed by a space and the name of the parameter.

■ If you have more than one parameter to list, type a comma, followed by a space, and then repeat step 15.

■ Type a close parenthesis to end the function signature and press Enter.

■ Type an open brace to start the body of the function and press Enter.

■ Type the code lines that perform the function task and press Enter.

■ Type **return**, followed by a space, the value to return from the function, a semicolon, and then press Enter.

■ The function return must be the same type as the declared return type.

Apply It

While all functions require a return type, not all functions actually need to return a value. If you do not want to return a value from a function, use `void` as the return type of the function. A function that returns no value requires no `return` statement.

TYPE THIS:

```
#include "stdafx.h"
#using <mscorlib.dll>
using namespace System;
void TestRange(int val) {
    if (val < 0) return;
    if ((val >= 0) && (val < 11))
        System::Console::WriteLine("val is between 0 and 10.");
    else
        System::Console::WriteLine("val is greater than 10.");
}
int main(void) {
    int value = 25;
    TestRange(value);
    return 0;
}
```

RESULT:

```
val is greater than 10.
```

Press any key to continue

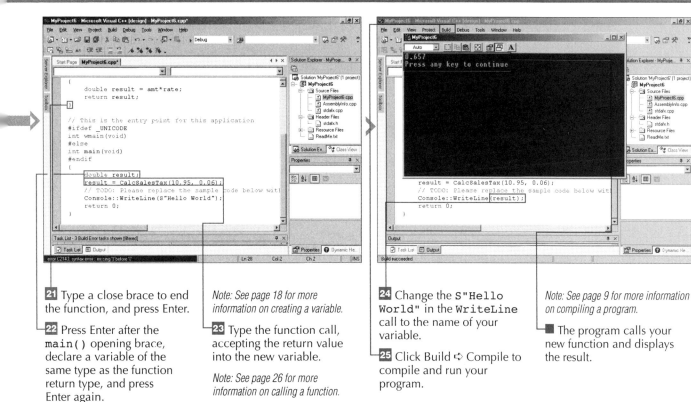

21 Type a close brace to end the function, and press Enter.

22 Press Enter after the `main()` opening brace, declare a variable of the same type as the function return type, and press Enter again.

Note: See page 18 for more information on creating a variable.

23 Type the function call, accepting the return value into the new variable.

Note: See page 26 for more information on calling a function.

24 Change the `S"Hello World"` in the `WriteLine` call to the name of your variable.

25 Click Build ▷ Compile to compile and run your program.

Note: See page 9 for more information on compiling a program.

■ The program calls your new function and displays the result.

CREATE A FUNCTION PROTOTYPE

Function prototypes enable you to place a function anywhere in your program, without being concerned with where the program calls the function. Moreover, function prototypes provide you with quick information about return types, names, and arguments of functions.

When you compile your program, the compiler needs to know information about all of the functions in your program. Because of the way the compiler works, if it runs into a function call before it has information about the function, the compiler generates an error. To avoid this error, you must place all function definitions in the program before where they are called or create function prototypes.

A function prototype is much like the first line of a function. That is, it includes the return type of the function, the name of the function, and the arguments required by the function. The only difference between the prototype and the first line of the actual function is that you need only provide the argument types, and you must place a semicolon at the end of the prototype. If you want to, you can also provide names for the arguments. However, the names you provide are informational only and have nothing to do with the names you choose for the actual arguments.

CREATE A FUNCTION PROTOTYPE

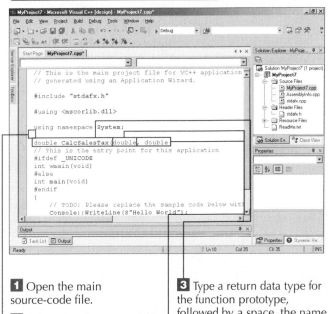

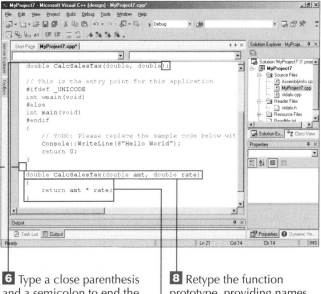

1 Open the main source-code file.

2 Position the cursor on the blank line following **using namespace System** and press Enter to start a new line.

3 Type a return data type for the function prototype, followed by a space, the name of the function, and an open parenthesis.

4 Type a data type for the first parameter.

5 Add a comma, space, and data type for more parameters.

6 Type a close parenthesis and a semicolon to end the prototype, and then press Enter.

7 Position the cursor on a blank line at the end of the program and press Enter.

8 Retype the function prototype, providing names for the parameters, and do not end with a semicolon.

9 Type the body of the function.

Note: See page 26 for information on calling a function.

Apply It

Structuring your program can be difficult without the use of function prototypes. You would be forced to write your program with the functions always preceding the calls to the functions. But often you will want to include calls to a function anywhere in the source, regardless of where the function is actually located.

```
#include "stdafx.h"
#using <mscorlib.dll>
using namespace System;
int main(void)
{
    int value = 25;
    TestRange(value);
    return 0;
}

void TestRange(int val)
{
    if (val < 0) return;
    if ((val >= 0) && (val < 11))
        System::Console::WriteLine("val is between 0 and 10.");
    else
        System::Console::WriteLine("val is greater than 10.");
}
```

```
error C2065: 'TestRange': undeclared identifier
error C2365: 'TestRange': redefinition; previous definition
    was a 'formerly unknown identifier'
```

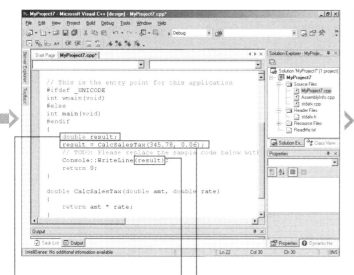

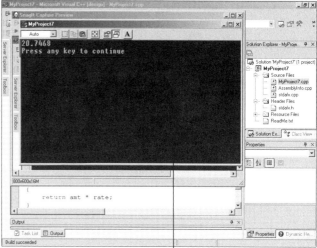

10 Press Enter after the `main()` opening brace and declare a variable of the same type as the function return type.

Note: See page 18 for more information on creating a variable.

11 Press Enter and type the function call, accepting the return value into the new variable.

Note: See page 26 for more information on calling a function.

12 Change the `S"Hello World"` in the `WriteLine` call to the name of your variable.

13 Click Build ⇨ Compile to compile and run your program.

Note: See page 9 for more information on compiling and running a program.

■ The program calls your new function and displays the result.

CREATE A FOR LOOP

By creating a `for` loop, you enable your program to perform one or more commands a specified number of times. For example, suppose you have a text file that contains ten lines of text, and you need to read each line of text into your program. A `for` loop is the perfect solution, because you can specify the number of times — in this case ten — that you want to read a line from the file.

If you are used to `for` loops in another computer language, you may at first be a little thrown by the syntax C++ uses to create these loops. However, the C++ way is actually more flexible than the method used in many other languages, giving you more powerful control over the loop-control variable.

The *loop-control* variable is a variable that the program uses to count the number of times the loop has executed. A more professional way of saying this is that the loop-control variable counts the number of loop iterations, an iteration being a single time through the loop. In C++, a single statement takes care of initializing the loop-control variable, adding or subtracting from the variable — called incrementing and decrementing, respectively — and comparing the variable to the expression that determines when the loop will end.

The loop statement consists of the keyword `for`, followed by an open parenthesis, followed by three clauses separated by commas. The first clause initializes the loop variable; the second clause is a test for whether to continue the `for` loop; and the final clause states what to do at the end of each loop, such as increment the loop variable by one. The statement then ends with a close parenthesis, followed by the code to be executed in the loop.

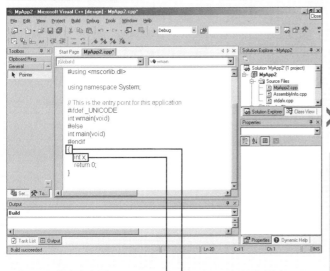

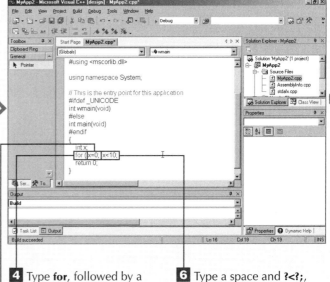

1 Open the main source-code file.

Note: See pages 5 and 6 for more information on opening a solution and its source-code file.

2 Position the cursor after the open brace in the `main()` function and press Enter to start a new line.

3 Type **int ?;**, replacing ? with the name you want for the loop-control variable, and press Enter.

4 Type **for**, followed by a space, and an open parenthesis.

5 Type **?=0;**, replacing ? with the loop variable name.

6 Type a space and **?<?;**, replacing the first ? with the loop variable name and the second ? with the number of times the loop should iterate.

Apply It

You do not have to start your loop variable at 0, and you can increment it by more than 1 each time through the loop.

TYPE THIS:

```
#include "stdafx.h"
#using <mscorlib.dll>
using namespace System;
int main(void) {
    int x;
    for (x=5; x<45; x+=5) {
        Console::WriteLine(x);
    }
    return 0;
}
```

RESULT:

```
5
10
15
20
25
30
35
40
```

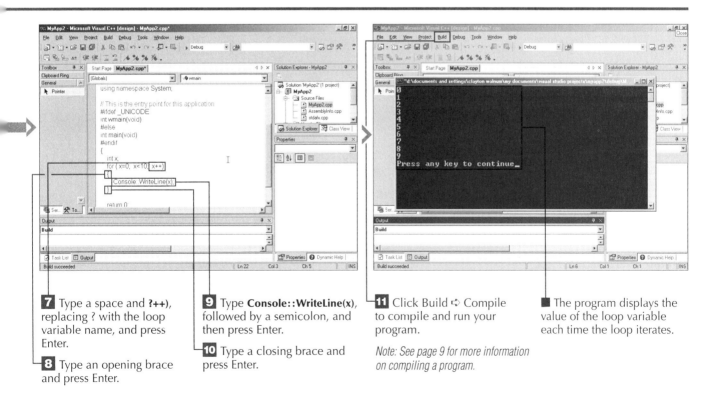

7 Type a space and **?++)**, replacing ? with the loop variable name, and press Enter.

8 Type an opening brace and press Enter.

9 Type **Console::WriteLine(x)**, followed by a semicolon, and then press Enter.

10 Type a closing brace and press Enter.

11 Click Build ⇨ Compile to compile and run your program.

Note: See page 9 for more information on compiling a program.

■ The program displays the value of the loop variable each time the loop iterates.

CREATE A WHILE LOOP

A while loop enables your program to perform a series of commands over and over as long as a specified condition remains true. A common example would be reading from a file, where you want to read the entire contents of the file, but you do not know how much data the file contains. In this case, you can set up a while loop that continues reading from the file until the file is empty.

A while loop may execute 0 or more times. That is, it is possible that a while loop will never execute, depending on how you set up the loop conditional, which is the expression that determines whether the loop will continue. Suppose, for example, you are reading from a file until the end, but the file contains no data. Assuming that the loop is supposed to continue until the file is empty, the while loop will never execute, because the file starts off empty.

The fact that a while loop may not execute at all makes coding them a little tricky. You must be sure to set up the loop conditional properly, which includes initializing the loop control variable before the loop starts. Also, it is important to handle the loop variable properly inside the loop. Otherwise, the loop could run forever.

Because the code that sets up the situation for ending the while loop must be inside the loop code rather than the while statement itself, a common error is to forget to include such code. For example, if a while loop executes while x is less than 10, a common error is to forget to increment x. Therefore if your while loop runs without quitting, you should check to see if you forgot the increment code.

CREATE A WHILE LOOP

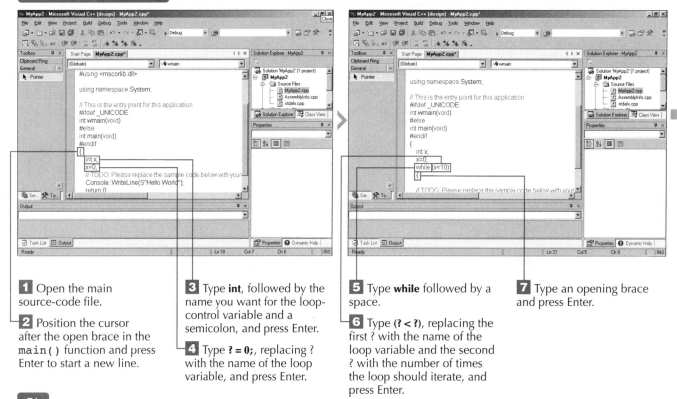

1 Open the main source-code file.

2 Position the cursor after the open brace in the main() function and press Enter to start a new line.

3 Type **int**, followed by the name you want for the loop-control variable and a semicolon, and press Enter.

4 Type **? = 0;**, replacing ? with the name of the loop variable, and press Enter.

5 Type **while** followed by a space.

6 Type **(? < ?)**, replacing the first ? with the name of the loop variable and the second ? with the number of times the loop should iterate, and press Enter.

7 Type an opening brace and press Enter.

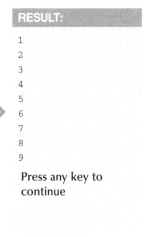

Apply It

The thing to remember about while loops is that you must initialize the loop variable before the loop starts, as well as update the variable inside the loop. For example, if the loop reads to the end of a file, you must read a line before the loop starts and then read lines while inside the loop.

As a shortcut, you can update the loop-control variable inside the while statement. This relieves you from doing the update inside the loop itself.

TYPE THIS:

```
#include "stdafx.h"
#using <mscorlib.dll>
using namespace System;
int main(void)
{
    int x;
    x=0;
    while((++x)<10)
    {
        Console::WriteLine(x);
    }
    return 0;
}
```

RESULT:

```
1
2
3
4
5
6
7
8
9
```

Press any key to continue

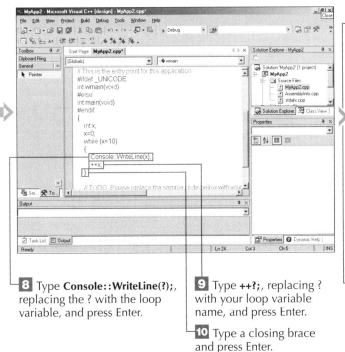

■8 Type **Console::WriteLine(?);**, replacing the ? with the loop variable, and press Enter.

■9 Type **++?;**, replacing ? with your loop variable name, and press Enter.

■10 Type a closing brace and press Enter.

■11 Click Build ➪ Compile to compile and run your program.

Note: See page 9 for more information on compiling a program.

■ The program displays the value of the loop variable each time the loop iterates.

CREATE A DO-WHILE LOOP

ike other types of loops, a do-while loop enables
your program to perform a series of commands over
and over as long as a specified condition remains true.
The difference between a do-while loop and a regular
while loop is that, with the former, the loop conditional —
which is the expression that controls the loop — comes at
the end of the loop instead of at the beginning. This means
that, whereas a while loop can execute 0 or more times, a
do-while loop always executes at least once.

Suppose, for example, you want the user to enter a list of
names into your program and that the user must give the
program at least one name. This would be a perfect task for

a do-while loop. When the program enters the loop, it
asks the user for a name. After the user has entered the
name, the loop checks its conditional expression to
determine whether to loop. If so, the loop goes back to the
beginning and asks for another name. Otherwise, the loop
ends after having received only a single name. In any case,
the loop requires that the user enter at least one name.

To code a do-while loop, you type the keyword do, and
follow with the code that will loop, surrounded by braces.
After the closing brace, you type the keyword while,
followed by the condition in parentheses.

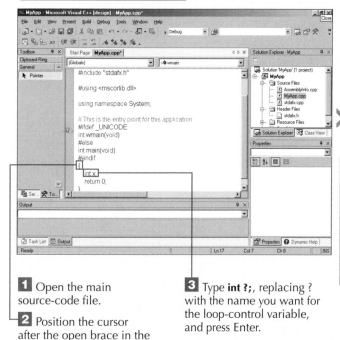

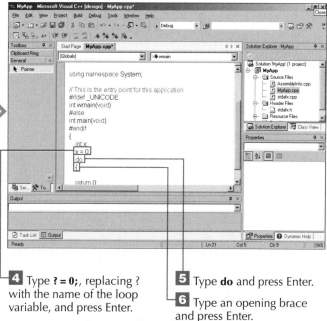

1 Open the main
source-code file.

2 Position the cursor
after the open brace in the
main() function and press
Enter to start a new line.

3 Type **int ?;**, replacing ?
with the name you want for
the loop-control variable,
and press Enter.

4 Type **? = 0;**, replacing ?
with the name of the loop
variable, and press Enter.

5 Type **do** and press Enter.

6 Type an opening brace
and press Enter.

You can use more complex loop conditionals than the ones you have used so far. For example, you can have your do-while loop iterate a given number of times or until the user enters a specified value.

TYPE THIS:

```
#include "stdafx.h"
#using <mscorlib.dll>
using namespace System;
int main(void)
{
    int i;
    char c;
    int x=0;
    do
    {
        Console::WriteLine(x);
        ++x;
        Console::WriteLine("Enter Q to quit:");
        // Get the character.
        i = Console::Read();
        c = (char)i;
        // Get the cr/lf.
        i = Console::Read();
        i = Console::Read();
    }
    while ((x < 10) && (c != 'Q') && (c != 'q'));
    return 0;
}
```

RESULT:

```
0
Enter Q to quit:
r
1
Enter Q to quit:
e
2
Enter Q to quit:
u
3
Enter Q to quit:
w
4
Enter Q to quit:
q
```

Press any key to continue

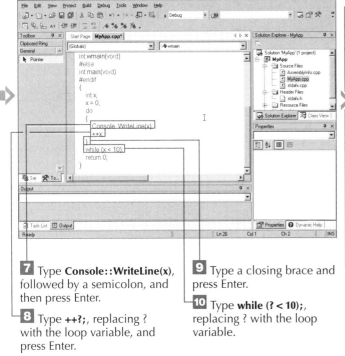

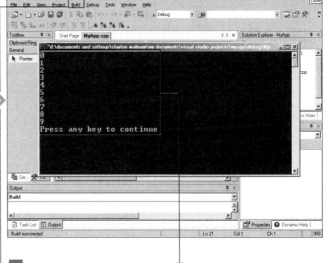

7 Type **Console::WriteLine(x)**, followed by a semicolon, and then press Enter.

8 Type **++?;**, replacing ? with the loop variable, and press Enter.

9 Type a closing brace and press Enter.

10 Type **while (? < 10);**, replacing ? with the loop variable.

11 Click Build ➪ Compile to compile and run your program.

Note: See page 9 for more information on compiling a program.

■ The program displays the value of the loop variable each time the loop iterates.

CREATE AN IF STATEMENT

The if statement enables your program to branch to different code based on a comparison. In this way, your programs can analyze data and make decisions on that data. The simplest form of an if statement evaluates a single comparison and then either branches or not. However, if statements can also make decisions based on compound comparisons. Also, by adding an else clause to an if statement, you can provide a default outcome.

The if statement evaluates a Boolean expression, which is an expression that can be either true or false. For example, the expression $x == 5$ is true if x equals five, but is false if x is any other value. Notice the use of the double equals sign as the expression's operator. This is how C++ differentiates between an assignment statement like $x = 5$ and a Boolean expression like $x == 5$.

If an if statement's Boolean expression evaluates to true, the program executes the code that makes up the body of the if statement, and then continues on to the next line in the program. If the Boolean expression evaluates to false, program execution skips the body of the if statement and continues with the next program line after the statement.

Probably the most common C++ programming error is to forget to use two equal signs in a row for testing equality. The compiler does not tell you if you make this mistake. Instead it treats the clause as an assignment statement and then treats it as a true statement. If you have an if statement that tests for equality and you find that the code inside the if block always executes whether the condition is true or not, then you probably used a single equals sign instead of a double equals sign.

CREATE AN IF STATEMENT

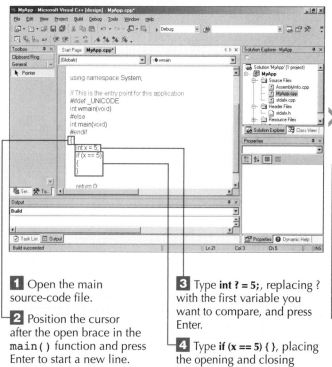

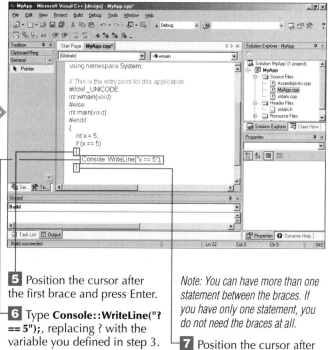

■1 Open the main source-code file.

■2 Position the cursor after the open brace in the main() function and press Enter to start a new line.

■3 Type **int ? = 5;**, replacing ? with the first variable you want to compare, and press Enter.

■4 Type **if (x == 5) { }**, placing the opening and closing braces on separate lines.

■5 Position the cursor after the first brace and press Enter.

■6 Type **Console::WriteLine("? == 5");**, replacing ? with the variable you defined in step 3.

■7 Position the cursor after the second brace and press Enter.

Note: You can have more than one statement between the braces. If you have only one statement, you do not need the braces at all.

Apply It

When writing `if` statements, be careful not to confuse the `==` operator with the `=` operator. If, for example, you write `x = 5` when you really mean `x == 5`, the program will assign 5 to `x` and will consider the expression to be true.

You can combine `else` clauses with `if` statements to give your programs more choices.

TYPE THIS:

```
#include "stdafx.h"
#using <mscorlib.dll>
using namespace System;
int main(void)
{
    Console::WriteLine("Enter a letter:");
    int i = Console::Read();
    char c = (char) i;
    if (c == 'a')
        Console::WriteLine("c == a");
    else if (c == 'b')
        Console::WriteLine("c == b");
    else if (c == 'c')
        Console::WriteLine("c == c");
    else
        Console::WriteLine("c is invalid");
    return 0;
}
```

RESULT:

```
Enter a letter:
c
c == c
```

Press any key to continue

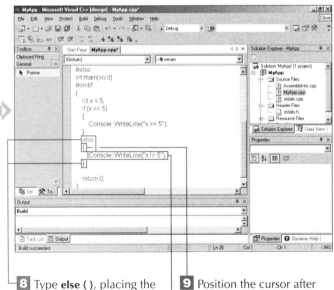

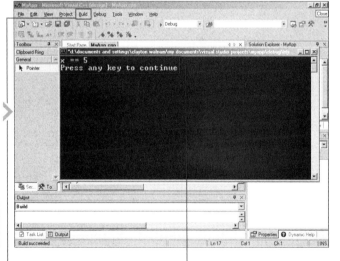

8 Type **else { }**, placing the opening and closing braces on separate lines.

9 Position the cursor after the `else` clause's first brace and press Enter.

10 Type **Console::WriteLine("? != 5");**, replacing ? with the variable you defined in step 3.

11 Click Build ➪ Compile to compile and run your program.

Note: See page 9 for more information on compiling a program.

■ The program's `if` statement uses the value of your variable to determine which message to display.

CREATE A SWITCH STATEMENT

A switch statement is a replacement for if statements that require many comparisons. Using a switch statement instead of a lengthy if statement cuts down on the amount of typing you need to do and makes your program easier to read. A switch statement can handle a long list of comparisons, and when looking over the program, you can quickly find the ones you want.

Instead of else clauses, a switch statement uses the case keyword. The first line of the switch statement specifies the value to compare and a list of case clauses follows, one case for each value to which you want to compare the value. Each case clause can contain one or more program lines, all of which the program will execute if the case evaluates to true.

The switch statement relies on the break keyword to know when to end. Unlike an if statement that ends as soon as it determines the result of the comparison, a switch statement continues through case clauses until it reaches a break statement. When the program reaches a break statement, program execution branches to the first line after the entire switch statement. This means that if you leave off a break statement, the code for the next case clause will also execute. A common error is to forget the break statement; therefore, if you have strange occurrences in your code near a case statement, the first thing you might check is whether you forgot the break statement.

CREATE A SWITCH STATEMENT

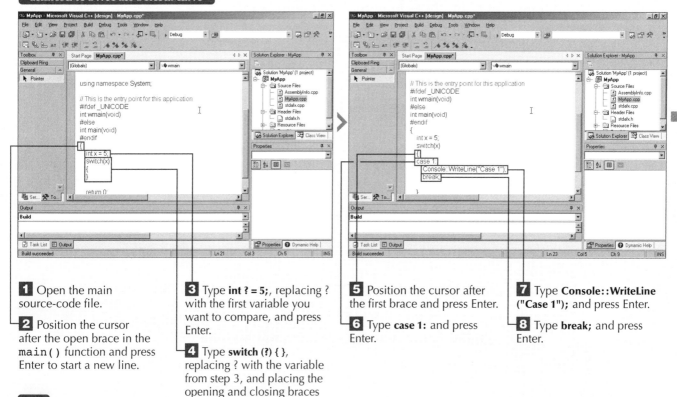

1 Open the main source-code file.

2 Position the cursor after the open brace in the main() function and press Enter to start a new line.

3 Type **int ? = 5;**, replacing ? with the first variable you want to compare, and press Enter.

4 Type **switch (?) { }**, replacing ? with the variable from step 3, and placing the opening and closing braces on separate lines.

5 Position the cursor after the first brace and press Enter.

6 Type **case 1:** and press Enter.

7 Type **Console::WriteLine ("Case 1");** and press Enter.

8 Type **break;** and press Enter.

Apply It

Just as you can use an `else` clause to provide a default path of execution for an `if` statement, so too can you use the `default` clause with a `switch` statement. The program executes the code associated with the `default` clause only when none of the `case` clauses evaluate to true.

TYPE THIS:

```
#include "stdafx.h"
#using <mscorlib.dll>
using namespace System;
int main(void)
{
    int x = 2;
    switch (x)
    {
    case 1:
        Console::WriteLine("Case 1");
        break;
    case 5:
    case 6:
        Console::WriteLine("Case 5 or 6");
        break;
    default:
         Console::WriteLine("Default case");
    }

    return 0;
}
```

RESULT:

```
Default case
```
Press any key to continue

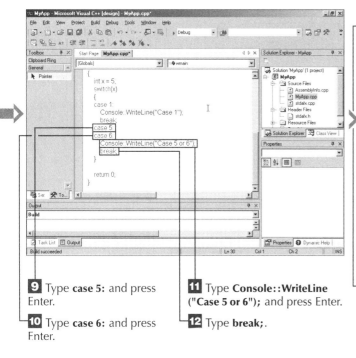

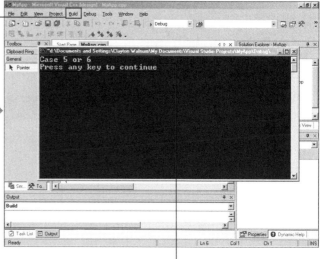

9 Type **case 5:** and press Enter.

10 Type **case 6:** and press Enter.

11 Type **Console::WriteLine ("Case 5 or 6");** and press Enter.

12 Type **break;**.

13 Click Build ➪ Compile to compile and run your program.

Note: See page 9 for more information on compiling a program.

■ The program displays the results of the comparisons.

DECLARE A STRUCTURE TYPE

Modeling complex data can make your programs very powerful by handling sophisticated data types. When you are modeling data that is more complex than the basic types such as `int` and `char`, you can declare a structure type. A *structure type* is a set of basic types grouped together and used as a single type. The individual parts making up the structure are called the *members of the structure*.

The idea behind a well-formed structure type is that you will likely have multiple instances of the structure type, and each of these instances carries with it all the members that form the structure. For example, a `CompactDisc` structure type might have as members character strings called `Name` and `Artist`, and an integer called `YearReleased`. When you create two variables of type `CompactDisc`, each will actually be a combination of three members, `Name`, `Artist`, and `YearReleased`. Similarly, a `ComputerProgram` structure type might have as members

a character string called `ProgramName` representing the name of the program, and a character string called `FullPath` representing the full path and filename of the executable file.

Because a structure type name is an identifier, it must begin with a letter or underscore, and can be followed by any combination of letters, numbers, and underscores. Similarly, the members of the structure must follow the same naming rules.

To declare a structure type, you type the word **struct**, the name of the structure, and an opening brace {. You then list the members, starting each with the type name, the member name, and ending each with a semicolon. If you have multiple members in sequence each having the same type, you can group them together by starting with the type, and then listing the members separated by commas, and ending with a semicolon.

DECLARE A STRUCTURE TYPE

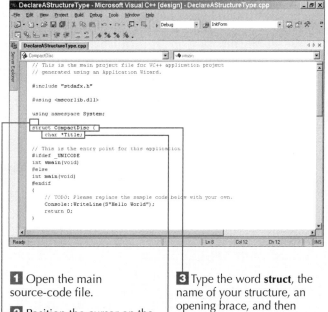

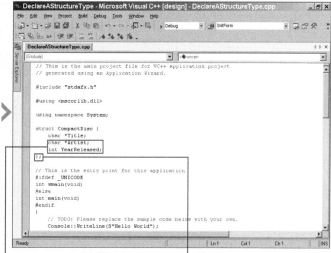

1 Open the main source-code file.

2 Position the cursor on the line after the `using namespace System` line and press Enter.

3 Type the word **struct**, the name of your structure, an opening brace, and then press Enter.

4 Enter the type of the first member, the member name, a semicolon, and then press Enter.

5 Type the remaining members, with one name per line, followed by a semicolon, and then press Enter.

6 Type a closing brace, followed by a semicolon, and then press Enter.

Extra

Structures can also contain members that are structures, in addition to the basic types such as integers and strings. These members can be defined either as structures or as pointers to structures.

Example:
```
struct ArtistInfo {
    char *Name;
    char *DateOfBirth;
    char *HomeTown;
};

struct CompactDisc {
    char *Title;
    char *Artist;
    ArtistInfo Info;
    int YearReleased;
};
```

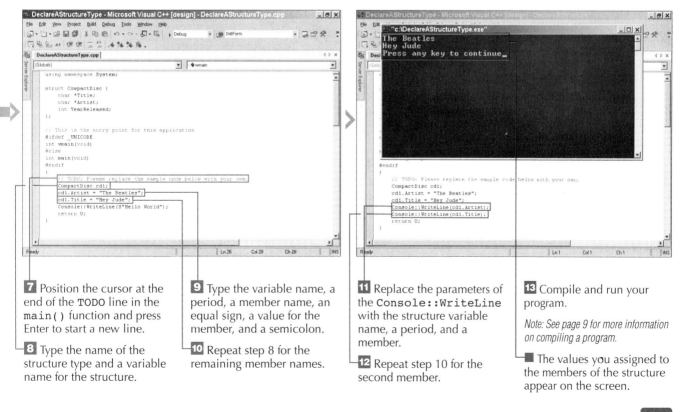

7 Position the cursor at the end of the TODO line in the main() function and press Enter to start a new line.

8 Type the name of the structure type and a variable name for the structure.

9 Type the variable name, a period, a member name, an equal sign, a value for the member, and a semicolon.

10 Repeat step 8 for the remaining member names.

11 Replace the parameters of the Console::WriteLine with the structure variable name, a period, and a member.

12 Repeat step 10 for the second member.

13 Compile and run your program.

Note: See page 9 for more information on compiling a program.

■ The values you assigned to the members of the structure appear on the screen.

CREATE A STRUCTURE

A structure is a form of user-defined data type. When you define a structure, you create a custom data type that can hold several different types of data simultaneously. For example, you might want to create a structure that organizes information about an employee into a single data type. In this case, you would create a structure that contained data fields for the employee's name, address, age, salary, and so on.

You can think of a structure as a container for related pieces of data. Each piece of data stored in a structure is called a *member* of the structure. Each member is much like a

variable in that each has its own name and data type. The members of a structure can be simple data types such as int and double or can be complex data types such as instances of another structure.

Because a structure is like any other data type, the data itself does not exist until you create an instance of the structure. You do this just as you would with any type of variable. Then, to access a member of a structure, you type the structure instance name, followed by a period, and the name of the member. See page 18 for more information on creating a variable.

CREATE A STRUCTURE

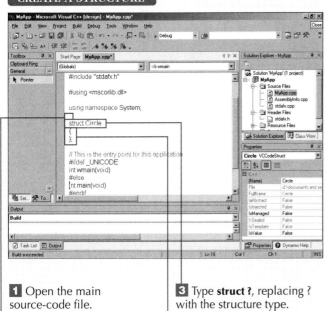

1 Open the main source-code file.

2 Position the cursor on the line after the using namespace System line and press Enter.

3 Type **struct ?**, replacing ? with the structure type.

4 Type **{ };**, placing the opening brace on a line, and then the closing brace and a semicolon on a separate line.

5 Position the cursor after the opening brace and press Enter to start a new line.

6 Type a data type, a space, a member name, a semicolon, and then press Enter.

Note: The variable is called a member of the structure.

7 Repeat step 6 for each member you want to add to the structure.

8 Position the cursor after the main( ) function's opening brace and press Enter to start a new line.

Apply It

You can create complex data that contains smaller data, allowing you to model data that consists of more than just numbers and strings.

TYPE THIS:

```
#include "stdafx.h"
#using <mscorlib.dll>
using namespace System;
struct Point { int x; int y; };
struct TwoPoints { Point point1; Point point2; };
int main(void)
{
    TwoPoints myPoints;
    myPoints.point1.x = 10;
    myPoints.point1.y = 15;
    myPoints.point2.x = 13;
    myPoints.point2.y = 25;
    Console::WriteLine(myPoints.point1.x);
    Console::WriteLine(myPoints.point1.y);
    Console::WriteLine(myPoints.point2.x);
    Console::WriteLine(myPoints.point2.y);
    return 0;
}
```

RESULT:

```
10
15
13
25
```

Press any key to continue

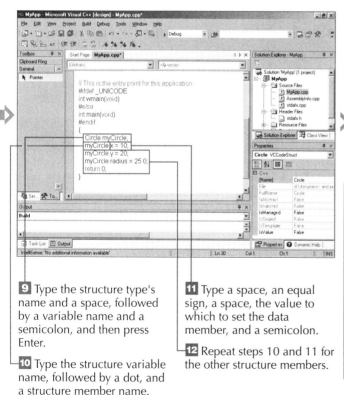

9 Type the structure type's name and a space, followed by a variable name and a semicolon, and then press Enter.

10 Type the structure variable name, followed by a dot, and a structure member name.

11 Type a space, an equal sign, a space, the value to which to set the data member, and a semicolon.

12 Repeat steps 10 and 11 for the other structure members.

13 Type **Console::WriteLine(?.?);**, replacing the first ? with the structure variable name and the second ? with a structure member name.

14 Repeat step 13 for each structure member.

15 Compile and run your program.

Note: See page 9 for more information on compiling a program.

■ The program displays the values of the members of the structure.

INITIALIZE A STRUCTURE

When you have a structure type, there are different ways in which you can create and initialize structures of the type. The first way is to create a variable of the structure type by typing the structure type name, followed by one of more variable names, separated by commas, and ending with a semicolon. This creates uninitialized structures and is analogous to declaring an integer by typing int followed by a variable name and a semicolon. Like the integer, the structure's contents are initially undefined. To initialize the structure, you follow each variable name with an equals sign, an open brace {, initializing data separated by semicolons, and finally a closing brace }. There is one item of initializing data for each member in the structure, and the types must match. For example, if you have an integer member, the initializing data for that member must be an integer as well.

The second way is to create the structure in memory, and to create a variable whose type is a pointer to the structure. To do this, you declare the variable by typing the structure type name, and one or more variables starting with an asterisk followed by the variable name, separated by commas, and ending with a semicolon. Each variable is preceded by its own asterisk; otherwise only the first will be a pointer to a structure and the remaining will simply be structures. As with the first approach, the pointer variable is uninitialized. To initialize it, type an equals sign after the variable name, followed by the new keyword, followed by the structure type name. This creates a new structure in memory and initializes your pointer variable with the address of the structure.

INITIALIZE A STRUCTURE

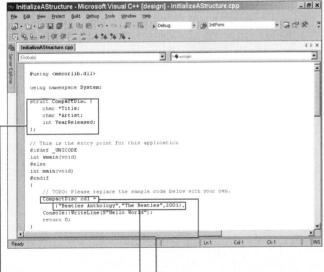

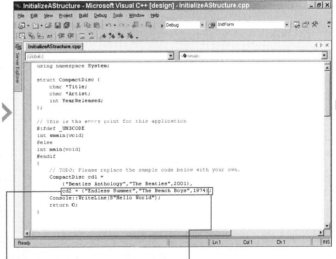

1 Open the main source-code file.

2 Declare a structure type.

Note: See page 42 for more information on declaring a structure type.

3 Position the mouse before the WriteLine line and type the name of the structure type, a space, a variable name, an equal sign, and then press Enter.

4 Press Tab and type an opening brace, the initialization values separated by commas, and a closing brace.

5 Repeat steps 3 and 4 for additional structures, separate each with a comma.

6 To end, type a semicolon and press Enter.

Apply It

Structures can contain constructor methods. This example shows how a constructor can be used to initialize the items in a structure.

TYPE THIS:

```cpp
struct CompactDisc {
    char *Title;
    char *Artist;
    int YearReleased;
    CompactDisc(char *t, char *a, int y) {
        Title = t; Artist = a; YearReleased = y;
    }
};

int main(void)
{
    CompactDisc cd1("Beatles Anthology","Beatles",2001);
    CompactDisc *cd3 = new CompactDisc("Endless Summer","Beach Boys",1974);
    Console::WriteLine(cd1.Artist);
    Console::WriteLine(cd3->Artist);
    return 0;
}
```

RESULT:

```
Beatles
Beach Boys
```

Press any key to continue

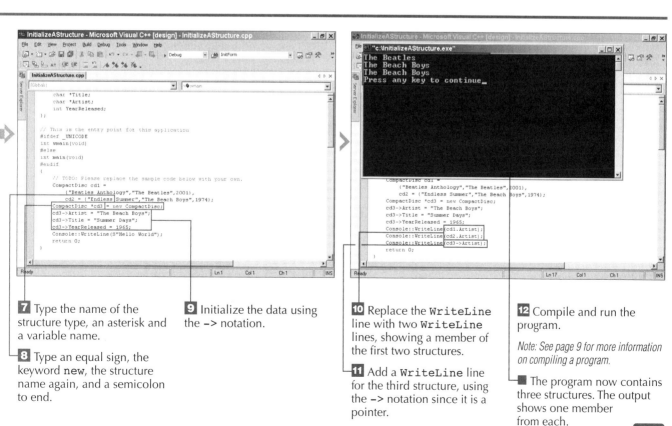

7 Type the name of the structure type, an asterisk and a variable name.

8 Type an equal sign, the keyword **new**, the structure name again, and a semicolon to end.

9 Initialize the data using the **->** notation.

10 Replace the WriteLine line with two WriteLine lines, showing a member of the first two structures.

11 Add a WriteLine line for the third structure, using the **->** notation since it is a pointer.

12 Compile and run the program.

Note: See page 9 for more information on compiling a program.

■ The program now contains three structures. The output shows one member from each.

ACCESS A STRUCTURE

By accessing the individual parts of a structure, your manipulations can either focus on the entire structures or the individual portions of the structures. To access the individual portions of a structure, you simply specify the structure name, a period, and the member name. When you access the individual members, you can treat them as regular variables. For example, you can pass the individual members to a function, or you can use standard operators such as ++ on them.

You can even take the address of a single member as you would any variable. For example, suppose you have a structure of type GroceryItem, and the structure is called VanillaIceCream, with member Inventory, which is an int. If you have a function called ProcessInventory that takes a pointer to int, you can pass the single member ProcessInventory(&(VanillaIceCream.Inventory)).

Notice there is an extra set of parentheses around VanillaIceCream.Inventory. Although not always necessary, since most compilers can sort through it, it is good practice for clarity when humans read it. Here, the order of operations is obvious that you are instructing the computer to take the address of VanillaIceCream.Inventory.

The usual ++ and arithmetic operators work on members, provided they are types that use these operators. For example, you can increment the Inventory member using VanillaIceCream.Inventory++. When dealing with the members of a structure for which you have a pointer, you can still use the same operators, combined with the -> notation, as in CurrentGroceryItem->InventoryCount++.

ACCESS A STRUCTURE

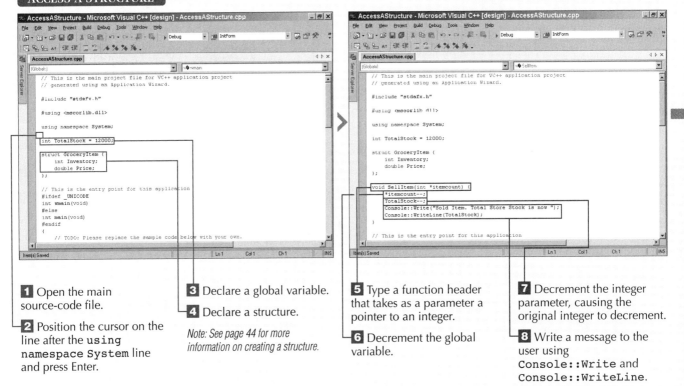

■1 Open the main source-code file.

■2 Position the cursor on the line after the **using namespace System** line and press Enter.

■3 Declare a global variable.

■4 Declare a structure.

Note: See page 44 for more information on creating a structure.

■5 Type a function header that takes as a parameter a pointer to an integer.

■6 Decrement the global variable.

■7 Decrement the integer parameter, causing the original integer to decrement.

■8 Write a message to the user using Console::Write and Console::WriteLine.

Apply It

You can pass the individual members of a structure to a function. For example, if you have a structure that contains a member that is an integer, and you have a function that takes an integer as a parameter, you can pass the member to the function.

TYPE THIS:

```
struct MyInfo {
        int x,y;
};

int square(int a) {
        return a * a;
}
int main(void) {
        MyInfo info;
        info.x = 10;
        info.y = 20;
        Console::WriteLine(square(info.x));
}
```

RESULT:

```
100
```

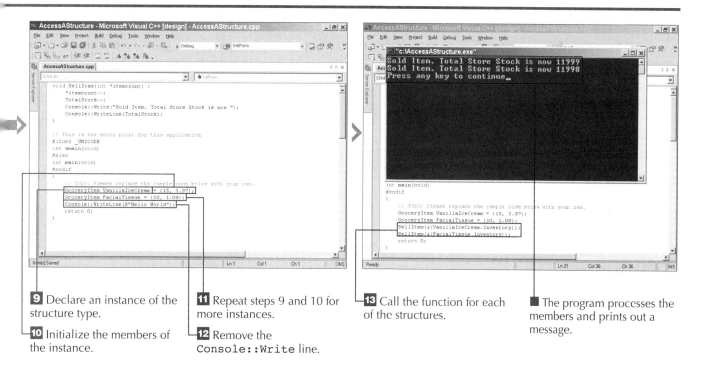

9 Declare an instance of the structure type.

10 Initialize the members of the instance.

11 Repeat steps 9 and 10 for more instances.

12 Remove the `Console::Write` line.

13 Call the function for each of the structures.

■ The program processes the members and prints out a message.

CREATE AN ARRAY OF STRUCTURES

A structure is a handy way to group related data. But because a structure is just a template for a custom data type, you can create as many instances of the structure as you like. This enables you to build a database of records, such as information about a group of employees. A good way to store each record of this database is in an array, where you can access each record with an index.

The ability to access a structure by way of an index means that you can process the records efficiently within loops, no matter how many records the array holds. For example, if

you created ten instances of a structure separately, you would have to initialize each structure with its own lines of code. If you store the instances in an array, however, you can initialize each structure with only a single line for each member.

For only a couple of structure instances, an array may not save much coding or processing time. However, when you start talking about databases with hundreds, thousands, or even millions of records, using an array to organize records as structure instances is the only way to go.

CREATE AN ARRAY OF STRUCTURES

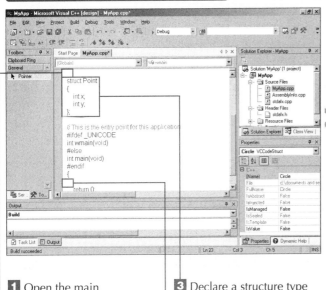

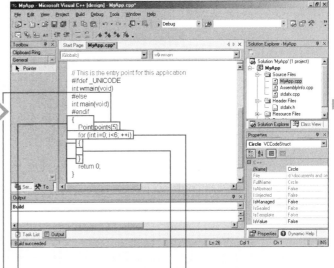

1 Open the main source-code file.

2 Position the cursor on the line after the `using namespace System` line and press Enter.

3 Declare a structure type with two members.

Note: See page 44 for more information on creating a structure.

4 Position the cursor after the `main()` function's opening brace and press Enter.

5 Type the structure type's name, followed by a space and a name for the structure array.

6 Type [?];, replacing ? with the number of structure instances minus 1 that you want to store in the array, and press Enter.

7 Type **for (int i=0; i<?; ++i)**, replacing ? with the number of structures in the array.

8 Type { }, placing the opening and closing braces on separate lines.

9 Position the cursor after the **for** loop's opening brace and press Enter.

Extra

Things can get confusing when you have an array of structures, each structure of which contains other structures. Remember, to access a member of the inner-most structure, you need to create a kind of roadmap to the member. You always start with the array name, followed by the index of the structure in the array. After the index, you type a period, the name of the structure that is contained in the outer structure, another period, and then the member name. You end up with something that looks like this: `points[i].point1.x`. If you have structures within structures within structures, you might end up with something like this: `points[i].myPoints.point1.x`.

When you create an array of structures, you can keep the array size down if you store pointers to structures within the array, instead of the structures themselves. This will also help keep your program running quickly.

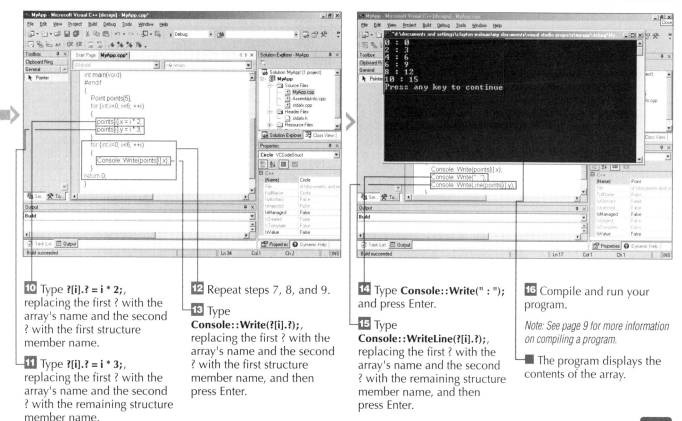

10 Type **?[i].? = i * 2;**, replacing the first ? with the array's name and the second ? with the first structure member name.

11 Type **?[i].? = i * 3;**, replacing the first ? with the array's name and the second ? with the remaining structure member name.

12 Repeat steps 7, 8, and 9.

13 Type **Console::Write(?[i].?);**, replacing the first ? with the array's name and the second ? with the first structure member name, and then press Enter.

14 Type **Console::Write(" : ");** and press Enter.

15 Type **Console::WriteLine(?[i].?);**, replacing the first ? with the array's name and the second ? with the remaining structure member name, and then press Enter.

16 Compile and run your program.

Note: See page 9 for more information on compiling a program.

■ The program displays the contents of the array.

PASS A STRUCTURE POINTER TO A FUNCTION

When you start programming with structures, you will need to pass them between functions as arguments. To do this, you want to use structure pointers, because passing a pointer is much more efficient than passing an entire structure.

The problem with passing structures as arguments is that a structure can be very large. Because a structure acts as a container to its members, the size of the structure is the sum of the sizes of all of its members. That is, whereas a single integer is 4 bytes, a structure that contains five integer members is 20 bytes. If you pass this structure as an

argument to a function, the system must duplicate all 20 bytes and pass them to the function. When you are dealing with extremely large structures and many function calls, this can cause a serious efficiency problem in your program.

The way to cut down on duplicating and passing data is to pass a pointer to the structure rather than the actual value of the structure. When you pass something using a pointer, you do not pass a copy of the data, but instead just the address of the data. Pointers are always the same size, so passing a pointer to a structure works for structures of any size, from a few bytes to many kilobytes.

PASS A STRUCTURE POINTER TO A FUNCTION

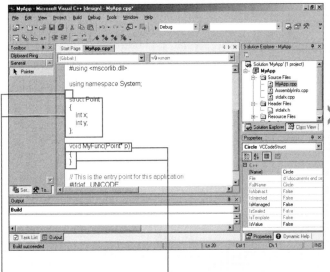

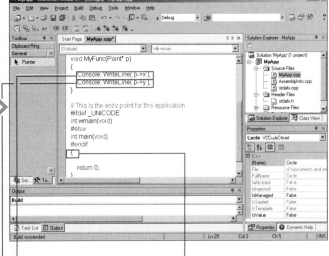

1 Open the main source-code file.

2 Position the cursor on the line after the **using namespace System** line and press Enter.

3 Declare a structure type with two members.

Note: See page 44 for more information on creating a structure.

4 Type **void MyFunc(?* p)**, replacing ? with the structure type's name.

5 Type **{ }**, placing the opening and closing braces on separate lines.

6 Inside the function, type **Console::WriteLine(p->?);**, replacing ? with the name of the first structure member, and press Enter.

7 Type **Console::WriteLine(p->?);**, replacing ? with the name of the second structure member.

8 Position the cursor after the **main( )** function's opening brace and press Enter.

Apply It

If a structure is small enough, you can pass it to a function just like any other type of data. Just remember that the size of the structure is the sum of the sizes of all its members, and all of this data must be duplicated and passed to the function.

TYPE THIS:

```
#include "stdafx.h"
#using <mscorlib.dll>
using namespace System;
struct Point {int x; int y;};
void MyFunc(Point p)
{
    Console::WriteLine(p.x);
    Console::WriteLine(p.y);
}
int main(void)
{
    Point point;
    point.x = 10;
    point.y = 20;
    MyFunc(point);
    return 0;
}
```

RESULT:

```
10
20
```

Press any key to continue

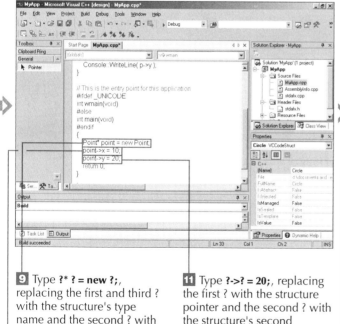

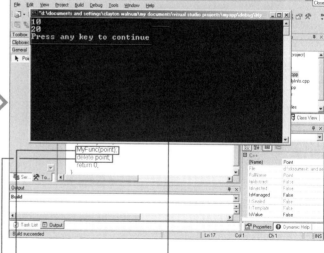

9 Type **?* ? = new ?;**, replacing the first and third ? with the structure's type name and the second ? with the name for the structure pointer, and then press Enter.

10 Type **?->? = 10;**, replacing the first ? with the structure pointer and the second ? with the structure's first member.

11 Type **?->? = 20;**, replacing the first ? with the structure pointer and the second ? with the structure's second member, and press Enter.

12 Type **MyFunc(?);**, replacing ? with the name of the structure pointer, and press Enter.

13 Type **delete ?;**, replacing ? with the name of the structure pointer.

14 Compile and run your program.

Note: See page 9 for more information on compiling a program.

■ The program displays the contents of the array.

CREATE A STRUCTURE CONTAINING FUNCTIONS

I f you need to perform actions on the members of a structure, you can place the functions that perform these actions inside the structure. Including the functions that operate on structure members within the structure makes a compact and cohesive package for managing data.

When you create more than one instance of the structure, you can think of each structure as having its own member data, and its own member functions. The member functions can operate on the member data for the particular structure.

To create a member function, you write a function header inside the class declaration. For example, if you have a structure called Amount, and it has a function called `Add` that takes an integer and returns a void, you would place the function header `void Add(int x);` inside the class declaration.

To declare the code for the function, after the structure definition you type the function header again, except with the structure name preceding the function name, followed by two colons, as in `void Amount::Add(int x)`. You then provide the code for the function inside braces as you would with any function.

The code inside the function can then refer to the members of the structure directly. For example, if the structure has an integer member called `Value`, the code in the function can simply use the variable `Value`. Thus, if you have two instances of the structure, and you call the function for the first instance, the variable `Value` inside the function refers to the `Value` member for the first instance. You call the member function in the same way you access the data members of the function using a -> (pointer-access notation) or a . (pointer notation), depending on whether you have a pointer or not, respectively.

CREATE A STRUCTURE CONTAINING FUNCTIONS

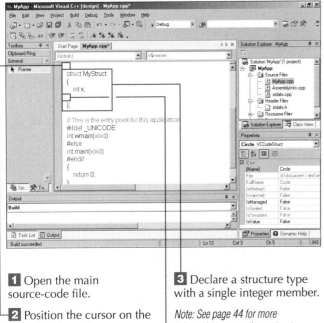

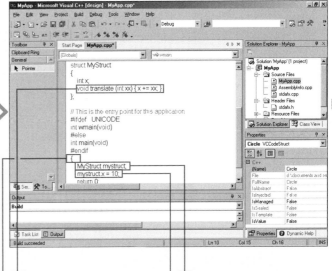

1 Open the main source-code file.

2 Position the cursor on the line after the `using namespace System` line and press Enter.

3 Declare a structure type with a single integer member.

Note: See page 44 for more information on creating a structure.

4 Position the cursor after the data member of the structure and press Enter to start a new line.

5 Type **void translate (int xx) { ? += xx; }**, replacing ? with the name of the structure's single integer member.

6 Position the cursor after the `main()` function's opening brace and press Enter to start a new line.

7 Type the structure type name, followed by a space, the name for the structure instance, and a semicolon.

8 Type **?.? = 10;**, replacing the first ? with the structure instances name and the second ? with the structure member name.

54

Apply It

Like classes, a structure can use access specifiers like `private` and `public` to determine what parts of the structure can be accessed from code outside of the structure.

TYPE THIS:

```
struct Point {
private: int x;
public:
    void translate(int xx){x += xx;}
    void setX(int xx){x = xx;}
    int getX(){return x;}
};
int main(void) {
    Point point;
    point.setX(10);
    point.translate(10);
    Console::Write("x = ");
    Console::WriteLine(point.getX());
    return 0;
}
```

RESULT:

```
20
```

Press any key to continue

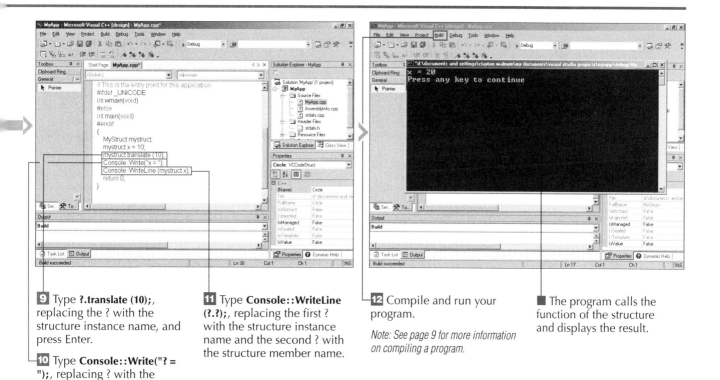

■9 Type **?.translate (10);**, replacing the ? with the structure instance name, and press Enter.

■10 Type **Console::Write("? = ");**, replacing ? with the structure member name, and press Enter.

■11 Type **Console::WriteLine (?.?);**, replacing the first ? with the structure instance name and the second ? with the structure member name.

■12 Compile and run your program.

Note: See page 9 for more information on compiling a program.

■ The program calls the function of the structure and displays the result.

CONVERT DATA WITH C-STYLE CASTS

B y using C-style casts to convert between data types, you enable your programs to perform actions that normally the compiler does not allow. For example, your C++ compiler does not complain when you try to assign an integer to a `long` integer, because no data is lost in the conversion. The compiler performs this type of conversion implicitly, meaning that you do not have to tell the compiler what to do. However, trying to assign a `long` integer to an integer means losing half the data. In most cases, your compiler complains when you try to do this.

You can stop the compiler from generating errors by using a cast, which tells the compiler that you are not accidentally converting data, but rather that you want to do it even though it may result in lost data. This is called an *explicit* conversion, because you are explicitly telling the compiler what to do.

To perform a C-style cast, just preface the value you want to convert with the new data type enclosed in parentheses. Before you do such conversions, however, be sure that you really do know what you are doing. In many cases, a cast results in truncated values, where the computer throws away bits of information in order to fit the data into the new type.

CONVERT DATA WITH C-STYLE CASTS

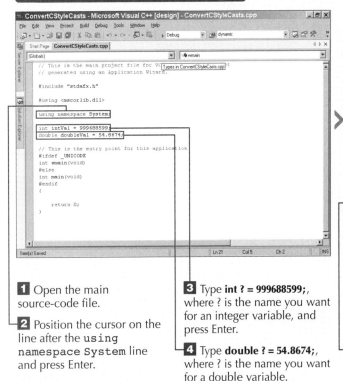

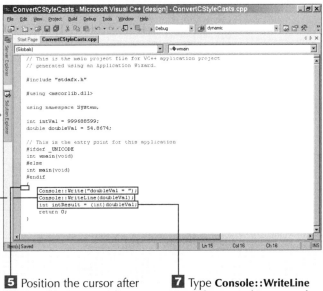

1 Open the main source-code file.

2 Position the cursor on the line after the `using namespace System` line and press Enter.

3 Type **int ? = 999688599;**, where ? is the name you want for an integer variable, and press Enter.

4 Type **double ? = 54.8674;**, where ? is the name you want for a double variable.

5 Position the cursor after the opening brace of the **main( )** function and press Enter to start a new line.

6 Type **Console::Write("? = ");**, where ? is the name of the double variable, and press Enter.

7 Type **Console::WriteLine (?);**, where ? is the name of the double variable, and press Enter.

8 Type **int intResult = (int) ?;**, where the ? is the name of the double variable, and press Enter.

Apply It

You do not need to perform conversions by assigning the results of a conversion to variable. You can perform a cast wherever you need to.

TYPE THIS:

```
#include "stdafx.h"
#using <mscorlib.dll>
using namespace System;
int intVal = 999688599;
double doubleVal = 54.8674;
int main(void)
{
    Console::Write("doubleVal = ");
    Console::WriteLine(doubleVal);
    Console::Write("Result = ");
    Console::WriteLine((int)doubleVal);
    Console::Write("intVal = ");
    Console::WriteLine(intVal);
    Console::Write("Result = ");
    Console::WriteLine((short)intVal);
    return 0;
}
```

RESULT:

```
doubleVal = 54.8674
Result = 54
intVal = 999688599
Result = 2455
```

Press any key to continue

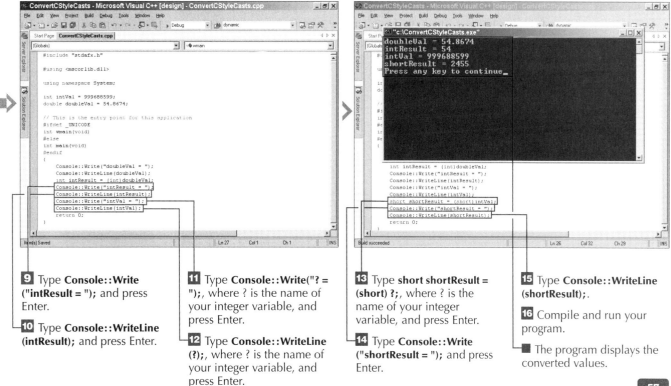

9 Type **Console::Write ("intResult = ");** and press Enter.

10 Type **Console::WriteLine (intResult);** and press Enter.

11 Type **Console::Write("? = ");**, where ? is the name of your integer variable, and press Enter.

12 Type **Console::WriteLine (?);**, where ? is the name of your integer variable, and press Enter.

13 Type **short shortResult = (short) ?;**, where ? is the name of your integer variable, and press Enter.

14 Type **Console::Write ("shortResult = ");** and press Enter.

15 Type **Console::WriteLine (shortResult);**.

16 Compile and run your program.

■ The program displays the converted values.

CONVERT BETWEEN POINTERS AND NUMBERS

Often during the course of a programming project, you need to convert one type of pointer into another or even pointers to numbers and vice versa. For example, your program may call a memory allocation function that returns the address of the allocated memory as a pointer to `void`. In this case, you need to convert the pointer to the type you need, such as `char`, `int`, `long`, and so on.

Because most C++ compilers do not allow you to make such conversions implicitly, you must use a cast to transform the pointer into the type you need. You can use

the regular C-style casts in these cases, but such casts are now considered to be outdated. Programmers should now use the C++ new-style casts. In the case of casting between pointer types and numbers, you would use the `reinterpret_cast` operator.

The `reinterpret_cast` operator takes as arguments the type to which to convert and the type to be converted. The type to convert to appears between angle brackets, whereas the type to convert appears in parentheses after the angle brackets. The operator returns the requested type.

CONVERT BETWEEN POINTERS AND NUMBERS

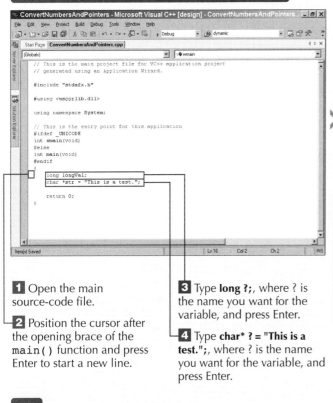

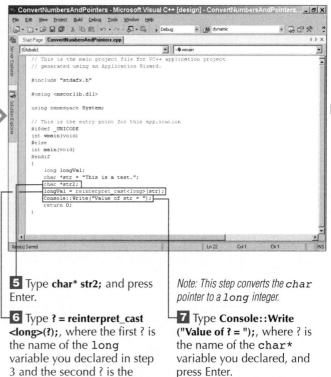

1 Open the main source-code file.

2 Position the cursor after the opening brace of the `main()` function and press Enter to start a new line.

3 Type **long ?;**, where ? is the name you want for the variable, and press Enter.

4 Type **char* ? = "This is a test.";**, where ? is the name you want for the variable, and press Enter.

5 Type **char* str2;** and press Enter.

6 Type **? = reinterpret_cast <long>(?);**, where the first ? is the name of the `long` variable you declared in step 3 and the second ? is the `char\*` variable you declared in step 4, and press Enter.

Note: This step converts the `char` pointer to a `long` integer.

7 Type **Console::Write ("Value of ? = ");**, where ? is the name of the `char\*` variable you declared, and press Enter.

Apply It

The most common use of the `reinterpret_cast` operator is to convert one type of pointer to another.

TYPE THIS:

```
#include "stdafx.h"
#using <mscorlib.dll>
using namespace System;

int main(void)
{
    char* pStr = "A";
    int* pInt = reinterpret_cast<int*>(pStr);
    Console::WriteLine("As string: ");
    Console::WriteLine(pStr);
    Console::WriteLine("As integer: ");
    Console::WriteLine(*pInt);
    return 0;
}
```

RESULT:

```
As string:
A
As integer:
65
```
Press any key to continue

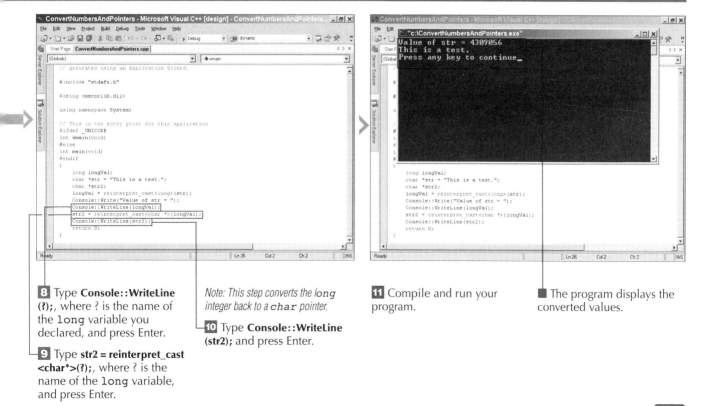

8 Type **Console::WriteLine (?);**, where ? is the name of the `long` variable you declared, and press Enter.

9 Type **str2 = reinterpret_cast <char*>(?);**, where ? is the name of the `long` variable, and press Enter.

Note: This step converts the long integer back to a char pointer.

10 Type **Console::WriteLine (str2);** and press Enter.

11 Compile and run your program.

■ The program displays the converted values.

CONVERT BETWEEN CLASS POINTERS

When you start working with polymorphic classes, you may sometimes need to know exactly what type of class a specific pointer represents. For example, you might have an array of class pointers, each pointer of which points to either a base class or one of several classes derived from the base class. When processing the pointers in this array, you can use the dynamic_cast operator to convert between classes, as well as to determine the type of class to which a pointer points.

The dynamic_cast operator gets its name from the fact that it performs its conversions dynamically, which means at runtime. This is the opposite of a static conversion, which happens when you compile your program. The static_cast operator handles static conversions.

In order to use the dynamic_cast operator, you must have run-time type information, also called RTTI, turned on for the project. You can do this by bringing up the Project Properties dialog box, selecting the C/C++ language options, and setting Enable Run-Time Type Info to Yes. If you fail to set this option, the compiler gives you a warning about the cast possibly causing unpredictable results, and your program may crash when it tries to perform the conversion.

CONVERT BETWEEN CLASS POINTERS

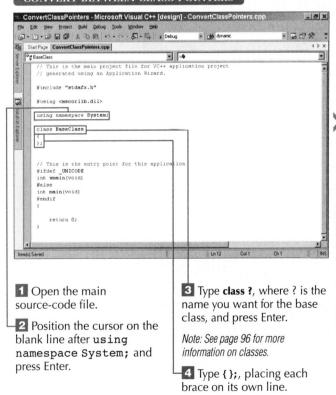

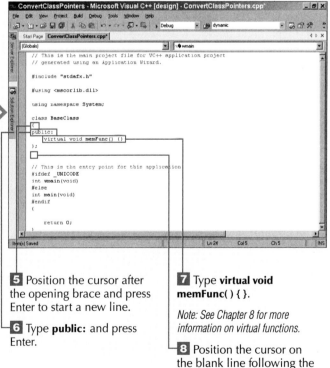

1 Open the main source-code file.

2 Position the cursor on the blank line after `using namespace System;` and press Enter.

3 Type **class ?**, where ? is the name you want for the base class, and press Enter.

Note: See page 96 for more information on classes.

4 Type **{ };**, placing each brace on its own line.

5 Position the cursor after the opening brace and press Enter to start a new line.

6 Type **public:** and press Enter.

7 Type **virtual void memFunc( ) { }.**

Note: See Chapter 8 for more information on virtual functions.

8 Position the cursor on the blank line following the class you just defined and press Enter.

Extra

If you are designing a set of classes, and you know that you will be converting between different classes, the only way you can successfully convert the classes is if they are related to each other; that is, if one is derived from another. The derived class can either be directly derived from the other, or it can be derived from a class that is derived from the other.

For this reason, if you are working with a commercially-available class library, which is a set of classes that somebody else developed, you will likely notice that the classes are arranged in a very large family tree fashion, often with one class at the very top. This top class is known as the root class and all other classes are derived from it. When you look at the different classes in this tree, those that are vertically connected through base classes and derived classes can be converted. Those that are analogous to siblings and cousins, which share a common ancestor but are not derived from each other, cannot be converted between each other.

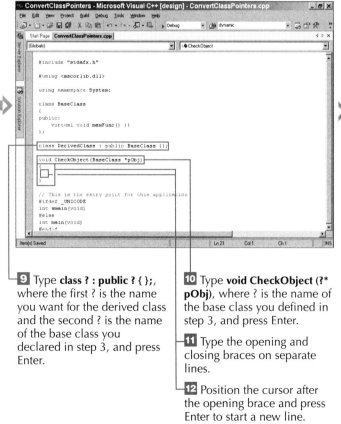

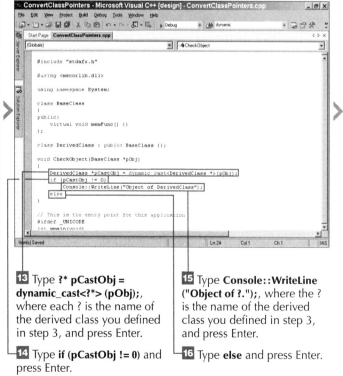

9 Type **class ? : public ? { };**, where the first ? is the name you want for the derived class and the second ? is the name of the base class you declared in step 3, and press Enter.

10 Type **void CheckObject (?* pObj)**, where ? is the name of the base class you defined in step 3, and press Enter.

11 Type the opening and closing braces on separate lines.

12 Position the cursor after the opening brace and press Enter to start a new line.

13 Type **?* pCastObj = dynamic_cast<?*> (pObj);**, where each ? is the name of the derived class you defined in step 3, and press Enter.

14 Type **if (pCastObj != 0)** and press Enter.

15 Type **Console::WriteLine ("Object of ?.");**, where the ? is the name of the derived class you defined in step 3, and press Enter.

16 Type **else** and press Enter.

CONTINUED

CONVERT BETWEEN CLASS POINTERS (CONTINUED)

The `dynamic_cast` keyword takes two parameters. The first is the type to which you are casting, and it is specified with angle brackets on either side of it, as in `<NewType>`. The second parameter is inside parentheses, and it is the value that you are casting.

If the cast is successful, the result of the cast is a pointer to an object of the type specified as a parameter to `dynamic_cast`.

If, however, the runtime library cannot perform the cast, the call to `dynamic_cast` will return a value of 0. This would be the case, for example, if you have an instance of a class and are trying to cast it to a derived class, but it is not an instance of the derived class. It will also happen if you attempt to cast two objects that are not related at all.

In your code, then, you can check whether `dynamic_cast` returns a 0. If it does, then that means the cast did not work. Otherwise, it will return a pointer to the original object, except cast as the new type.

In general, you would use `dynamic_cast` when you have a function that takes as a parameter a pointer to a certain class and you are passing to the function a pointer to a derived class. Inside the function, you would include a call to `dynamic_cast` to test whether the object can be cast to the derived class. If it can, and you receive a pointer from the cast, then it is indeed an instance of the derived class. If it cannot, and you receive a value of 0 instead of a pointer, then it is an instance of the base class.

CONVERT BETWEEN CLASS POINTERS (CONTINUED)

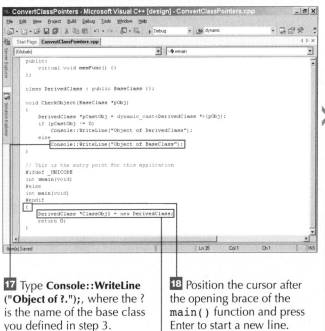

17 Type **Console::WriteLine ("Object of ?.");**, where the ? is the name of the base class you defined in step 3.

18 Position the cursor after the opening brace of the **main()** function and press Enter to start a new line.

19 Type **?* ClassObj1 = new ?;**, where the ? is the name of the derived class you defined in step 3, and press Enter.

20 Type **?* ClassObj2 = new ?;**, where each ? is the name of the base class you defined in step 3, and press Enter.

21 Type **CheckObject (ClassObj1);** and press Enter.

22 Type **CheckObject (ClassObj2);** and press Enter.

23 Type **delete ClassObj1;** and press Enter.

24 Type **delete ClassObj2;**.

Apply It

You can also use the `dynamic_cast` operator to convert a pointer to a derived class into a pointer to the base class.

TYPE THIS:

```
#include "stdafx.h"
#using <mscorlib.dll>
using namespace System;

class BaseClass { virtual void F(){} };
class DerivedClass : public BaseClass {};

int main(void)
{
    DerivedClass* a = new DerivedClass;
    BaseClass* b = dynamic_cast<BaseClass*>(a);
    if (b != 0)
        Console::WriteLine("Conversion to base class successful.");
    else
        Console::WriteLine("Conversion to base class unsuccessful.");
    delete a;

    return 0;
}
```

RESULT:

```
Conversion to base class
successful.
Press any key to continue
```

Converting a base class pointer to a derived class pointer is called *downcasting*. This operation gets its name from the fact that the pointer conversion moves down the class hierarchy, from the more general classes to the more specialized classes. Converting a derived class pointer to a base class pointer is called *upcasting*, because the operation moves up the class hierarchy, from more specialized classes to the classes from which the specialized classes are derived.

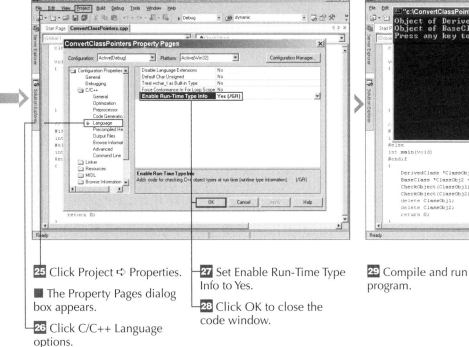

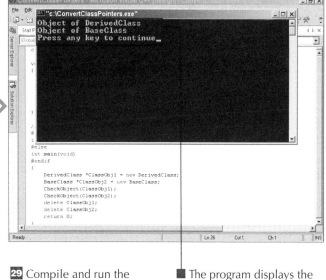

25 Click Project ➪ Properties.

■ The Property Pages dialog box appears.

26 Click C/C++ Language options.

27 Set Enable Run-Time Type Info to Yes.

28 Click OK to close the code window.

29 Compile and run the program.

■ The program displays the class types passed as arguments to the `CheckObject()` function.

CONVERT BETWEEN CLASS REFERENCES

References are a handy way to pass large objects like class instances and structures in and out of functions. This is because a reference enables you to use simpler syntax, as compared to a pointer, when accessing the referenced object, while still offering most of the benefits of a pointer. However, unlike pointers, a reference cannot have a null value, a fact that changes the way you deal with reference conversions when using the `dynamic_cast` operator.

When using a pointer, the `dynamic_cast` operator can return a null value if the conversion fails. References,

however, cannot have null values, so the mechanism by which the `dynamic_cast` operator indicates an error must be different. When used with a reference, the `dynamic_cast` operator throws a `bad_cast` exception in the case of an error. This means that you must enclose the cast in a `try` program block and provide error handling in a `catch` program block.

Other than the way the program handles a failed cast, the syntax for the cast is nearly the same, except that you do not need to accept the result of the cast into a variable and all the cast arguments are references rather than pointers.

CONVERT BETWEEN CLASS REFERENCES

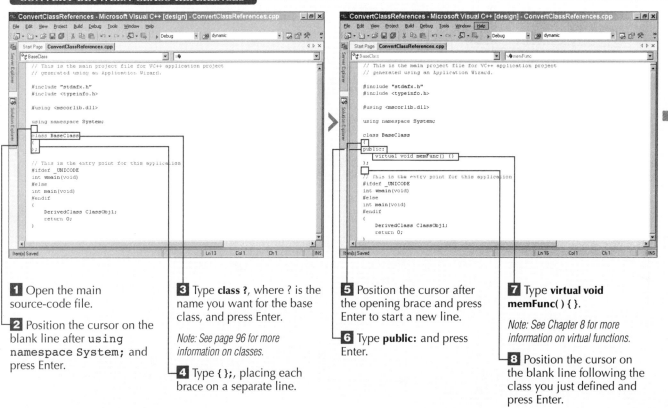

1 Open the main source-code file.

2 Position the cursor on the blank line after `using namespace System;` and press Enter.

3 Type **class ?**, where ? is the name you want for the base class, and press Enter.

Note: See page 96 for more information on classes.

4 Type **{ };**, placing each brace on a separate line.

5 Position the cursor after the opening brace and press Enter to start a new line.

6 Type **public:** and press Enter.

7 Type **virtual void memFunc( ) { }.**

Note: See Chapter 8 for more information on virtual functions.

8 Position the cursor on the blank line following the class you just defined and press Enter.

Extra

As with pointers, you can also use the `static_cast` keyword to convert references. However, remember that no type checking occurs at runtime. Therefore, if there is a problem and the classes you are converting are not compatible, you will see unpredictable behavior. Therefore, only use `static_cast` if you know for sure in the code you are writing that the cast will succeed.

A common place where you would type the code to convert between references is in a function that takes as a parameter a base class from which other classes are derived. However, as an alternative, you can make the function a member function of the base class, and override the function in the derived classes.

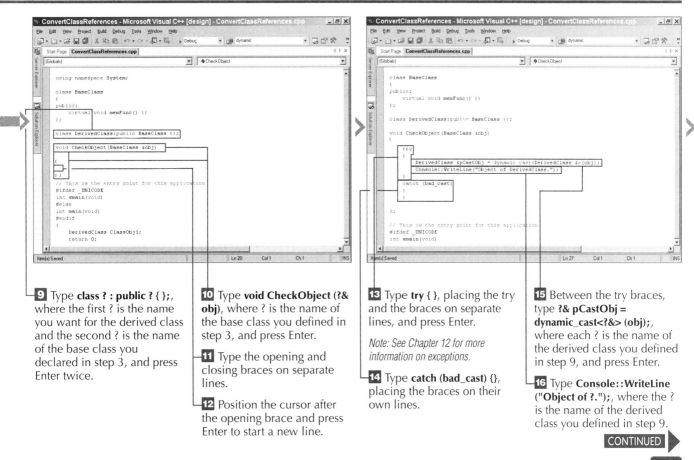

9 Type **class ? : public ? { };**, where the first ? is the name you want for the derived class and the second ? is the name of the base class you declared in step 3, and press Enter twice.

10 Type **void CheckObject (?& obj)**, where ? is the name of the base class you defined in step 3, and press Enter.

11 Type the opening and closing braces on separate lines.

12 Position the cursor after the opening brace and press Enter to start a new line.

13 Type **try { }**, placing the try and the braces on separate lines, and press Enter.

Note: See Chapter 12 for more information on exceptions.

14 Type **catch (bad_cast) {}**, placing the braces on their own lines.

15 Between the try braces, type **?& pCastObj = dynamic_cast<?&> (obj);**, where each ? is the name of the derived class you defined in step 9, and press Enter.

16 Type **Console::WriteLine ("Object of ?.");**, where the ? is the name of the derived class you defined in step 9.

CONTINUED ▶

CONVERT BETWEEN CLASS REFERENCES (CONTINUED)

To use the `dynamic_cast` for references, you call `dynamic_cast` passing as the first parameter the new reference type to which you are casting. You surround this type with angled brackets, as in `<NewType&>`. You must make sure to include the ampersand (`&`) after the type name so the compiler knows that this is a reference type. Without it, the compiler assumes it is the basic type and generates an error message.

After you type the class name in angled brackets, type the name of the object you are converting, surrounding it by parentheses.

Because you are putting the cast inside a `try` block, you can type the lines of code that immediately follow the cast

with the assumption that the cast succeeded. That is because if the cast did not succeed, the program will not execute these lines of code that follow the cast. Instead, the program will execute the exception handler code inside the `catch` block.

This can make it slightly more difficult for you to construct your code. Your best approach is to put the cast inside a `try` block, along with any code specific to the situation when the cast succeeds. Then inside the `catch` block put any code specific to the situation when the cast does not succeed. Finally, after the `catch` block, put the code common to both. This common code will execute after either the `try` or `catch` block, whichever occurs.

CONVERT BETWEEN CLASS REFERENCES (CONTINUED)

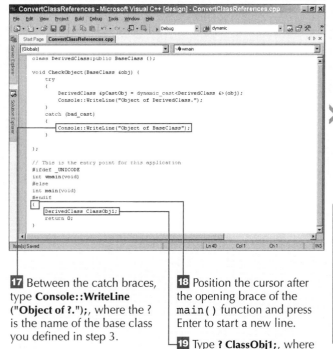

17 Between the catch braces, type **Console::WriteLine ("Object of ?.");**, where the ? is the name of the base class you defined in step 3.

18 Position the cursor after the opening brace of the **main()** function and press Enter to start a new line.

19 Type **? ClassObj1;**, where the ? is the name of the derived class you defined in step 9, and press Enter.

20 Type **? ClassObj2;**, where ? is the name of the base class you defined in step 3, and press Enter.

21 Type **CheckObject (ClassObj1);** and press Enter.

22 Type **CheckObject (ClassObj2);**.

Apply It

You can also use `dynamic_cast` operator to convert a reference to a derived class into a reference to the base class.

TYPE THIS:

```
#include "stdafx.h"
#include <typeinfo.h>
#using <mscorlib.dll>
using namespace System;
class BaseClass { virtual void F(){} };
class DerivedClass : public BaseClass {};
int main(void)
{
    DerivedClass a;
    DerivedClass& aa = a;
    try
    {
        BaseClass& b = dynamic_cast<BaseClass&>(aa);
        Console::WriteLine("Conversion to base class successful.");
    }
    catch (bad_cast)
    {
        Console::WriteLine("Conversion to base class unsuccessful.");
    }
    return 0;
}
```

RESULT:

```
Conversion to base class successful.
Press any key to continue
```

Visual C++ .NET provides many library files that define values and objects that you need in your programs. For example, the typeinfo.h header file contains the definition of the `bad_cast` exception, which you need to use when casting between object references with the `dynamic_cast` operator. If you get an undefined symbol error when referencing a value defined by the Visual Studio .NET library or include files, you probably forgot to add the appropriate `#include` directive to the top of your program. The MSDN documentation tells you which header files to include. Just look up the appropriate symbol, such as `bad_cast`, in the documentation.

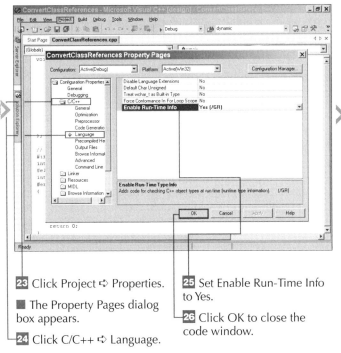

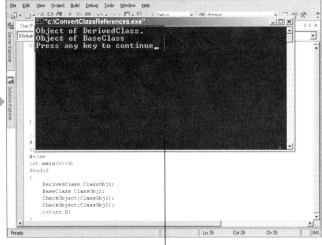

23 Click Project ➪ Properties.

■ The Property Pages dialog box appears.

24 Click C/C++ ➪ Language.

25 Set Enable Run-Time Info to Yes.

26 Click OK to close the code window.

27 After the line `#include "stdafx.h"`, type **#include <typeinfo.h>**.

Note: This header file contains the definition for the `bad_cast` exception.

28 Compile and run the program.

■ The program displays the object types of the `CheckObject()` function arguments.

CONVERT BETWEEN CLASSES STATICALLY

The dynamic_cast operator provides the safest mechanism for converting one type of class pointer to another. However, this run-time type checking requires a certain amount of overhead, not only in that you need to turn on run-time type checking in your project, but the system also needs to perform type-checking operations at runtime when you call upon the dynamic_cast operator. By using the static_cast operator, you can avoid these complications.

The static_cast operator performs similar conversion operations, when compared with dynamic_cast, except that it does the type checking when you compile your program, rather than when you run it. That is, if there is a problem with the conversion you request, the program does not compile. The downside of static type checking is that no type checking is done at runtime. However, as long as you do not try to manipulate pointers in dangerous ways, such as by performing C-style casts on them, the static_cast operator is a safe conversion mechanism.

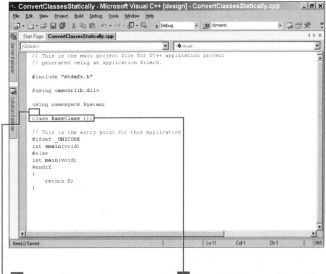

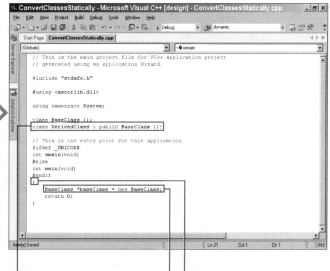

1 Open the main source-code file.

2 Position the cursor on the line after the using namespace System line and press Enter.

3 Type **class ?{ };**, where ? is the name you want for the base class, and press Enter.

Note: See page 96 for more information on creating classes.

4 Type **class ? : public ? {};**, where the first ? is the name you want for the derived class, and the second ? is the name you gave the base class.

Note: See Chapter 8 for more information on class inheritance.

5 Position the cursor after the opening brace of the main() function and press Enter to start a new line.

6 Type **?* baseClass = new ?;**, where ? is the name you chose for the base class, and press Enter.

Extra

Although a `static_cast` operation is relatively safe, if you are at all unsure about the resulting conversion, use `dynamic_cast` instead. The extra overhead required to perform run-time type checking is usually a problem only in programs that are already pushing the processor hard. Most programs will suffer no noticeable degradation when using the `dynamic_cast` operator in place of `static_cast`. However, `dynamic_cast` can be used only on pointers and references, whereas `static_cast` can also be used with numeric data types, such as when you need to convert between `char` and `int`.

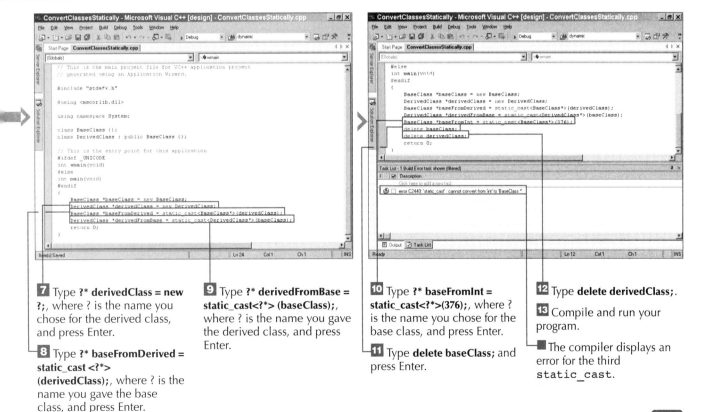

7 Type **?* derivedClass = new ?;**, where ? is the name you chose for the derived class, and press Enter.

8 Type **?* baseFromDerived = static_cast <?*> (derivedClass);**, where ? is the name you gave the base class, and press Enter.

9 Type **?* derivedFromBase = static_cast<?*> (baseClass);**, where ? is the name you gave the derived class, and press Enter.

10 Type **?* baseFromInt = static_cast<?*>(376);**, where ? is the name you chose for the base class, and press Enter.

11 Type **delete baseClass;** and press Enter.

12 Type **delete derivedClass;**.

13 Compile and run your program.

■ The compiler displays an error for the third `static_cast`.

REMOVE THE CONST ATTRIBUTE WITH A CAST

The `const_cast` operator enables your program to temporarily turn off a `const` attribute.

`Const` is an attribute that disallows changes to a data-member value. By declaring class member functions as `const`, those member functions, and only those member functions, become available to `const` objects created from the class. However, a `const` member function can never modify data members of the class. If you try to modify a data member within a `const` member function, your program will not compile.

While this limitation is logical considering that `const` data in any form is not allowed to be changed, it does create problems within classes. For example, a `const` member

function may need to modify a data member that is not part of the public interface of the class. Such a value may have no effect on how the class looks to a program creating an object of the class, so it does not need to be protected from change in a `const` object of the class.

Using the `const_cast` operator gets around this limitation, but only for the single line in which the operator is used. Using the `const_cast` operator is similar to using the other C++ new-style casts, in that you provide the data type you want to end up with in angle brackets and the data type you want to convert in parentheses following the angle brackets. However, in the case of `const_cast`, both the data types are the same. The only difference is that the converted data type will no longer be `const`.

REMOVE THE CONST ATTRIBUTE WITH A CAST

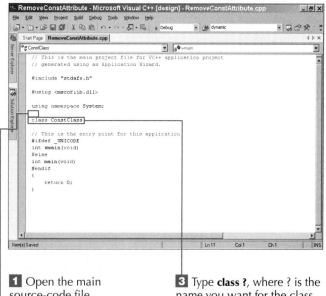

1 Open the main source-code file.

2 Position the cursor on the line after the `using namespace System` line and press Enter.

3 Type **class ?**, where ? is the name you want for the class, and press Enter.

Note: See page 96 for more information on classes.

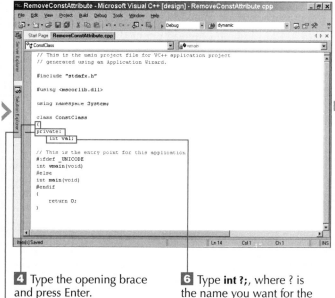

4 Type the opening brace and press Enter.

5 Type **private:** and press Enter.

6 Type **int ?;**, where ? is the name you want for the member variable, and press Enter.

Extra

When you carefully design your classes, you will find that some member functions do not modify the members of the class. You can make these functions const functions. However, you may find that your classes have such functions, but they need to modify certain private members of the function that are, for example, only for logging purposes or debugging purposes. In these cases, you can make the member function a const function, and use const_cast when you need to modify these certain members.

You cannot use const_cast between classes. If you have an object of a certain class, you cannot use const_cast to convert it to another class, even if the other class is a base class of the object. const_cast only works within a single class.

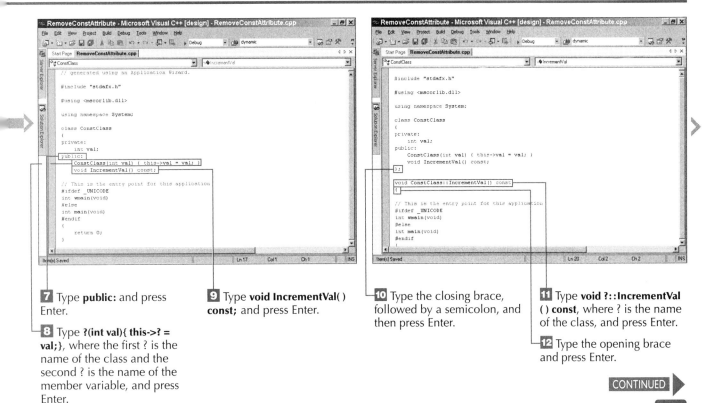

7 Type **public:** and press Enter.

8 Type **?(int val){ this->? = val;}**, where the first ? is the name of the class and the second ? is the name of the member variable, and press Enter.

9 Type **void IncrementVal( ) const;** and press Enter.

10 Type the closing brace, followed by a semicolon, and then press Enter.

11 Type **void ?::IncrementVal ( ) const**, where ? is the name of the class, and press Enter.

12 Type the opening brace and press Enter.

CONTINUED

REMOVE THE CONST ATTRIBUTE WITH A CAST (CONTINUED)

When using the `const_cast` keyword, you do not need to check the return value of the cast, as it will always succeed, provided the value you pass to it is valid.

Once place you would use the `const_cast` keyword is inside a member function for a class, and only inside those member functions where you have specified the function as `const`. But another place you might find this keyword useful is if you are in a function that has been passed a `const` object, and you need to call a function that does not take a `const` object. In order to pass the object to the latter function, you would cast the object using `const_cast` before casting it.

You can easily accomplish this within the parameters to the function call itself, as in

```
myfunction (const_cast<ClassType *>(a));
```

where a is a pointer to a `const` ClassType.

The `const_cast` keyword works both with pointers and with references. Thus, you can also use it as in

```
myfunction2 (const_cast<ClassType &>(b));
```

where b is a `const` object of type ClassType.

REMOVE THE CONST ATTRIBUTE WITH A CAST (CONTINUED)

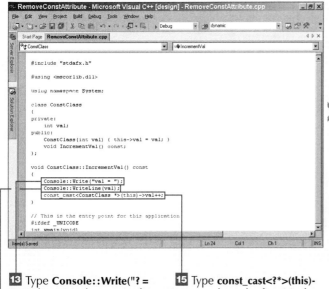

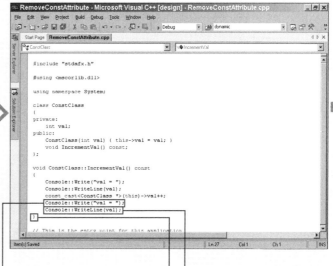

13 Type **Console::Write("? = ");**, where ? is the name of the member variable, and press Enter.

14 Type **Console::WriteLine (?);**, where ? is the member variable, and press Enter.

15 Type **const_cast<?*>(this)->?++;**, where the first ? is the name of the class and the second is the name of the member variable, and press Enter.

16 Type **Console::Write("? = ");**, where ? is the name of the member variable, and press Enter.

17 Type **Console::WriteLine (?);**, where ? is the name of the member variable, and press Enter.

18 Type the closing brace and press Enter.

Apply It

It can be difficult to understand the need for the `const_cast` operator until you start working with `const` objects of a class. When you create a `const` object of a class, only the `const` member functions of the class can be called. This leads to the problem of not being able to change data-member values, because such values cannot be changed in a `const` member function, but only `const` member functions are available to your `const` object.

TYPE THIS:

```
#include "stdafx.h"
#using <mscorlib.dll>
using namespace System;
class MyClass
{
private:
    int t;
public:
    MyClass(int num) { t=num; }
    int get() const { return t; }
    void myFunc(){};
};
void main(void)
{
    const MyClass a(10);
    Console::WriteLine(a.get());
    // a.myFunc(); // This line will not compile.
}
```

RESULT:

10
Press any key to continue

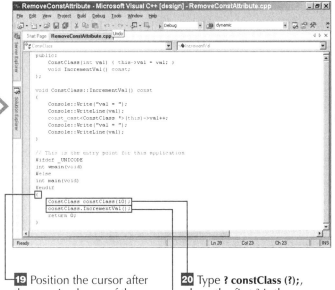

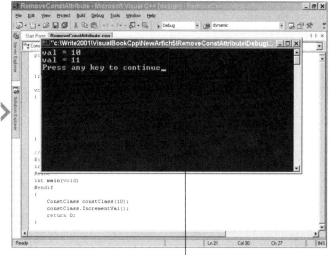

19 Position the cursor after the opening brace of the `main()` function and press Enter to start a new line.

20 Type **? constClass (?);**, where the first ? is the name of the class and the second is the value to which you want to set the member variable, and press Enter.

21 Type **constClass.IncrementVal ();**.

22 Compile and run your program.

■ The program displays the value of the member variable before and after incrementing it.

SAFELY CAST A BASE CLASS TO A DERIVED CLASS

You can cast a base class to a derived class to ensure that you can access all the members of the class, not just those in the base class. There are two ways to cast a base class to a derived class, and which one you choose depends on your goal: You can either cast without any runtime checking, which is not always safe but faster, or you can cast with runtime checking, which is always safe, but a bit slower. Knowing the difference helps you make your programs as robust as possible.

Casting of objects almost always involves pointers. When you know at coding time that the class you are casting is indeed a derived class, then you can safely use a standard "c-style" cast. This is the first approach. Using this approach, you simply place the name of the derived class in parentheses before the instance name along with an asterisk denoting the pointer, as in this example: `(DerivedClass *)MyObject`. You declare `MyObject` as a pointer to `BaseClass` even though it points to a

`DerivedClass`. You use this type of casting in a call to a function that expects an object of the derived class.

The compiler creates derived classes by taking the base class and adding data onto the end of the actual storage of the base class information. If you have a pointer to a derived class, this data will automatically be present. But if instead you have a pointer to a base class, and you cast to the derived class, the program assumes the presence of the extra data, but there is no data there. This could result in unexplained crashes and other problems in your program. Therefore, when you do not know at coding time if the object is indeed a derived class, you should use the second approach of casing, known as the safe cast using the `dynamic_cast` keyword. `dynamic_cast` is part of the C++ language standard, and it uses runtime type information to verify that the cast is indeed legitimate. If it is not, it will return a null pointer equal to 0. It is therefore wise to include code to check for 0.

SAFELY CAST A BASE CLASS TO A DERIVED CLASS

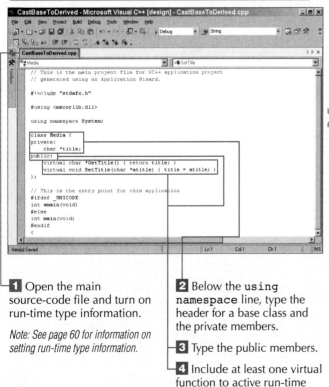

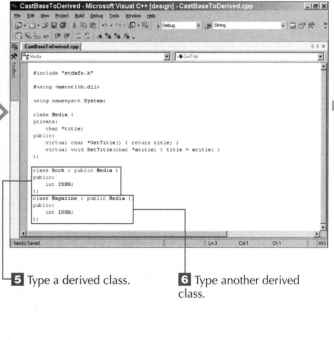

1 Open the main source-code file and turn on run-time type information.

Note: See page 60 for information on setting run-time type information.

2 Below the `using namespace` line, type the header for a base class and the private members.

3 Type the public members.

4 Include at least one virtual function to active run-time type information.

5 Type a derived class.

6 Type another derived class.

Extra

In general, you can safely cast a base class to a derived class when you write a function that takes as a parameter a pointer to a base class object. Because of inheritance, anytime a function expects a pointer to a base class object, you can pass any type of object as long as it is derived from the base class. The compiler stops you from passing a different object by generating a compile-time error. Inside the function, you can include a call to `dynamic_cast` to determine the exact type of derived class at runtime.

If you create a lot of classes derived from the same base class, you can make your programs more robust by incorporating the override capabilities of member functions. If you intend to write a function that takes a pointer to a base class as a parameter, and you use `dynamic_cast` in the function to test for various types of derived classes, you can alternatively create the function as a virtual function, and override it within the derived classes. You place the code specific to the derived class inside the derived class methods.

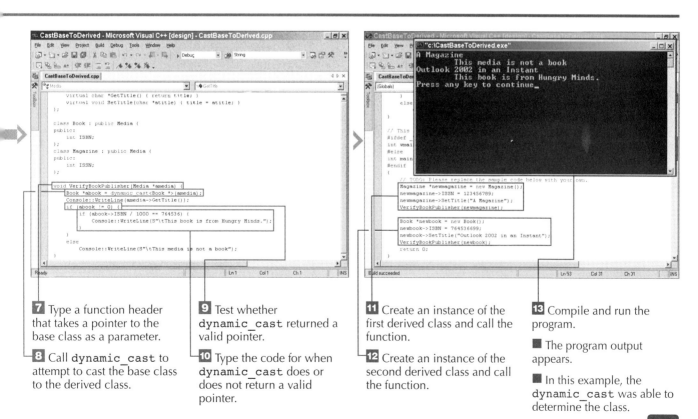

7 Type a function header that takes a pointer to the base class as a parameter.

8 Call `dynamic_cast` to attempt to cast the base class to the derived class.

9 Test whether `dynamic_cast` returned a valid pointer.

10 Type the code for when `dynamic_cast` does or does not return a valid pointer.

11 Create an instance of the first derived class and call the function.

12 Create an instance of the second derived class and call the function.

13 Compile and run the program.

■ The program output appears.

■ In this example, the `dynamic_cast` was able to determine the class.

CAST WITHOUT RUN-TIME CHECKING

As you program, when you are sure about your types and variables, you can perform a cast without any run-time checking. This speeds up the execution of your program, and simplifies the conversion of data. Normally you only do this when casting between basic types such as `int` to `float` and vice versa.

When casting between such types, the compiler uses a built-in library to do the conversion for you. Thus you can simply do the cast as `x = (float)n;` where n is an integer containing a value, and x is a float. After the cast, x will contain the same value as n, but in a floating-point notation rather than as an integer.

When you make this cast in the other direction, such as from an integer to a float as in `n = (int)x;` the compiler converts the floating pointer number to an integer, and rounds it off if necessary.

Because of the round-off, you will want to be careful if you are casting important data or information. For example, if you have a floating-point value such as 5.3 and you cast it to an integer, it will be rounded to 5. Then if later you cast it back to a float, it will have the floating-point value 5.0, not 5.3. In other words, you lost some of the precision.

You can also use a cast without run-time checking in one specific situation: When you are casting from a derived class to a base class. In this case, the compiler automatically knows how to do this cast, so you do not need to do anything. If you have a variable D of class `MyDerived` which is derived from class `MyBase`, and you need to cast D as `MyBase`, you can simply cast it as `(MyBase)D`.

CAST WITHOUT RUN-TIME CHECKING

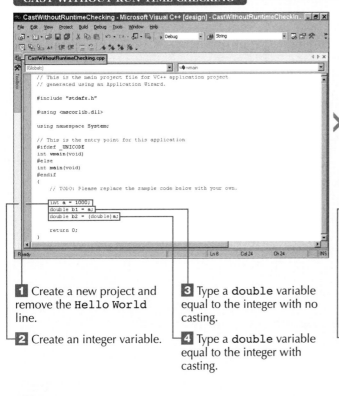

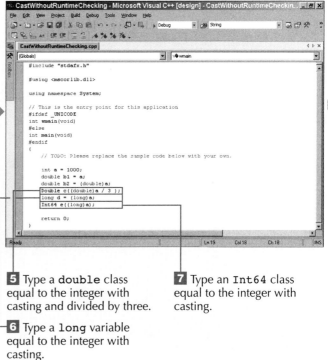

1 Create a new project and remove the `Hello World` line.

2 Create an integer variable.

3 Type a **double** variable equal to the integer with no casting.

4 Type a **double** variable equal to the integer with casting.

5 Type a **double** class equal to the integer with casting and divided by three.

6 Type a **long** variable equal to the integer with casting.

7 Type an **Int64** class equal to the integer with casting.

Extra

Casting without run-time checking is often good practice when it seems you do not need a cast. For example, if you cast from an `int` to a `double`, you can leave off the cast, since the compiler generates code for the cast automatically. However, it is good practice to include the cast so that when other programmers look at the code for maintenance purposes, they can easily see what is happening. By including the cast, you make a clear comment to other programmers about your intentions and how the program should properly behave. Further, if the code ever gets ported to another platform outside of .NET, then including the casts helps ensure that the code compiles correctly.

The `dynamic_cast` and `static_cast` keywords are new to ANSI C++. ANSI C++ is the standard version of C++ approved in 1998 by the National Committee for Information Technology Standards. If you are working with older C++ programs, it is likely you will not see `dynamic_cast` and `static_cast`.

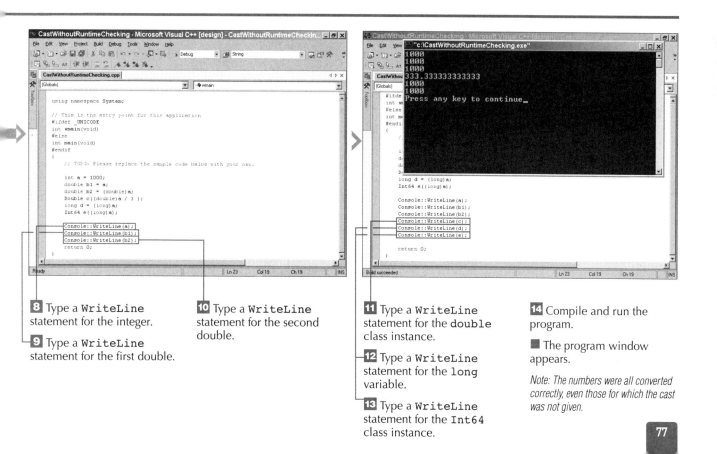

8 Type a `WriteLine` statement for the integer.

9 Type a `WriteLine` statement for the first double.

10 Type a `WriteLine` statement for the second double.

11 Type a `WriteLine` statement for the **double** class instance.

12 Type a `WriteLine` statement for the **long** variable.

13 Type a `WriteLine` statement for the **Int64** class instance.

14 Compile and run the program.

■ The program window appears.

Note: The numbers were all converted correctly, even those for which the cast was not given.

77

REPLACE MOST C-STYLE CASTS

When you convert an older program to run under .NET, you can make the program more robust by replacing the C-style casts with the newer `dynamic_cast` and `static_cast` functions. The C-style casts should contain a type inside parentheses before an expression that you want to cast. The compiler does little, and the runtime library does no type checking for such a cast. At runtime, the program simply accepts the data inside memory as the new type. This can cause problems if the types are not compatible.

While coding, if you know the exact types to and from which you are converting, you use the `static_cast`. The `static_cast` function does no type checking at runtime, just like the old C-style casts. At compile time, however, the `static_cast` function makes sure the cast is acceptable. If

it is not, the compiler shows you an error message. Further, if you convert between basic types such as integers and enums, you must use `static_cast`, rather than `dynamic_cast`.

If, while coding, you do not know the exact type to which you are converting, and you are dealing with pointers or references, you need to use `dynamic_cast`. The `dynamic_cast` function checks the type at runtime rather than compile time making it best to use when casting an object from one class to another. You can test the results of the `dynamic_cast` for 0, which means the conversion was not acceptable. Your code can then include error handling as necessary. If you do the same conversion with a C-style cast, you cannot readily predict the computer response and you may receive some sort of exception error.

REPLACE MOST C-STYLE CASTS

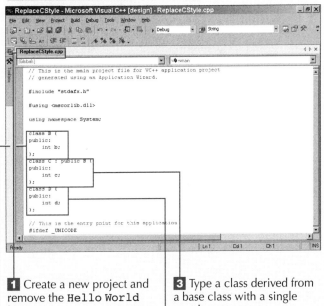

1 Create a new project and remove the `Hello World` line.

2 Type a base class with a single member.

3 Type a class derived from a base class with a single member.

4 Type another class with a single member but not derived from the base class.

5 Create two instances, one of the second and one of the third class.

6 Type a `WriteLine` statement with a `C-cast` of the second class to the first.

Note: This is a safe cast.

7 Type a `WriteLine` statement with a `C-cast` of the third class to the first.

Note: This is not safe because they are not related.

Extra

If you use pointers or references to classes, and you are not sure whether to use `dynamic_cast` or `static_cast`, it is best to always use `dynamic_cast`. The `dynamic_cast` keyword handles error situations much better, allowing you to include exception handler code. The `const_cast` will actually perform a cast if it is not correct, resulting in erroneous data. Further, the program will not throw an exception, nor will it allow you to test for a NULL value. Therefore `const_cast` should only be used when you are absolutely sure in your code that the cast will succeed.

Before you can use `dynamic_cast` on a class, the class must have at least one virtual function in it. If you do not have any virtual functions in the classes, you can easily define an empty member function.

Example:
```
virtual void nothing() { }
```

Place this function in the base class from which you derive the other classes. This provides the class with enough capabilities to make it work with `dynamic_cast`. The one function will force the class to become a virtual class. Then you can also use `dynamic_cast` on any classes derived from the class.

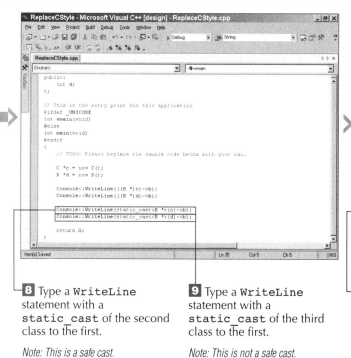

8 Type a `WriteLine` statement with a `static_cast` of the second class to the first.

Note: This is a safe cast.

9 Type a `WriteLine` statement with a `static_cast` of the third class to the first.

Note: This is not a safe cast.

10 Attempt to compile the program.

■ The compilation fails.

■ In this example, the complier did not catch the unsafe C-style cast, but did catch the unsafe `static_cast`.

WORK WITH POINTERS

When you create a variable in a computer program, the variable takes up space in the computer memory. Memory is organized sequentially inside the computer, and each position in memory has a number associated with it. This number is similar to the addresses on a city street. Indeed, the number for the memory location is called an address and represents the location within memory. Each location in memory consists of eight bits of information that together are known as a single byte.

Each variable takes up a certain amount of memory depending on the type of the variable. Integers typically take up four bytes. A character takes up one byte. A structure will take up as much memory as the total of all the members of the structure. For example, if a structure contains three integers, then the structure will take up to 12 bytes. The amount of memory an array takes up depends on how many elements are in the array, and the type of items in the array. For example, an array of 10 integers will take up 40 bytes.

DETERMINING SIZE

You can determine the size of a variable by calling the `sizeof` function, passing the variable whose size you wish to determine. For example, `x = sizeof(y);` would save the size of `y` inside `x`. The size itself is an integer. All variables of a single type will have the same size. For this reason, you can also pass a type to the `sizeof` function, as in `x = sizeof(int);`.

If you call `sizeof(y)` where `y` is an instance of a class or a structure, the size will be approximately the sum of the member data. The size will be approximate because sometimes the compiler rounds the size up to an even number of bytes. Further, the member functions do not impact the size. Even if rounding up does occur, it will occur consistently. Thus, the size of an instance of a class will always be the same as the size of any other instance of that same class.

ADDRESS-OF OPERATOR

You can determine the address of a variable by using the `address-of` operator, which is the ampersand character `&`. For example, if you have a variable called `Count`, and it contains the value 3, you can determine where the variable is stored in memory by calling `&Count`. This will return a number that represents the

location in memory where `Count` is stored. Because `Count` contains a 3 and is an integer, which takes up four bytes, the four bytes contain the number 3. If you change `Count` to 150, then the four bytes that compose `Count` will instead store the number 150.

A POINTER VARIABLE

If you take the address of a variable, you can store the resulting address in another variable. The address is just a number, but you have to store it in a type of variable called a *pointer variable*. Further, the variable must be declared not only as a pointer, but also as a pointer to the type of the variable whose address you are obtaining. For example, if you want to obtain the address of an integer, then you would store the address in a variable of type pointer-to-integer. You declare such a variable by using an asterisk * notation. First you declare the type that the variable points to, type the *,

and then the name for the pointer variable, as in `int *mypointer;`. You can then save the address of `Count` in `mypointer`, as in `mypointer = &Count;`. If you are declaring several pointer variables of the same type, it is important that each variable has the * symbol before it. For example, if you declare x, y, and z to be pointers-to-integer, you can declare this as `int *x, *y, *z;`. A common mistake is to only put the * symbol before the x. However, that would only declare x as a pointer-to-integer. In that case, y and z would simply be an integer.

TYPES OF MEMORY

When you declare a variable, the variable is stored inside a special place of memory specifically allocated for the function where you declare the variable. For example, if you have a function called `MyFunction`, and somewhere inside the function you declare an integer with `int a;`, that integer's memory is allocated inside the memory space for `MyFunction`. This is called the *stack space* for `MyFunction`. However, the computer lets you store variables in a place outside the stack called the *heap*. To declare variables inside the heap, you use the `new` keyword. For example, you would type `a = new int;` to allocate an integer on the heap. However, because the `new` keyword returns only pointers, you must precede this line with a

statement to allocate the variable a as a pointer-to-integer, as in `int *a;`.

You can use the `new` keyword to declare any type of variable. You can create, for example, a new instance of a class called `MyClass` with `MyClass *inst = new MyClass();`. If the class has a constructor requiring parameters, you include these parameters inside the parentheses. A common error is to forget to allocate the instance. You can simply declare `MyClass *inst;`. This is a valid instruction because it declares a pointer variable call `inst`, but does not initialize the pointer. If you then attempt to access the members of inst; as in `inst->data = 5;`, you will get a runtime error.

DEREFERENCING A POINTER

When you have a pointer variable and need to access the actual data that it points to, you can use a * symbol to *dereference* the variable. For example, if you have a pointer-to-integer called x and it points to a value in

memory containing the number 150, then there are actually two values associated with x. The actual value of x is the address of the memory containing 150. However, if you dereference x, you find the value 150.

ACCESS DATA THROUGH A POINTER

You can use a pointer variable to get the address of a variable and then use the pointer variable to change or retrieve the contents of the original variable. With this method, you can create powerful programs by manipulating multiple data structures, one after the other, by using a single pointer variable. You set the pointer to the first variable, modify it, then set the pointer to the next, and so on. You can use pointer variables as parameters to a function.

To get the address of the variable, you use the address-of operator, &. You can then save the resulting address into a pointer variable. By using the pointer variable, you can read or change the original variable with the asterisk * notation. The asterisk (*) is called the *dereference operator*.

For example, if you have an integer called Count, you can determine its address and store it into a pointer variable

mypointer **using** int *mypointer = &Count;. **If you want to read the value of** Count **using** mypointer, **you can read the value of** Count **by typing** *mypointer, **as in** int y = *mypointer. **In this case,** y **will contain the same value as** Count.

You can also modify the value of Count **in the same manner, as in** *mypointer = *mypointer + 5;, **which will add 5 to the value of** Count, **by going through** mypointer.

If you have a function that uses pointers in its parameters, you can call the function, passing the address of the variable, rather than the variable itself. You can then have the function manipulate the original variable through the pointer it receives. You do this by using the (*) **notation as before. This is called** *dereferencing* **the pointer.**

ACCESS DATA THROUGH A POINTER

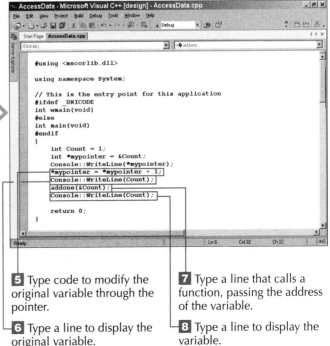

1 Create a new project and remove the Hello World line.

2 Type code to initialize a variable.

3 Type code to obtain the address of the variable.

4 Type code to dereference the variable.

5 Type code to modify the original variable through the pointer.

6 Type a line to display the original variable.

7 Type a line that calls a function, passing the address of the variable.

8 Type a line to display the variable.

Extra

You can avoid errors if you recognize the difference between a pointer variable and a non-pointer variable. If you have a variable `int Count;` and a pointer variable `int *mypointer = &Count;`, you can store the dereferenced value into another variable, as in `int y = *mypointer;`. If you then change the value of `Count`, `y` will not change, because the variable `y` does not point to `Count`. Rather, `y` simply contains the same value that `Count` originally contained.

You can change what the pointer points to by simply re-assigning it. For example, if you have `int *mypointer = &Count;` and then call `mypointer = &Value`, `mypointer` will then point to `Value` instead of `Count`.

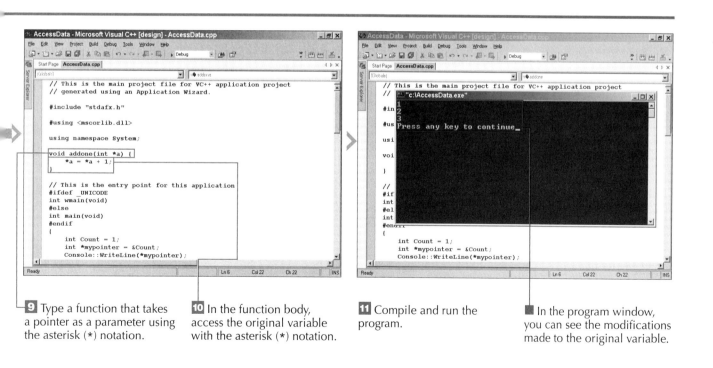

9 Type a function that takes a pointer as a parameter using the asterisk (*) notation.

10 In the function body, access the original variable with the asterisk (*) notation.

11 Compile and run the program.

■ In the program window, you can see the modifications made to the original variable.

WORK WITH NEW AND DELETE

You can declare a pointer variable and create an associated variable that it points to without giving a name to the associated variable. To declare the pointer, you use the new keyword. You first allocate a pointer variable, but instead of setting it to the address of another variable, you set it to the result of a call to new, as in the following:

```
int *mypointer = new int;
```

This code creates a new integer variable, but does not give a name to it. The address of the new integer is then stored in the pointer variable. You can apply this technique to any type, not just integers. After you have declared such a variable, you can use it as you would any other pointer variable. The difference here is that the variable itself has no name. You can only deal with the variable through the pointer.

The process of calling new is called *memory allocation*, because the computer allocates a portion of the memory for the new variable. Each time you call new in your program, the computer allocates more of the memory. If you have a variable that you use only for a short time and no longer need, you can remove it from memory by using another keyword called delete.

To use the delete keyword, you call delete followed by the name of the pointer variable, as in the following:

```
delete mypointer;
```

Remember that you are dealing with two variables here, one unnamed variable, and a pointer variable pointing to the unnamed variable. Although it is the unnamed variable you are deleting, you pass the pointer variable to delete. The reason is that the unnamed variable has no name by itself, and there is no way to refer to it directly in your program.

WORK WITH NEW AND DELETE

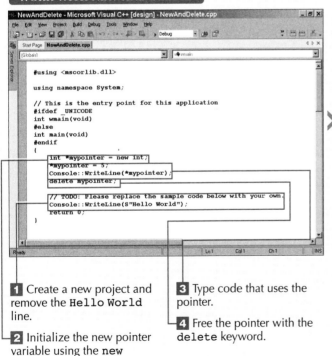

1 Create a new project and remove the Hello World line.

2 Initialize the new pointer variable using the new keyword.

3 Type code that uses the pointer.

4 Free the pointer with the delete keyword.

5 Compile and run the program.

■ The program window opens showing the results of the variable.

CREATE A .NET POINTER

Microsoft .NET includes an entire library of classes that you can use in your programs. For example, there are numerous classes for handling file operations and string operations. To use these classes, you must use .NET pointers.

There are two areas of memory where you can store your variables. These two areas are known as the *heap* and the *stack*. The stack is the area reserved for the functions, and the variables you create that are not pointers are stored in the stack. When you use the .NET classes and types, you can only declare them in the heap. You cannot declare the .NET variables in the memory space for the function. Therefore, when you declare a variable that is of a type found in the .NET framework, you must make the variable a pointer and use the `new` keyword.

If you attempt to create a variable with the .NET framework that is not a pointer, as in `String name("Visual Blueprint");`, you will get an error at compile time. You will see the following error message:

```
error C3149: 'System::String' : illegal use
of managed type 'System::String'; did you
forget a '*'?
```

Instead of `System::String`, you will see the name of the type that you used. The clue here is the suggestion that you forgot a *, which is used for a pointer declaration. Therefore, if you see this error, it means you must change your variable to a pointer as in `String *name = new String ("Visual Blueprint");`. This change will ensure that you declare your variable on the heap. The compile will then proceed normally.

CREATE A .NET POINTER

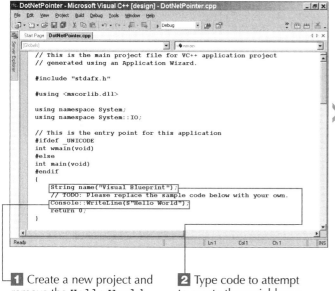

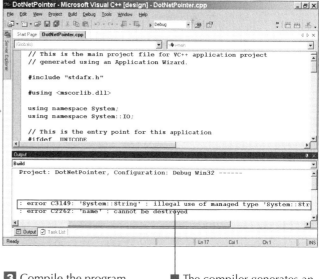

1 Create a new project and remove the `Hello World` line.

2 Type code to attempt to create the variable on the stack.

3 Compile the program.

■ The compiler generates an error. To fix the error, use the `new` keyword.

PASS BY REFERENCE

Y ou can simplify your functions that use pointers by passing parameters by reference. For example, suppose you have a function that takes an integer as a parameter. If you call this function by passing an integer variable and the function modifies the integer, the original integer does not change. Only the copy inside the function changes.

If you pass a pointer to the function, the function can dereference the pointer and modify the original variable. However, this can sometimes create code that is cumbersome if you have to dereference the pointer numerous times.

You can avoid the need to dereference pointers if you pass by reference. In the function header, you precede the variable name with an ampersand & symbol, as in void MyFunction(int &a). Inside the body of the function, you can make changes directly to the parameter without the use of a pointer, for example, a=a+1; . Unlike standard passing without pointers or references, changing the

parameter changes the original variable. Thus, if you declare a variable and call your function as shown here, the original variable will change:

```
int x =10;
MyFunction(x);
```

After these two lines execute, the variable x will contain 11. The function not only modified its parameter; it modified the original as well.

You can pass structures in this manner, as well. The advantage to passing structures by reference rather than with a pointer is that inside the function you can use the standard . notation instead of the -> pointer notation.

For example, if you have a function void MyFunction2(MyStruct &mys), then the function code can have, for example, mys.member = 10;, which will modify the original structure passed into the function.

PASS BY REFERENCE

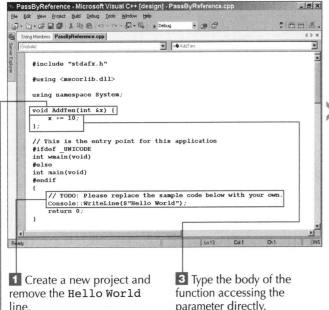

1 Create a new project and remove the Hello World line.

2 Type a function header using the & notation representing pass-by-reference.

3 Type the body of the function accessing the parameter directly.

4 Type code to create a new variable and initialize it.

5 Type code to print out the value of the variable.

Extra

You can avoid errors if you take great care in using the pass-by-reference feature. Sometimes when you are working inside a function, writing new code or modifying existing code, it is easy to forget that you are modifying the original variable, and not just a temporary copy.

You can pass classes by reference in the same manner that you can pass structures by reference. As with structures, when you pass an instance of a class by reference, the code uses the . notation to access the members of the instance, instead of the -> notation. As with passing other variables by reference, any changes to the instance affect the original instance as well.

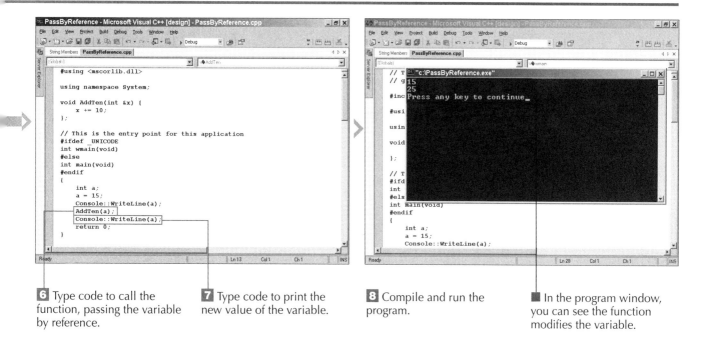

6 Type code to call the function, passing the variable by reference.

7 Type code to print the new value of the variable.

8 Compile and run the program.

■ In the program window, you can see the function modifies the variable.

RETURN A POINTER FROM A FUNCTION

When you write a function, you can allocate a variable and return a pointer to the variable. This lets you have greater control over the management of the variables and their memory in your program. For example, you might have a function that needs to create a very large structure with many data members. Because of the way the compiler works, it is faster for you to return a pointer to a structure rather than return an entire structure. Further, if you return a structure and not a pointer, you are actually returning a copy of the structure. By returning a pointer, you return the actual structure itself.

Inside the function, create a new instance of the variable whose address you wish to return. Note that you must

create this variable on the heap by using the new keyword. Although the compiler enables you to return the address of a variable declared on the stack without the new keyword, you should not do this because the memory is no longer valid after the function finishes.

After you create the instance, you return it by using the return keyword followed by the name of the pointer variable. When you consider this, you see that the reason you return the pointer variable is that you are really returning the contents of the pointer variable, which happens to be the address of the allocated variable itself.

RETURN A POINTER FROM A FUNCTION

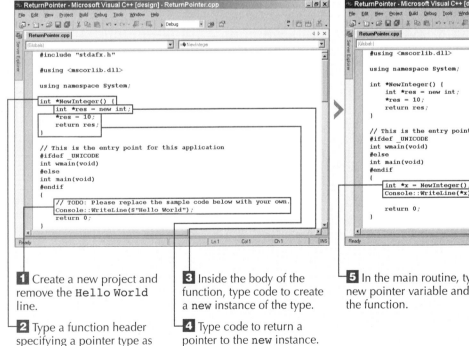

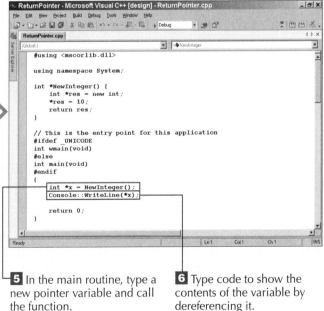

1 Create a new project and remove the Hello World line.

2 Type a function header specifying a pointer type as the return type.

3 Inside the body of the function, type code to create a new instance of the type.

4 Type code to return a pointer to the new instance.

5 In the main routine, type a new pointer variable and call the function.

6 Type code to show the contents of the variable by dereferencing it.

Extra

You can keep your programs operating correctly by considering proper memory management. Whenever you call `new`, somewhere in your program you should call `delete` to clear the variable, even if you call it at the very end of your program. If your function calls `new`, the part of your program that calls the function should call `delete` when it is finished with the variable.

Example:
```
int *NewInteger() {
    int *res = new int;
    *res = 10;
    return res;
}
int main(void)
{
    int *x = NewInteger();
    delete x;
    return 0;
}
```

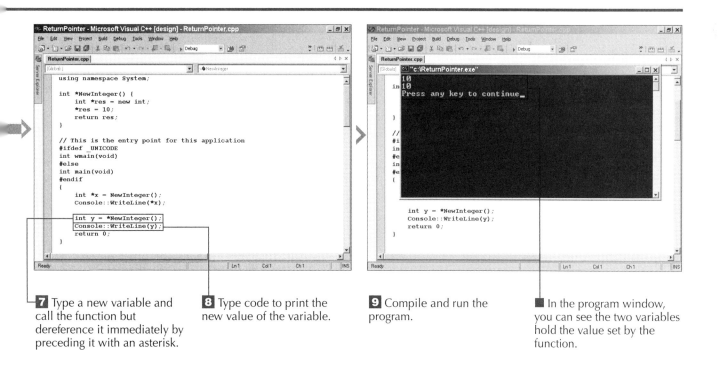

7 Type a new variable and call the function but dereference it immediately by preceding it with an asterisk.

8 Type code to print the new value of the variable.

9 Compile and run the program.

■ In the program window, you can see the two variables hold the value set by the function.

DECLARE A POINTER TO AN ARRAY

You can get the most power out of your arrays if you recognize the connection between pointers and arrays. The name of the array serves as a pointer and points to the first member of the array. Thus, if you have an array int MyArray[10];, to denote an array of ten integers, you can access the members the usual way with MyArray[0], MyArray[1], and so on. Or, you can access the first member by recognizing that MyArray is a pointer to the first member. Thus, *MyArray is the first member, and *MyArray = 10; stores the number 10 in the first member.

You cannot change what the array name points to; it always points to the first member. Therefore, it is often convenient to copy the value to another pointer variable. For example, you can set int *MyPointer = MyArray;. Then, MyPointer will point to the first member of the array.

Although you cannot change the value of MyArray from pointing to something other than the first member, you can use it to access the remaining members of the array by simply adding 1 to it to get the second member, 2 to get the third member, and so on. Therefore, if you set int *MyPointer2 = MyArray + 1;, then MyPointer2 will point to the second member of the array.

After you have a pointer to the second member, you can set the contents of the second member by dereferencing the second pointer, as in *MyPointer2 = 60. Therefore, you have two ways to access the array members. The first is through the standard bracket notation, as in MyArray[0], MyArray[1], and so on, and the second is through the pointers *MyArray, *(MyArray+1), and so on. Note that you should enclose MyArray+1 in parentheses before you dereference it.

DECLARE A POINTER TO AN ARRAY

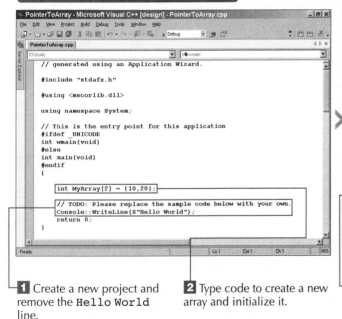

1 Create a new project and remove the Hello World line.

2 Type code to create a new array and initialize it.

3 Create a new pointer variable that points to the first position in the array.

4 Create a second pointer variable that points to the second position in the array.

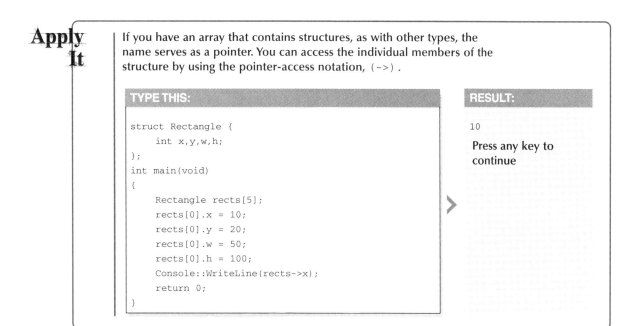

Apply It

If you have an array that contains structures, as with other types, the name serves as a pointer. You can access the individual members of the structure by using the pointer-access notation, `(->)`.

TYPE THIS:

```
struct Rectangle {
    int x,y,w,h;
};
int main(void)
{
    Rectangle rects[5];
    rects[0].x = 10;
    rects[0].y = 20;
    rects[0].w = 50;
    rects[0].h = 100;
    Console::WriteLine(rects->x);
    return 0;
}
```

RESULT:

```
10
```

Press any key to continue

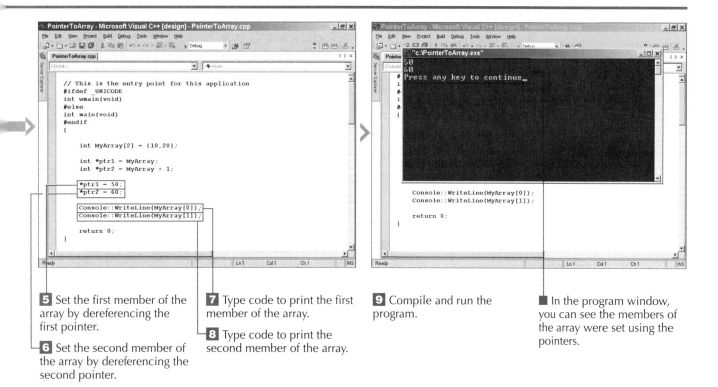

5 Set the first member of the array by dereferencing the first pointer.

6 Set the second member of the array by dereferencing the second pointer.

7 Type code to print the first member of the array.

8 Type code to print the second member of the array.

9 Compile and run the program.

■ In the program window, you can see the members of the array were set using the pointers.

DECLARE A STRUCTURE POINTER

You can make your programs efficient by manipulating pointers to structures, rather than the structures themselves. This is especially helpful when you pass structures into functions, because structures can take up a great deal of memory. For example, if you need to pass ten very large structures to a function, it is faster to pass ten pointers.

Another benefit of passing pointers into functions is that the function receives a *copy* of the structure. In the function, all your changes to the structure reside on the copy, and do not affect the original structure.

When you want the function to modify the original structure, you can pass a pointer to the structure. The function can use the pointer to find the original structure, and work directly on the original structure, not a copy.

To pass the address of a structure, you use an &, for example:

```
SetPhoneExtension(&TheEmployee);
```

In this example, the function SetPhoneExtension receives a pointer to the TheEmployee structure.

Inside the function, you must use the -> notation, because you have a pointer. For example:

```
void SetPhoneExtension(Employee
    *CurrentEmployee) {

    CurrentEmployee->PhoneExtension = 1212

}
```

where CurrentEmployee is a pointer to a structure, and is declared in the function header as a pointer to the structure type Employee.

You can also create a new structure where you only have a pointer variable accessing it, and no other variables, by using the new keyword, for example:

```
Employee *AnotherEmployee = new Employee;
```

Think of new as a function that creates a new instance of the structure and returns a pointer, and that you are assigning that pointer to the AnotherEmployee variable.

DECLARE A STRUCTURE POINTER

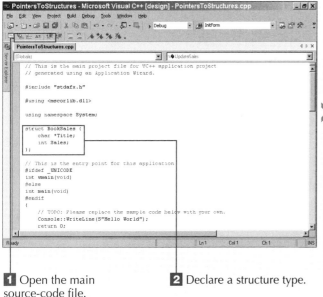

1 Open the main source-code file.

2 Declare a structure type.

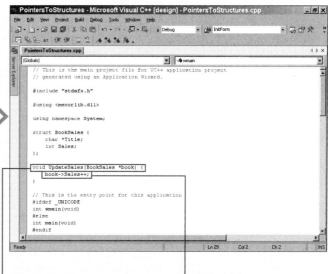

3 Type a function that takes as a parameter a pointer to the structure.

4 Type the -> notation to access the members of the structure.

Extra

When inside a function, if you prefer to work directly with the structure rather than a pointer to the structure, you can pass the structure by reference. In this manner, you can access the structure using the . notation rather than the -> notation. The following example shows how you change the UpdateSales method to use references.

Example:
```
void UpdateSales(BookSales &book) {
    book.Sales++;
}
```

When you call the function, you do not need to use the & operator as illustrated in the following example. The compiler still passes a pointer to the structure, but this notation makes it much easier with which to work. Be mindful that you are working with the original and not a copy.

Example:
```
BookSales book1 =
    {"PHP: Visual Blueprint", 10000};
UpdateSales(book1);
```

If you already have a pointer to the structure and you want to pass it to this function expecting a reference, you can dereference the pointer using the * notation.

Example:
```
BookSales *book2 = new BookSales;
book2->Title = "ASP.NET: Visual Blueprint";
book2->Sales = 12035;
UpdateSales(*book2);
Console::WriteLine(book2->Sales);
```

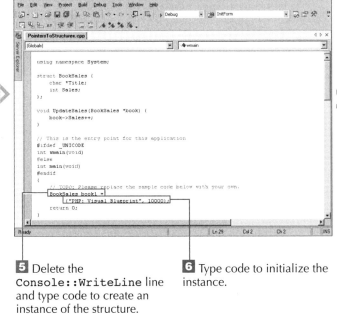

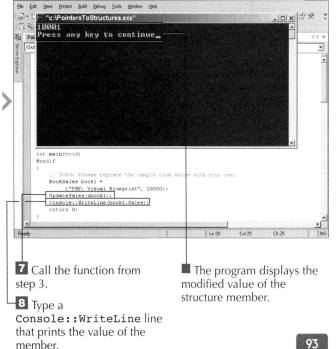

5 Delete the Console::WriteLine line and type code to create an instance of the structure.

6 Type code to initialize the instance.

7 Call the function from step 3.

8 Type a Console::WriteLine line that prints the value of the member.

■ The program displays the modified value of the structure member.

PERFORM POINTER MATH

You can take advantage of the advanced capabilities of pointers to make your program efficient. If you have an array and you have a pointer to a member of the array, then you can easily move about within the array by adding to or subtracting from the pointer. The pointer must be the same type as a member of the array. Adding 1 to the pointer will change the pointer so it points to the next element in the array. If you subtract 1 from the pointer, it will move the previous element in the array.

You can also add or subtract more than 1 to move multiple positions in the array. For example, if you add 3 to the pointer, it will move ahead three positions in the array. The key, however, is that the type the pointer points to matches

the type of the elements of the array. The way this works is the compiler knows the size of the type the pointer points to, and it uses that number of bytes to calculate how far to move.

To move a pointer, you simply add a number to it or subtract a number from it. For example, if MyPointer is a pointer to an integer, and it points to the first element of an integer array, then MyPointer = MyPointer + 2; will move the pointer ahead two positions in the array. You can also use the standard ++ and -- notation to add one and subtract one, respectively. For example, MyPointer++; will move the pointer forward one position, and MyPointer--; will move the pointer back one position.

PERFORM POINTER MATH

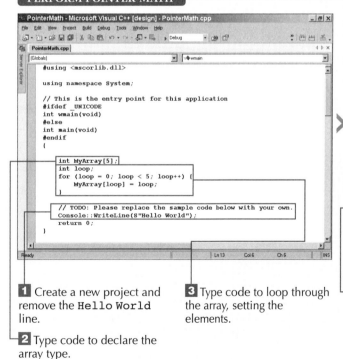

1 Create a new project and remove the **Hello World** line.

2 Type code to declare the array type.

3 Type code to loop through the array, setting the elements.

4 Type code to initialize a pointer variable with the address of the first element of the array.

5 Type a header for a loop.

Pointer math works with any data type. You can have an array of structures, and you can still move forward and backward through the data. If you have a pointer such as `MyPointer`, and it points to a structure in the array, you can access the members with pointer notation. For example, if the structure has members `x` and `y`, you can access the members as `MyPointer->x`, `MyPointer->y` as you normally would. When you advance the pointer with `MyPointer++`, `MyPointer->x` will be the `x` member of the next item in the array.

Pointer math is very useful when dealing with large amounts of data. If you have large arrays of information, you can easily move forward and backward through the data without having to keep track of exactly which element you are on. When you create the array, you can store a special number in the first and last members, such as 0 or -1, or whatever is appropriate for your own data. Then, when you are moving about the array through ++ and --, you can test the current value to determine if you are at the beginning or end of the data.

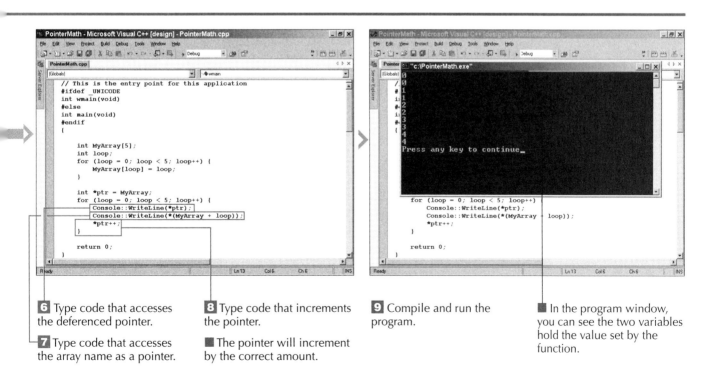

6 Type code that accesses the deferenced pointer.

7 Type code that accesses the array name as a pointer.

8 Type code that increments the pointer.

■ The pointer will increment by the correct amount.

9 Compile and run the program.

■ In the program window, you can see the two variables hold the value set by the function.

CREATE A CLASS

When you are creating data in your programs, you can keep your data organized using classes. The encapsulation of methods and data into a single logical entity is known as a *class*. Classes are the building blocks from which you can construct object-oriented applications.

Although you can write C function libraries that contain collections of related procedures, these functions do not define *public* and *private* interfaces for access to *methods* and *local variables* in any consistent way.

In fact, the interface between methods and classes is one of the main design features of the C++ language. Classes are designed to be self-contained units that describe a specific kind of data and the operations that can be performed on it.

One of the best features of C++ classes is that you can design them to be models of real data and processes, and

their properties can be *inherited* by other classes. Thus, a generic design for a car might define all elements common to a car, such as steering wheel, trunk, tires, and engine. A specific design for a sports car might inherit these generic properties and include class-specific features, such as a sunroof and turbo transmission. A specific sports car object can then be instantiated within a specific application, inheriting the properties of the abstract class and the class that defines the sports car. Thus, a specific sports car might have a leather steering wheel, small trunk, 15-inch tires, a 2.5-liter engine, and red paint.

You can create a simple class `Rectangle` that represents a `Rectangle` object. Once created, you can use this class to model all activities on a computer by defining appropriate local methods and variables — collectively known as *members*.

CREATE A CLASS

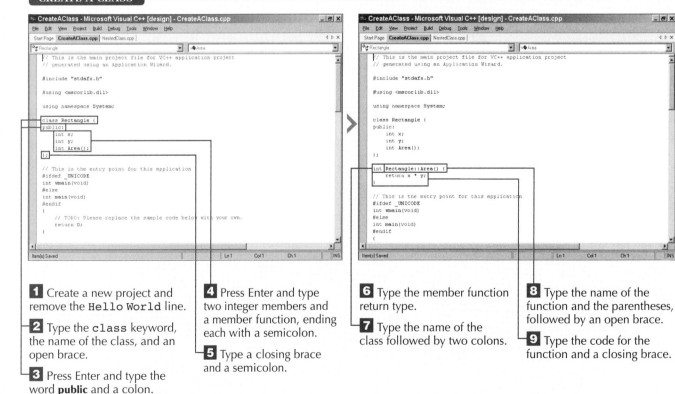

1 Create a new project and remove the `Hello World` line.

2 Type the `class` keyword, the name of the class, and an open brace.

3 Press Enter and type the word **public** and a colon.

4 Press Enter and type two integer members and a member function, ending each with a semicolon.

5 Type a closing brace and a semicolon.

6 Type the member function return type.

7 Type the name of the class followed by two colons.

8 Type the name of the function and the parentheses, followed by an open brace.

9 Type the code for the function and a closing brace.

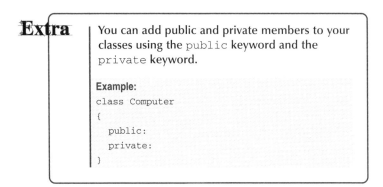

Extra

You can add public and private members to your classes using the `public` keyword and the `private` keyword.

Example:
```
class Computer
{
  public:
  private:
}
```

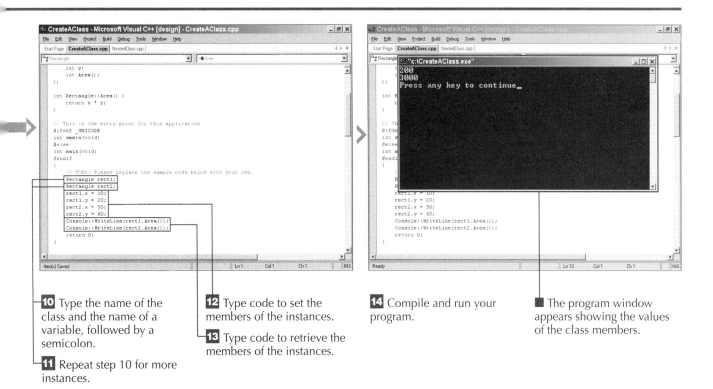

-10 Type the name of the class and the name of a variable, followed by a semicolon.

-11 Repeat step 10 for more instances.

12 Type code to set the members of the instances.

13 Type code to retrieve the members of the instances.

14 Compile and run your program.

■ The program window appears showing the values of the class members.

WRITE A CONSTRUCTOR

When a class is instantiated as an object, it is often useful to insert a general initialization method that establishes default values for member variables. Visual C++ uses an initialization method for each class that is known as a *constructor*. A constructor is usually declared in the public section of the class and can receive variables as parameters that can be operated upon.

A constructor sets up all the values of object variables that must be in place before any operations can occur. To allow the compiler to identify a method as a constructor method, it always has the same name as the class.

Constructors can receive values to initialize members of the instantiated class. Alternatively, you can define multiple

constructors that can be called with differing numbers and types of parameters. You can create a constructor to initialize a class for all conceivable scenarios.

You can also define a *default constructor* that takes no parameters and simply instantiates the class. If you do not enter a default constructor (or any other constructor), a default constructor is automatically generated for you although it will not appear in the source code.

If you have a simple `Computer` class, you might want to initialize the speed of the computer's CPU when the `Computer` object is instantiated. You can do this conveniently in the constructor. In this case, the class `Computer` has a constructor method called `Computer`.

1 Position the cursor after the declaration of the **public:** section in the class and press Enter.

2 Type the name and type of the variable that will be initialized in the constructor and press Enter.

3 Type the name of the constructor and press Enter.

4 Type **private:** and press Enter.

5 Type the name of the class followed by two colons and the name of the constructor.

Extra

Because CPUType is a private variable, it cannot be modified by members external to the class. Its value can be initialized through the constructor as shown. However, if you want to change the value of CPUType from an external main() method after the class is instantiated and initialized, you would need to create an accessor method. For example, to create an accessor method called UpdateCPUType that updates the value of CPUType, you simply need to declare it in the public section of the class and define it in the body of the class as shown below.

Example:
```
class Computer {
    public:
        Computer();
        void UpdateCPUType(String newType);
private:
        String CPUType;
};
Computer::Computer() {
    CPUType="Pentium";
}
void Computer::UpdateCPUType(String newType) {
    CPUType=newType;
}
```

Most class variables are private, since the whole point of encapsulation is to prevent external methods from operating on data that they are not supposed to be able to change. You can initialize a private variable called CPUType in Computer::Computer(), using the following class definition.

Example:
```
class Computer {
    public:
        Computer();
private:
        String CPUType;
};

Computer::Computer() {
    CPUType="Pentium";
}
```

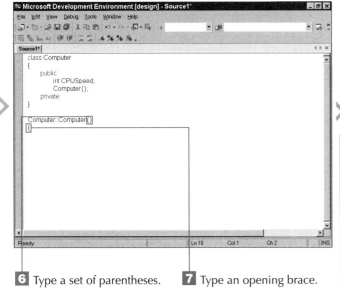

6 Type a set of parentheses. **7** Type an opening brace.

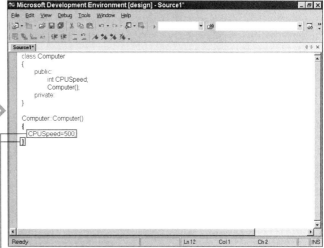

8 Type the appropriate value to initialize the variable.

9 Type a closing brace.

■ Your class now has a constructor that initializes the member data.

WRITE A DESTRUCTOR

When you develop a class, you can include a special function that contains cleanup code. This function is called a *destructor*. When you declare an instance of a class as shown in the following code, the computer will delete the instance at the end of the function containing the instance.

```
int main() {
....MyClass inst;
}
```

At the end of the function, in this case main, the computer will delete the instance called inst. If you include a destructor in your class, the computer will call the destructor just before it deletes the instance called inst. Then it will delete the instance, and the function will be finished.

To declare a destructor, you specify a member function in the class that has the same name as the class, except preceded by a tilde character, ~. The destructor does not

have a return type, nor does it have parameters. Thus, for your class MyClass, your destructor would be declared as ~MyClass().

Inside the code for the destructor, you can include any code that you would like to run before the instance is deleted. For example, you can print out a message on the console that the instance is being deleted.

During destruction, the instance still exists, so you can access any member variables in the destructor. For example, if you have an integer member called Count, you can type Console::WriteLine(Count); to display the value of Count on the console.

You can also call other member functions from within the destructor. However, you cannot call the constructor. If you decide to call other member functions, the member functions will run before the destructor finishes. The computer will not actually delete the instance until after the destructor is finished running.

WRITE A DESTRUCTOR

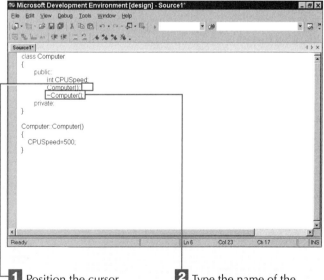

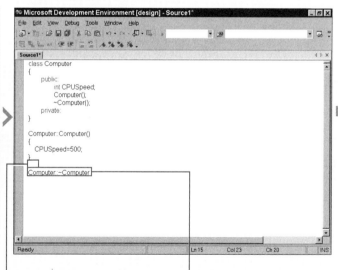

1 Position the cursor after the declaration of the **public:** section in the class and press Enter.

2 Type the name of the destructor and press Enter.

3 Position the cursor after the end of the **private:** section of the class and press Enter.

4 Type the name of the class followed by two colons and the name of the destructor.

Extra

You must use destructors to free memory occupied by pointers that are no longer required. This makes your application more memory-efficient, which can be important where many pointers are concurrently declared in memory. To delete a pointer, simply use the `delete` keyword, as shown in the following class definition.

Example:
```
class Computer
{
public:
    int *CPUType;
    Computer();
    ~Computer();
private:
    CPUType=new int;
};

Computer::~Computer()
{
    delete CPUType;
}
```

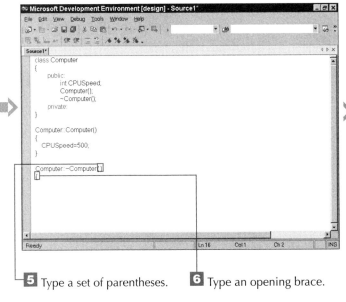

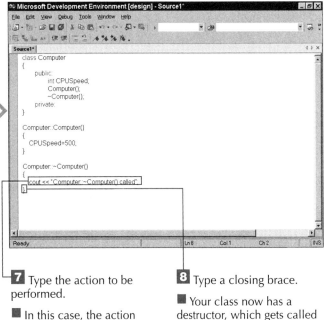

5 Type a set of parentheses.

6 Type an opening brace.

7 Type the action to be performed.

■ In this case, the action is to print a log message to standard output.

8 Type a closing brace.

■ Your class now has a destructor, which gets called when the object is destroyed.

ADD A MEMBER VARIABLE

Member variables are class variables marked as either publicly or privately accessible, depending on whether they are declared in the public or private section of the class. Variable types supported by Visual C++ include integers, characters, and floating-point numbers, as indicated by the `char`, `int`, and `float` keywords respectively.

Public member variables can be modified or updated by any of the methods within a class or by any other function. For example, an authentication class might have a personal identification number integer variable called PIN. If the `int` variable PIN is declared in the public section of the class, then its value could be modified by the calling method. If the method was a `main()` method, or if the authentication object was instantiated in the calling class,

then it might be appropriate to initialize the value of PIN directly.

However, you would more commonly prevent direct access to the value of PIN by external methods because of security concerns. Imagine if the calling method was able to modify and update the value of PINs without any kind of checks, particularly if the authentication object updated a database record for the PIN when the destructor was called. It is much safer, in this instance, to declare PIN as a private member variable and define accessor methods to retrieve or update its value. These accessor methods would be declared as public. You might have two accessor methods for the one variable, one that sets the PIN and another that retrieves it. Or, instead of retrieving it, you might have one that simply tests a user-entered number against the existing PIN.

ADD A MEMBER VARIABLE

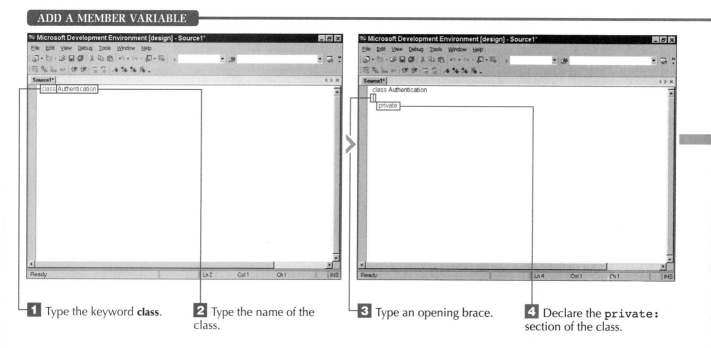

1 Type the keyword **class**.

2 Type the name of the class.

3 Type an opening brace.

4 Declare the **private:** section of the class.

Extra

In most cases, member variables should be initialized to a default value when declared, usually through a class constructor. The following example assigns the default value 9999 to the PIN variable in the constructor of the Authentication class.

Example:
```
class Authentication
{
  public:
    Authentication();
  private:
    int PIN;
};
Authentication::Authentication()
{
  PIN=9999;
}
```

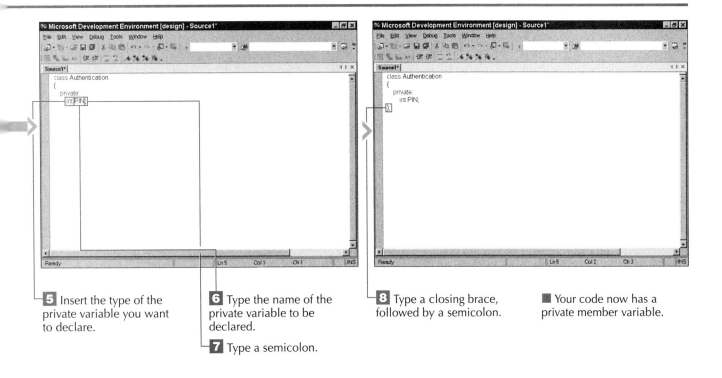

■5 Insert the type of the private variable you want to declare.

■6 Type the name of the private variable to be declared.

■7 Type a semicolon.

■8 Type a closing brace, followed by a semicolon.

■ Your code now has a private member variable.

ADD A STATIC VARIABLE

You can give your classes data that is common to all instances of the class, letting you share information between the instances. Such data is called *static data*, and is associated with a class, not an individual instance. When you create an instance of the class, the object you create can access the static data as if it is a member of the instance, but the same data item is shared among all instances. Thus, any changes the one instance makes to the data will be reflected in all the instances. This is unlike non-static member data where each instance gets its own copy of the data.

To make a data member static, type the word `static` immediately before its declaration in the class, as shown in the following code:

```
class MyClass {
public:
static int a;
};
```

However, when you create static data, you must manually supply the memory storage for it. The way you do this is include in your code a line such as this:

```
int MyClass::a;
```

Member functions can also be static. When you declare a member function as static, the function can access any of the static data members of the class, but it can not access non-static members. The reason is that each instance gets its own set of non-static members, and the static functions are not associated with a particular instance. Thus the compiler would have no way to know which instance the members are associated with; therefore, a member function can not access non-static members.

Typically you would use static members to keep track of class-wide information, such as how many instances there are. You would accomplish this by including in the constructor a line that increments a static `int count` member.

ADD A STATIC VARIABLE

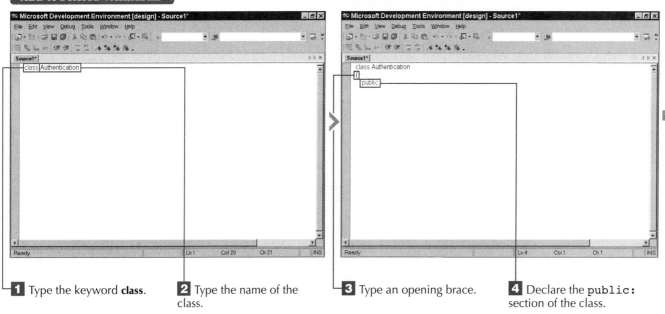

1 Type the keyword **class**.

2 Type the name of the class.

3 Type an opening brace.

4 Declare the **public:** section of the class.

Apply It

In a situation where data is being shared between different instantiations of an object, such as static member variables, it is important to initialize the affected variables sensibly. In the following example, you initialize the nPIN variable in the class constructor, and then retrieve the number of PINs in the system. When each Authentication object is destructed, you decrement nPIN to accurately reflect the number of objects.

TYPE THIS:

```cpp
#include <iostream.h>
class Authentication {
  public: static int nPIN;
  Authentication();
  ~Authentication();
  private: int PIN;
};
int Authentication::nPIN=0;
Authentication::Authentication()
{ PIN=9999; nPIN++ };
Authentication::~Authentication()
{ nPIN--; };
int main() {
  Authentication a;
  cout << "nPIN" << Authentication::nPIN << endl;
  Authentication b;
  cout << "nPIN" << Authentication::nPIN << endl;
}
```

RESULT:

```
nPIN: 1
nPIN: 2
```

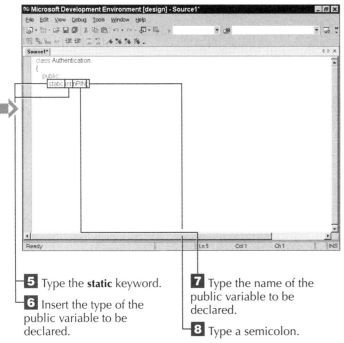

-5 Type the **static** keyword.

-6 Insert the type of the public variable to be declared.

7 Type the name of the public variable to be declared.

8 Type a semicolon.

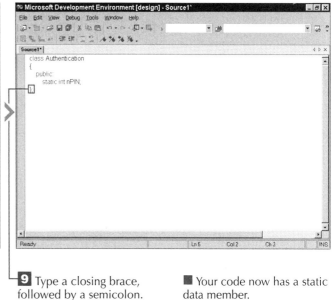

-9 Type a closing brace, followed by a semicolon.

■ Your code now has a static data member.

WRITE METHODS

Methods are functions that belong to a specific class. The main difference between procedural programming and object-oriented programming is the class, and classes have two members: variables and methods. In this section, you learn how to define and use methods in classes.

There are two main reasons for writing methods in a class: modularity and repetition. Modular methods are designed to be executed once and improve the logical layout of an application. For example, a program that generates Web pages might have a method called `printHeader()`, `printBody()`, and `printFooter()`. Although the functions of each section could very well be performed in line within the class, using methods in this way separates each of the major functions of the class. A second advantage of modularity is code reuse. In the HTML generation example, while the body of individual pages often changes, the header and footer are generally consistent across all pages. Thus, it would be wasteful to write ten separate but identical headers and footers for ten HTML pages.

Repetition involves the use of loops to perform tasks iteratively, depending on whether some condition has been fulfilled. For example, a calendar-printing program needs to repeat the act of incrementing the day of the month and printing it to the screen 31 times for the month of January. It would be extremely wasteful to do this manually:

```
day=0;
day++;
cout << "Day: " << day;
day++;
cout << "Day: " << day;
day++;
cout << "Day: " << day;
...
```

It is much more efficient to write a method that can print out a list of days.

WRITE METHODS

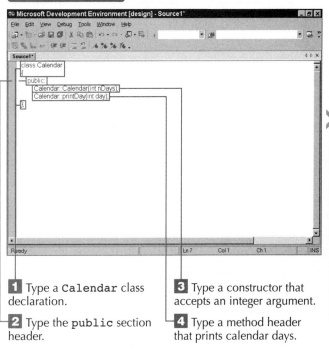

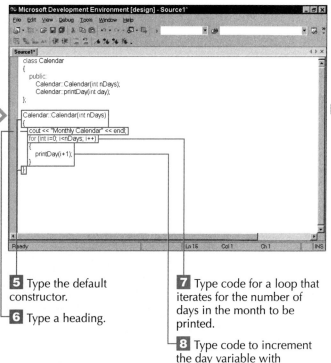

1 Type a `Calendar` class declaration.

2 Type the `public` section header.

3 Type a constructor that accepts an integer argument.

4 Type a method header that prints calendar days.

5 Type the default constructor.

6 Type a heading.

7 Type code for a loop that iterates for the number of days in the month to be printed.

8 Type code to increment the day variable with iteration.

Extra

If you decide to include your class definition in a header file, you can make sure the program will compile correctly by putting the code for the method in a source file, not in the header file. You only want one copy of the code. You will likely want to put all the methods for a single class inside a single source file.

You can keep your programs error-free by making sure the members used only by other methods within the class are kept private. If you make such methods public, you are allowing other programmers who might use your class to call these methods. If, for example, you write a method that increments the number of instances, and you make this method public, other parts of the program can call this method, making the value incorrect.

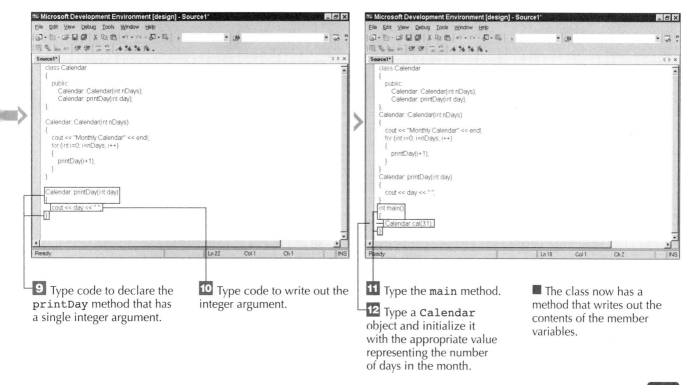

9 Type code to declare the `printDay` method that has a single integer argument.

10 Type code to write out the integer argument.

11 Type the `main` method.

12 Type a `Calendar` object and initialize it with the appropriate value representing the number of days in the month.

■ The class now has a method that writes out the contents of the member variables.

WRITE STATIC METHODS

When you create a class with static variables, the static variables are shared among all instances of the class. You can think of the static variables as being associated with the class itself. For more information on creating static variables, see page 104.

You can also write member functions that are static. These are called *static methods*. Like static variables, static methods are associated with the class and are shared among all instances. Because a static method is not associated with a particular instance of the class, it cannot access the non-static member variables. It can only access the static member variables.

To declare a static member function, you type the word **static**, followed by the function definition. For example, if you have a function called Add that takes an integer and returns a void, and it is a static function, you would declare it as the following.

```
static void Add(int x)
```

This declaration would go inside the class.

Inside the static function, you can refer to the static variables simply by specifying their names. For example, if the above function refers to a static variable called Amount, you could write Amount = 10;. You do not specify an instance, because static variables do not have an instance. Because this is inside the static function code, you do not need to specify the class name.

Your static functions can return any type and take any type as a parameter. This is the same as non-static functions. Further, you can call a static function within a non-static function by simply calling it as you would any other member function, as in Add(10);. Remember that when you call a static method from within a non-static function, the static method still cannot access the members that are not static.

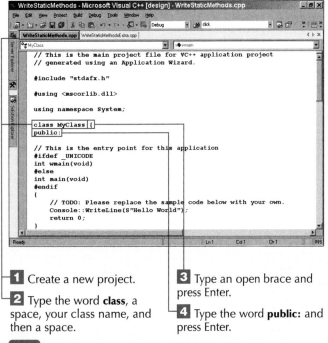

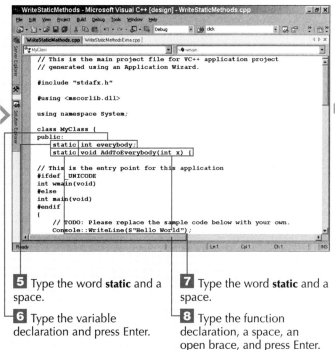

1 Create a new project.

2 Type the word **class**, a space, your class name, and then a space.

3 Type an open brace and press Enter.

4 Type the word **public:** and press Enter.

5 Type the word **static** and a space.

6 Type the variable declaration and press Enter.

7 Type the word **static** and a space.

8 Type the function declaration, a space, an open brace, and press Enter.

Extra

You can access the public static member functions from anywhere in your code, not just from within member functions. To do this, type the name of the class, then two colons, and then the name of the function. Follow it with parentheses and the parameters. Further, you can refer to the static members as if they are members of the individual instances. However, when you do so, they are still shared among all instances.

Example:
```
MyClass inst1;
MyClass inst2;
MyClass::everybody = 10;
MyClass::AddToEverybody(5);
Console::WriteLine(inst1.everybody);
Console::WriteLine(inst2.everybody);
```

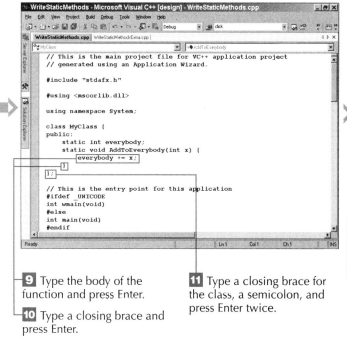

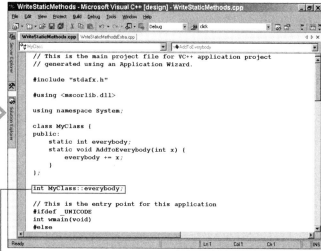

9 Type the body of the function and press Enter.

10 Type a closing brace and press Enter.

11 Type a closing brace for the class, a semicolon, and press Enter twice.

12 Type the storage for the static variable.

Note: For more information on static variable storage, see page 104.

■ Your program now has a static method that accesses a static variable.

OVERLOAD METHODS

You can use a feature of C++ called *overloading* to write a class that has multiple methods that are named the same but perform slightly different tasks. For example, sometimes you need to use a function in more than one way. For example, you may want to write a calculator program that adds together two numbers of different types, such as integer plus integer or integer plus floating-point number. You can overload methods with C++ by creating methods with the same name that have different numbers and types of arguments. This allows equivalent functions to be carried out without crowding the namespace with redundant names. A generic add() is easier to interpret and program than methods created for all operations, such as addTwoFloats(), addTwoInts(), and addIntAndFloat().

You can overload an add() method by creating methods that have the same name but accept different variable types

as parameters. In C, declaring functions with the same name would cause a compiler error; however, such a practice is perfectly legal in C++ as long as the parameter types and ordering are distinct between the overloaded method names. This flexibility overcomes the age-old problem of wanting to access particular methods for data operations that sometimes use floating-point numbers and sometimes use integers.

Often your overloaded function names will appear within a single class, although they can be standalone functions as well. You can also put one function in a base class, and an overloaded function in a derived class. The derived class will have both functions available, while the base class will have only the first function available.

OVERLOAD METHODS

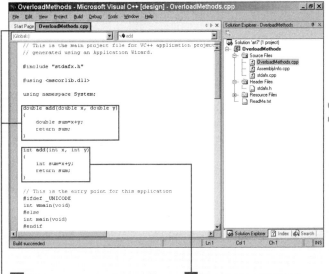

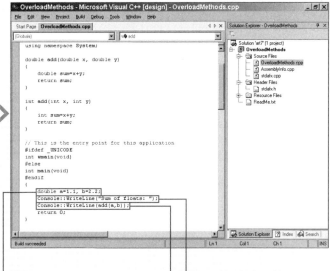

1 Create a new project and remove the Hello World line.

2 Type a function that takes one type of parameter.

3 Type an overloaded function of the same name with a different type of parameter.

4 Type code to declare variables for use in the function call.

5 Type a statement that displays a message to the user.

6 Type a line that calls the first overloaded function.

Apply It

You can make your classes more powerful by using overloaded functions in them. Member functions within classes can be overloaded in the same way standard functions can be.

TYPE THIS:

```cpp
class MyMath {
public:
    double Add(double x, double y);
    int Add(int x, int y);
};
double MyMath::Add(double x, double y) {
    return x + y;
}
int MyMath::Add(int i, int j) {
    return i + j;
}
void main(void)
{
    MyMath inst;
    Console::WriteLine(inst.Add(10,20));
    Console::WriteLine(inst.Add(1.5,2.7));
}
```

RESULT:

```
30
4.2
```

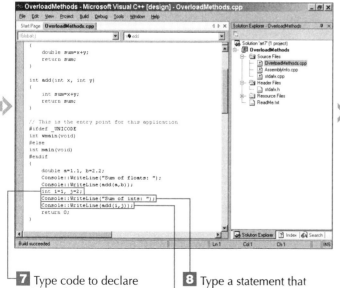

7 Type code to declare variables for use in the second function call.

8 Type a statement that displays a message to the user.

9 Type a line that calls the second overloaded function.

10 Compile and run the program.

■ The program will run showing that the proper overloaded function was called.

SPECIFY MEMBER ACCESS

When you create a class, you will have member variables that you will want to manipulate from within the member functions. However, you may not want other classes and functions to access these member variables. To ensure that other classes and functions do not have access to these member variables, you can declare them as private. You can also declare member functions as private, and only the other member functions can call the private functions.

When you are designing a class, you will want to have limited ways the other classes and functions can use the class. For example, if you have a class called ToyotaCamry, you might have member functions called OpenDoor, CloseDoor, Drive, and Park. But internally, to make these member functions work, you might include a function called CoolEngine. You would not want functions outside the class to be calling the CoolEngine function directly. Instead, your Drive function may need to occasionally call this function. Therefore, you would declare the CoolEngine function as private.

Further, the ToyotaCamry class might have a member data item called GasolineLevel. You might want the Drive function to decrease this level, but you would not want another class or function to be able to decrease it. Again, you would make GasolineLevel private.

The methods, OpenDoor, CloseDoor, Drive, and Park would be public because any other classes and functions can call these functions. Together these public functions would represent the *public interface* to the class. They are the functions that other classes and functions use for manipulating the class.

When you design a class, you will want to carefully think about how you want other classes and functions to interact with the class. You will then only make certain functions and variables public.

SPECIFY MEMBER ACCESS

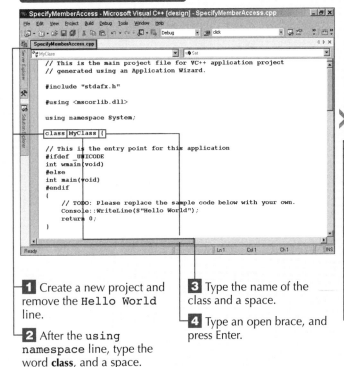

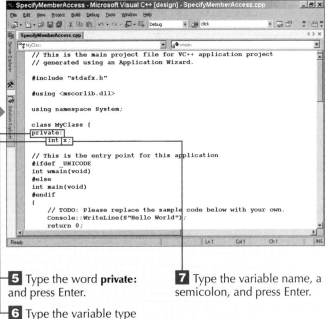

1 Create a new project and remove the `Hello World` line.

2 After the `using namespace` line, type the word **class**, and a space.

3 Type the name of the class and a space.

4 Type an open brace, and press Enter.

5 Type the word **private:** and press Enter.

6 Type the variable type and a space.

7 Type the variable name, a semicolon, and press Enter.

Apply It

You can check whether you are accessing private members incorrectly by noting the compile errors. If you incorrectly attempt to access a private member, you will see the message *cannot access private member.*

TYPE THIS:

```
#include "stdafx.h"
#using <mscorlib.dll>
using namespace System;
class MyClass {
private:
    int x;
public:
    int y;
};
int main(void) {
    MyClass inst;
    inst.x = 10;
}
```

RESULT:

```
error C2248: 'MyClass::x' :
cannot access private member declared in class 'MyClass'
```

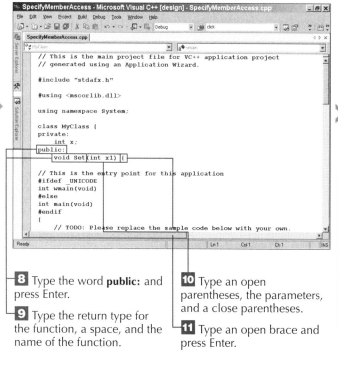

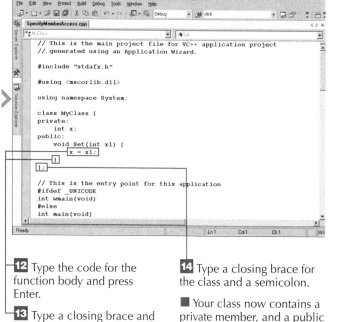

8 Type the word **public:** and press Enter.

9 Type the return type for the function, a space, and the name of the function.

10 Type an open parentheses, the parameters, and a close parentheses.

11 Type an open brace and press Enter.

12 Type the code for the function body and press Enter.

13 Type a closing brace and press Enter.

14 Type a closing brace for the class and a semicolon.

■ Your class now contains a private member, and a public function that accesses the private member.

ADD FRIEND VARIABLES AND METHODS

Sometimes when you write a class that has private members, you may wish to allow another class to access those private members. A class that can access the private members of another class is called a *friend class*.

To create a friend class, you specify the friend class name in the original class definition. For example, if you have a class called MyPoint, and you want to allow the class called MyRectangle to access the private members of MyPoint, you would include a line in your MyPoint definition as follows.

```
friend class MyRectangle;
```

The member functions of the class MyRectangle can then create instances of MyPoint, and can access the private members. For example, if MyPoint has a member variable called X declared in the private section, a member function for MyRectangle can include the following code.

```
void Set(int x1, int y1) {
    mypoint->X = x1;
    mypoint->Y = y1;
}
```

If you write code outside of the member functions for MyPoint and MyRectangle, you cannot access the private variables in this manner. You will receive an error when you try to compile your code.

Be careful when using friend classes. You normally choose to make members private because you do not want other functions and classes modifying them. Instead, you normally want to provide public methods that modify the member data. That way you can control exactly how the private data is set. For example, if you have a private integer variable, and never want it to be set to 0, you can put an if statement in the member functions that attempt to set it. This if statement would test for 0 and instead set it, for example, to 1. However, if you create a friend class, the code in the friend class can directly set the private integer to 0.

ADD FRIEND VARIABLES AND METHODS

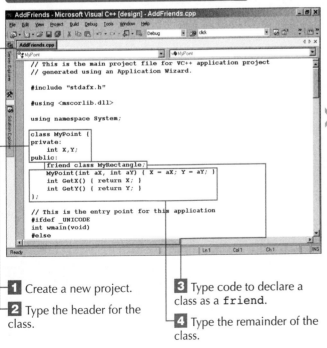

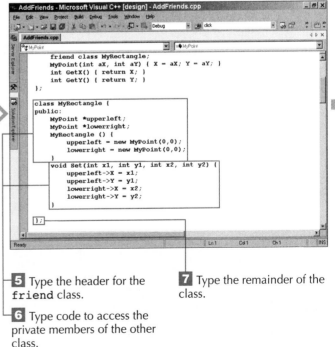

1 Create a new project.

2 Type the header for the class.

3 Type code to declare a class as a **friend**.

4 Type the remainder of the class.

5 Type the header for the **friend** class.

6 Type code to access the private members of the other class.

7 Type the remainder of the class.

Extra

Imagine that a defense system is being created using a class called Enemy. It cannot have any public members to ensure that all private data is secure, and cannot be externally accessed by using accessor methods. This seems like an exercise in overzealous security, since a class with no publicly addressable accessor methods would not be very useful.

This is a situation where a friend class would be very useful. A friend class called Buddy could be used to access any private methods defined in Enemy without requiring any public accessor methods.

Example:
```
class Enemy
{
public:
friend class Buddy;
private:
int secretBusiness();
};
int Enemy::secretBusiness()
{
count << "You have discovered the secret business";
}
```

In this situation, Buddy can access the secretBusinesss method by directly calling the private method, because it has friend status. No other classes can do this.

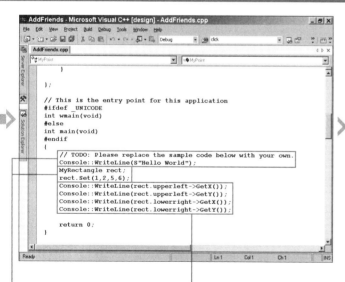

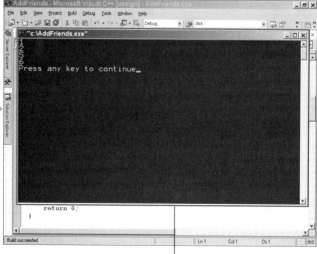

8 Remove the Hello World lines.

9 Type code that creates an instance of the friend class and calls the functions that access the private members.

10 Type code to call the public members of the other class.

■ You cannot access the private members of the other class in the main function.

11 Compile and run the program.

■ The program window opens. The console shows the results of the access to the public members.

ADD A NESTED CLASS

Using friend classes is one way of allowing another class to have full and trusted access to its members. However, if you are reluctant to allow unrestricted external access to members, an alternative is *nested classes*. A nested class is literally located within another class and is typically private to its containing class. Using a nested class is most appropriate when one class is only ever called by one other class. This approach simplifies design and ensures the integrity of objects instantiated by the nested class.

You will encounter two main variants of nested classes in C++. A *static nested class* only allows access to its enclosing classes methods through accessor methods when

instantiated. *A non-static nested class* — also called an *inner class* — does not have this restriction.

An example of how to use a nested class is a class `Printer` that models all of the properties and actions of a printer. Inside the printer is an ink level monitor that is modeled by the class `InkLevel`. While a `Printer` class such as `SerialPort` (representing the serial port) may need to access an external class (such as `Computer`), the `InkLevel` class only ever needs to interact with the `Printer` class. Thus, it makes sense to declare `SerialPort` a friend of the `Printer` class, but declare the `InkLevel` class a nested class.

ADD A NESTED CLASS

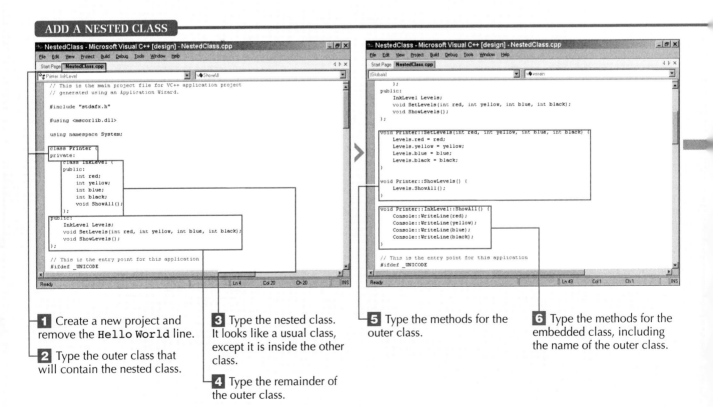

1 Create a new project and remove the **Hello World** line.

2 Type the outer class that will contain the nested class.

3 Type the nested class. It looks like a usual class, except it is inside the other class.

4 Type the remainder of the outer class.

5 Type the methods for the outer class.

6 Type the methods for the embedded class, including the name of the outer class.

An enclosing class can have more than one nested class associated with it. The following example defines two nested classes: The `InkLevel` class models the level of ink in a printer, and the `PaperOutDetector` represents the status of the paper level in the printer.

Example:
```
class Printer
{
class InkLevel;
friend class Printer::InkLevel;
class PaperOutDetector;
friend class Printer:: PaperOutDetector;
// Printer members go here
};
class Printer::InkLevel
{
// InkLevel methods go here
};
class Printer::PaperOutDetetcor
{
// PaperOutDetector methods go here
};
```

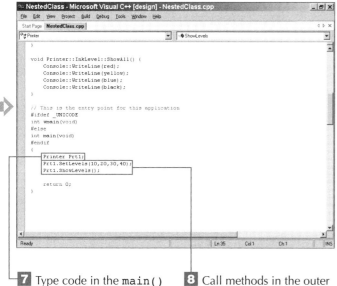

7 Type code in the `main()` function to create a new instance of the outer class.

8 Call methods in the outer class.

9 Compile and run the program.

■ The program runs, executing the code in the outer and embedded classes.

INTRODUCING INHERITANCE

When you model data, you use a C++ class as a self-contained unit that describes an object and the operations it can perform. When you consider data in the real world, you will notice that there are different types of objects, but often there are some close similarities. For example, a Honda Accord automobile and a Navistar tow truck have certain similarities; they both have wheels, doors, a steering wheel, brakes, they can both be driven, and so on. But they have differences as well, the most obvious being the fact that the tow truck has a tow mechanism and the Honda Accord does not. Therefore, when modeling data for an Accord and a Navistar tow truck, you would likely create two distinct classes.

The problem with making them two distinct classes, however, is that they have certain common traits and capabilities, and you would then end up duplicating the code. Duplicating code is never a good idea because if situations change over time and you need to modify the code, then you need to modify it in more than one place, which can be difficult. It can also cause errors, because if

two programmers are working on a project and they both modify the duplicate code separately, one might modify it slightly differently from the other, and one might cause a bug in the program where the two parts of code are expected to perform the same.

The way to prevent such troubles is to recognize the common features in the models, and to first create a single class holding these common features. This single class might be called Vehicle. The class Vehicle would have common data members such as the number of tires, the number of doors, and common member functions such as Drive, Stop, and Park.

Then, to provide the features for the individual types of vehicles, you would create classes that inherit the features of Vehicle, and then extend or modify Vehicle to model the particular type of vehicle. This process is called *Inheritance* and is used often in C++ programming. Very rarely do you find professional programs that do not use inheritance.

LEVELS OF INHERITANCE

Inheritance does not restrict you to only one level. You can inherit from one class, and then inherit from that class, as many times as you wish, with each inherited class becoming more and more specialized. Many professional class libraries will have hundreds of classes available, with perhaps eight or more levels of inheritance.

When you inherit a class, and then inherit again, the class in the middle serves as both a base and a derived class. Also, the process of inheriting is usually called deriving: You derive a class from a base class.

INDIVIDUAL INSTANCES OF A CLASS

When you derive a class, such as Honda Accord, from a base class, such as Vehicle, you are not actually creating an object of type Honda Accord. Rather, you are creating a type. This type serves as a model for actual objects or instances. Thus, you might have a class called Honda Accord with a data member called Color. You might then create three instances of Honda Accord, one with color Black, one with color Red, and one with color Blue. These instances represent an

actual, individual car. The class, on the other hand, does not represent an actual, individual car. Instead, the class simply describes the type of car.

The actual, individual car is called either an instance or an object. Thus, in programming, you say that you are creating an instance of type Honda Accord, or you say that you are creating an object of type Honda Accord. Both terms are equally useful and mean the same thing.

COMPLEX MODELS AND INSTANCES

Therefore, when you are inheriting, you will likely develop a rather sophisticated tree diagram where you have one class at the top from which you derive several classes, and then you might continue deriving from each of the derived classes. You may end up with dozens of classes, with multiple levels. However, nowhere in this inheritance tree are you actually creating any objects. You are only describing the types of objects, also called the classes of objects. One way to look at it is to treat it analogous to a species classification in the animal kingdom. You might have a class called `Animal`, from which you would derive two classes, `Vertebrate` and `Invertebrate`, referring to animals that either have or do not have a backbone. From `Vertebrate`, you might derive the five classes `Mammal`, `Bird`, `Fish`, `Reptile`, and `Amphibian`. From `Mammal` you might continue following the classification created by zoologists, and

derive a class called `Carnivore`, as well as others. From `Carnivore` you might derive a class called `Feline`, as well as others. The `Feline` class might have further classifications under it to describe cats the way zoologists classify them.

But throughout this large classification of animals, there are no actual animals. You are simply describing kinds of animals. Only when you encounter a group of actual cheetahs in the wild or at a zoo would you have actual instances of the cheetah species.

The same holds for programming. When you model the data, you are creating the types. Then after creating the types, you can create the instances or objects. Thus, the class `Honda Accord` is a type of `Vehicle`, not an instance of `Vehicle`.

INHERITANCE AND PROTECTION

There are many ways you can handle the data members when you derive new classes. For example, when you write a function in a base class, you might want to allow the functions in the derived class to call this base class function. Or you might want to only allow other functions in the base class to call this particular function. Or, you might want to allow any method or function within your entire program to call it.

There are three possibilities here. The first is that the function is *public*, meaning it can be called from anywhere within your program. The second is that the function is *protected*, meaning the function can only be called from within the base class functions, and within the derived class functions. The third is that the function is *private*, meaning the function can only be called from within functions of the base class itself, and nowhere else.

DERIVE A CLASS

*D*erivation describes the process, in a child class, of inheriting members from a parent class. This process means that members available in the parents become available to the child class after it has been declared. Parent classes are known as *base classes* because they are the base from which these inherited features are derived.

Child classes are also known as *derived classes*. In addition to the inherited members from a base class, a derived class can declare any number of its own members which are not inversely inheritable. That is, these members are not available for use by the base class. If a member is identified in the base class that must be accessible from the base class, it should be moved back into the base class, and inherited by the derived class.

The member functions in a child class may only access those inherited members that are either public or protected. Private members in the base class can only be accessed by the member functions in the base class. Because protected members cannot be accessed by code outside the class, this shows the difference between protected and private: Although neither can be accessed outside the class, private cannot be accessed by derived classes, whereas protected can.

To derive a class from another class, declare the class, and after the class name, add a colon followed by the word public, followed by the name of the base class.

DERIVE A CLASS

1 Type the **class** keyword.

2 Type the name of the derived class.

3 Type the colon operator (**:**).

4 Type the **public** keyword.

Extra

Your derived classes can overload member functions, which means they can have their own versions of a function that is in the base class. To do this, you must supply the keyword `virtual` to the function in the base class, and then code the function in the derived class using the same function name, parameters, and return type.

Example:
```cpp
class BaseClass {
public:
    virtual void MyFunction() {
        Console::WriteLine("Inside Base class");
    }
};
class DerivedClass : public BaseClass {
public:
    virtual void MyFunction() {
        Console::WriteLine("Inside Derived class");
    }
};
void main() {
    BaseClass base;
    DerivedClass derived;
    base.MyFunction();
    derived.MyFunction();
}
```

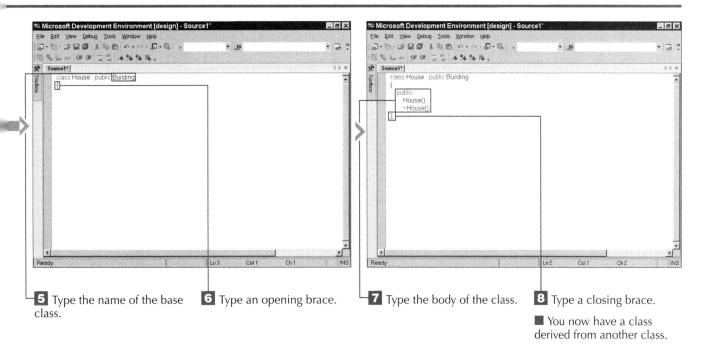

5 Type the name of the base class.

6 Type an opening brace.

7 Type the body of the class.

8 Type a closing brace.

■ You now have a class derived from another class.

INITIALIZE THE BASE CLASS

When you derive and inherit classes, classifying members as private in the base class would prevent them from being accessed by the derived class. Private members are the one exception to inheritance. Instead, the protected keyword is used to indicate that data should be private from all classes except those that are descendents of the base class.

For example, the Building class is called the base class, and the class that inherits the features is called the derived class. Because the member limits is private, it would not be accessible by its children (such as Home). Instead, the protected members nRooms, nWalls, and roofType are given private protection from all but descendent classes.

You can access members from a base class after a derived class has been declared in three ways: accessing public

members as if they were members of the derived class; accessing protected members as if they were members of the derived class; and accessing private data members of the base class by using a public or protected method of the base class.

However, before you can access any base members, you must invoke two constructors to instantiate the class. The first constructor to be called is the constructor of the base class. The second constructor to be called is the constructor of the derived class. It is important to understand how this sequence affects the instantiation of the derived class. If the base class constructor initializes a public member of the base class and the derived class does the same, then the net effect of both constructor actions is equivalent to the action of the derived class constructor alone.

INITIALIZE THE BASE CLASS

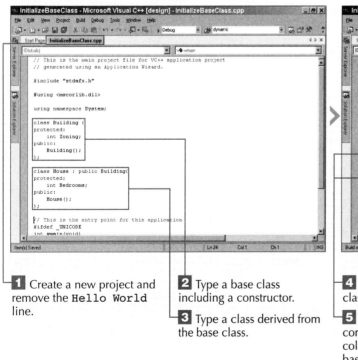

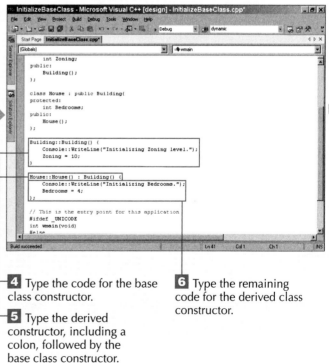

1 Create a new project and remove the **Hello World** line.

2 Type a base class including a constructor.

3 Type a class derived from the base class.

4 Type the code for the base class constructor.

5 Type the derived constructor, including a colon, followed by the base class constructor.

6 Type the remaining code for the derived class constructor.

Extra

You can initialize the members of the data base class using a notation similar to the constructor initialization. If you want to initialize the members for each instance, you type a colon after the constructor name in the class definition, followed by the name of the member, and then the initial value in parentheses.

Example:
```
class Building
{
    public:
        Building():nRooms(1);
        ~Building();
        int nRooms;
};
class House : public Building
{
    public:
        House():nRooms(2);
        ~House();
};
```

7 Type code that creates an instance of the derived class.

8 Compile and run the program.

■ The program window opens, demonstrating that first the base class constructor runs, then the derived class constructor.

CALL A BASE METHOD

When you derive a class from another class, you often override some of the member functions using the `virtual` keyword. If you call the method of a derived class object, the code in the derived class will execute. Sometimes, however, you may have code in the base class version of the overridden method that needs to run. For example, you might have a program that models some graphics objects and draws them on the screen. The base class might be called `Shape`, and it might have a `draw` method. The draw method could check if there is supposed to be a rectangular border around the shape, and if so, draw it. You might then have a derived class called `Circle`, which draws a circle through the overridden `draw` method. But when you call the `draw` method on a `Circle` class object, the code in the `Shape` class for drawing the border will not get called.

The solution is to write your overridden `draw` method in the `Circle` class, and to have it in turn call the base class

method. The way to call the base class method is by specifying the name of the base class, then the method name, and then the parameters. For example

```cpp
void Circle::draw(int x, int y) {
    Shape::draw(x,y);
    // Remaining Circle::draw code goes here.
}
```

You can only do this in the derived class method. If you try to put such code outside of a derived class method, you will receive a compiler error.

Note that when you call the base class method, you do not need to pass the same parameters that you received in the derived class method. For example, you can modify them mathematically, and then pass them. However, you do need to pass some parameters, even if they are modified.

CALL A BASE METHOD

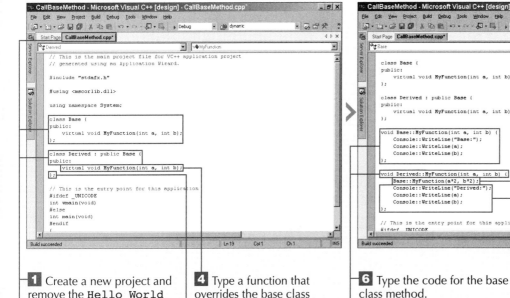

1 Create a new project and remove the `Hello World` line.

2 Type a declaration for a base class.

3 Type the header for a class derived from the base.

4 Type a function that overrides the base class function.

5 Type a closing brace and semicolon.

6 Type the code for the base class method.

7 Type the header for the derived class method.

8 Type code to call the base class method.

9 Type the remaining code for the derived class method.

Apply It

You can call the base class destructor automatically by making the destructor `virtual`. Then, when you delete an instance, you do not need to manually call the base class destructor.

TYPE THIS:

```
class Base {
public:
    virtual ~Base() {
        Console::WriteLine("Base cleanup");
    };
};
class Derived : public Base {
public:
    virtual ~Derived() {
        Console::WriteLine("Derived cleanup");
    };
};
int main(void) {
    Derived instance;
    return 0;
}
```

RESULTS:

Derived cleanup

Base cleanup

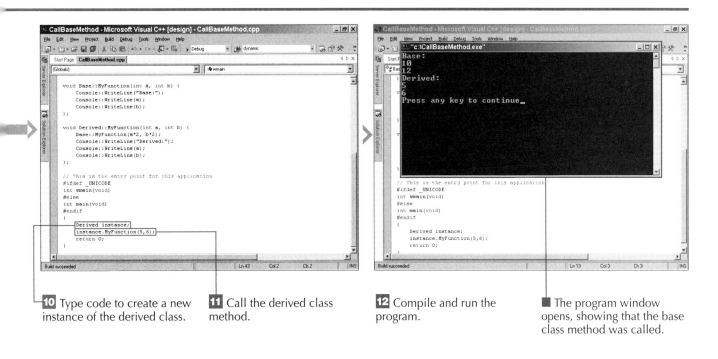

10 Type code to create a new instance of the derived class.

11 Call the derived class method.

12 Compile and run the program.

■ The program window opens, showing that the base class method was called.

CREATE CLASSES USING POLYMORPHISM

Y ou can use a feature of inheritance to add code reuse to your programs. C++ provides a level of interrelation between derived classes and a base class by *polymorphism*, which from Greek means many forms. Polymorphism plays on the fact that derived classes are descendents of base classes, allowing virtual functions to select the appropriate derived class methods to be invoked, ahead of base class methods of the same name and type.

This is an important feature for separating the functionality of base and derived classes. The base class constructor has precedence over a derived class constructor, because it is called first. In addition, a method defined in a base class has precedence over a method called in a derived class. For example, if an accessor method called printStatus() was defined in the base class Building, it would be

invoked in preference to a printStatus() method defined in the derived class House. A feature of inheritance is that all inherited members are selected over local members, unless those members are declared as VIRTUAL MEMBERS.

Using virtual members allows a public method to be defined in a base class that is then inherited by its descendents. If no member with the same name is defined in a derived class, then the base class method has precedence. However, if the derived class defines a method with the same name as the virtual member of the base class, then the derived class member has precedence. This allows derived class methods to override their base class counterparts if local customization is required.

CREATE CLASSES USING POLYMORPHISM

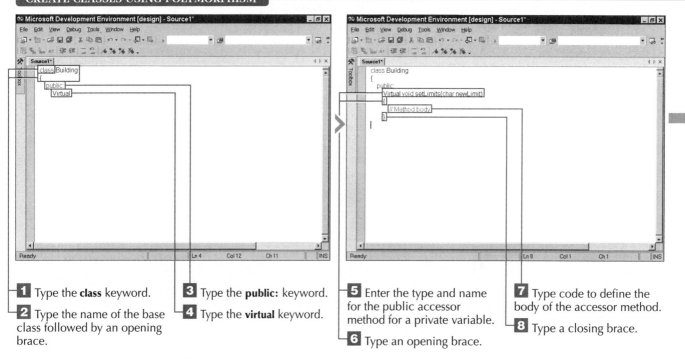

1 Type the **class** keyword.

2 Type the name of the base class followed by an opening brace.

3 Type the **public:** keyword.

4 Type the **virtual** keyword.

5 Enter the type and name for the public accessor method for a private variable.

6 Type an opening brace.

7 Type code to define the body of the accessor method.

8 Type a closing brace.

Extra

To see how virtual members work, declare a base class `Building` and a derived class `House`, and two methods in each class: a set method and a get method. The `set` method in the base class is declared `virtual`. Thus, it is called only if there is no corresponding member in the derived class. In contrast, the `get` method is not declared `virtual` in the base class. Thus, the derived class `get` method should never be called.

Example:
```
class Building {
    public:
        Building();
        ~Building();
        char getLimits() { return limits; }
        virtual void setLimits(char newLimit) { }
    private:
        char limits='N';
};
class House : public Building {
    public:
        House();
        ~House();
        virtual void setLimits(char newLimit) { limits=newLimit; }
        char getLimits() { return 'N'; }
};
```

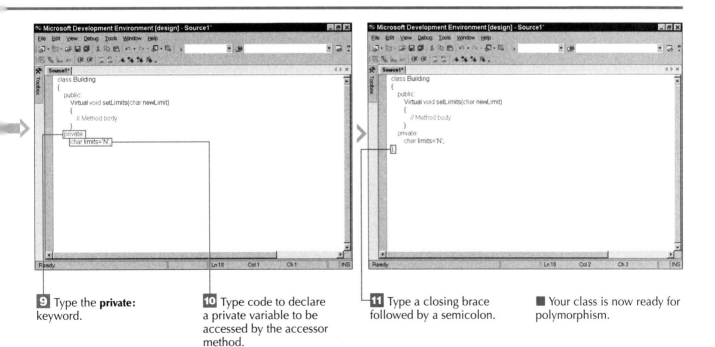

9 Type the **private:** keyword.

10 Type code to declare a private variable to be accessed by the accessor method.

11 Type a closing brace followed by a semicolon.

■ Your class is now ready for polymorphism.

CREATE ABSTRACT CLASSES

You can organize your classes by finding common portions, and placing the common portions in a single class. You can then derive from the single class. For example, if you have a class called House and a class called Factory, you will likely find that these two classes have many common elements. For example, each has a number of walls and a number of floors. You can group these common elements in a single class called Building. You can then derive House and Factory from Building.

While you can then create instances of House and Factory, you might not want to be able to create instances of Building. Building might contain just generic information that is common to all types of buildings. Such a class is called *abstract*.

To declare an abstract class, you need to declare at least one function as virtual. Instead of giving the function a body, you type an equal sign after the declaration, then a 0,

then a semicolon. This declares the function as *pure abstract*. For example, the following declares a pure abstract function called MyFunction.

```
virtual void MyFunction() = 0;
```

By including a pure abstract function in your class, you automatically designate the class as abstract.

After you declare an abstract class, the compiler will not allow you to create an instance of the class. If you try to, it will generate an error when you compile the code. You will see this message: "cannot instantiate abstract class." It will then list the names of the pure virtual functions. Thus, you must derive new classes from the abstract class, and in the derived class, you must overload the MyFunction method, providing code for it. You can then create instances of the derived class.

CREATE ABSTRACT CLASSES

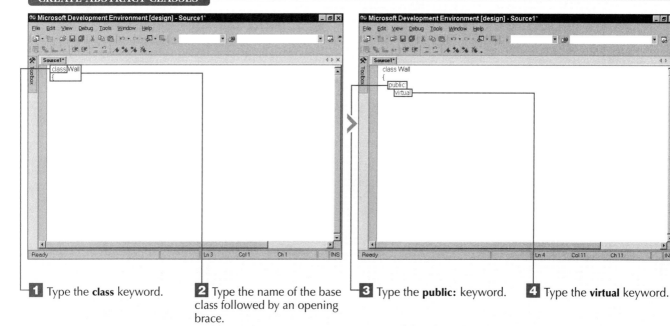

1 Type the **class** keyword.

2 Type the name of the base class followed by an opening brace.

3 Type the **public:** keyword.

4 Type the **virtual** keyword.

Extra

You can include constructors and destructors in your base class, even if the class is abstract. You can have the base class constructor and destructor provide initialization code and cleanup code that is common to all the derived classes.

Example:
```cpp
class Wall {
    public:
        Wall();
        ~Wall();
        virtual void paint()=0;
};
class Brick : public Wall {
    public:
        Wall();
        ~Wall();
        void paint() {
            cout << "Painting has commenced";
        }
};
```

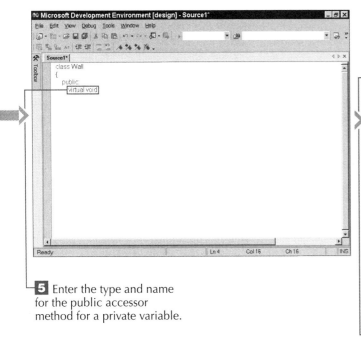

5 Enter the type and name for the public accessor method for a private variable.

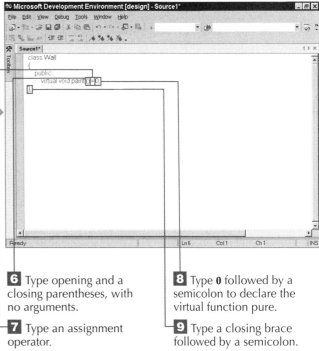

6 Type opening and a closing parentheses, with no arguments.

7 Type an assignment operator.

8 Type **0** followed by a semicolon to declare the virtual function pure.

9 Type a closing brace followed by a semicolon.

■ Your class is now abstract.

DERIVE A CLASS FROM AN ABSTRACT CLASS

You can declare a class as abstract if you want to ensure that you cannot create instances of it. You declare it as abstract by including a pure virtual function. See page 128 for more information.

After you have an abstract class, you can derive classes from it. You can then create instances of the derived classes, provided you fill in the abstract functions. The abstract class defines at least one pure virtual function. Your derived class must supply code for the pure virtual functions. Otherwise, the derived class will also be abstract and the compiler will not allow you to create an instance of it.

To fill in the code for the pure virtual function, you write your class and include a function definition for the function by the same name as the pure virtual function, with the same return type and parameters. However, you do not include the =0 notation. Instead, you supply a function body.

For example, if MyAbstract contains the pure virtual function

```
virtual void MyFunction() = 0;
```

then you can derive MyDerived from MyAbstract, including a new function definition for MyFunction, as in the following.

```
class MyDerived : public MyAbstract {
    void MyFunction() {
    }
};
```

Inside the braces, you can supply the code for the function. Then the function will not be pure abstract for the MyDerived class. Thus, you can create instances of it.

You will sometimes see the word virtual in the function definition in the abstract class, as in virtual void MyFunction(). The word virtual here is optional, and many programmers always include it as a reminder to themselves that they are overriding a function.

DERIVE A CLASS FROM AN ABSTRACT CLASS

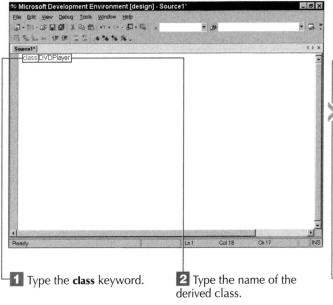

1 Type the **class** keyword.

2 Type the name of the derived class.

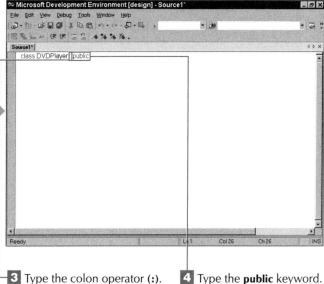

3 Type the colon operator (:).

4 Type the **public** keyword.

Extra

This example shows that the derived class DVDPlayer is related to the base class HiFiSystem. The HiFiSystem class defines two public methods (a constructor and destructor) and three protected variables that are inherited by all descendent classes. A private variable called serialNumber is not inherited by any descendent classes and can be accessed only by an accessor method.

Example:
```
class HiFiSystem
{
    public:
        HiFiSystem();
        ~HiFiSystem();
    protected:
        int volumeControl;
        int toneControl;
        char muteControl;
    private:
        int serialNumber=0;
};
class DVDPlayer : public HiFiSystem
{
    public:
        DVDPlayer();
        ~DVDPlayer();
    protected:
        char outputType;
        int regionCode;
};
```

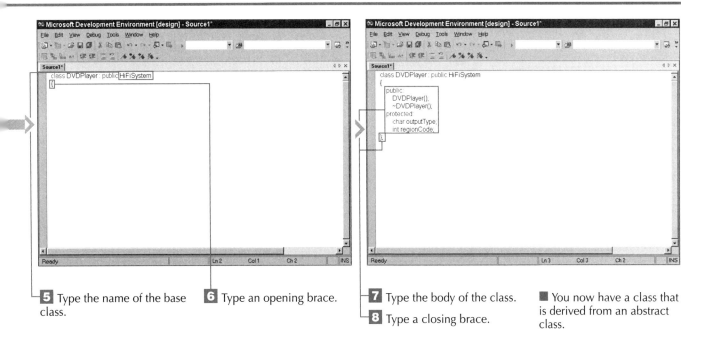

█5 Type the name of the base class.

█6 Type an opening brace.

█7 Type the body of the class.

█8 Type a closing brace.

■ You now have a class that is derived from an abstract class.

CREATE A DEBUGGING EXECUTABLE

One of the most challenging tasks for programmers is identifying coding errors and errors in logic which have occurred in a program. Although the C++ compiler flags most errors outright, identifying semantic errors is much more difficult. This is because the compiler contains a parser which validates that all of the statements you enter into a program's source code are syntactically correct — however, the compiler does not have the ability to identify the intention of a programmer who arranges syntactically correct statements into a particular sequence. Because sequencing is critical to the logical integrity of an application, a programmer (or more commonly, a tester) needs to validate the semantics of all applications manually.

Consider the example of a bank account program, where a customer deposits and withdraws money in a specific sequence. The sequence of banking events is critical to the integrity of the business process — if a customer has a $10 balance, deposits $20, and withdraws $30, then the account has a balance of $0, but is never overdrawn. However, if the withdrawal transaction is processed before the deposit

transaction, then the withdrawal may be rejected, because the account would appear to be overdrawn. In many cases, incorrect sequencing of statements and errors in logic can lead to serious runtime problems.

Fortunately, Visual C++ provides a number of tools to assist in the debugging of applications. Commonly used debugging methods include stepping through each statement in a program as it is executing, and watching how key variables (such as bank account balances) are updated by various statements. It is also possible to step into a function or method call, or bypass a specific method call, if it is suspected to be causing a bug.

Before any of these tools can be used, a debugging executable must be created in your project. In the following example, you learn how to create a debugging executable, which contains all of the symbolic information required to step through an application, by configuring the debugging requirements for the current project.

CREATE A DEBUGGING EXECUTABLE

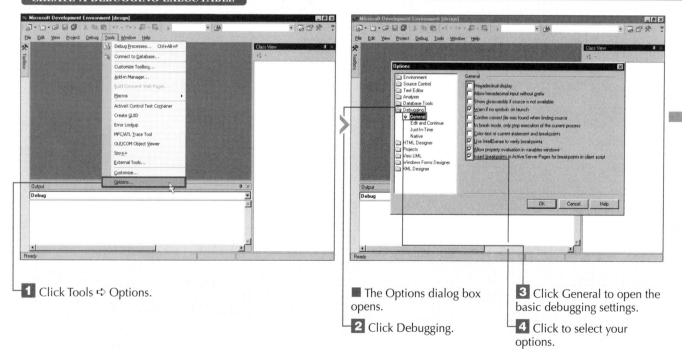

1 Click Tools ➪ Options.

■ The Options dialog box opens.

2 Click Debugging.

3 Click General to open the basic debugging settings.

4 Click to select your options.

Extra

After an application has been debugged and is ready for production use, all symbolic debugging information should be stripped, which provides a smaller, leaner executable.

During debugging, any optimization features should be disabled, because optimizing algorithms have been known to interfere with the sequencing of statements, especially in loops.

The return values of functions called in the application are shown in the Autos watch list, while local variable values are shown in the Locals watch list.

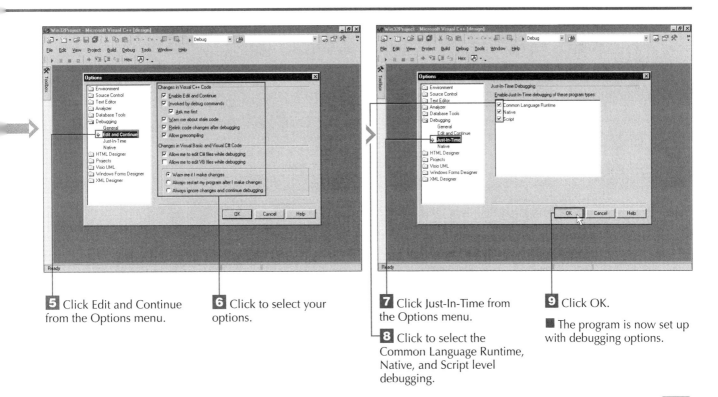

5 Click Edit and Continue from the Options menu.

6 Click to select your options.

7 Click Just-In-Time from the Options menu.

8 Click to select the Common Language Runtime, Native, and Script level debugging.

9 Click OK.

■ The program is now set up with debugging options.

STEP THROUGH A PROGRAM

Stepping through a program involves literally executing each statement sequentially through the application, as the .NET environment pauses on each line. This debugging approach is very useful for determining a specific method or code block that is giving rise to runtime errors. In addition, variable watches can be set to keep track of the value of specific variables during execution. Unlike distributed systems, where code may be executed on a number of different servers, locally executed code can be executed statement by statement.

The Step Into feature can be activated by clicking the Step Into button on the Debug toolbar. This toolbar can be activated by selecting Debug from the Toolbar submenu of the View menu.

During the Step Into process, a yellow arrow points to the line of code that is currently being executed. To step into

the next statement, you simply click the yellow arrow that appears on the Debug toolbar, next to the Step Into button. The yellow arrow in the source code window should then move to the next executed statement, and so on, until the program terminates normally (or abnormally, if there is a runtime error).

While stepping through the code, you will also see several other windows that you may find useful. One shows the order that functions are called; this is called the *Call Stack*. When you step into a function, you will see the name of the function appear at the top of the list in the Call Stack. When you step into yet another function, that function is added to the top, showing the previous function below it. When you step out of a function, the name of the function is removed from the Call Stack.

STEP THROUGH A PROGRAM

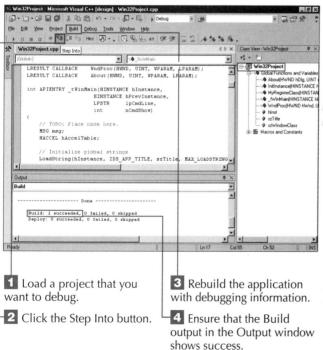

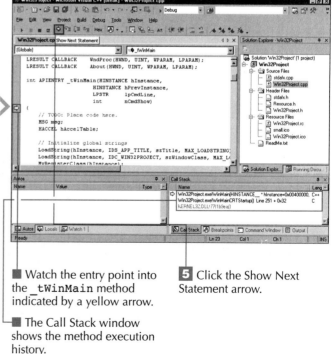

1 Load a project that you want to debug.

2 Click the Step Into button.

3 Rebuild the application with debugging information.

4 Ensure that the Build output in the Output window shows success.

■ Watch the entry point into the `_tWinMain` method indicated by a yellow arrow.

■ The Call Stack window shows the method execution history.

5 Click the Show Next Statement arrow.

Extra

Using the Step Into technique, walking through entire methods which are called from the application's entry point is possible. This is very useful if you need to watch some specific variable values in the Autos window. However, if you are sure that your methods are bug free — they have been supplied by a component developer and fully tested — then you can simply click the Step Over button to avoid stepping into a specific method.

When you step line by line through your source code, you can easily determine the values of your variables by moving the mouse pointer on top of the variable. The value of the variable will momentarily appear in a small tip window. This usually works best with simple variables such as integers and floats, because information on classes will not appear in the small tip window. If you want to see those items, right-click the item and select Quick Watch.

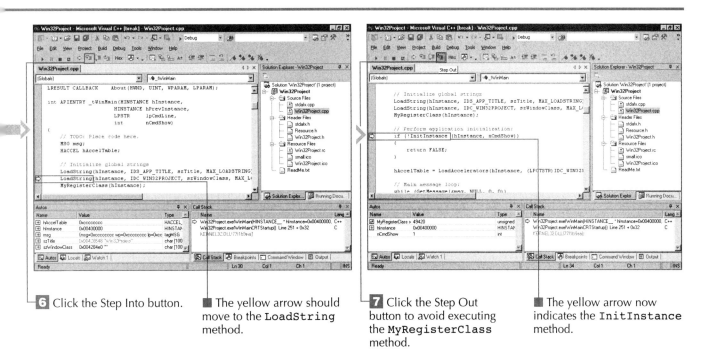

6 Click the Step Into button.

■ The yellow arrow should move to the **LoadString** method.

7 Click the Step Out button to avoid executing the **MyRegisterClass** method.

■ The yellow arrow now indicates the **InitInstance** method.

STEP INTO A FUNCTION

The most powerful aspect of debugging is the ability to trace through a program and its associated functions line by line. Although you may not care how some functions execute, such as those written by other people, you will want to trace through the functions that you write. When you trace through them, you can examine them carefully for accuracy and to make sure they perform correctly. You can trace functions in one of two ways: You can trace through the code leading up to the function and then trace into the function. Alternately, you can place a breakpoint at the beginning of the function, and run the program, allowing it to stop only once to arrive at a function.

To step into a function from the code leading up to it, you use the Step Into command on the Debug menu, or the F11 button.

To set a breakpoint that begins at the function, find the function in the source code editor and then use the Insert Breakpoint command on the right-click menu after selecting the first line of the function. When you run the program, it stops at the first line in the function. Note that if you place the break point on the function header, the program will stop on the first line within the function, instead of the header line.

If you end up in a function in which you did not intend to enter, you can use the Step Out button to tell the computer to run the rest of the function without displaying any of the code in it. The remaining lines execute without showing up in the debugger, until you are out of the function. After that you can continue tracing as before.

STEP INTO A FUNCTION

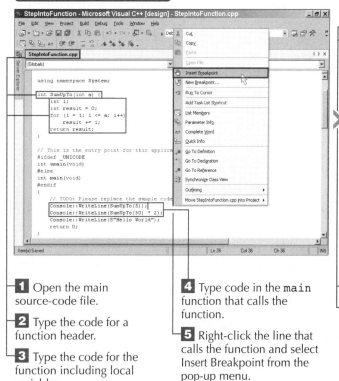

1 Open the main source-code file.

2 Type the code for a function header.

3 Type the code for the function including local variables.

4 Type code in the `main` function that calls the function.

5 Right-click the line that calls the function and select Insert Breakpoint from the pop-up menu.

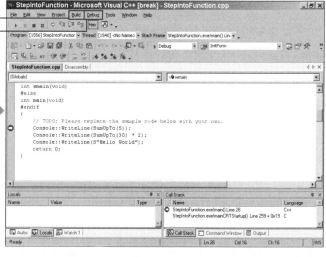

6 Build the program.

7 Click Debug ➪ Start to run the program.

■ The program opens in the debugger and stops at the line containing your breakpoint.

Extra

Sometimes when debugging a function, you need to look at the variables in the routine that called the function. Viewing these variables helps you become more aware of the state of the program, and helps you debug more successfully. If you debug a function and you want to look at the source code to the routine that called the function, open up the stack window, find the function, and double-click it. The function's source code appears, and the Locals window shows the local variables for that particular function, along with their values.

If you are in a function that has been called recursively several times and you want to step out of the entire recursion, stepping out of the function only takes you out one level. To step all the way out, switch to the Call Stack window, and scroll down until you are past the recursive function calls. Right click that function, and click Insert Breakpoint. Next, click Continue in the Debug toolbar. The program takes you to the breakpoint and out of the recursion.

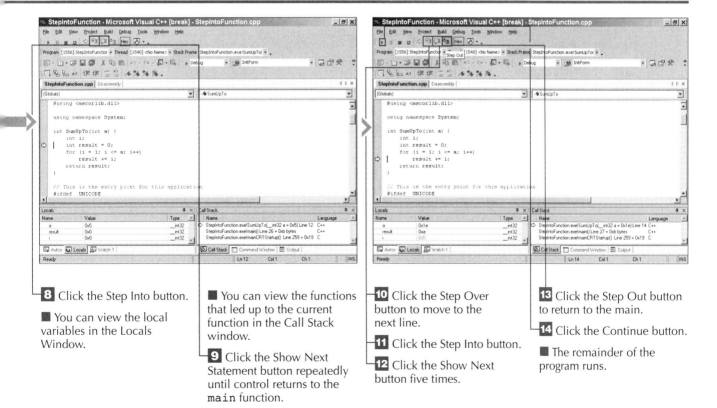

■8 Click the Step Into button.

■ You can view the local variables in the Locals Window.

■ You can view the functions that led up to the current function in the Call Stack window.

■9 Click the Show Next Statement button repeatedly until control returns to the `main` function.

■10 Click the Step Over button to move to the next line.

■11 Click the Step Into button.

■12 Click the Show Next button five times.

■13 Click the Step Out button to return to the main.

■14 Click the Continue button.

■ The remainder of the program runs.

137

WATCH A VARIABLE

The main reason for stepping through a program's methods is to identify statements that fail at runtime. Failure, in this sense, means incorrectly or inappropriately responding to input that is provided at runtime. For example, the _tWinMain method expects a certain number and type of parameters at runtime. If these values are incorrect, or simply null, then the program terminates abnormally.

There are two ways to check whether an application is seeing expected values at any point in its execution. The first technique is to print the value of specific variables to standard output and watch them on the console. However, this can quickly grow tiresome, as code for printing the contents of new variables needs to be explicitly added into each part of the program where the variable is used. After debugging is complete, that code then needs to be

removed; otherwise it may interfere with other agents that use standard output, such as a logging agent.

Fortunately, Visual C++ provides an easy way to watch the value of all local variables during execution of specific methods. Simply by enabling the display of the Autos window, current variable values can be watched as the application steps through each statement in the normal order of execution.

In the following example, you step into a sample Win 32 application and watch the values of key variables. Starting at the _tWinMain(HINSTANCE hInstance, HINSTANCE hPrevInstance, LPSTR lpCmdLine, int nCmdShow) method, you step through the application and view variable values in the Autos window.

WATCH A VARIABLE

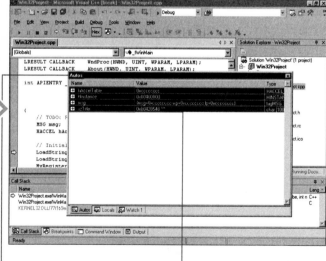

1 Load the project you want to debug.

2 Click the Step Into button.

3 Rebuild the application with debugging information.

■ Check to make sure the Build output in the Output window shows success.

4 Maximize the Autos windows, showing the values of current variables.

■ The name, value, and type of each variable appears.

Extra

If you want to stop the execution of an application at a specific point in the code, it is possible to set a breakpoint from the Debug menu. This allows potentially thousands of lines of code to execute before you examine the watch list. This is very useful for examining bugs that lie deep inside code that is executed only during runtime.

Alternatively, in Debugging mode, it is possible to identify a point in the code by selecting it with a cursor and executing Run To Cursor from the Debug Menu. Doing so ensures that the application is executed only up to the specific statement indicated.

After you have identified a code segment which is faulty, it is possible to edit the code, rebuild the class affected, and continue execution of the application. This is very useful when reproducing the bug takes several minutes of user interaction or CPU time, and you need to know whether a bug fix works with the current application state.

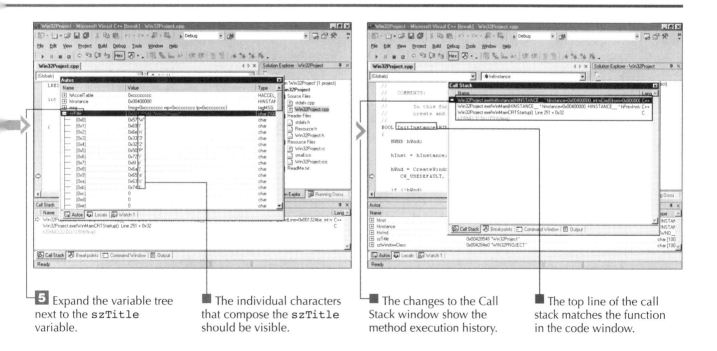

5 Expand the variable tree next to the `szTitle` variable.

■ The individual characters that compose the `szTitle` should be visible.

■ The changes to the Call Stack window show the method execution history.

■ The top line of the call stack matches the function in the code window.

SET A BREAKPOINT

While function-based stepping in and out of calling methods is useful if your application has issues with functions, if you have noticed an exception occurring at a specific line of code, you may wonder if it is possible to halt execution up to that point and then watch variables change as the offending lines are executed. Fortunately, Visual C++ allows you to halt the execution of an application at a specific point in the code. This is known as setting a breakpoint.

A breakpoint can be set from the Debug menu, and allows hundreds and thousands of lines of code to execute, before the watch list is displayed, with all variables updated prior to breaking. Using breakpoints is particularly useful for tracing the effects and source of runtime errors, which do not show up during normal testing. Some of these bugs may only occur when a specific sequence of events occurs, and may not be easy to predict from standard test cases.

In the following example, you will set a breakpoint in a sample Win 32 application, and watch the values of key variables.

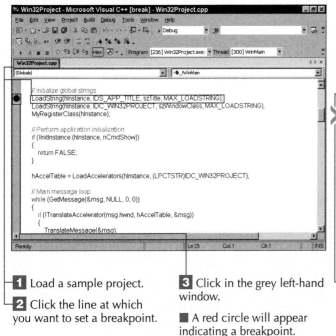

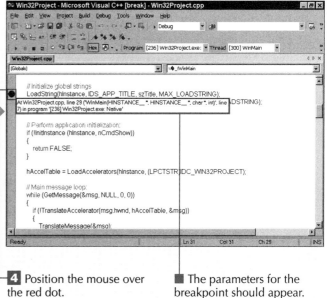

1 Load a sample project.

2 Click the line at which you want to set a breakpoint.

3 Click in the grey left-hand window.

■ A red circle will appear indicating a breakpoint.

4 Position the mouse over the red dot.

■ The parameters for the breakpoint should appear.

Extra

Visual C++ defines three other types of breakpoints: function breakpoints, address breakpoints, and data breakpoints. A function breakpoint is used to halt execution at a designated place within a function. An address breakpoint is designed to halt execution when a specific place in memory is addressed. A data breakpoint is used to track variable changes, and when the value of a specific variable changes, execution is halted. The latter can be particularly useful when trying to determine why a specific result is not obtained after execution for a target variable.

Another advanced feature of breakpoints is the ability to specify logical conditions for breakpoints. If a logical condition is not satisfied when the specific line of code (or address or function line) is reached, then execution is not halted. The Hit Count condition, for example, specifies that the line must have been reached a certain number of times before execution is halted. For example, stack overflow issues occurring at runtime might not surface for 64,000 or more iterations of a loop; thus, you need to start watching variables and setting breakpoints at 64,001 hits. In addition, any valid C++ expression can be evaluated as a logical precondition for the execution of a breakpoint.

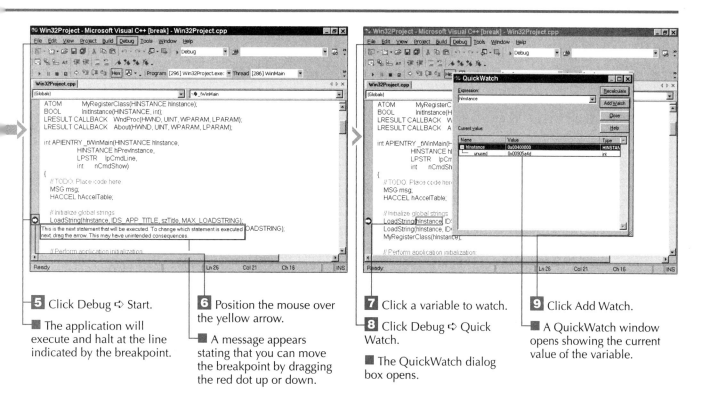

5 Click Debug ➪ Start.

■ The application will execute and halt at the line indicated by the breakpoint.

6 Position the mouse over the yellow arrow.

■ A message appears stating that you can move the breakpoint by dragging the red dot up or down.

7 Click a variable to watch.

8 Click Debug ➪ Quick Watch.

■ The QuickWatch dialog box opens.

9 Click Add Watch.

■ A QuickWatch window opens showing the current value of the variable.

RUN TO THE CURSOR LOCATION

Running to the cursor location is similar to setting a breakpoint: Your goal is to try and solve a debugging mystery by halting execution at a pre-defined stage. When you run to the cursor, you position the cursor by clicking in the source code. You then right-click and select Run To Cursor from the pop-up menu. Your program will run, and it will halt as if there is a breakpoint on the line where you clicked. This is similar to placing a breakpoint, except it is only a temporary. If this line is executed again, it will not stop there unless you still have the cursor there and you again select Run to the Cursor.

Once the program halts at your chosen line, you can perform the same activities you can as if the program halted at a breakpoint. You can inspect the variables by right-clicking them and selecting Quick Watch. You can continue to step line-by-line through the program.

While breakpoints are geared towards variable watching, running to the cursor location allows you to access disassembly information. Indeed, running to the cursor location can be executed either in the source window or the disassembly window. Thus, if you are a hexadecimal specialist, you might prefer to work directly in the disassembly window, until a specific command is executed.

In the following example, you will run to the cursor location from the message handler method associated with opening the About window in the sample application (About(hDlg, message, wParam, lParam)). You will then switch to the Disassembly mode to review the associated hexadecimal code.

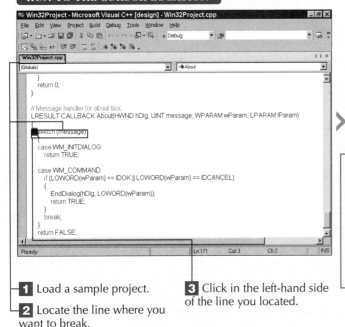

1 Load a sample project.

2 Locate the line where you want to break.

3 Click in the left-hand side of the line you located.

4 Right-click anywhere inside the editor window and select Run To Cursor from the pop-up menu.

Extra

To view the value of a variable in the Disassembly window, double-click the variable concerned, and then right-click the selection. Select QuickWatch, and the QuickWatch window will appear with the current variable's hexadecimal value.

After your program stops at the current cursor location, if you decide you want to add a breakpoint at that location, you can simply press F9. You will see a red marker appear to the left of the line, denoting a breakpoint. However, if after the program halted you clicked somewhere else in the source code, you will have to click back on the line before pressing F9, or right-click the line and select Insert Breakpoint from the pop-up menu. If you want to continue running the program, you can press F5, or click Debug ⇨ Continue.

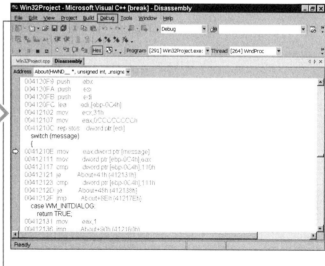

■ The application stops at the line chosen in step 2.

5 Click the Step Over button.

■ A yellow arrow appears at the next line to be executed.

6 Click Debug ⇨ Windows ⇨ Disassembly.

■ The editor window switches to Disassembly mode, showing the assembler code.

INTRODUCTION TO STRINGS

hroughout your programming, you may need to manipulate a string of characters, commonly referred to simply as a string. For example, you might have a program that stores the name of a person, and you need to change the name to uppercase before printing it on a business card. The .NET platform supports several different types of strings for use in C++, the two most common being C-style strings and the new .NET String class.

You find the C-style strings in all other C++ platforms, not just .NET and Windows. To manipulate them, you use a set of standard functions providing capabilities such as calculating the length of a string and searching for a substring.

Although other .NET languages such as Visual Basic and C# support it in addition to C++, the .NET String class is

specific to .NET. Further, the String class provides many sophisticated capabilities that make string handling far easier than the C-style strings. You can easily compare and manipulate strings. You can also perform such functions as pad strings with spaces, trim spaces and white space off a string, replace certain parts of a string, convert a string to uppercase or lowercase, and split a string into substrings.

The C++ you find in .NET includes a special language enhancement providing built-in support for the String class. If you specify a capital letter S followed by a string of characters inside double quotes, as in S"Hello World", the compiler generates an instance of a String class and fills it with the specified characters, in this case Hello World. You can then manipulate the string using the methods available to the String class.

INTRODUCTION TO STRINGS

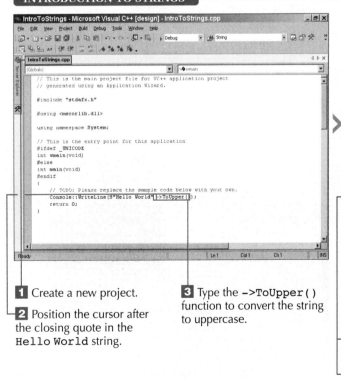

1 Create a new project.

2 Position the cursor after the closing quote in the Hello World string.

3 Type the ->ToUpper() function to convert the string to uppercase.

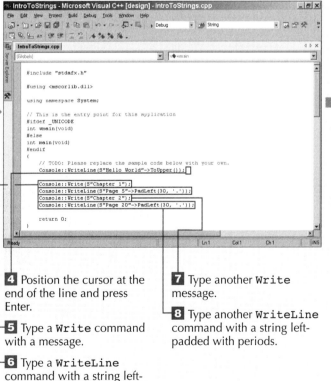

4 Position the cursor at the end of the line and press Enter.

5 Type a Write command with a message.

6 Type a WriteLine command with a string left-padded with periods.

7 Type another Write message.

8 Type another WriteLine command with a string left-padded with periods.

Extra

The `String` class provides several methods, and most of these methods provide several different versions. When you become familiar with the large number of methods available, you can begin to appreciate how powerful this class is, and how useful it is in your programs. The following table shows some of these methods.

METHOD	FUNCTION
CopyTo	Copies characters from the String to a standard c-style unicode string
Join	Joins together multiple strings into a single string, combining a separator character between them
Length	Gets the length of the string
EndsWith	Determines whether the string ends with a particular substring
IndexOf	Finds a substring and reports the index where it begins
Insert	Inserts a substring into the string
Remove	Removes characters from the string
Replace	Replaces a substring of the string
StartsWith	Determines whether the string begins with a particular string

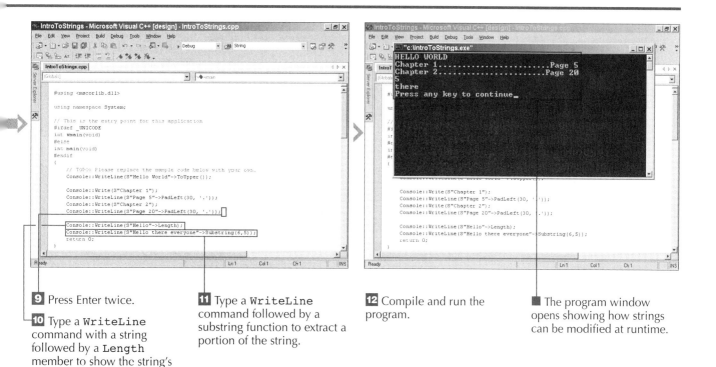

9 Press Enter twice.

10 Type a `WriteLine` command with a string followed by a `Length` member to show the string's length.

11 Type a `WriteLine` command followed by a substring function to extract a portion of the string.

12 Compile and run the program.

■ The program window opens showing how strings can be modified at runtime.

CREATE A STRING

A string is simply an array of characters terminated by a null character '\0'. The characters in the array have an ordinal relationship — the first character of an array precedes the second character, and so on. However, in C++ terms, there is nothing special about a string. It is just a null-terminated array of characters. Very few restrictions apply to the contents of strings. You can use all ASCII characters to construct strings.

Strings have a wide variety of uses. You can use them to store user data, such as names, addresses, and phone numbers, and use them for more low-level tasks, such as buffering and concatenation. Depending on your specific application, strings are widely used to store any

non-numeric data, even special types such as dates, where no user-defined class exists to define them.

After you have declared a string as an array of characters, you can add new characters to the string and modify its contents. Because a string is simply an array, you can use all of the standard methods for accessing the elements of an array to operate on the characters contained within a string.

You can create a string in C++ in two ways: by explicitly declaring all of the elements of the array as characters, including the terminating null character, or by using a shorthand method that declares the string outright and using double quotes to indicate that the set of characters defined is a string.

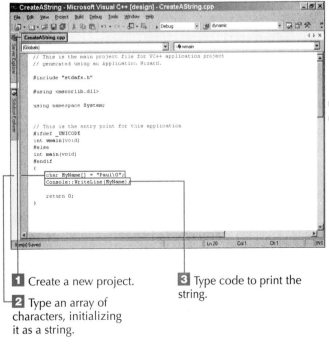

1 Create a new project.

2 Type an array of characters, initializing it as a string.

3 Type code to print the string.

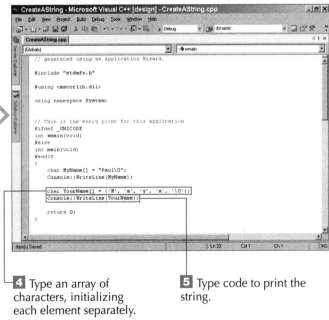

4 Type an array of characters, initializing each element separately.

5 Type code to print the string.

Apply It

You can add new character elements to a string, individually or recursively in a loop. To add new characters to a .NET String instance, use the `Concat` member function.

TYPE THIS:

```
#include "stdafx.h"
#using <mscorlib.dll>
using namespace System;
void main(void) {
    String *Digits = S"";
    for (int i=0; i<5; i++) {
        Digits = String::Concat(Digits, i.ToString(S"d"));
        Console::WriteLine(Digits);
    }
}
```

RESULT:

```
0
01
012
0123
01234
```

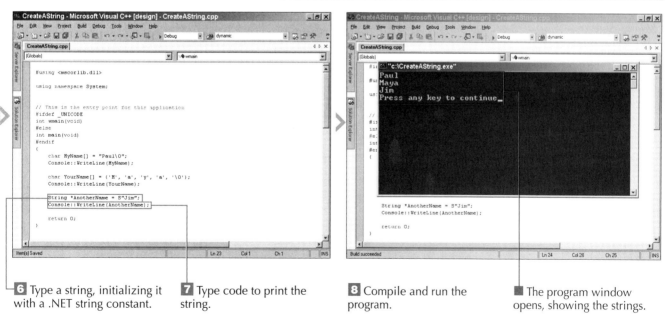

6 Type a string, initializing it with a .NET string constant.

7 Type code to print the string.

8 Compile and run the program.

■ The program window opens, showing the strings.

INITIALIZE A STRING

After you have declared an array of characters, it is important to initialize the values of the individual elements to a value that your program can handle rather than a null value. Otherwise, your program might encounter a null pointer problem when it tries to access an uninitialized element later on as the program is running, when processing the string that comprises the elements in the char array. It often makes sense to initialize numeric values to an empty character, or a space, for arrays of type char.

You can initialize array elements at specific locations, and you do not need to initialize all elements at once. For example, your program might allocate 1,024 characters to a large string for storing a comment field from a database.

You could initialize the array 256 bytes at a time, with each further segment of 256 bytes being initialized only if required by the application. This saves needless processing time because an overhead is incurred for each initialization.

The most common method for initializing the elements of a string is to use a for loop to iterate through all character array elements, and assign a common initial value — an empty character or a space — to each element.

The alternative is to specify the initial values using a set of comma-delimited initial values enclosed by braces and terminated by a null character. You must null-terminate all strings. Thus, the total number of characters available for a string is the length of the array minus one.

INITIALIZE A STRING

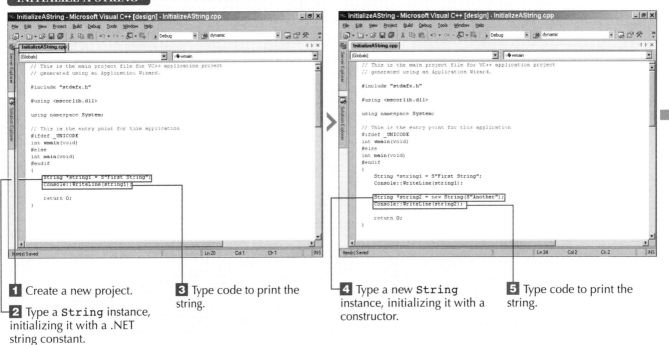

1 Create a new project.

2 Type a String instance, initializing it with a .NET string constant.

3 Type code to print the string.

4 Type a new String instance, initializing it with a constructor.

5 Type code to print the string.

Extra

The size of any array to be initialized is limited by the amount of free space available on the stack. The amount of free space depends on the memory model the compiler uses. To create larger arrays, you might need to use an array of pointers to objects, rather than storing an object itself in an array. Whether or not this is possible depends on your specific application.

The .NET framework treats a string constant in quotes preceded with an S as a .NET String instance initialized with the characters inside the quotes. When you create a String instance using String *mystring = S"My String"; you are actually creating a new string instance and saving a pointer to it in the mystring variable.

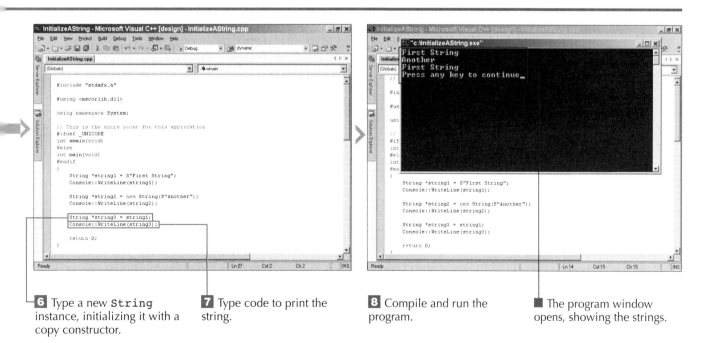

6 Type a new **String** instance, initializing it with a copy constructor.

7 Type code to print the string.

8 Compile and run the program.

■ The program window opens, showing the strings.

CHANGE THE CASE OF A STRING

When you are working with strings, there may be times where you will allow the users of your program to enter in some information, but you will want to save the information in either all uppercase or all lowercase. For example, you might be writing a mailing label program where the users of your program can enter in a name and address. But to satisfy postal requirements, you may want to print the information in all uppercase.

Or, you might be saving the name and address information into a database, and the database administrators at your company have determined that they want the information in all lowercase to provide easier comparisons.

The .NET String class includes two routines that make conversion of case very easy. These routines are ToUpper and ToLower; the first converts a string to uppercase, and the second converts a string to lowercase. They are both members of the String class, and like other members you

can use them on an existing constant string.

For example, you can either create a String instance, initialize it with a string of characters, and then call ToUpper on this instance. In this case, the ToUpper method will return a new String instance with the string converted to uppercase. Or, you can take a string constant preceded by the letter S and call ToUpper, as in S"another string"->ToUpper(). This is because the S identifier instructs the compiler to treat the following string of characters as an object of the String class, providing you with all the functionality in the String class.

The ToLower method works similarly, and you can either call it on an existing String instance, or on a string constant that is preceded by an S. Like ToUpper, the ToLower function returns a pointer to a new String instance.

CHANGE THE CASE OF A STRING

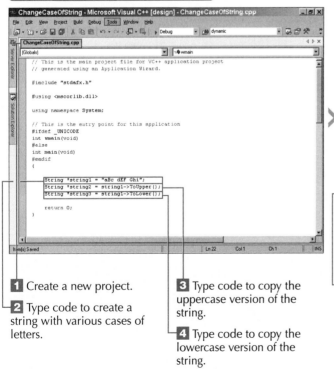

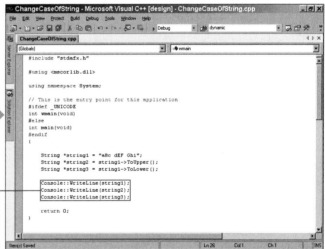

1 Create a new project.

2 Type code to create a string with various cases of letters.

3 Type code to copy the uppercase version of the string.

4 Type code to copy the lowercase version of the string.

5 Type lines of code to print the values of each string.

150

Extra

If you want to change only a portion of a string, you need to divide the string up into separate parts, and change the case of only those parts you need changed, and then combine them back together into a single string. To break up a string, you use the Split function, and to join them together you use the Join function. When used in conjunction with the ToUpper or ToLower function, you can easily convert only portions of a string.

Example:
```
Char separators[] = {' '};
String *parts[] = S"george washington"->Split(separators);
for (int i=0; i<parts->Count; i++) {
    String *converted = String::Concat(
        parts[i]->Substring(0,1)->ToUpper(),
        parts[i]->Substring(1, parts[i]->Length-1));
    parts[i] = converted;
}
String *final = String::Join(S" ",parts);
Console::WriteLine(final);
```

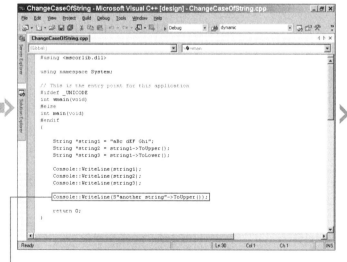

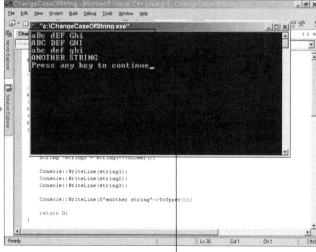

6 Type code that takes a new instance using an **S** constant and converts it to uppercase.

7 Compile and run your program.

■ The program window opens, showing the strings in various cases.

SPLIT A STRING

You can modify your strings by using the String class. You can make your program flexible by allowing any number of spaces before the first name and after the last name. For example, you can allow a user to enter a first name, a space, and then a last name. By using the String class, you can easily find the first and last name inside this single string.

To split a string, you must remove any spaces at the beginning and end of a string. There are three routines in the String class that let you split a string. The first is TrimStart, which removes spaces at the beginning of a string. The second is TrimEnd, which removes spaces at the end of a string. The third is Trim, which removes spaces at both the beginning and the end. These functions also remove any character that shows up as white space, including tabs.

After you have removed the spaces from the beginning and end of the string, you are ready to split the string. The String class includes a function called Split, which breaks a string into several smaller strings. It breaks up the string based on a set of characters that you provide. For example, if you provide a space and a tab, the function will break up the string wherever it finds either a space or a tab.

The Split function returns an array of strings, which you can then loop through to obtain the individual strings.

Note that the Trim, TrimStart, TrimEnd, and Split functions do not actually modify the string itself. Instead, they return a new string with the appropriate modifications. Thus, it is common to assign the new string back to the original string pointer variable, as in mystring = mystring->Trim();.

SPLIT A STRING

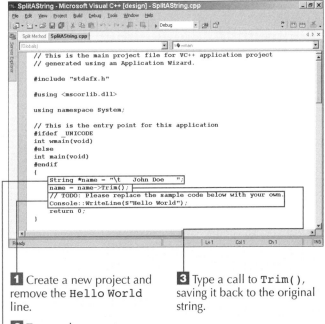

1 Create a new project and remove the Hello World line.

2 Type code to create a new String instance with leading and ending spaces and/or tabs.

3 Type a call to Trim(), saving it back to the original string.

4 Type a new character array containing the split characters.

5 Type a call to split the string.

Apply It

You can trim characters other than white spaces. For example, if you have a string that begins and ends with mixture of leading spaces, periods, and asterisks, you can remove all these characters using the `Trim` function, if you pass an array of characters.

TYPE THIS:

```
#include "stdafx.h"
#using <mscorlib.dll>
using namespace System;
int main(void)
{
    String *name = ".* **. John Doe ..** ";
    Char chars[] = {' ','.','*'};
    name = name->Trim(chars);
    Console::WriteLine(name);
    return 0;
}
```

RESULT:

John Doe

Press any key to continue

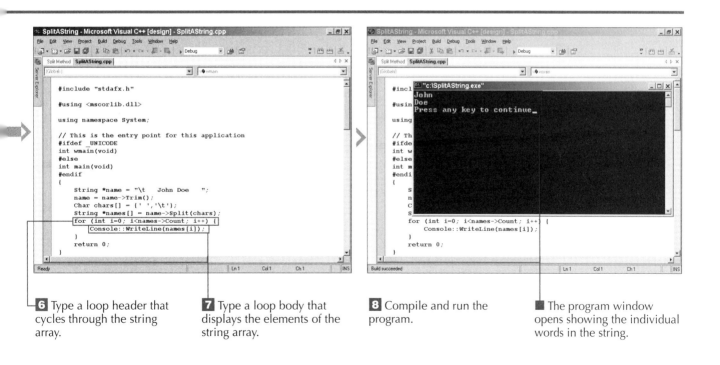

6 Type a loop header that cycles through the string array.

7 Type a loop body that displays the elements of the string array.

8 Compile and run the program.

■ The program window opens showing the individual words in the string.

EXTRACT SUBSTRINGS

One of the most powerful things you can do with strings is to scan through them and find substrings. The .NET String class provides you with several methods for doing this very easily. For example, you may have a string that contains a sentence, and you need to determine whether the word "hello" is in the sentence, Using the substring and searching features of the .NET String class, you can easily locate items within a string.

The first method allows you to find a substring by specifying the position and length of the substring. This is useful when you know that you want the characters from an exact position of a string but do not know exactly what the characters are. For example, you might have a string that always has ten characters for the first name, ten for the middle, and ten for the last, separated by a series of spaces

to fill up the string. To find the middle name, you can tell the String object that you want the substring starting at the ninth position and spanning the next ten characters. Note that the first position is considered position zero, and that is why you start at the ninth position to find the tenth character.

Another method is called Split and it allows you to break apart a string based on a separator character that you specify. For example, if you provide the string S"Hello there everyone" and you split it up based on spaces, then you will obtain three separate strings, S"Hello", S"there", and S"everyone". You can specify any character or set of characters for the separators. If there are two separator characters in a row, you will get an empty string representing the string between the two separators.

EXTRACT SUBSTRINGS

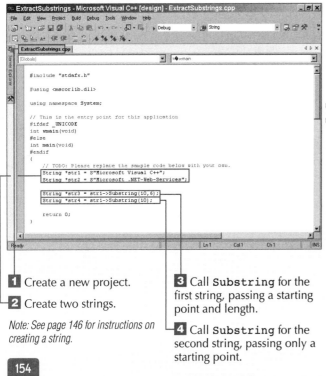

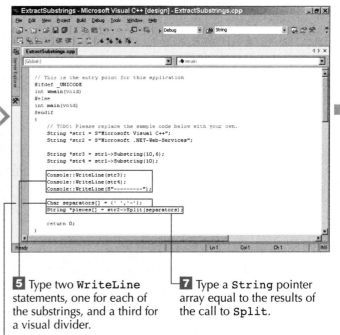

1 Create a new project.

2 Create two strings.

Note: See page 146 for instructions on creating a string.

3 Call Substring for the first string, passing a starting point and length.

4 Call Substring for the second string, passing only a starting point.

5 Type two WriteLine statements, one for each of the substrings, and a third for a visual divider.

6 Type a character array denoting the separators for use in the Split method.

7 Type a String pointer array equal to the results of the call to Split.

Apply It

Sometimes you may know the substring and simply want to know its position. If so, you can use the `IndexOf` method. This method takes as a parameter the string you are looking for and it returns an index. You can optionally pass an index that represents the position to start looking; any characters before this position are not searched. Finally, you can use this method to determine whether a string contains a substring. The return -1 means the substring is not present in the string.

TYPE THIS:

```
#include "stdafx.h"
#using <mscorlib.dll>
using namespace System;
int main(void)
{
    Console::WriteLine(S"This is a string"->IndexOf(S"a string"));
    Console::WriteLine(S"Some strings have multiple strings"->IndexOf(S"strings",10));
    Console::WriteLine(S"Sometimes a substring is not present"->IndexOf("another"));
    return 0;
}
```

RESULT:

```
8
27
-1
```

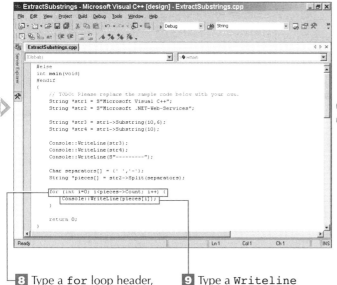

8 Type a `for` loop header, with lower bounds 0, and upper bounds the array's count member.

9 Type a `Writeline` statement for the individual array element.

10 Compile and run the program.

■ The program window opens showing the results of the various comparisons.

COMPARE STRINGS

Often when programming, you will encounter the need to compare two strings. For example, if a user enters a password, you might need to compare it to an existing string to determine if the password is correct. The .NET `String` class provides many methods for comparing two strings.

The first method simply tests whether two strings are identical using the `==` operator in the same way you would compare two numbers. For example, `S"abc" == S"def"` would yield `false` since abc and def are different. You can also perform this same comparison by explicitly calling the `compare` method in the `String` class, as in `String::compare(S"abc",S"def")`.

Another method lets you specify whether to ignore uppercase and lowercase differences among letters when making the comparison. Here, again, you call the `compare`

method, but you add a third parameter, `true`. Setting this parameter to `true` means *ignore case sensitivity*.

Yet another method of comparing strings is to only compare a portion of the strings, called a substring comparison. In this case you call the `compare` method, but after each string you pass a number denoting where in the string to begin the search. You then follow the second number's index with a number denoting the length of the substrings to compare. You only specify one length, since the substrings must be the same size. Optionally, you can include a final parameter of `true` to specify that the substrings are to be compared without regard to case. Notice, however, that when you compare substrings, you can determine whether the substring is present or not in the string, but you will not be able to determine where the substring is in the string. If you need to find the location of the substring, use the `IndexOf` method, described on page 155.

COMPARE STRINGS

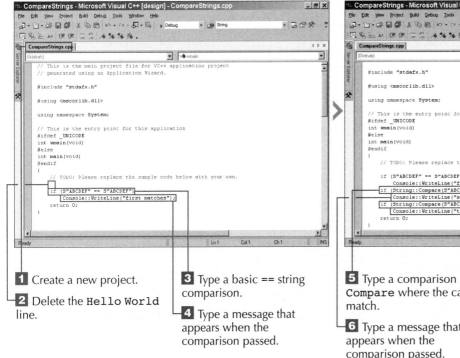

1 Create a new project.

2 Delete the `Hello World` line.

3 Type a basic `==` string comparison.

4 Type a message that appears when the comparison passed.

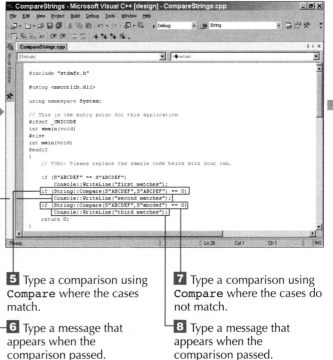

5 Type a comparison using **Compare** where the cases match.

6 Type a message that appears when the comparison passed.

7 Type a comparison using **Compare** where the cases do not match.

8 Type a message that appears when the comparison passed.

Apply It

If you are looking for a quick and easy way to compare strings without using the extra features of `CompareString`, you might consider the `Equals` method. Whereas `CompareString` returns a number and you need to test it against zero, `Equals` returns a true or false, making it ideal for `if` statements. It does not have the optional case insensitivity comparison.

```
#include "stdafx.h"
#using <mscorlib.dll>
using namespace System;
#ifdef _UNICODE
int wmain(void)
#else
int main(void)
#endif
{
    String *a = S"abc";
    String *b = S"def";
    if (a->Equals(b))
        Console::WriteLine("a and b are the same");
    else
        Console::WriteLine("a and b are different");
    return 0;
}
```

RESULT:

```
a and b are different
```
Press any key to continue

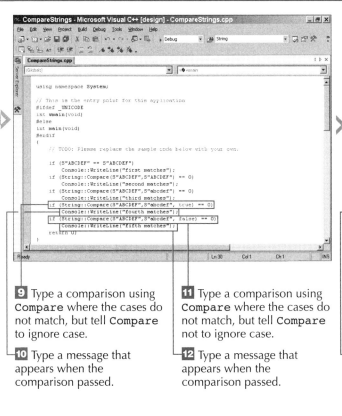

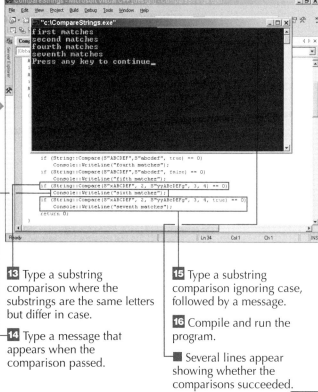

9 Type a comparison using **Compare** where the cases do not match, but tell **Compare** to ignore case.

10 Type a message that appears when the comparison passed.

11 Type a comparison using **Compare** where the cases do not match, but tell **Compare** not to ignore case.

12 Type a message that appears when the comparison passed.

13 Type a substring comparison where the substrings are the same letters but differ in case.

14 Type a message that appears when the comparison passed.

15 Type a substring comparison ignoring case, followed by a message.

16 Compile and run the program.

■ Several lines appear showing whether the comparisons succeeded.

CONVERT NUMBERS TO STRINGS

The System module provides several structures that provide additional functionality for basic types such as integers and doubles. Like classes, these structures include methods that let you operate on the basic types. With these methods, you can easily convert numbers to strings. This is an important feature that allows you to write numbers to a text file for example, or send them to another program where they must be in a text format. Two of these structures are Int32 and Double. Each of these structures contains a method called ToString, allowing you to easily convert a number to a string.

To use the ToString method of the Int32 structure, you simply call Int32::ToString, passing an integer. The integer you pass can either be an integer constant or an int variable. The method returns a String instance. Note that the method is static, meaning it is associated with the structure and not a single instance. Therefore, you do not need to create an instance of Int32 to call its ToString method.

To use the ToString method of the Double structure, you call Double::ToString, passing a floating-point value. This floating-point value can either be a double constant or a double variable. This method also returns a String instance. And like Int32::ToString, the Double::ToString method is static. You do not need an instance of Double to call it.

If you are dealing with unsigned integers, single-point floats, or long integers, you can use the UInt32, Single, and Int64 structures respectively. These structures represent the additional numeric types you are likely to use in your programming. Each structure has a ToString method, which will convert the numbers to a string. You use these functions in the same way you do with the Int32 and Double structure ToString methods.

CONVERT NUMBERS TO STRINGS

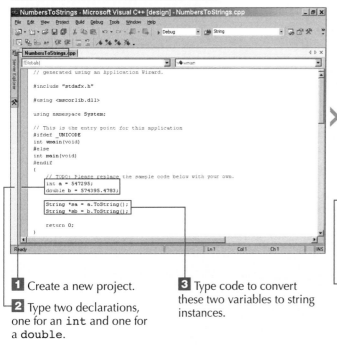

1 Create a new project.

2 Type two declarations, one for an int and one for a double.

3 Type code to convert these two variables to string instances.

4 Type two WriteLine statements, one for a message and one to print out the first string.

5 Type two more WriteLine statements, one for a message and one to print out the second string.

Apply It

You can optionally pass as a parameter a string known as a format specifier when calling `Int32:ToString` or `Double::ToString`. Depending on the specifier you choose, the number will be formatted in various ways including currency, exponential notation, or fixed point.

TYPE THIS:

```
#include "stdafx.h"
#using <mscorlib.dll>
using namespace System;
int main(void) {
    int a = 547295; double b = 574395.4783;
    Console::WriteLine(a.ToString(S"c"));
    Console::WriteLine(a.ToString(S"d"));
    Console::WriteLine(a.ToString(S"e"));
    Console::WriteLine(a.ToString(S"f"));
    Console::WriteLine(b.ToString(S"c"));
    Console::WriteLine(b.ToString(S"e"));
    return 0;
}
```

RESULT:

```
$547,295.00
547295
5.472950e+005
547295.00
$574,395.48
5.743955e+00
```

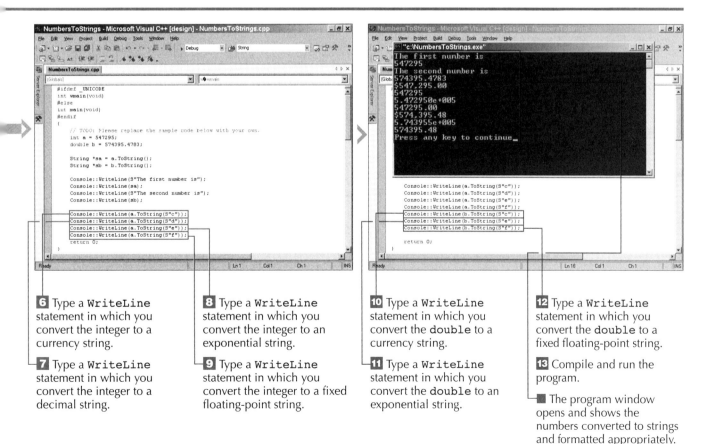

6 Type a `WriteLine` statement in which you convert the integer to a currency string.

7 Type a `WriteLine` statement in which you convert the integer to a decimal string.

8 Type a `WriteLine` statement in which you convert the integer to an exponential string.

9 Type a `WriteLine` statement in which you convert the integer to a fixed floating-point string.

10 Type a `WriteLine` statement in which you convert the **double** to a currency string.

11 Type a `WriteLine` statement in which you convert the **double** to an exponential string.

12 Type a `WriteLine` statement in which you convert the **double** to a fixed floating-point string.

13 Compile and run the program.

■ The program window opens and shows the numbers converted to strings and formatted appropriately.

CONVERT STRINGS TO NUMBERS

When you are dealing with information, often there are times that you need to convert from strings to numbers. For example, if you are writing a program that connects to an external server to download a list of information, some of this information could be numbers represented in a string format. It is quite likely, then, that you will need to convert the strings to an actual number, so that you can perform mathematical manipulations on them.

There are several structures inside the System module that allow you to convert between numbers and strings. Each structure represents a separate data type. For example, Int32 represents 32-bit integers and Double represents double-precision floating points.

Each of these structures has a Parse method that allows you to convert a string containing a textual form of a number to either to an int or a double.

The Parse method is a static method, meaning you do not need to have an instance of Int32 or Double to call it. Instead, you simply call either Int32::Parse, passing the string to convert to an integer, or Double::Parse, passing the string to convert to a double.

You can also convert from a string to a single-precision floating-point number using the Single::Parse method. Other structures for conversion include UInt32 for unsigned integers and Int64 for long integers.

CONVERT STRINGS TO NUMBERS

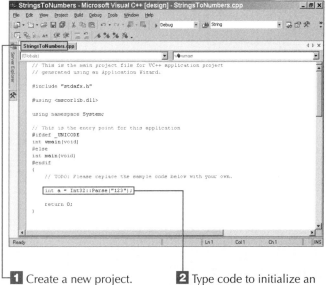

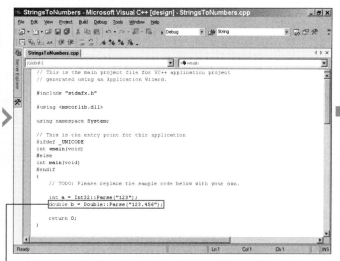

1 Create a new project.

2 Type code to initialize an integer variable by calling the Parse member of Int32, passing a string.

3 Type code to initialize a double variable by calling the Parse member of Double, passing a string.

■ The Parse method will convert the string to a numeric value.

Apply It

You can use format specifiers when converting strings to numbers. This will let your program accept numbers in many different formats, making it more user-friendly. Unlike converting numbers to strings, you have to make use of a special class called `NumberStyles`. To use this class, you need to include a statement `using namespace System::Globalization;` (or you can precede each instance of `NumberStyles` with `System::Globalization`). Notice in this code the `Parse` function is taking as input a fully-formatted string, and converting it to a non-formatted number.

TYPE THIS:

```
int main(void) {
    int a = Int32::Parse(S"123");
    int b = Int32::Parse(S"$547,295.00",NumberStyles::Currency);
    double c = Double::Parse("123.456");
    double d = Double::Parse("5.743955e+005",NumberStyles::Any);
    Console::WriteLine(a);
    Console::WriteLine(b);
    Console::WriteLine(c);
    Console::WriteLine(d);
    return 0;
}
```

RESULT:

```
123
547295
123.456
574395.5
```

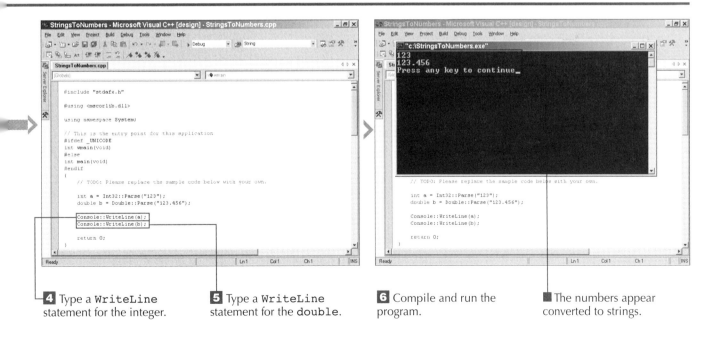

4 Type a `WriteLine` statement for the integer.

5 Type a `WriteLine` statement for the **double**.

6 Compile and run the program.

■ The numbers appear converted to strings.

INTRODUCTION TO .NET ARRAYS

When you have several instances of the same type of data, such as several integers or several instances of a structure, you can easily group the items all into a single entity called an *array*. An array is a list of items that you can access using a number, much like slots in the mailroom of a business. Each slot has a number, and the first is 0, then 1, then 2, and so on. These numbers are called the *index*. The array itself has a name, and you use the name in conjunction with the index to refer to a single element in the array.

Every element in an array must be the same type. For example, you can have an array of 20 integers. Alternatively, you can have an array of 50 instances of `MyStructure`. Or, you can have an array of 100 pointers to `MyClass`. You cannot have an array that holds both integers and characters.

DECLARING AN ARRAY

When you declare an array, you declare a single variable that will hold the array. You specify the type of item the array will hold, and the number of items it will hold, called the *size* of the array. You can then access the individual items in the array using the index by placing the index inside brackets after the array name. For example, `MyArray[0]` accesses the first element in the array, and `MyArray[10]` accesses the eleventh element in the array. In C++, because the first item in an array is 0, the arrays are called *zero-based*. For this reason, you will always want to be careful when you are referring to the elements in the array. The size is always one more than the highest index. The index number and the position are always off by one. For example, Index 0 is the first position, index 5 is the sixth position, and so on.

An array of size 10 does not have an index of 10. The indexes in an array of size 10 range from 0 through 9.

You can calculate the total number of bytes in an array by taking the size of the individual elements and multiplying the result by the number of elements in an array. For example, if you declare an array as `int MyArray[50]`, then the total bytes the array occupies is 50 times the size of an integer. The size of an integer is four bytes, so the total bytes the array occupies is 50 times 4, or 200. Alternatively, you can call the `sizeof` function for the array name, for example `sizeof(MyArray)`. The result will be the total number of bytes the array occupies.

ARRAYS OF POINTERS

When you work with arrays that hold instances of structures or classes, instead of placing the actual instance in the array, you can declare the array so it holds pointers to the instances. This will make the array smaller and allow you to refer to the same instance in more than one array. You must allocate the instances using the `new` keyword to obtain a pointer. You can then place that pointer inside the array.

ARRAYS OF CLASSES

When you have an array that holds pointers to a certain class, you can place pointers to instances of that class into the array, or pointers to instances of any class derived from that class.

MULTIDIMENSIONAL ARRAYS

You can think of an array as holding your elements in a long, straight line, all side by side. However, you can also create arrays that store items in a grid fashion, with rows and columns. Such an array is called a *multidimensional* array. Instead of having a single index, these arrays have two indexes, one that represents the row position, and one that represents the column position. When you declare such an array, you specify the type that the array holds, and you specify the two sizes. When you access the elements, you specify the indexes in separate brackets, as in `MyArray[5][7]`. Finally, you can actually create arrays that have more than two dimensions, although such arrays tend to be very large and take up a lot of memory, and can be difficult for you, as a programmer, to keep track of. Rarely will you see professional programmers use arrays of more than two dimensions.

You can easily calculate the size of a multidimensional array. The total number of elements is the product of all the dimensions. For example, if you declare an array as `int MyArray[20][60]`, the total number of elements is 20 times 60, or 1,200. Because each element holds an integer and integers are each four bytes, the total number of bytes is 1,200 times 4, or 4,800.

.NET ARRAYS

With the .NET framework, you can create arrays that contain instances of the .NET classes. Because you must declare instances of .NET classes on the heap using pointers, the .NET arrays must contain pointers. When you create a .NET array, you can take advantage of special features such as sorting and searching. This is because a .NET array is actually a class called `Array`.

This class contains several useful member functions that provide the sorting and searching features. You can also obtain the size of a .NET array through the `Count` property. If you create an array that does not contain instances of .NET classes, you do not have access to the extra sorting, searching, and counting features.

CREATE A C++ ARRAY

I f you have several instances of the same type of data, you can easily store them in an array. To create an array, you need to specify the type of items the array will hold, and the size of the array. To declare the array, you first give the type, then you specify a name, then an open bracket, the size, and a closing bracket. For example, the declaration int MyArray[10]; declares an array of ten integers called MyArray.

To access the elements of the array, you give the name of the array, followed by the index in brackets, such as MyArray[3]. For MyArray, there are ten items, and so the indexes range from 0 through 9. The first index is always 0, and the highest index is always one less than the size.

You can also create a multidimensional array by adding more brackets with sizes, one for each dimension. Thus, int MultiArray[5][6]; declares a five-by-six array

called MultiArray that holds integers. To access the elements of the multidimensional array, you specify the indexes in separate brackets, such as MultiArray[3][2].

If you want to access every member of the array, you will typically write a for loop that loops from 0 through one less than the size of the array. You would then use the loop variable as the index, as in MyArray[n] to access the elements of the array. For a multidimensional array, you need to use several loops, one for each dimension. Thus, a two-dimensional array would require two loops, and you would access the array using the loop indexes, as in MultiArray[m][n].

Always make sure when you loop through an array that you only go through one less than the size of the array. An array of size 10 does not have an element with index 10.

CREATE A C++ ARRAY

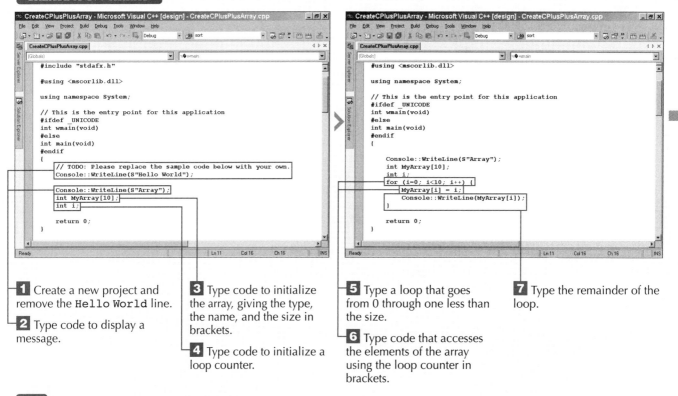

■1 Create a new project and remove the Hello World line.

■2 Type code to display a message.

■3 Type code to initialize the array, giving the type, the name, and the size in brackets.

■4 Type code to initialize a loop counter.

■5 Type a loop that goes from 0 through one less than the size.

■6 Type code that accesses the elements of the array using the loop counter in brackets.

■7 Type the remainder of the loop.

Extra

You will typically want to initialize every member of an array to a basic value such as 0 if the array holds integers. To do this, create a loop that runs through the array, setting every item to 0. The following code demonstrates this.

Example:
```
int main(void)
#endif
{
    int MyArray[10][20];
    int x,y;
    for (x=0; x<10; x++) {
        for (y=0; y<20; y++) {
            MyArray[x][y] = 0;
        }
    }
    return 0;
}
```

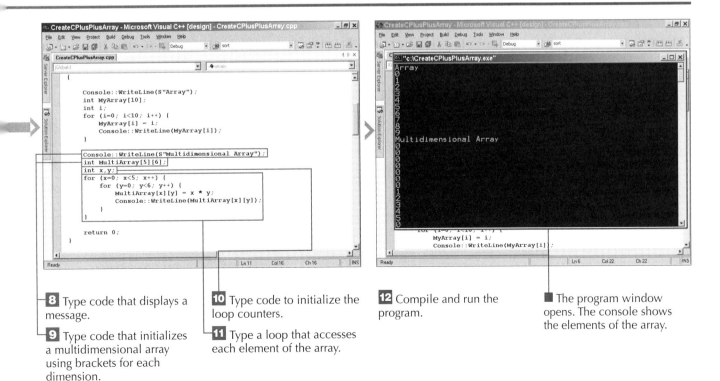

8 Type code that displays a message.

9 Type code that initializes a multidimensional array using brackets for each dimension.

10 Type code to initialize the loop counters.

11 Type a loop that accesses each element of the array.

12 Compile and run the program.

■ The program window opens. The console shows the elements of the array.

CREATE AN ARRAY OF POINTERS

If you have several instances of a class, you can create an array of the instances by storing pointers to the instances in the array. You can do this instead of storing the actual instances in the array. For example, you might have a class that contains a name, address, and account balance, along with member functions to process the account balance. If you have, say, 100 instances of this class, you can easily create an array of size 100, containing the addresses of the 100 instances.

You would store pointers instead of the actual instances because large programs often have a separate function that creates an instance of a class, fills it, and perhaps processes it. This function probably returns a pointer. Because you have a pointer, then, you can easily put it into an array. Further, you can have multiple arrays, and one instance can be in both arrays by having each array contain a pointer to the same instance. If you put the actual instance in the arrays, this is not possible; the arrays would have to have copies of the instance.

You create an array of pointers in the same way you create any other array, except you include the pointer symbol *, as in the following:

```
MyClass *MyArray[10];
```

To access the elements of the array, you specify the name of the array, and the element number in brackets, as in MyArray[3].

You can then store a pointer in the array as in the following:

```
MyArray[3] = new MyClass();
```

To access the members of an array element, you use the pointer notation for member access ->, as in MyArray[3]->name.

CREATE AN ARRAY OF POINTERS

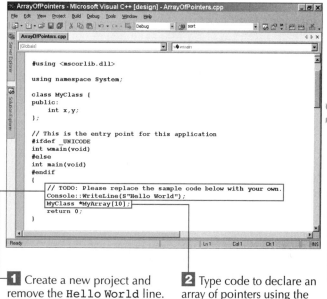

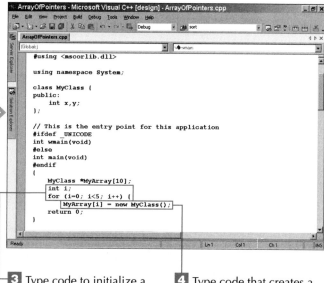

1 Create a new project and remove the `Hello World` line.

2 Type code to declare an array of pointers using the pointer symbol (*).

3 Type code to initialize a loop variable and loop through the array.

4 Type code that creates a new instance and stores it in the current array element.

Extra

You can initialize the elements of an array of pointers to 0. As you create instances, you can save the pointers in the array. Then, before accessing the members of the array elements, you can first test if the array element is not 0 before you attempt to access it. If it is 0, it means there is no instance for that element. If it is not 0, then there is an instance.

Example:
```
MyClass *MyArray[10];
int i;
for (i=0; i<5; i++) {
    MyArray[i] = 0;
}
MyArray[3] = new MyClass();
MyArray[3]->x = 3;
MyArray[3]->y = 6;
for (i=0; i<5; i++) {
    if (MyArray[i] != 0) {
        Console::WriteLine(MyArray[i]->x);
        Console::WriteLine(MyArray[i]->y);
    }
}
```

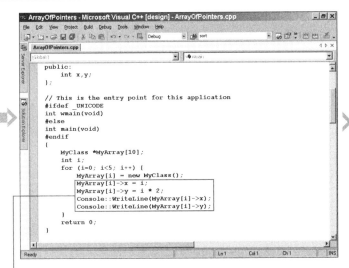

5 Type code to access the members of the current array element, using the class pointer notation (->).

6 Compile and run the program.

■ The program window opens. The console displays the members of the array elements.

CREATE A .NET ARRAY

You can create an array that holds instances of the classes in the .NET framework. For example, you can declare an array that holds String instances, or you can create an array that holds instances of Int32.

When you create a .NET array, you do not immediately declare a size. Instead, you declare it without a size using two empty brackets preceded by a __gc keyword. Then you type an equals sign, followed by the new keyword, the type the array holds, another __gc keyword, and finally the size in brackets. For example, if you want to create an array of Int32 of size 12, you would declare it as Int32 MyArray __gc[] = new Int32 __gc[12];. Note that this statement is really a declaration of a general array of unspecified size, followed by an initialization where you actually create an array of specified size.

When you create instances of value classes in the .NET framework, which are the classes that mirror the basic

types, such as Int32, which corresponds to the basic int type, you can store the instances directly in the array.

However, when you create instances of the managed classes in the .NET framework such as String, you can only create them on the heap, meaning you must create pointers to them. Thus, when you create an array that holds managed classes, the array must hold pointers. Therefore, you need to carefully declare the array with the pointer notation. The syntax becomes somewhat cumbersome; thus, you will want to carefully understand the various portions. For example, to declare an array of size 15 that holds pointers to .NET strings, you would use the following:

```
String *y __gc[] = new String *__gc[15];
```

Notice the pointer symbol * follows the type String, and the __gc keyword precedes the brackets.

CREATE A .NET ARRAY

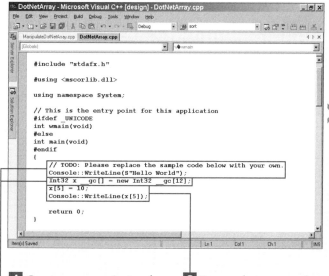

1 Create a new project and remove the Hello World line.

2 Type code to declare an array of value classes.

3 Type code to access the elements using the bracket notation.

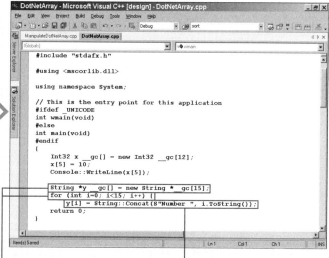

4 Type code to declare an array of managed classes.

5 Type a **for** loop that loops through the elements of the array.

6 Type code to access the elements of the array.

You can create a .NET array to hold any .NET instance.
For example, you can have an array of `StreamWriter`
pointers if your program needs to manage multiple files.
To do this, you declare an array of pointers using the
`__gc` notation, and then you store the `StreamWriter`
pointers in each element. Note that `StreamWriter`
pointers are the results of a call to `File::CreateText`.

Example:
```
StreamWriter *StreamArray __gc[] = new StreamWriter
*__gc[5];
for (int i=0; i<5; i++) {
    String *filename =
        String::Concat(S"c:\\temp\\File",
        i.ToString(), S".txt");
    Console::WriteLine(filename);
    StreamArray[i] = File::CreateText(filename);
    StreamArray[i]->WriteLine("hi");
    StreamArray[i]->WriteLine(i);
    StreamArray[i]->Close();
}
```

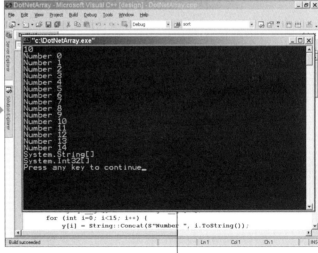

-7 Type code that shows the array types.

■ You can inspect the array types to be sure they are holding the correct type.

8 Compile and run the program.

■ The program window opens. The console shows the elements of the arrays, and the types of the arrays.

MANIPULATE A .NET ARRAY

When you create an array that holds instances of the .NET classes, whether they are value classes such as Int32 or managed classes such as String, the compiler automatically creates an instance of the Array class, also found in the .NET framework. This class contains many useful member functions for manipulating arrays, such as functions for reversing and sorting the arrays.

The name of the array variable becomes the name of the Array class instance. You can then, for example, find out the size of the array by inspecting its Count property, as in MyArray->Count. Most of the methods in the Array class, however, are static methods, which means they are not associated with a particular instance of Array. To use them, you call the method directly, preceding it with Array::.

For example, if you declare an array that holds .NET strings using notation such as

```
String *y __gc[] = new String *__gc[6];
```

you can then reverse the elements of this array by calling the reverse method of the Array class as in the following:

```
Array::Reverse(y);
```

You can also sort the array by calling Array::Sort(y). For example, if the array contains String instances, the elements are sorted in alphabetical order. If the array contains Int32 instances, the array is sorted in numerical order.

You can search the array for a particular element using the IndexOf method. This is a static method. You call Array::IndexOf, passing the name of the array and the element for which you are searching. If the element is found, the function will return the index where it was found. For example, if you have an array of String instances, you can call Array::IndexOf(y, S"SomeString"); to locate the element containing the string SomeString.

MANIPULATE A .NET ARRAY

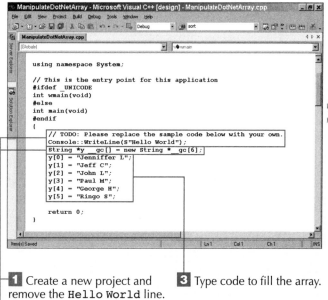

1 Create a new project and remove the **Hello World** line.

2 Type code to create a new .NET array.

3 Type code to fill the array.

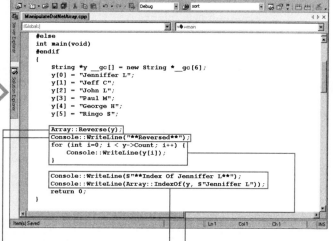

4 Type code to reverse the elements of the array.

5 Type code to show a message.

6 Type code to print the elements of the array.

7 Type code that shows a message and searches for a particular element.

Apply It

If you have .NET class instances stored in an array, and you want to find the final element that contains a particular item, you can use the `Array::LastIndexOf` method. For example, if you have an array that holds `String` instances, and three of the elements contain the string abc, you can find the final one using the `LastIndexOf` method.

TYPE THIS:

```
int main(void)
#endif
{
    String *MyArray __gc[] = new String *__gc[15];
    MyArray[0] = S"abc";
    MyArray[1] = S"def";
    MyArray[2] = S"def";
    MyArray[3] = S"abc";
    MyArray[4] = S"abc";
    Console::WriteLine(Array::LastIndexOf(MyArray, S"abc"));
    return 0;
}
```

RESULT:

4

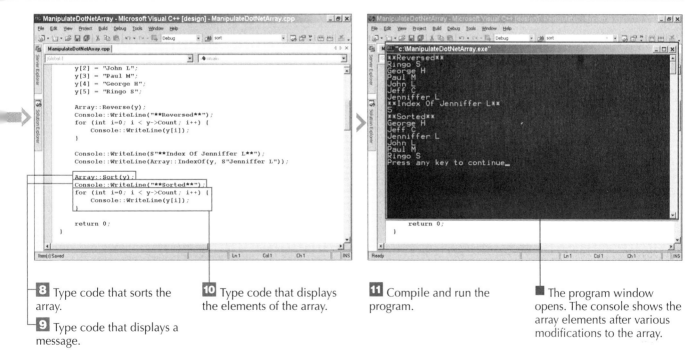

8 Type code that sorts the array.

9 Type code that displays a message.

10 Type code that displays the elements of the array.

11 Compile and run the program.

■ The program window opens. The console shows the array elements after various modifications to the array.

CREATE A CONTAINER

The .NET framework includes some special classes meant for holding pointers to instances of other .NET classes. You can use these classes when you have special requirements for managing data. For example, one such class is called Stack. It is similar to an array in that it stores instances of classes; however, the way you store items in it and access them is different from an array. A Stack instance mimics a stack of papers on a desk. You can put items one-by-one onto a stack, and you can only take items one-by-one off the top of a stack. You cannot take items out from the middle.

For example, if you have a Stack instance that holds strings, you can place the string a on the stack, then the string b, and finally the string c. To access these strings, first you must take the c string off the stack, and only then can

you access the b string. After you take the b string off the stack, only then can you access the a string.

The process of putting an item on the stack is called *pushing* the item, and the process of taking an item off the stack is called popping the item.

To use the Stack class, you create a new instance of Stack. Then you create the instances of the classes you wish to put on the stack. Unlike arrays, these instances do not all have to be the same type. You can put instances of any .NET class on a single stack.

To push an item on the stack, you call the Push method. To remove the top item from the stack, you call the Pop method.

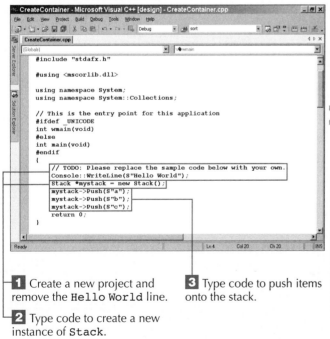

1 Create a new project and remove the **Hello World** line.

2 Type code to create a new instance of **Stack**.

3 Type code to push items onto the stack.

4 Type code to pop an item off the stack.

5 Type code to display the item.

6 Repeat steps 4 and 5 for popping more items.

Extra

You can use an interesting data structure called a *queue* to hold data. A queue works like people waiting in line. You can put items one-by-one at the end of the line, but only access the items one-by-one from the front of the line. You can continue adding more items to the end of the line as the line gets longer, as you occasionally access the item at the front of the line. The .NET framework includes a class called `Queue`. To add an item at the end of the line, you call `Enqueue`. To remove an item from the front, you call `Dequeue`.

Example:
```
Queue *myqueue = new Queue();
myqueue->Enqueue(S"a");
myqueue->Enqueue(S"b");
myqueue->Enqueue(S"c");

Object *front = myqueue->Dequeue();
Console::WriteLine(front->ToString());

front = myqueue->Dequeue();
Console::WriteLine(front->ToString());

myqueue->Enqueue(S"d");
front = myqueue->Dequeue();
Console::WriteLine(front->ToString());
```

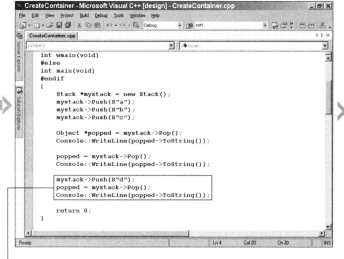

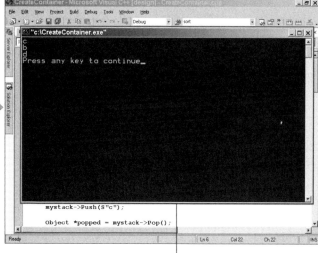

7 Type code to push and pop more items on and off the stack.

8 Compile and run the program.

■ The program window opens. The console shows the items as they are popped off the stack.

PROGRAMMING EXCEPTIONS

One of the most common experiences of .NET developers is writing code that builds without errors, runs well in a test environment, but does not run properly for some unexplained reason in production. This kind of error is not a bug because the application was built successfully, nor is it an error in logic because the application passed all of the tests required to put the system into production. A runtime error of this kind is an exception because it is the exception to a rule, rather than the normally observed behavior of a program.

While bugs and errors in logic might seem to be very different from exceptions, in reality, non-programmers are unlikely or unwilling to distinguish between them. Users are typically only concerned with status — whether the system actually runs perfectly in real time or not. This apparent disregard for the technicalities of error handling may frustrate developers. Fortunately, however, C++ provides sophisticated mechanisms for identifying, trapping, and handling run-time errors, in the form of exception handling.

In order for an exception to be handled properly, you must place it inside a `try` block. When an exception is thrown in a `try{}` block, all statements located within the corresponding `catch{}` block are executed sequentially. Possible actions arising from the execution of a `catch{}` are virtually unlimited. However, common actions include halting the application, warning the user that an error has occurred, asking the user what to do next, or simply logging the error and allowing the user to proceed. The specific action you choose for a certain exception entirely depends on how critical the error is. For example, if a user enters an invalid character into an input field, it would be silly to shut down the application. It would be more appropriate to either ask the user to reenter a valid character or simply to strip the illegal character from the input stream before processing it or storing it in a database.

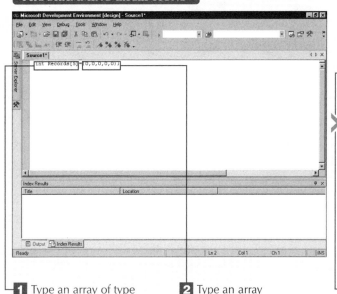

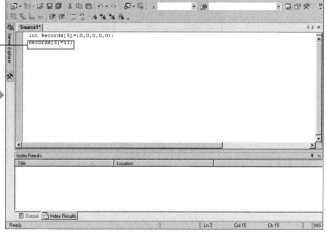

1 Type an array of type `integer` with five elements.

2 Type an array initialization.

3 Type code to insert a value into one of the array items.

■ When executed, the code will produce unexpected results.

Extra

By using `try/catch` blocks, you can reduce the number of loops in your program and increase the readability of your code. You may already be used to writing code that tests logical conditions, using `if` statements to determine whether a method returned a particular code. For example, your methods might return an integer where 1 indicates success, and -1 indicates failure. You then write an `if/then/else` loop to evaluate the return value of your method. One problem that this creates is that the number of branches in your program multiplies as a function of the number of methods with potential return error code values, multiplied by the number of possible return codes from each method. Thus, a program with 100 method calls, possibly returning three error codes per method, gives a total of 300 `if/then/else` loops that do nothing but check return codes. In distributed systems, where you might be waiting on a return code invoked on another server, your loop might loop infinitely if the other system is down, and you do not have an exception to handle that possibility.

There is another good reason to use exceptions in object-oriented programming. If a constructor fails at run-time, there is no way that it can return an error code because constructors do not have a return type. Thus, if an accessor method is called on an object that was not instantiated, a null pointer error would occur because an error code could not be returned. Throwing an exception in the constructor would handle this situation.

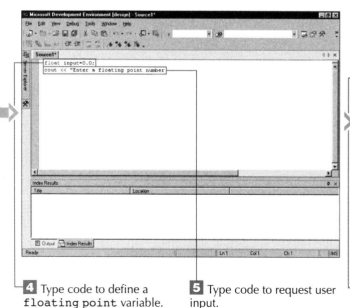

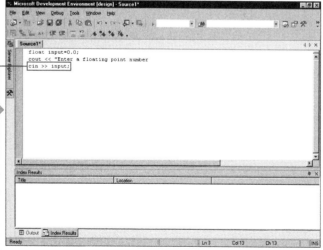

■4 Type code to define a **floating point** variable.

■5 Type code to request user input.

■6 Type code to capture a non-numeric value and assign it to **input**.

■ When executed, the code will produce unexpected results.

CATCH AN EXCEPTION WITH A TRY/CATCH BLOCK

You can catch an exception by using a `try`/`catch` block. When you write some code, if the code could fail and produce an exception, you can put that code inside a `try` block. You then write a `catch` block, which handles the exception.

To write a `catch` block, you type the word try, an open brace, and then the code that could fail. Then you end with a closing brace.

Next, you type the word **catch**, followed by a set of parentheses containing a pointer to the type of exception you are handling, such as the following.

```
catch (Exception *e)
```

You then type an open brace, followed by the handler code, and a closing brace.

There are several types of exceptions that can occur with most being derived from a single class called `Exception`.

These exception classes handle various types of exceptions, based on the situation.

Alternatively, if you do not care what type of exception you are catching, you can put three periods inside the parentheses, as follows.

```
catch (...)
```

Your handler can then catch any exception, regardless of the type of exception that occurred.

You can do several things inside your exception handler. You might display a message to the user of your program, explaining that an error occurred. You might then ask the user whether to continue, to try again, or to end the program. Alternatively, you might attempt to fix the situation yourself, if possible. For example, if the problem is that the data you read from a file was incorrect, you might read more data to try to remedy the situation.

CATCH AN EXCEPTION WITH A TRY/CATCH BLOCK

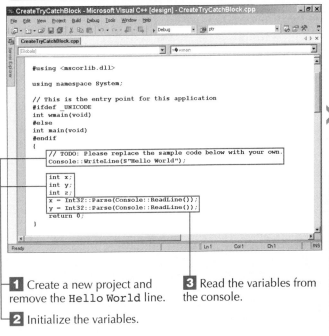

1 Create a new project and remove the `Hello World` line.

2 Initialize the variables.

3 Read the variables from the console.

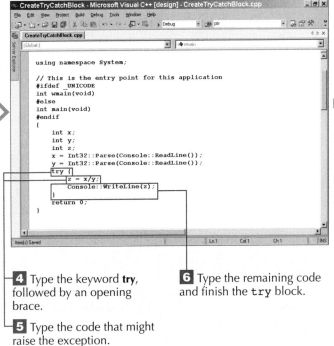

4 Type the keyword **try**, followed by an opening brace.

5 Type the code that might raise the exception.

6 Type the remaining code and finish the `try` block.

Extra

If you call a function or perform an action that can raise an exception, you can put the call inside a `try` block and follow it with a `catch` block. However, if the code that makes the call is itself inside a function and is called elsewhere, you can put the `try` block in the outer function. You can even put the `try` block inside your main function.

Example:
```
void MyFunction() {
    int x,y,z;
    x = Int32::Parse(Console::ReadLine());
    y = Int32::Parse(Console::ReadLine());
    z = x/y;
    Console::WriteLine(z);
}
int main(void)
{
    try {
        MyFunction();
    }
    catch (...) {
        Console::WriteLine(
            "Exception. Unable to complete the operation.");
    }
    return 0;
}
```

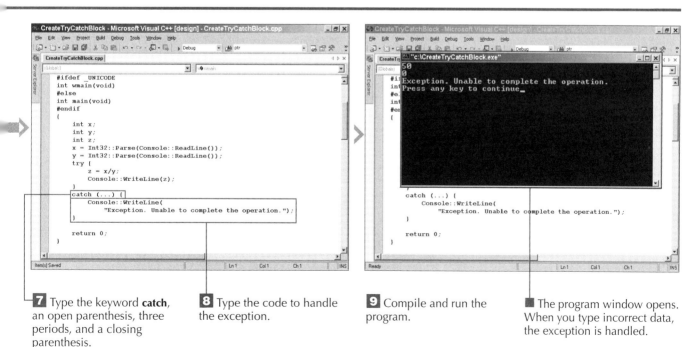

7 Type the keyword **catch**, an open parenthesis, three periods, and a closing parenthesis.

8 Type the code to handle the exception.

9 Compile and run the program.

■ The program window opens. When you type incorrect data, the exception is handled.

THROW AN EXCEPTION

While you can use exceptions to catch errors, you can also throw your own exceptions. Often you would throw an exception inside a function, and the code that calls the exception would be inside a `try` block, with an accompanying `catch` block.

To throw an exception, you create a new instance of `Exception`, or any class derived from `Exception`, and call `throw`, passing a pointer to the new instance. You can do this in one line of code, such as `throw new Exception();`. Note that you do not need to use parentheses with the `throw` keyword.

Normally in your function, you would test for various conditions, and if the conditions were not met, you would throw an exception. For example, if you have a routine that processes two numbers, but have the requirement that neither number can be 0, you can write an `if` statement

testing the numbers for 0. If either is 0, you can throw an exception as an efficient means of handling errors that your functions may encounter.

Exceptions work well for handling error situations if there are multiple levels of function calls. For example, if you have a function that calls a function that in turn calls another function, several times deep, and the innermost function encounters an error, it would be cumbersome for it to return an error message to the function that called it, and that function must check for that error message and return it, and so on. Instead, the innermost function can throw an exception. The outermost function, the one that made the first call, can have a `try/catch` block to handle the error. That way the other functions do not have to do their own error handling.

CATCH MULTIPLE EXCEPTIONS

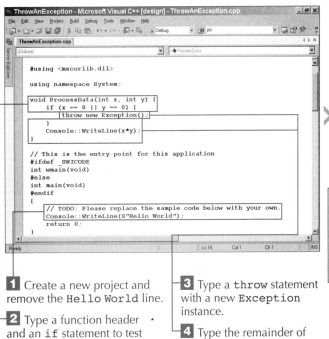

1 Create a new project and remove the `Hello World` line.

2 Type a function header and an `if` statement to test the data.

3 Type a `throw` statement with a new `Exception` instance.

4 Type the remainder of the function.

5 Initialize the variables.

6 Type code to read from the console into the variables.

Apply It

You can store a message in the exception, which the handler can retrieve.

Example:
```
void ProcessData(int x, int y) {
    if (x == 0 || y == 0) {
        throw new Exception("Zero encountered");
    }
    Console::WriteLine(x*y);
}
int main(void) {
    int x;
    int y;
    x = Int32::Parse(Console::ReadLine());
    y = Int32::Parse(Console::ReadLine());
    try {
        ProcessData(x,y);
    }
    catch (Exception *e) {
        Console::WriteLine(e->Message);
    }
    return 0;
}
```

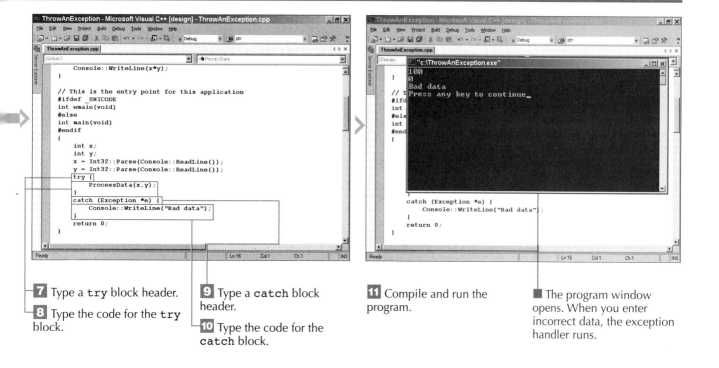

7 Type a `try` block header.

8 Type the code for the `try` block.

9 Type a `catch` block header.

10 Type the code for the `catch` block.

11 Compile and run the program.

■ The program window opens. When you enter incorrect data, the exception handler runs.

USING THE .NET EXCEPTIONS

You can make full use of all the advantages .NET offers by working with its exceptions. Because of the concept of managed code, which is a fundamental part of the .NET framework, the runtime library provides you with a whole set of additional exception features that work specifically with the .NET framework.

These exception features include a set of .NET exceptions, as well as built-in handling features if you do not write your own exception handlers. They work much like standard C++ exceptions in that you surround the code with a try block and put your handlers in the catch block.

The .NET framework provides you with a large set of possible exceptions, each for a specific type of error that

can occur. For example, the Int32::Parse method, which converts a string to an integer, has an associated FormatException class that gets thrown when the Parse method cannot convert the string to an integer. This situation might occur, for example, if you try to pass a string of letters to the Parse method. The idea is that you can write an exception handler that will respond, for example, if a user enters a string that cannot represent an integer. Your handler might respond by notifying the user of the error and asking him or her to try again.

The .NET framework has an entire class hierarchy of exceptions with SystemException as the base. These exceptions live in the System namespace, the same place you find classes such as String and Int32.

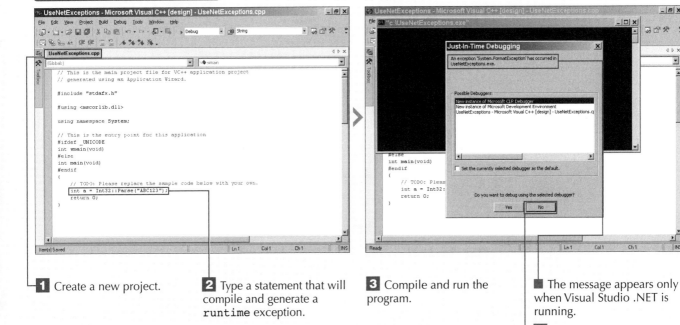

1 Create a new project.

2 Type a statement that will compile and generate a **runtime** exception.

3 Compile and run the program.

■ The message appears only when Visual Studio .NET is running.

4 Click No.

Extra

The .NET framework provides a wide range of exception handlers for different situations. The names are generally descriptive and indicate when the exception might occur. The following is a list of some useful exception classes.

ArgumentException	InvalidOperationException
ArithmeticException	NullReferenceException
ArrayTypeMismatchException	OutOfMemoryException
BadImageFormatException	SecurityException
DataException	StackOverflowException
FormatException	TimeoutException
IndexOutOfRangeException	VerificationException
InternalBufferOverflowException	WarningException
InvalidCastException	

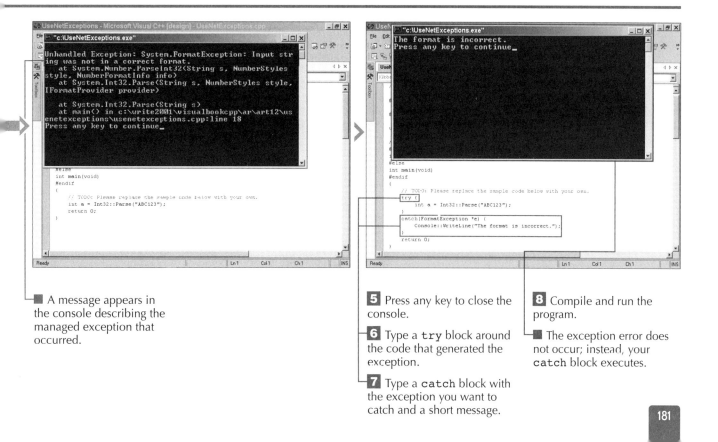

■ A message appears in the console describing the managed exception that occurred.

5 Press any key to close the console.

6 Type a **try** block around the code that generated the exception.

7 Type a **catch** block with the exception you want to catch and a short message.

8 Compile and run the program.

■ The exception error does not occur; instead, your **catch** block executes.

WRITE A .NET EXCEPTION HANDLER

With a large set of .NET exception classes available to you, you can easily write code that allows your program to respond to many different errors. One of the most common sources of errors is user input. It is difficult to control everything users will do with the software you develop, so the best goal would be to write code that handles errors in the input.

Many programs allow users to enter numbers. Although you could restrict the keys users can press and ensure they do not enter letters and other non-numeric digits, such a restriction can often frustrate users. Instead of adding restrictions, you can make users happy by allowing them to enter numbers in many different formats. For example, users often appreciate the ability to enter currency symbols and thousands separators along with their numbers. A good software package will let users enter any of the following variations: 53267, $53267, 53,267, or $53,267.

By using a proper exception handler along with the `Int32::Parse` method, you can easily give your program this feature with very little work.

You can also respond to other types of exceptions such as file input/output or communication exceptions. For example, you might be writing a program that receives information over the Internet, and in the middle of receiving the information, the dial-in connection goes down or the Internet library times out waiting. You might then include an exception handler for various communication exceptions.

Or, you might want to respond to mathematical errors. For example, you might have the user entering in numbers that your code processes. If while processing the numbers you suddenly find yourself dividing by 0, which is not allowed mathematically, you might have an exception handler that responds to a division by zero error.

WRITE A .NET EXCEPTION HANDLER

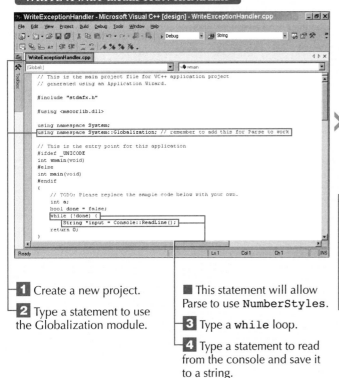

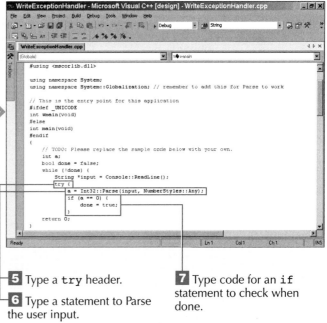

■1 Create a new project.

■2 Type a statement to use the Globalization module.

■ This statement will allow Parse to use **NumberStyles**.

■3 Type a **while** loop.

■4 Type a statement to read from the console and save it to a string.

■5 Type a **try** header.

■6 Type a statement to Parse the user input.

■7 Type code for an **if** statement to check when done.

Extra

It is good programming practice to become familiar with the exceptions that a method can generate. The online help includes a list of exceptions that a method can generate. For example, the entry for `Int32::Parse(String, NumberStyles)` lists `ArgumentNullException`, `ArgumentException`, `FormatException`, and `OverflowException`. When calling methods, it is always a good idea to study these exceptions and determine if it is possible for your program to generate these exceptions. If so, it is wise practice to include an exception handler for each kind that can occur. That way, you can be sure your programs will respond gracefully to the unusual errors that can happen when a program interacts with files, other programs, or humans.

You can keep your code simple by categorizing your exceptions. Many exceptions can be grouped together, covering a wide array of different errors. Because you certainly can not write code that covers every possible problem, instead you can write exception handlers for the general case of each type of exception. For example, you can not anticipate every possible file error that could occur; thus, you might instead have a general exception handler that responds to all file errors.

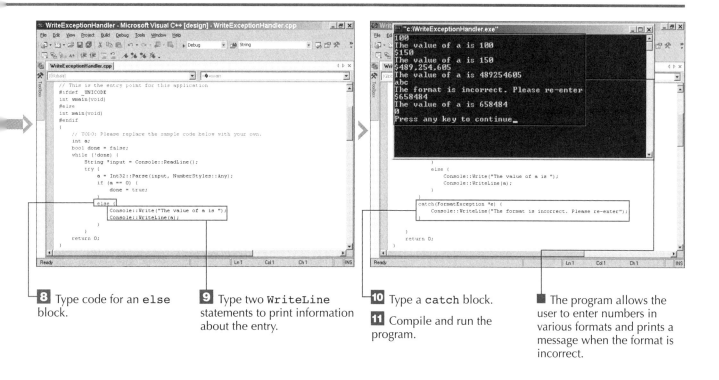

8 Type code for an `else` block.

9 Type two `WriteLine` statements to print information about the entry.

10 Type a `catch` block.

11 Compile and run the program.

■ The program allows the user to enter numbers in various formats and prints a message when the format is incorrect.

CREATE AN EXCEPTION CLASS

You can use the .NET framework to write your own exception classes, giving you strong control over exactly what errors your program recognizes and the ability to respond to these errors. When you look at the existing exception classes in the .NET framework, you find that they deal with specific error situations. For example, the FormatException class is used specifically by methods that expect a string formatted in a particular manner, and the methods raise this exception when the format is not correct. Similarly, the IndexOutOfRangeException is used by methods that operate on arrays, and they raise it when the index goes beyond the size of the array.

You can also create your own exception classes for use in specific situations. For example, you might be writing a program that reads data over the Internet, and the data must be a valid Web page. You would write the code to receive it and surround it by a try block. You might then create an exception class called IncorrectWebPage that you would throw if the file received is something other than a Web page. For example, it may be a straight graphics file or a file intended for a word processor or other type of viewer. After your try block, you would have a catch block in which you notify the user that the file is not a valid Web page, and perhaps ask what to do next: try again, give up, or look for a new Web page.

CREATE AN EXCEPTION CLASS

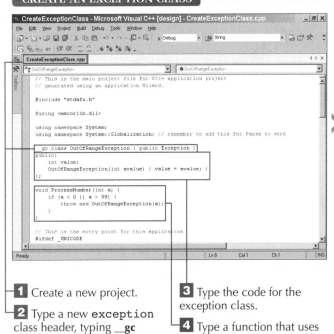

1 Create a new project.

2 Type a new **exception** class header, typing **__gc** before it to tell the compiler it is a managed class, and inheriting from class Exception.

3 Type the code for the exception class.

4 Type a function that uses the **exception** class and throws it when an error occurs.

5 Type code to get a string from the console input.

6 Type code that calls the function that raises the exception.

7 Compile and run the program.

8 Enter a number greater than 99.

■ The standard message uses the new exception name.

Extra

To make your programs as robust as possible, you should adopt two methods of error handling: using exceptions sparingly and handling errors without exceptions. For example, if you are testing whether a number is out of bounds, you can either test it in an `if` statement and display a message, or you can throw an exception. The one you choose depends on how deep you are within function calls. For example, if you write code that calls a function and that function in turn calls a function, and so on, but down at the innermost level an error occurs that you want to handle in the outermost level, that is an ideal situation for an exception. But if you are calling only a single function, it is more practical to have the function return an error code to which you can respond.

If you are writing code that uses a lot of exceptions, you can either create a few exception classes to handle a wide variety of cases, perhaps by just using the standard exceptions without writing your own, or you can write several exception classes, each of which handles a specific situation. The choice is yours, depending on how you want to manage your code. If you prefer to divide your work into multiple classes, then you can divide your exceptions into multiple classes. However, in general, most programs, even large-scale commercial applications, do not have more than six or seven exception classes. For additional exceptions, most commercial applications rely on built-in exceptions such as the .NET exceptions.

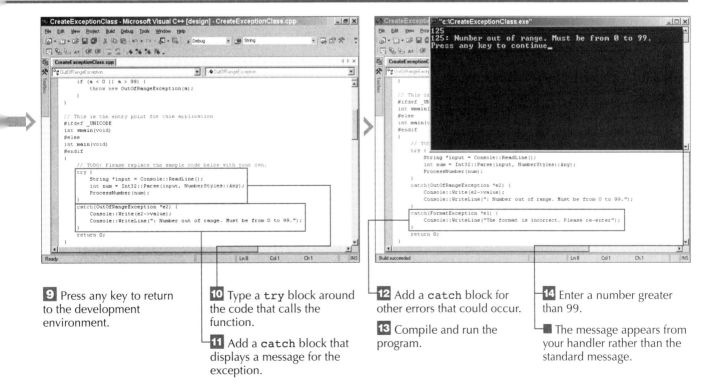

9 Press any key to return to the development environment.

10 Type a `try` block around the code that calls the function.

11 Add a `catch` block that displays a message for the exception.

12 Add a `catch` block for other errors that could occur.

13 Compile and run the program.

14 Enter a number greater than 99.

■ The message appears from your handler rather than the standard message.

CREATE A TEXT FILE

A text file is simply a file that contains data, usually ASCII code, that human beings can read. Text files generally have the .txt extension, although you are free to create a text file with any extension. You can have your program create a text file using the .NET framework. After you create a text file, you can easily store lines of ASCII data in the file. For example, if your program deals with e-mail messages, you can easily save the e-mail messages line by line to a text file.

The .NET framework provides a set of classes that you can use to deal with text file input/output easily. Calling the CreateText method of the class File, for example, creates a text file with the filename given as a parameter. The method returns an object of class StreamWriter that you can use for writing to the file.

To use the CreateText method, you do not need an instance of the File class; instead, you use the File class directly. The methods in the File class are static, so you simply call them with the word File followed by two colons, and then the CreateText method. You then pass the name of the path and file you wish to create.

If CreateText cannot create the file, it will throw an exception. This may happen, for example, if the directory does not exist. CreateText does not create directories, and so it can only create files in directories that already exist. You should, therefore, include a try/catch block around your call to CreateText.

Note that if the file already exists, CreateText will replace the file with a new, empty file. Also, after the call to CreateText, the file will be open, so you need to close it later by calling the Close method.

CREATE A TEXT FILE

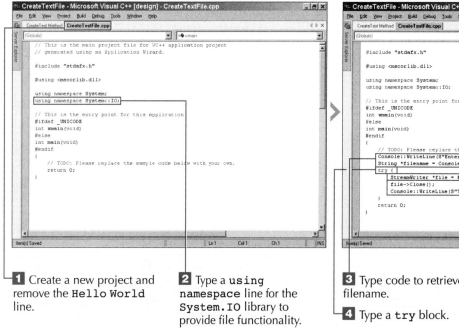

1 Create a new project and remove the **Hello World** line.

2 Type a **using namespace** line for the **System.IO** library to provide file functionality.

3 Type code to retrieve the filename.

4 Type a **try** block.

5 Type a line to create a text file, saving the results in a **StreamWriter** instance.

6 Type a line to close the new file and write a message.

Extra

In addition to using the `File` class, you can also create a text file using the `ofstream` class. You create an `ofstream` object with a string as the new filename.

Example:
```
void CcreateDlg::OnBnClickedOk() {
    ofstream textfile("textfile.txt");
    textfile.close()
}
```

When you create a text file, you can normally only write ASCII characters to the file. You do not normally write what is called *binary data* to the file. Binary data refers to any type of data that is stored in a file in a form that cannot be opened in a standard text editor such as Notepad or the editor in Visual Studio .NET. An example of a binary file is a program file with an .EXE extension.

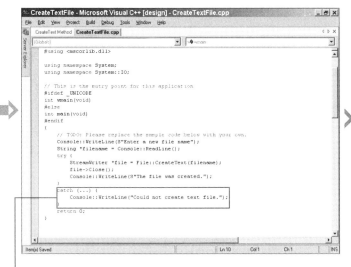

7 Type a `catch` block that runs if the file cannot be created.

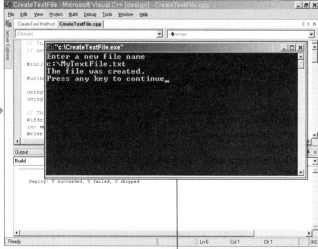

8 Compile and run the program.

■ The program window opens, letting you create a file.

OPEN A TEXT FILE

Y ou can open a text file in several different ways, depending on your purpose. You may want to open an existing file to read, write, or append to it. Alternatively, you may wish to create and open a blank file to write new data.

Calling the OpenText method of the File class with an existing filename opens the text file in read-only mode. The method returns a StreamReader object that you can use as the file handler.

After you have a StreamReader object, you can read from the file. The ReadLine method reads one line of text from the file and stores it in a String object. The ReadToEnd method reads data from a file, starting at the current position and continuing to the end of the file, and again stores it in a String object.

After you have read from the file, you can check the value of the String object. If it is the NULL pointer, then that means you have reached the end of the file. Otherwise, the String object will contain the text read in from the file.

A text file ends each line with a carriage return and linefeed; however, when you call ReadLine, your strings will not have a carriage return and linefeed at the end of them. Therefore you do not need to remove these when you are processing the strings.

You can also open a text file using an ifstream or ofstream object. You must first create a file object of either type, and then call the corresponding open method. The open method takes a string parameter as the filename, and a mode parameter that can be ios::in for reading in a file or ios::out for writing a file.

OPEN A TEXT FILE

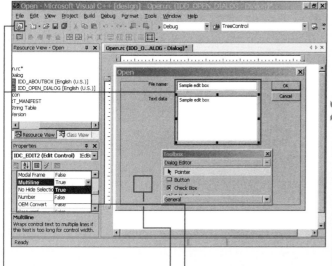

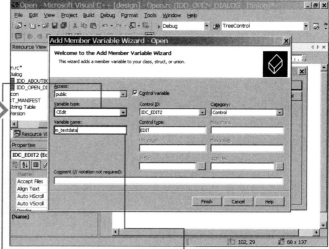

1 Create a new dialog-based project.

2 In the dialog editor, add two text boxes to the dialog box.

3 In the properties window, change the Multiline property to True and the Want Enter property to True.

4 Right-click the Open dialog box and select Add Variable from the pop-up menu.

5 In the Class Wizard, add a variable for the text box.

6 In the Class Wizard, add a variable **m_textdata**.

Extra

You can also read a text file using the `ifstream` class. First create an `ifstream` object and a buffer to hold the text data. You may then call the `getline` method to acquire data from the file. You will call this method over and over until you reach the end of the file.

Example:
```
void CWriteDlg::OnBnClickedOk()
{
    // TODO: Add your control notification handler code here
    Char buffer[256];
    ifstream textfile("textfile.txt");
    while(!textfile.eof()) {
        textfile.getline(buffer, 100);
        cout << buffer << endl;
    }
}
```

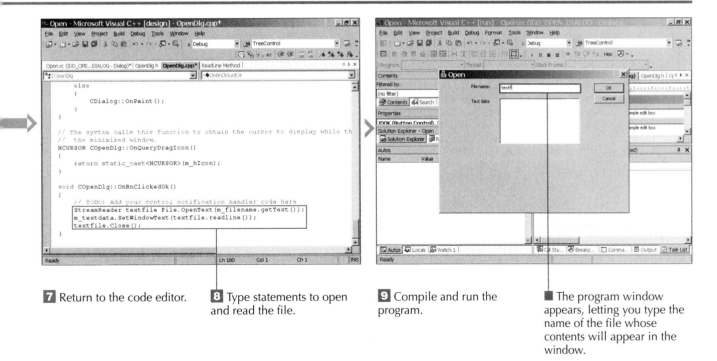

7 Return to the code editor.

8 Type statements to open and read the file.

9 Compile and run the program.

■ The program window appears, letting you type the name of the file whose contents will appear in the window.

WRITE TO A TEXT FILE

You can easily use the .NET framework to write to a text file. A text file is a file that contains the standard characters that you can type on the keyboard and see in a word processor program. A text file does not show formatting such as bold and italic. A text file also does not contain program information as you would find in the compiled executables you build with Visual Studio .NET. However, the code files you type into the editor in Visual Studio.NET are good examples of text files.

To create a text file with the .NET framework, you use the File class. The File class provides the CreateText method. To use this method, pass the name of the file you want to create. The CreateText method will create the file for you, open it, and give you back a StreamWriter object. The StreamWriter object will be in the form of a pointer.

From there, you can write to the text file using the methods of the StreamWriter class. This class includes the Write and WriteLine methods. The Write method writes a string. The WriteLine method writes a string and then writes a carriage return and linefeed so that the next text written will be on the next line.

For example, if you save the StreamWriter pointer in a variable called writer, then to write the string Hello World to a file, you would call writer->WriteLine(S"HelloWorld");. This would write the string and then start a new line. If you call Write or WriteLine again, the next text will be on the next line in the file.

After you create your text file, you can open it in the editor in the Visual Studio.NET environment.

WRITE TO A TEXT FILE

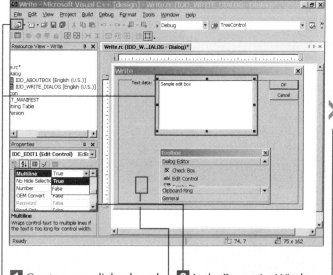

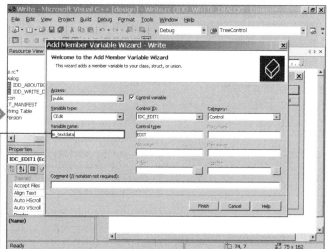

■1 Create a new dialog-based project.

■2 In the dialog editor, add a text box.

■3 In the Properties Window, change the Multiline property to True and the Want Enter property to True.

■4 Right-click the Write dialog box and select Add Variable from the pop-up menu.

■5 In the Class Wizard, add a variable for the text box.

Extra

When you use the `File::CreateText` method to create a new text file, you can write many types of data to the file in text form. The `StreamWriter::Write` and `StreamWriter::WriteLine` method supports the different data types. For example, you can write integers and floating-point numbers by simply passing them to the `Write` or `WriteLine` method.

Example:
```
#include "stdafx.h"
#using <mscorlib.dll>
using namespace System;
using namespace System::IO;
int main(void) {
    int x = 10;
    double n = 3.1415926;
    String *str = S"Hello World";
    Decimal big = Decimal::Parse(
        "79228162514264337593543950335");
    StreamWriter *writer =
        File::CreateText("c:\\textfile.txt");
    writer->WriteLine(x);
    writer->WriteLine(n);
    writer->WriteLine(str);
    writer->WriteLine(big);
    writer->Close();
}
```

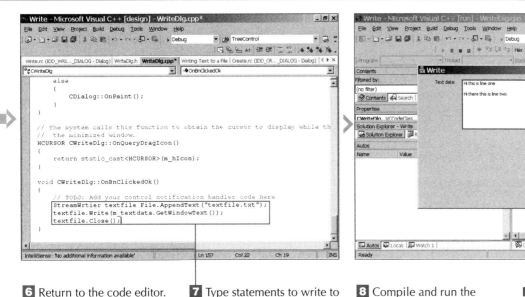

6 Return to the code editor.

7 Type statements to write to a file.

8 Compile and run the program.

■ The program opens, letting you append to a new file.

APPEND TO A TEXT FILE

I f your program writes to text files, the .NET framework provides several classes that can make your work easy. Within the `System.IO` namespace is the `File` class that includes a useful method called `AppendText` for appending text to a file. This method opens up an existing file and returns an instance of the class called `StreamWriter`. Like the `File` class, the `StreamWriter` class is a member of the `System.IO` namespace. The `StreamWriter` class includes methods similar to those in the `Console` class, including `Write` and `WriteLine`. These methods work similarly to their counterparts in the `Console` class, except they write to a text file rather than the console.

For example, you can open a text file by calling `StreamWriter *writer = File::AppendText`

`("MyFile.txt");`. You can then write a string to it by calling `writer->Write(S"Hello World");`. Or, you can write a string followed by a new line with `writer->WriteLine(S"Hello World");`.

After you are finished with the `StreamWriter` instance, you should close the file by calling the `Close()` method, as in the following.

```
writer->Close();
```

After the file is closed, you can open it in any text editor such as Notepad, or the editor in Visual Studio .NET and look at its contents. You will see the strings that you wrote using the Write and WriteLine methods.

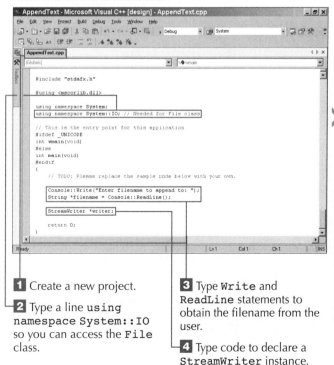

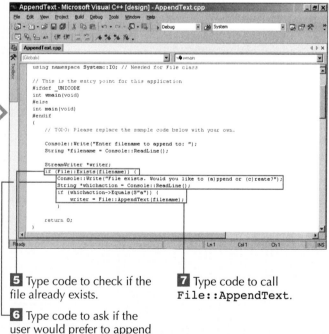

1 Create a new project.

2 Type a line using `namespace System::IO` so you can access the `File` class.

3 Type `Write` and `ReadLine` statements to obtain the filename from the user.

4 Type code to declare a `StreamWriter` instance.

5 Type code to check if the file already exists.

6 Type code to ask if the user would prefer to append or create a new file by that name.

7 Type code to call `File::AppendText`.

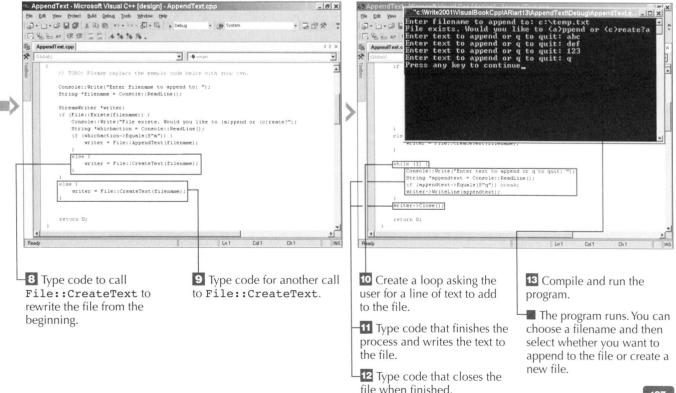

Extra

To get the most out of the `File` class, understand the difference between `File::Append` and `File::Create`. `File::Append` will either append to an existing file, or create a new file if it already exists. If your situation requires that you append to and never recreate a file from scratch, then you can use `Append`. But if you want to always create the file from scratch, even if it exists, in which case its contents will be deleted and it will start over new, then use `Create`.

As its name suggests, the `StreamWriter` class only writes to files. You cannot use it to read from a file, for it has no methods for doing so. If you need to read from a file, use its corresponding class called `StreamReader`. The `File` method `OpenText`, which is for reading a text file, returns a `StreamReader` instance.

■8 Type code to call `File::CreateText` to rewrite the file from the beginning.

■9 Type code for another call to `File::CreateText`.

■10 Create a loop asking the user for a line of text to add to the file.

■11 Type code that finishes the process and writes the text to the file.

■12 Type code that closes the file when finished.

■13 Compile and run the program.

■ The program runs. You can choose a filename and then select whether you want to append to the file or create a new file.

CREATE A BINARY FILE

A binary file is a file containing binary data, such as images, executable data, database files, or any other kind of non-ASCII data. Humans cannot read binary files; only applications and system software can read them. Consequently, binary file retrieval methods are different than the retrieval methods for text files.

The .NET framework provides the File class that uses the method Create to create a binary file. The method can take one parameter, Create(String *file_name), or two parameters, Create(String *file_name, int buff_size). The method returns a pointer of type FileStream, effectively a handler for the created file.

The FileStream class offers methods for both reading and writing to binary files. The FileStream class also provides methods for other operations on binary files, such as seeking and flushing data.

You can create a binary file by using the ofstream class. You simply create an ofstream object and call the open method. The method takes two parameters, a filename and a mode, with the form open(const char * filename, openmode mode). The open mode for a binary file may be a combination of modes, such as ios::out|ios::binary.

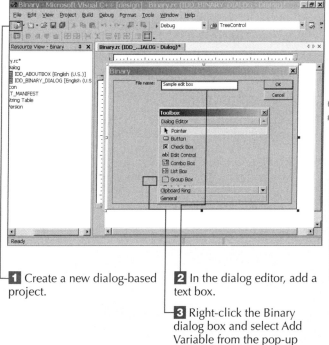

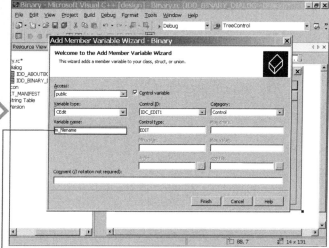

1 Create a new dialog-based project.

2 In the dialog editor, add a text box.

3 Right-click the Binary dialog box and select Add Variable from the pop-up menu.

4 In the Class Wizard, add a variable for the text box.

Extra

An alternative way to create a binary file is through the `ofstream` class. You first create an `ofstream` object, and then call the `open` method, which takes two parameters — a filename, and an open mode. The open mode used in the following example is for writing into a new binary file.

Example:

```
void CBinaryDlg::OnBnClickedOk()
{
    // TODO: Add your control notification handler code here
    ofstream binaryfile("file.bin",
ios::out|ios::trunc|ios::binary);
    binaryfile.Close();
}
```

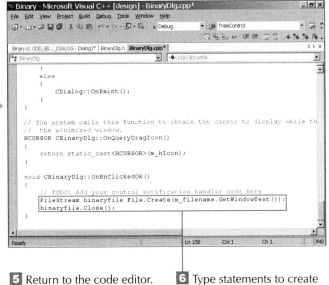

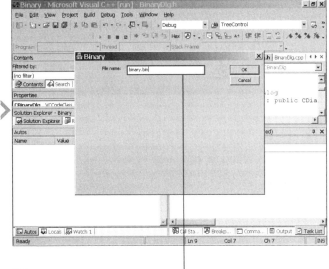

5 Return to the code editor.

6 Type statements to create a binary file.

7 Compile and run the program.

■ The program creates a new binary file.

195

READ A DISK DIRECTORY

With the help of the .NET framework, you can easily perform many operations regarding file directories. One of these is reading the contents of a directory.

The .NET framework includes a class in the `System.IO` namespace called `Directory`. This class provides several methods for manipulating directories. One of these methods, called `GetFiles`, reads all the files within a specified directory and returns them as an array of string instances. To call the method, you pass the name of the directory. Optionally, you can pass a string representing a file-matching pattern. This pattern can contain letters that match the names of the files, along with the wildcards `*` and `?`. The wildcard `*` means any string can match, while the wildcard `?` means any single character can match. For

example, if you wish to obtain a list of all files that start with the string net, such as NET.EXE, NETLOGON.DLL, and NETAPI32.DLL, you would specify the pattern as `net*`. If you wish to find all files that end with .cpp, your pattern would be `*.cpp`. If you want to find every file that has the letter a for the second character, your pattern would be `?a*`.

With the `Directory` class, you can also read the names of the subdirectories within a directory using the `GetDirectories` method. To use this method, you pass the name of the directory you wish to scan as a string. As with `GetFiles`, you can also pass an optional pattern to obtain only the subdirectories with names matching your specification.

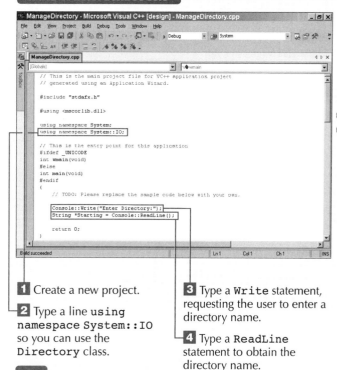

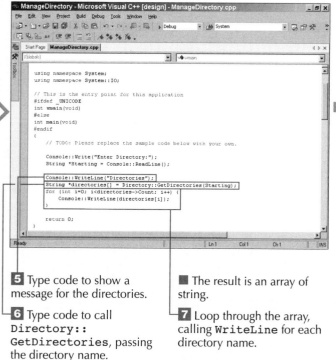

1 Create a new project.

2 Type a line using `namespace System::IO` so you can use the `Directory` class.

3 Type a `Write` statement, requesting the user to enter a directory name.

4 Type a `ReadLine` statement to obtain the directory name.

5 Type code to show a message for the directories.

6 Type code to call `Directory::GetDirectories`, passing the directory name.

■ The result is an array of string.

7 Loop through the array, calling `WriteLine` for each directory name.

Extra

Using some `ReadLine` and `WriteLine` statements in conjunction with some methods from the Directory class, you can easily make a basic command-line processor, much like the Windows command line. This command-line processor only has two commands, cd and dir, plus a quit command. To try this code you need to start with a new project, and you will type this code into the main block of the program. Presently this code does not check if a directory exists. As an exercise, you might think how you could use the `Directory::Exists` method to make sure the directory exists before switching to the directory.

Example:
```
Directory::SetCurrentDirectory("C:\\");
while (true) {
    Console::Write(Directory::GetCurrentDirectory());
    Console::Write(">");
    Char separators[] = {' ','-'};
    String *input[] = Console::ReadLine()->Split(separators, 2);
    String *cmd = input[0]->ToUpper();
    if (cmd->Equals(S"QUIT")) break;
    if (cmd->Equals(S"DIR")) {
        String *directories[] = Directory::GetDirectories(
            Directory::GetCurrentDirectory());
        for (int i=0; i<directories->Count; i++)
            Console::WriteLine(String::Concat("\t",directories[i]));
    }
    if (cmd->Equals(S"CD"))
        Directory::SetCurrentDirectory(
            String::Concat(Directory::GetCurrentDirectory(), "/", input[1]));
}
return 0;
```

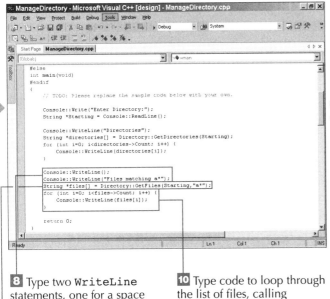

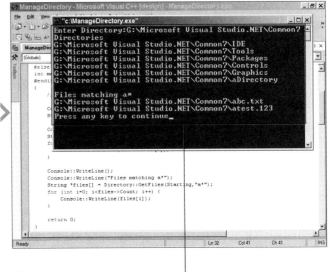

8 Type two `WriteLine` statements, one for a space and one for a message.

9 Type code to call `Directory::GetFiles`, passing the directory name and optionally a pattern.

10 Type code to loop through the list of files, calling `WriteLine` for each.

11 Compile and run the program.

■ A list of directories appears along with all files that begin with the letter a.

COPY A FILE

The File class in the System::IO namespace includes a Copy method for copying a file. You can copy a file into the same directory as the original, provided the new file has a different name than the original. If you copy a file into a different directory, you can use the same name as the original. To use the File::Copy method, you pass the name and path of the original file, called the source file, and the name and path of the new file, called the destination file. You also pass a Boolean variable that instructs the File::Copy method how to behave if a file with the same

name as the destination file already exists. If you specify true, the old destination file will be rewritten with a copy of the original source file.

In general, when copying files, it is good policy to first check whether the destination file already exists, and if so, ask the user whether to overwrite the existing file before proceeding. This rule will help you create software that is more user-friendly.

COPY A FILE

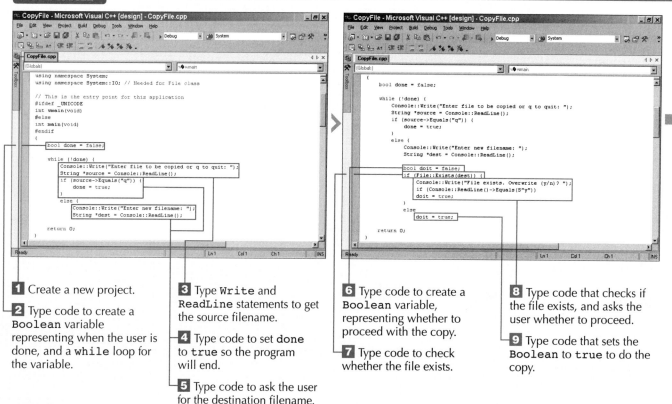

1 Create a new project.

2 Type code to create a Boolean variable representing when the user is done, and a while loop for the variable.

3 Type Write and ReadLine statements to get the source filename.

4 Type code to set done to true so the program will end.

5 Type code to ask the user for the destination filename.

6 Type code to create a Boolean variable, representing whether to proceed with the copy.

7 Type code to check whether the file exists.

8 Type code that checks if the file exists, and asks the user whether to proceed.

9 Type code that sets the Boolean to true to do the copy.

Extra

In order to make your programming as effective and user-friendly as possible, make sure you completely understand the difference between file copy, file move, and file rename operations. A copy takes an original file and makes a duplicate of it without removing the original file. A move takes an original file, makes a duplicate of it, and removes the original file, thereby simulating a move operation. A rename is a type of move in that the file is moved within the same directory. For that reason, the File class does not contain a rename method. You simply use the Move method.

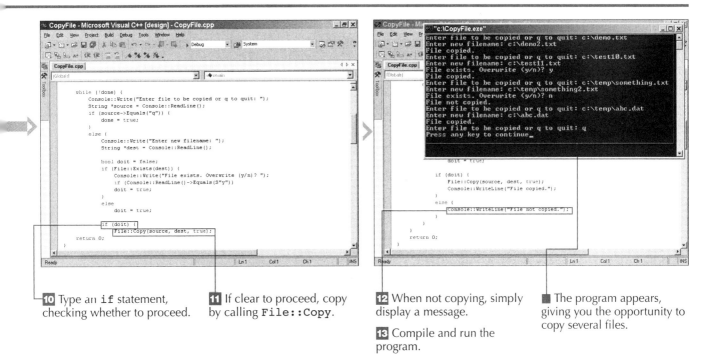

🔟 Type an if statement, checking whether to proceed.

1️⃣1️⃣ If clear to proceed, copy by calling File::Copy.

1️⃣2️⃣ When not copying, simply display a message.

1️⃣3️⃣ Compile and run the program.

■ The program appears, giving you the opportunity to copy several files.

DELETE A FILE

When writing a program, there will be times when your program needs to delete a file. Deleting a file is very easy with the .NET framework using the File class, found in the System::IO namespace. To use it, you simply specify the name of the file you wish to delete.

You can also delete directories using the Directory::Delete method. To use this method, specify the name of the directory, along with a Boolean variable that represents whether to delete all subdirectories and files underneath it. Be careful with this option, for if you set it to

true, it will remove everything under the directory. If you set it to false, and the directory is not empty, an exception will be raised.

Deleting a file is a very important ability that must be used with care. If your program needs to create any temporary files, or if your users want your program to remove a file, then your program should remove it. However, it is very easy for your program to accidentally remove a file that either you or the user does not want deleted. In general, then, it is good policy to ask the user before deleting a file.

DELETE A FILE

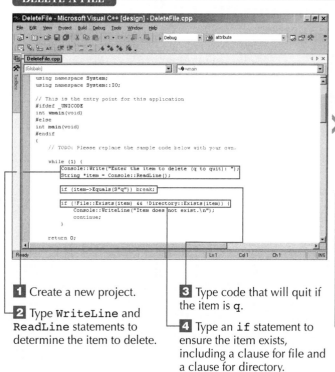

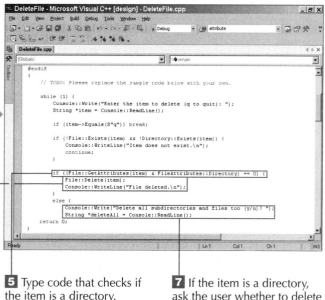

1 Create a new project.

2 Type WriteLine and ReadLine statements to determine the item to delete.

3 Type code that will quit if the item is **q**.

4 Type an **if** statement to ensure the item exists, including a clause for file and a clause for directory.

5 Type code that checks if the item is a directory.

6 Type code to delete the item if it is a file as opposed to a directory.

7 If the item is a directory, ask the user whether to delete all subdirectories and files underneath.

Extra

In some cases, you do not want to ask the user for permission to delete a file. The most common case is when your program creates a temporary file that holds interim information, and the user does not even know this file exists. When it is time to delete the file, if you ask the user for permission, the baffled user may not know how to answer the question.

For your program to be as user-friendly as possible, it is always good policy for the program to clean up any temporary files that it no longer needs, especially if these are not essential to the user. If you are dealing with multiple files, you can keep the names of them in a string array, and before your program exits, it can move through the array, extracting the filenames and deleting the temporary files associated with the names.

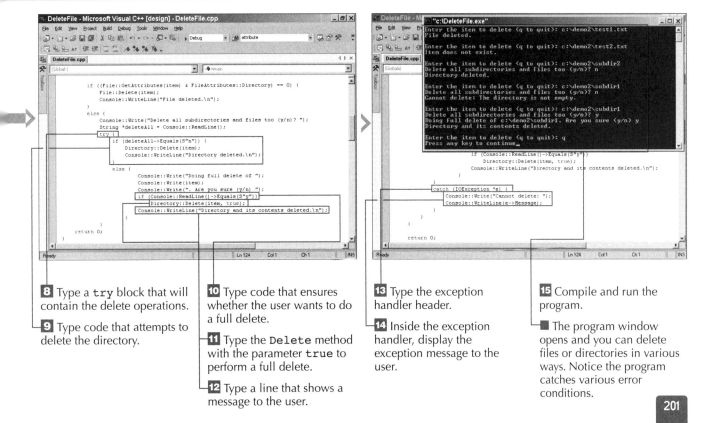

8 Type a `try` block that will contain the delete operations.

9 Type code that attempts to delete the directory.

10 Type code that ensures whether the user wants to do a full delete.

11 Type the `Delete` method with the parameter `true` to perform a full delete.

12 Type a line that shows a message to the user.

13 Type the exception handler header.

14 Inside the exception handler, display the exception message to the user.

15 Compile and run the program.

■ The program window opens and you can delete files or directories in various ways. Notice the program catches various error conditions.

SEEK TO ANY POSITION IN A FILE

I f you are working with binary files, you can use the .NET framework to easily move to any position within them to read or write individual bytes, all within the same file. The .NET framework includes several classes within the System::IO namespace that provide these features. Using the File class, you can open a file for binary read and write operations by calling the File::Create method, passing the name of the file. You receive back a pointer to a FileStream instance containing methods Read, Write, WriteByte, and Seek. The Read method reads an array of bytes, while the Write method writes an array of bytes. The WriteByte method writes a single byte. The file includes a current position from which the next Read, Write, or WriteByte method takes place. The Seek method moves this current position. With Seek, you also specify whether the position you are requesting is relative to the current position, the beginning, or the end.

When using the Read or Write methods, you need to work with a .NET managed array containing unsigned characters. In this case, a character is the same thing as a byte. To declare the array, you need to use the built-in __gc compiler keyword that tells the compiler the variable is a .NET managed object: unsigned char data __gc[] = {1,2,3,4,5};. The compiler translates the managed type unsigned character to a class called Byte. Thus, you can alternatively declare this as Byte data[] = {1,2,3,4,5}; . Either of these arrays can then be passed to the Write method.

For the Read method, you create an array, but do not need to initialize it. You can declare it in two ways: unsigned char readdata __gc[] = new unsigned char __gc[data->Count]; or Byte readdata[] = new Byte[data->Count];.

SEEK TO ANY POSITION IN A FILE

1 Create a new project.

2 Type a **namespace** line for **System::IO**.

3 Type code to create a new instance of **newfile**.

4 Type an array declaration, initializing it with some data.

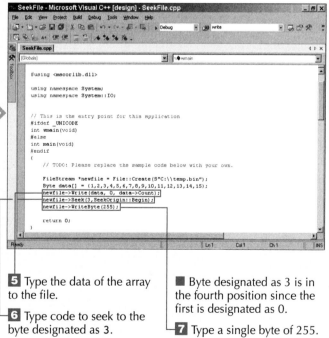

5 Type the data of the array to the file.

6 Type code to seek to the byte designated as **3**.

■ Byte designated as 3 is in the fourth position since the first is designated as 0.

7 Type a single byte of 255.

Extra

You can get more use out of binary files by writing typed data to a file and reading it back in. Using the `BinaryReader` and `BinaryWriter` classes found in the `System::IO` namespace, you can write a particular set of data types and later read in those data types following a protocol that you choose. The following example demonstrates a protocol that writes two integers, a float, and then a string.

Example:
```
FileStream *newfile = File::Create(S"C:\\temp.bin");
BinaryWriter *writer = new BinaryWriter(newfile);
writer->Write(100);
writer->Write(150);
writer->Write(200);
writer->Write(250);
writer->Write(S"Hello");
writer->Write((float)1.2345);
// Seek to the 4th integer position
writer->BaseStream->Seek(3 * sizeof(int), SeekOrigin::Begin);
writer->Write(251);
WriteSet2(writer);
newfile->Close();
```

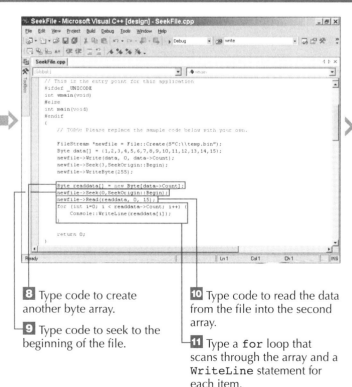

■**8** Type code to create another byte array.

■**9** Type code to seek to the beginning of the file.

■**10** Type code to read the data from the file into the second array.

■**11** Type a **for** loop that scans through the array and a **WriteLine** statement for each item.

■**12** Type a line to close the file.

■**13** Compile and run the program.

■ A window appears showing the entries of the **for** loop. The entries match what was written into the file, and the fourth byte is 255.

RENAME OR MOVE A FILE

Although users often use Windows Explorer to move and rename files, there are times when your program may need to move or rename a file. You can give your programs this ability with the help of the `File` class found in the `System::IO` namespace.

To move a file, you call the `File::Move` method. This method takes as parameters the name of the file you wish to move and the directory and filename you want to move it to. For example, if you want to move the file called c:\mydocument.doc to the c:\temp directory, you would call `File::Move (S"c:\\mydocument.doc", S"c:\\temp\\mydocument.doc");`. While moving the file, you can also rename it by supplying a different filename in the second parameter along with the directory you are moving it to.

To rename a file, you also call `Move`, except you specify the same directory. Renaming a file is actually a move operation in which you move the file within the same directory. Thus, if you want to rename the file c:\mydocument.doc to c:\letter.doc you would call `File::Move (S"c:\\mydocument.doc", S"c:\\letter.doc");`. This action would move the file to a new filename, or in other words, rename it.

When you use Windows Explorer to move a file, the computer actually just renames it with a new directory name and keeps the original filename. Thus all move and rename operations are actually just a rename. That is why moving a large folder with hundreds of files and subfolders is very quick under Windows Explorer. Windows is not copying the files and deleting the originals; instead each file is simply renamed with a new path.

RENAME OR MOVE A FILE

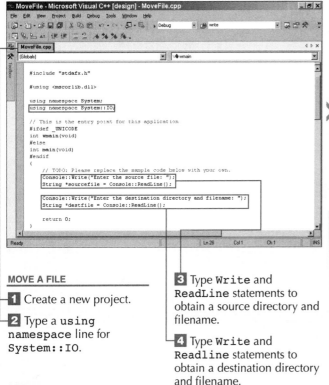

MOVE A FILE

1 Create a new project.

2 Type a `using namespace` line for `System::IO`.

3 Type `Write` and `ReadLine` statements to obtain a source directory and filename.

4 Type `Write` and `ReadLine` statements to obtain a destination directory and filename.

5 Type **File::Move** supplying the source and destination.

6 Type code that shows a message that the file was moved.

7 Compile and run the program.

■ The program window appears, allowing you to move a file.

Extra

You can move an entire set of files using a combination of the `Directory` class, the `File` class, and the `Path` class, all found in the `System.IO` namespace. You use the `Directory` class to get a list of files that match a certain pattern; you use the `Path` class to extract the path of each file and replace it with a new path; and you use the `File` class to move the file. This example code will move all files in the C:\Demo2 directory that match the pattern *.txt to the C:\Demo2\temp directory.

Example:
```
using namespace System::IO;
String *files[] = Directory::GetFiles(
    S"C:\\Demo2", S"*.txt");
for (int i=0; i < files->Count; i++) {
    String *oldfilename = Path::GetFileName(files[i]);
    String *newpathfile = Path::Combine(
        S"C:\\Demo2\\temp", oldfilename);
    File::Move(files[i], newpathfile);
}
```

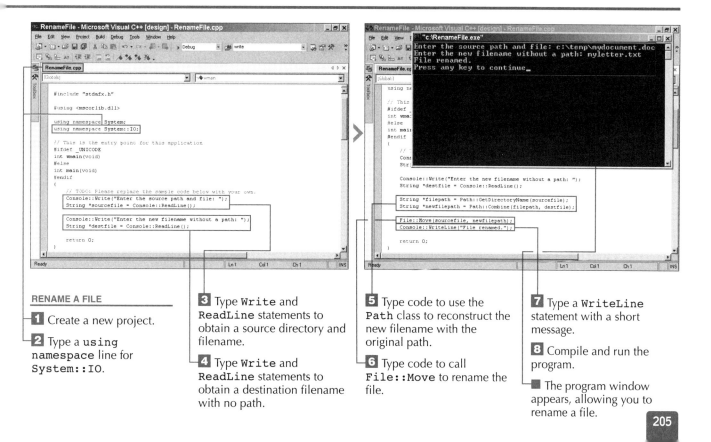

RENAME A FILE

1 Create a new project.

2 Type a **using namespace** line for **System::IO**.

3 Type **Write** and **ReadLine** statements to obtain a source directory and filename.

4 Type **Write** and **ReadLine** statements to obtain a destination filename with no path.

5 Type code to use the **Path** class to reconstruct the new filename with the original path.

6 Type code to call **File::Move** to rename the file.

7 Type a **WriteLine** statement with a short message.

8 Compile and run the program.

■ The program window appears, allowing you to rename a file.

CREATE A WINDOWS FORM

With the .NET framework of classes, you can create a window for your program in which you can place controls such as buttons and ListBox controls. In .NET terminology, a window is called a *form*.

To use the windowing features of .NET, you need to include several standard lines at the beginning of your program.

```
#using <System.DLL>
#using <System.Windows.Forms.DLL>
#using <System.Drawing.DLL>
```

These three lines instruct the compiler to make use of various libraries that support the windowing and graphics features. Additionally, you should include the following lines:

```
using namespace System::Windows::Forms;
using namespace System::Drawing;
```

These two lines simplify the use of the classes dealing with forms and graphics. Without the first line, the way you

would refer to the Form class would be as System::Windows::Forms::Form. This can be cumbersome to type every time; thus, the first line allows you to simply type **Forms**. The second line does similarly for various classes dealing with graphics and drawing.

To create a form, you create a new instance of Form, passing no parameters to the constructor. Next, you set its Width and Height properties to set its size. You can then set the Text property to control the text that appears in the title bar at the top of the form. To show the form, you call the form's ShowDialog() method. The ShowDialog method will display the form, and will not return until the form is closed.

After the call from ShowDialog returns, you can inspect the values of the various controls on the form to find out how the user of your program interacted with it. For more information on controls, see the remaining sections of this chapter.

CREATE A WINDOWS FORM

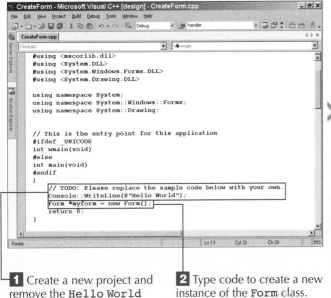

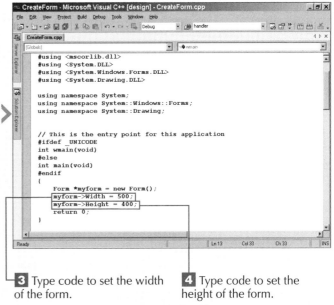

1 Create a new project and remove the Hello World line.

2 Type code to create a new instance of the Form class.

3 Type code to set the width of the form.

4 Type code to set the height of the form.

Extra

You can easily add a menu to your form. You must first create an instance of `MainMenu` and instances of `MenuItem`. Next, create a class containing the functions that run when the user of your program clicks a menu. Finally, connect these functions to the appropriate menu by creating an instance of a class called `EventHandler` and pass this instance to the `MenuItem` constructor.

Example:
```
// This class goes before the main function
__gc class HandlerClass {
public:
    Form *form;
    void ExitClick(System::Object* s, System::EventArgs* e) {
        form->Close();
    }
};
    // This is inside the main function, before ShowDialog.
    HandlerClass *handler = new HandlerClass();
    handler->form = myform;
    MainMenu *mainMenu1 = new MainMenu();
    MenuItem *FileMenu = new MenuItem("File");
    MenuItem *ExitItem = new MenuItem("Exit",
        new EventHandler(handler,HandlerClass::ExitClick));
    FileMenu->MenuItems->Add(ExitItem);
    mainMenu1->MenuItems->Add(FileMenu);
    myform->Menu = mainMenu1;
```

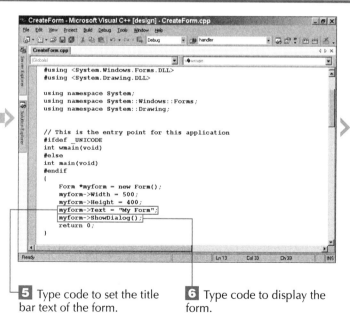

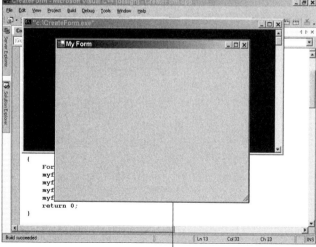

5 Type code to set the title bar text of the form.

6 Type code to display the form.

7 Compile and run the program.

■ The window opens with the proper height, width, and title bar.

ADD A BUTTON CONTROL

In most programs, the windows contain various buttons. A button provides an easy way for the user of your program to interact with your program. Typically, you write code so that a button causes some process to take place, such as opening another form or closing the current form. Or, your button might cause other controls on the form to change; for example, it might fill a `ListBox` control with various strings of text.

The .NET framework includes a `Button` class that allows you to easily add a button to your form. For each button you want to add to your form, you create a new instance of `Button`. Then you set the `Text` property to set the words that appear on the button.

Next, you need to write a function that contains the code that runs when the user clicks the button. Create a class and give it any name such as `Handlers` or `HandlerClass` and

then place the function inside this class. You can give the function whatever name you choose; but, it must have the following parameters and return type:

```
void button_Click(System::Object* s,
        System::EventArgs* e)
```

In the `main()` function where you are creating your buttons and your form, you create an instance of your `Handler` class. You then create a new instance of a class called `EventHandler`, passing the instance of the `Handler` class and the name of the function, in this case `button_Click`. Finally, you add this `EventHandler` instance to the button's `Click` property using the `+=` notation.

When the user clicks the button, the code `button_Click` runs.

ADD A BUTTON CONTROL

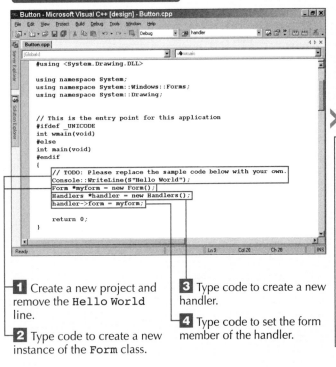

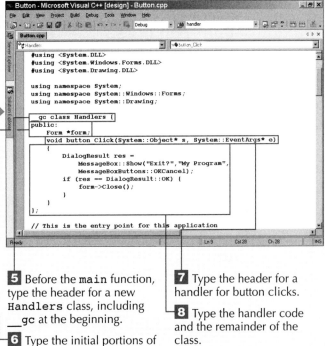

1 Create a new project and remove the `Hello World` line.

2 Type code to create a new instance of the `Form` class.

3 Type code to create a new handler.

4 Type code to set the form member of the handler.

5 Before the `main` function, type the header for a new `Handlers` class, including `__gc` at the beginning.

6 Type the initial portions of the class.

7 Type the header for a handler for button clicks.

8 Type the handler code and the remainder of the class.

Extra

You can add multiple buttons and other controls to a single form. To add multiple buttons, create the instances of the controls and then create a `Control` array containing the pointers to the controls. Next, call the `AddRange` method for the form's `Controls` property. Note that the order you place the controls in the array specifies the order in which the controls are highlighted when the user of your program presses the Tab key.

Example:

```
Form *myform = new Form();
myform->Width = 300;
myform->Height = 300;
Button *b1 = new Button();
b1->Text = "One";
b1->Left = 10;
b1->Top = 50;
Button *b2 = new Button();
b2->Text = "Two";
b2->Left = 110;
b2->Top = 50;
Control* controls[] = {b1, b2};
myform->Controls->AddRange(controls);
```

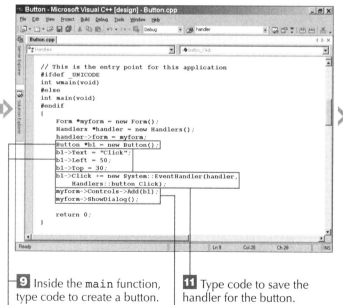

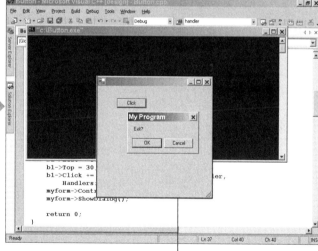

9 Inside the `main` function, type code to create a button.

10 Type code to set the properties of the button.

11 Type code to save the handler for the button.

12 Type code that stores the controls in the form and displays the form.

13 Compile and run the program.

■ The program window opens. When you click the button, the handler runs.

ADD A LABEL CONTROL

A *label* is a piece of text that displays on a form that the user of your program cannot type into or change. You can change the text on the label from within your program.

To use a Label control, you create an instance of the Label class. Like the other controls, you can find this class in the namespace System::Windows::Forms. Thus, you should include the statement using namespace System::Windows::Forms; in your program.

After you create an instance of the Label class, you set its position by setting its Left and Top properties. You set its size by setting the Width and Height properties. Finally, you set the text that displays in the control by setting its Text property.

If you are not sure how wide to make your label, you can set its AutoSize property to true. Then, when the label displays on the form, it will resize itself automatically to fit the text that you placed in the Text property.

If you prefer to choose the exact width of the Label control, and the text you choose is wider than the control, the text will wrap to a new line of text. In this case, you need to set the Height property of the control so it will accommodate the lines of text. There is no AutoSize property for height, so you will need to run your program and look at the label to make sure the text fits. If the Label control is not tall enough for the text, you will only see the first few lines of text. Finally, note that this text wrapping will occur at the spaces, meaning words will not be broken up unless the word is too wide for the control. If it is, the word is split.

ADD A LABEL CONTROL

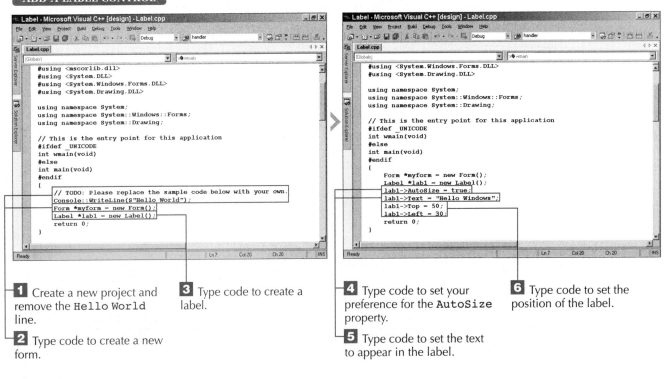

1 Create a new project and remove the Hello World line.

2 Type code to create a new form.

3 Type code to create a label.

4 Type code to set your preference for the **AutoSize** property.

5 Type code to set the text to appear in the label.

6 Type code to set the position of the label.

Extra

You can display an image inside a Label control. This will result in the text appearing superimposed on top of the image. If the Label control is smaller than the image, you will see only a portion of the image. The image will not shrink to fit inside the label box.

Example:
```
Form *myform = new Form();
Label *lab1 = new Label();
lab1->Text = "Name:";
lab1->Top = 50;
lab1->Left = 30;
lab1->Image = new Bitmap("c:\\winnt\\Santa Fe
Stucco.bmp");
myform->Controls->Add(lab1);
myform->ShowDialog();
```

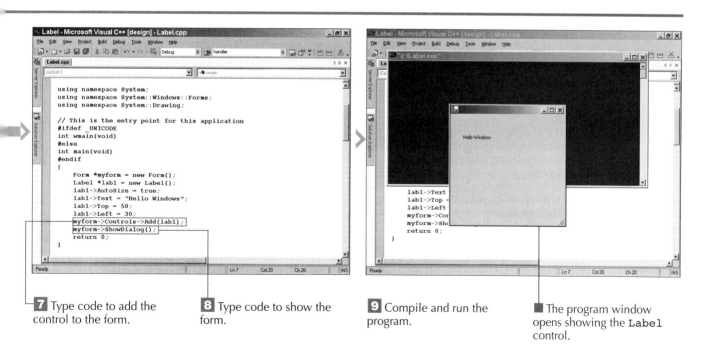

7 Type code to add the control to the form.

8 Type code to show the form.

9 Compile and run the program.

■ The program window opens showing the Label control.

ADD A TEXTBOX CONTROL

You can give the users of your program the ability to easily enter text. You can do this by creating a *TextBox control*. A TextBox control, sometimes called an Edit control, is a box that provides a blinking caret showing the current position where text is entered. When the user clicks the control, the caret appears, and when the user types at the keyboard, the text appears in the box. The user can use the mouse to drag portions of the text and copy or delete it. The user can also paste text into the control. The user can copy, paste, and delete by pressing Ctrl+C, Ctrl+V, and Ctrl+X, respectively. Alternatively, the user can right-click and choose these options from a small popup menu.

The TextBox control also includes a basic undo feature, which the user can perform by pressing Ctrl+V, or selecting Undo from the right-click pop-up menu.

To create a TextBox control, you create a new instance of the TextBox class. You then specify the Width, Height, Top, and Left properties to set the size and position. You can set the initial text by setting the Text property.

You can determine what the user entered by inspecting the Text property. For example, after the form closes, you can look at the Text property to see the contents; or, inside a button's click handler you can look at the Text property of the TextBox.

The TextBox provides for limited text entry features, but it does not provide advanced word processing features where each character can have a different font, style (such as bold or italic), and size. To provide for these features, see page 238.

see page 238.

ADD A TEXTBOX CONTROL

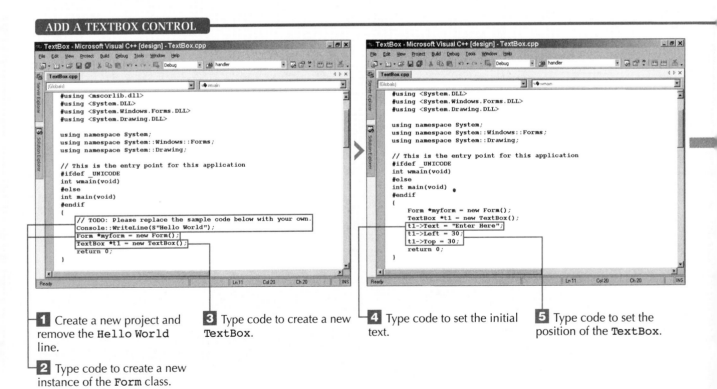

1 Create a new project and remove the Hello World line.

2 Type code to create a new instance of the Form class.

3 Type code to create a new TextBox.

4 Type code to set the initial text.

5 Type code to set the position of the TextBox.

Extra

You can set up a `TextBox` control to accept multiple lines of input by setting the `Multiline` property to true and `WordWrap` to true. Optionally, you can set `AcceptsReturn` to true and `AcceptsTab` to true, which specify that when the user presses Tab or Enter, these will result in a tab and carriage return being inserted into the TextBox. If these properties are not set, pressing Enter will result in the default button clicking, and pressing Tab will result in the next control being highlighted.

Example:

```cpp
Form *myform = new Form();
TextBox *t1 = new TextBox();
t1->Text = "Enter Here";
t1->Left = 30;
t1->Top = 30;
t1->Height = 150;
t1->Width = 150;
t1->Multiline = true;
t1->WordWrap = true;
t1->AcceptsReturn = true;
t1->AcceptsTab = true;
myform->Controls->Add(t1);
myform->ShowDialog();
Console::WriteLine(t1->Text);
```

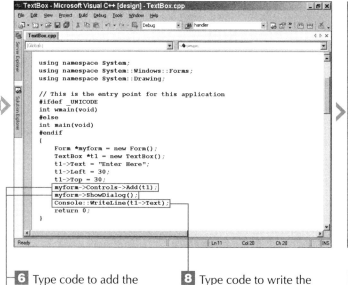

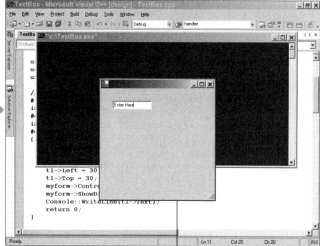

6 Type code to add the `TextBox` to the form.

7 Type code to display the form.

8 Type code to write the contents of the `TextBox`.

9 Compile and run the program.

■ The program window opens. When you type data in the `TextBox` and then close the form, the text shows on the console.

ADD A CHECKBOX CONTROL

With the .NET framework, you can give your users the ability to check off items on your form by using a CheckBox control. With the CheckBox control, you provide a string that appears beside a small box. When the user clicks on the box, a small check mark appears inside the box.

To use the CheckBox control, you create an instance of the CheckBox class. You then set its size and position by setting its Width, Height, Left, and Top properties. Next, you set the text that appears beside the box by setting the Text property.

You can then check the state of the CheckBox by inspecting its Checked property. If the property is set to true, it means the user has checked the box. Otherwise, the property is set to false.

You can also manually set the check in your program by either setting the Checked property to true to check it, or false to uncheck it.

When you create the CheckBox, you can decide where inside the entire control you want the box to appear. By default, the box appears on the left side of the control, to the left of the text. However, you can change this by setting the CheckAlign property. To set the box to appear on the right side instead of the left, set the CheckAlign property to ContentAlignment::MiddleRight. The choices for this property all start with ContentAlignment:: and then are BottomCenter, BottomLeft, BottomRight, MiddleCenter, MiddleLeft, MiddleRight, TopCenter, TopLeft, and TopRight. Note that the text will move accordingly, so the text and box will never appear on top of the other.

ADD A CHECKBOX CONTROL

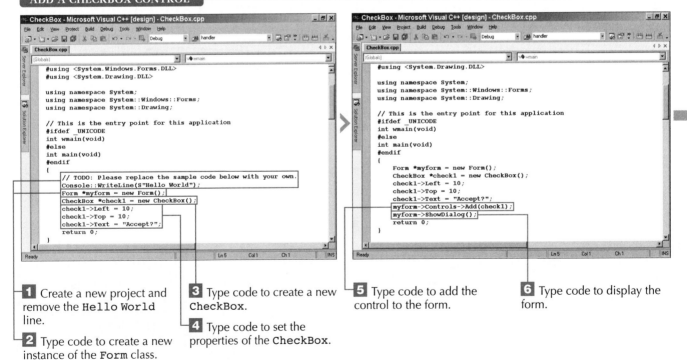

■1 Create a new project and remove the Hello World line.

■2 Type code to create a new instance of the Form class.

■3 Type code to create a new CheckBox.

■4 Type code to set the properties of the CheckBox.

■5 Type code to add the control to the form.

■6 Type code to display the form.

Apply It

You can use the `CheckBox` control to cause other controls on a form to become active or inactive if you have a form that represents a set of options. For example, you might have a `CheckBox` for extended options. When you check the `CheckBox`, several other controls on the form might become active.

Example:

```
// This goes before the main function
__gc class Handlers {
public:
    TextBox *text;
    CheckBox *check;
    void checkClick(System::Object* s, System::EventArgs* e) {
        text->Enabled = check->Checked;
    }
};
// This goes inside the main function
CheckBox *check1 = new CheckBox();
handler->check = check1;
check1->Text = "Include Name";
check1->Click += new System::EventHandler(handler, Handlers::checkClick);
TextBox *text1 = new TextBox();
handler->text = text1;
text1->Text = "Name";
text1->Enabled = false;
```

7 Type code to test if the `CheckBox` is checked.

8 Type code to test if the `CheckBox` is not checked.

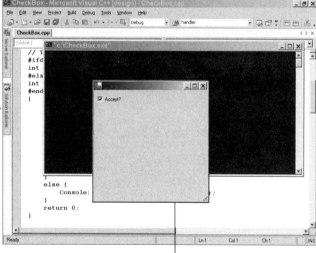

9 Compile and run the program.

■ The program window opens. When you close the form, a message displays stating whether the box is checked.

ADD A GROUPBOX WITH RADIOBUTTON CONTROLS

Often in forms with various programs, you will see a set of small round buttons with text next to them. These buttons, called *RadioButtons*, contain the round button plus a string of text. They are usually grouped together with a border drawn around them; this border is called a *GroupBox*. Of all the RadioButton controls inside the GroupBox, you can only click one RadioButton at a time. When you do, the RadioButton you click becomes selected, and the others become unselected. This is called *mutually-exclusive*.

To add a GroupBox control, you create a new instance of the class GroupBox. The only properties you typically set for GroupBox are Left and Top for its position, Width and Height for its size, and Text for a string that appears at the top of the GroupBox control.

After you have created a GroupBox control, you can create the RadioButton controls. To add a single RadioButton

control, you create a new instance of the RadioButton class. You then set its position through its Left and Top properties, and its size through its Width and Height properties. Optionally, you cannot set the Height property. A default height is chosen for you to accommodate the text. Then, you specify the words to appear beside the RadioButton's round button by setting its Text property.

Unlike other controls, you do not add the RadioButton controls to the Form's Controls list. Instead, the GroupBox has its own Controls list, and you add the RadioButtons to this list. Thus, you can have multiple GroupBox controls, each with their own set of RadioButtons.

To determine which RadioButton the user selected, you inspect the Checked property of each RadioButton instance. The one that is selected will have a true for this property; the others will have a false.

ADD A GROUPBOX WITH RADIOBUTTON CONTROLS

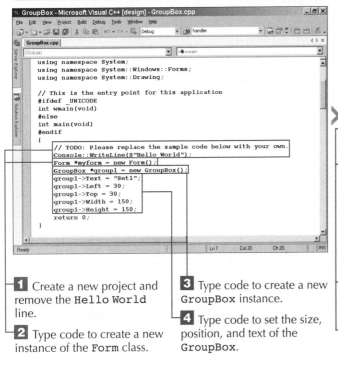

1 Create a new project and remove the Hello World line.

2 Type code to create a new instance of the Form class.

3 Type code to create a new GroupBox instance.

4 Type code to set the size, position, and text of the GroupBox.

5 Type code that creates a new RadioButton instance and sets its properties.

6 Repeat step 5 for any number of RadioButton instances.

7 Type code to add the RadioButton instances to the GroupBox.

Extra

You can change the position of the round button inside the
`RadioButton` by setting its `CheckAlign` property. For example, to
make the button appear on the right side of the control, set the
`CheckAlign` property to `ContentAlignment::MiddleRight`. This
is the same as the `CheckAlign` property of the `CheckBox` control.

If you want an action to occur as soon as the user of your program
clicks a `RadioButton`, you can add an event handler. This event
handler works the same way as it does with a button. For example, you
can create a handler class and add a line such as:

```
radio1->Click += new System::EventHandler(handler,
    Handlers::radio_Click);
```

For more information on button click events, see page 208.

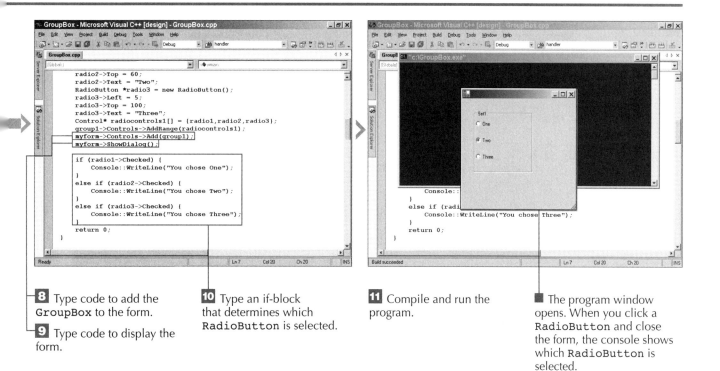

8 Type code to add the **GroupBox** to the form.

9 Type code to display the form.

10 Type an if-block that determines which **RadioButton** is selected.

11 Compile and run the program.

■ The program window opens. When you click a **RadioButton** and close the form, the console shows which **RadioButton** is selected.

ADD A PICTUREBOX CONTROL

I f you are writing a program that handles graphics and bitmapped images, or if you want to give your program a sophisticated user interface, you can use a PictureBox control on a form that you create. The PictureBox control displays graphical images from several formats including BMP, JPG, GIF, and WMF.

To create a PictureBox control on a form, you create an instance of PictureBox without passing any parameters to the constructor. You then set the various properties inherited from Control. The most common ones you will need are Location, Dock, and BorderStyle. Location specifies the upper-left coordinate of the control; Dock specifies whether the PictureBox control stays up against the sides of the form; and BorderStyle specifies whether the control has a border.

Two properties unique to PictureBox and not inherited from Control are SizeMode and Image. SizeMode

describes the location and stretching of the image within the control. The SizeMode property is a PictureBoxSizeMode enumeration and can be either AutoSize, CenterImage, Normal, or StretchImage. If you specify AutoSize, the PictureBox resizes automatically to fit the image inside it. CenterImage centers the image within the PictureBox. An image smaller than the PictureBox has empty spaces around it. If the image is larger, it is clipped. StretchImage stretches the image horizontally and vertically so it always fits within the PictureBox. The horizontal and vertical stretching are independent of one another, so the image may appear distorted. The StretchImage value works well with the Dock property set to DockStyle::Fill to ensure that the PictureBox control always fills the window even if the window is resized, and the image also always fills the control, allowing the user to reshape and resize the appearance of the image by resizing the window.

ADD A PICTUREBOX CONTROL

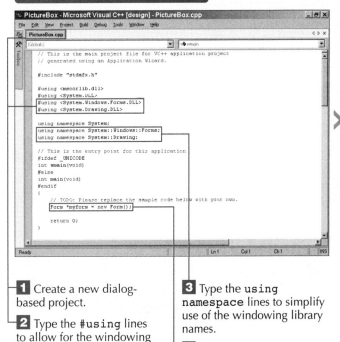

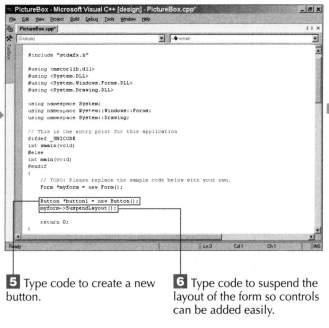

1 Create a new dialog-based project.

2 Type the #using lines to allow for the windowing libraries.

3 Type the using namespace lines to simplify use of the windowing library names.

4 Type code to create a new form object.

5 Type code to create a new button.

6 Type code to suspend the layout of the form so controls can be added easily.

Extra

You can add code that runs in response to a user clicking on the `PictureBox`. The `PictureBox` class inherits mouse response methods from the `Control` class including `Click` and `MouseDown`. If you do not need to know where the user clicked, you can use `Click`. If you need to know the location, you can use `MouseDown`. The following example code demonstrates the `MouseDown` event. Add this class definition outside of your function.

Example:
```
__gc class Handlers {
public:
    void picturebox_mousedown(System::Object* sender, MouseEventArgs* e)
    {
        Console::WriteLine(e->X);
        Console::WriteLine(e->Y);
    }
};
```

Then add this code to the rest of your property initializations:

```
Handlers *handlers = new Handlers();
picturebox->MouseDown += new MouseEventHandler(handlers,
    Handlers::picturebox_mousedown);
```

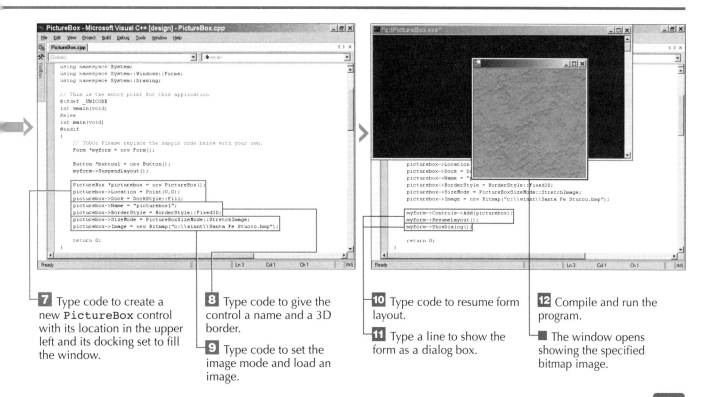

7 Type code to create a new **PictureBox** control with its location in the upper left and its docking set to fill the window.

8 Type code to give the control a name and a 3D border.

9 Type code to set the image mode and load an image.

10 Type code to resume form layout.

11 Type a line to show the form as a dialog box.

12 Compile and run the program.

■ The window opens showing the specified bitmap image.

ADD A LISTBOX CONTROL

With the .NET framework, you can include a ListBox control on your form. A ListBox control simply displays a set of strings in a vertical list inside a box. If the set of strings extends beyond the vertical dimensions of the ListBox, the ListBox will include a scrollbar on the right-hand side.

When the users of your program work with the ListBox, they can scroll through the items and click various items to make a selection. You can set up the ListBox so that the user can choose either one item or multiple items.

To use the ListBox, you create an instance of the ListBox class. You specify the Height and Width properties to choose the size, and the Left and Top properties to choose the position of the ListBox control. You then add strings to the ListBox control by calling the Add method of the control's Item property.

You can determine which items the user chose in the list by inspecting the SelectedIndices property. This property is an array that contains a list of indexes representing the items in the list that the user chose. Note that the first item has index 0. Then, for each index in the SelectedIndices property, you can determine the string in the list by looking at the Item array of the Items property.

To specify whether the user can choose only one item or multiple items, set the SelectionMode property of the ListBox. This property can have the values SelectionMode::MultiSimple, SelectionMode::One, and SelectionMode::MultiExtended. With SelectionMode::MultiSimple, when the user clicks an item in the list, its selection state switches from either selected to unselected. With SelectionMode::MultiExtended, the user can hold down Ctrl and Shift to make multiple selections.

ADD A LISTBOX CONTROL

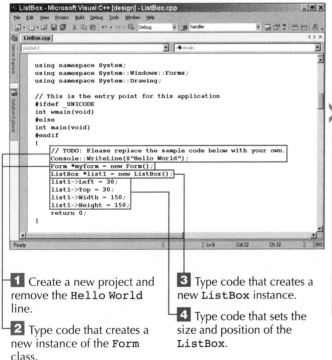

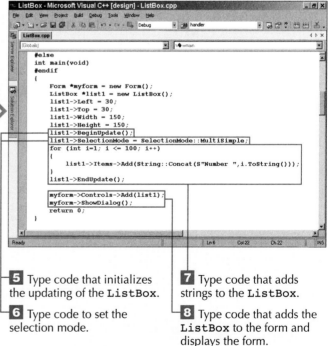

■1 Create a new project and remove the Hello World line.

■2 Type code that creates a new instance of the Form class.

■3 Type code that creates a new ListBox instance.

■4 Type code that sets the size and position of the ListBox.

■5 Type code that initializes the updating of the ListBox.

■6 Type code to set the selection mode.

■7 Type code that adds strings to the ListBox.

■8 Type code that adds the ListBox to the form and displays the form.

Extra

The `ListBox` class includes a searching feature. You can search for items in the list using the `FindString` method and the `FindStringExactmethod`. `FindString` searches without regard to case, while `FindStringExact` searches with regard to case. To use `FindString`, you specify the string for which you want to search.

Example:
```
// Create the list box and then:
list1->Items->Add(S"Jenniffer");
list1->Items->Add(S"John");
list1->Items->Add(S"Jane");
list1->Items->Add(S"Frank");
list1->Items->Add(S"Jeff");
list1->Items->Add(S"Elizabeth");
// Then later, search:
int found = list->FindString("jenniffer");
Console::WriteLine(found);
found = list->FindString("jeff");
Console::WriteLine(found);
found = list->FindString("mark");
Console::WriteLine(found);
```

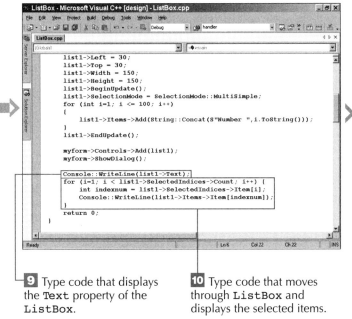

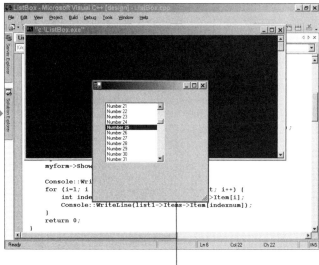

9 Type code that displays the **Text** property of the **ListBox**.

10 Type code that moves through **ListBox** and displays the selected items.

11 Compile and run the program.

■ The program window opens. When you select items in the **ListBox** and close the window, the console displays the text and selected items.

ADD A CHECKEDLISTBOX CONTROL

You can give your users the ability to check items off in a list using the `CheckedListBox` control. This control displays items in a vertical list. Each item in the list includes a small check box to the left. The users can scroll through the list and check the check box beside the items. Your program can manipulate the list by adding items, removing items, or clearing all the items from the list by calling various methods within the `Item` property. These methods include `Add` for adding a single item, `AddRange` for adding an array of items, `RemoveAt` for removing an item based on its index, and `Clear` for removing all the items.

The `CheckedListBox` class includes a `CheckedIndices` property that is an array containing the items that are currently checked. Your program can determine whether an item is checked by inspecting whether its index is in the

array. Alternatively, your program can inspect the `CheckedItems` property, an array containing all the items that are checked.

The `CheckedListBox` class also includes various properties for setting its appearance. You can set the `Font` property with a new `Font` instance to specify the font for the text. You can set `ThreeDCheckBoxes` to `true` to give the boxes a 3D look.

The `CheckedListBox` class also includes properties that it inherits from the `Control` class, such as `Location` for specifying its position on the form, `DockStyle` for specifying if it stays against one edge of the form or perhaps fills the form, and `BorderStyle` for specifying whether it has a single border, a 3D border, or no border at all.

ADD A CHECKEDLISTBOX CONTROL

1 Create a new dialog-based project.

2 Type the lines to give the program access to the windowing and graphics libraries.

3 Type a code that creates a new form.

4 Type code to create a new `CheckedListBox`.

5 Type code to suspend the form layout.

6 Type code that sets the location and docking of the `CheckedListBox`.

7 Type code that sets the border style and font for the control, and turns on a 3D look.

Extra

Because the `CheckedListBox` is inherited from `ListBox`, you can respond to events as if it were a standard `listbox`. For example, the user can select a line in the `listbox` without checking it, and you can respond to this event through the `SelectedValueChanged` event. The following code attaches the handler.

Example:
```
checkedlistbox->SelectedValueChanged +=
    new EventHandler(handler,Handlers::changed);
```

The following code responds to the event:

```
__gc class Handlers {
public:
    void changed(System::Object* sender, EventArgs* e) {
        Console::WriteLine(S"Changed");
    }
};
```

You can list checked items to discover what items the user checked by looping through the `CheckedItems` property container.

Example:
```
for (int i=0; i<checkedlistbox->CheckedItems->Count; i++) {
    Console::WriteLine(checkedlistbox->CheckedItems->Item[i]);
}
```

8 Type a list of items to put in the checklist.

9 Type code that adds the items to the `CheckedListBox`.

10 Type code that adds the `CheckedListBox` to the form and resumes the layout.

11 Type code to show the form as a dialog box.

12 Compile and run the program.

■ The `CheckedListBox` appears in the form.

ADD A COMBOBOX CONTROL

Many Windows programs include a control that appears as a TextBox with a small arrow to the right of it pointing downward. When you click this arrow, a ListBox appears. You can click an item in the list to appear inside the TextBox. Together, this TextBox and drop-down ListBox are known as a ComboBox.

You can add a ComboBox to your form with the help of the ComboBox class found in the .NET framework. This class provides methods and properties for creating the list that appears in the drop-down list. Further, you can specify whether the user is permitted to type into the EditBox, or if the user can only choose an item from the drop-down list.

To add a ComboBox, you create an instance of the ComboBox class. You set its size by setting the Width property. Note that although the Height property exists, you do not need to set it because the ComboBox will

assume a default height for the text box. You set the position with the Left and Top properties. Next, you specify the DropDownStyle. Set this to ComboBoxStyle::DropDownList to allow the user to choose an item from the list, but not to type into the TextBox control. To allow the user to type into the TextBox control, set this property to ComboBoxStyle::DropDown.

Next, you can specify the strings that appear in the list by calling the Add item of the ComboBox control's Items property. You pass a string to this function. Call this method for each item that you want to add to the list.

Finally, you can determine which item the user chose by inspecting the ComboBox control's Text property to get the text; or, you can inspect the SelectedIndex property to get the index into the list.

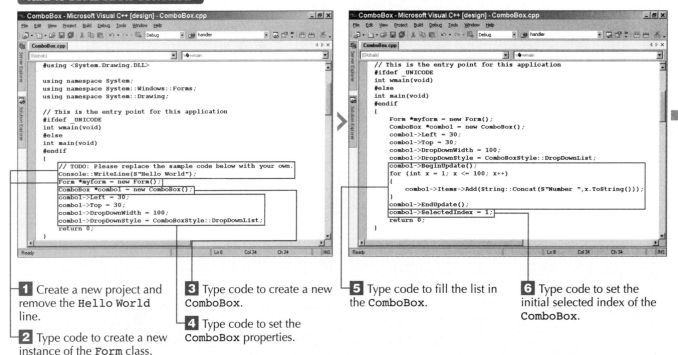

1 Create a new project and remove the Hello World line.

2 Type code to create a new instance of the Form class.

3 Type code to create a new ComboBox.

4 Type code to set the ComboBox properties.

5 Type code to fill the list in the ComboBox.

6 Type code to set the initial selected index of the ComboBox.

Extra

You can change the size of the drop-down `ListBox` by specifying the maximum number of items that can appear in it before a scroll bar is added. You do this by setting the `MaxDropDownItems` property. For example, if you want at most ten items to appear in the list, you would type the following:

```
combo1->MaxDropDownItems = 10;
```

If the list contains ten or fewer items, all will appear in the ListBox. If the list contains more than ten items, only ten will appear at any time with a scrollbar, allowing the user to scroll through all the items.

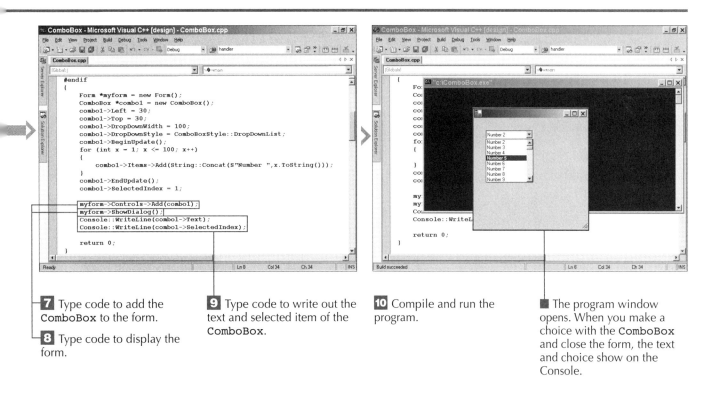

7 Type code to add the **ComboBox** to the form.

8 Type code to display the form.

9 Type code to write out the text and selected item of the **ComboBox**.

10 Compile and run the program.

■ The program window opens. When you make a choice with the **ComboBox** and close the form, the text and choice show on the Console.

ADD A PROGRESSBAR CONTROL

Windows provides you with a standard control called a *ProgressBar*. The ProgressBar appears as a horizontal bar filled with small blocks that gradually fill up from left to right. This control usually serves as an indicator to the user representing how much work has been done and how much is remaining. As the bars grow from left to right, the work is closer to being finished.

The .NET framework provides you with the ProgressBar class that makes it easy for you to include a ProgressBar control on your form.

The ProgressBar class is easy to use. You simple create a new instance of ProgressBar, and then, like the other controls, set its Width, Height, Top, and Bottom properties to specify its size and position. Then, you specify a range of numbers that the bar represents by setting its

Minimum property and its Maximum property. Typical values for these are 0 and 100, respectively.

You can then set the position of the blocks within the ProgressBar by setting the Value property. You can set this property anywhere from the value set in Minimum to the value set in Maximum. As your program performs its work, you can change the Value property.

If your program is doing a great deal of work, the ProgressBar is a useful control for letting the user know that there is still work to be done. Further, it helps prevent the user from growing frustrated, because he or she can get an idea of how much time is left before your program is finished. If you do not include such a notification, the user might not realize your program is still functioning, and may think that it has stopped.

ADD A PROGRESSBAR CONTROL

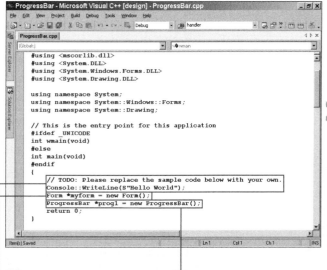

1 Create a new project and remove the Hello World line.

2 Type code to create a new instance of the Form class.

3 Type code to create a new ProgressBar.

4 Type code that sets the position of the ProgressBar.

5 Type code that sets the range of the ProgressBar.

6 Type code that sets the value and width of the ProgressBar.

■ You can set these properties in any order.

Extra

Instead of setting the `Value` property of the `ProgressBar` directly, you can set the `Value` property to a starting point. Then, you can set the `Step` value to an incremental amount. Next, each time you call the `PerformStep()` method, the `ProgressBar` will automatically increase the `Value` property by the amount in the `Step` property. Further, each time you call `PerformStep()`, you can update a label control with the `Value` property.

Example:
```
// This would go outside your main function
__gc class Handlers {
public:
    ProgressBar *prog;
    Label *lab;
    void button_Click(System::Object* s, System::EventArgs* e) {
        prog->PerformStep();
        lab->Text = String::Concat(prog->Value.ToString(), S"%");
    }
};
// This would go inside your main function
prog1->Step = 5;
Handlers *handler = new Handlers();
handler->prog = prog1;
handler->lab = lab1;
b1->Click += new System::EventHandler(handler,
    Handlers::button_Click);
```

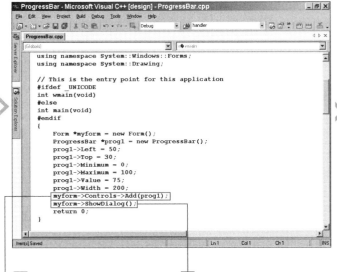

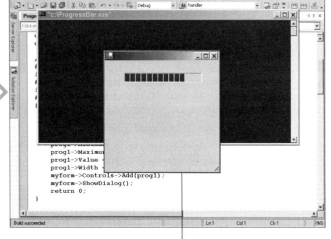

7 Type code that adds the `ProgressBar` to the form.

8 Type code that displays the form.

9 Compile and run the program.

■ The program window opens, showing the progress bar at the value you chose.

ADD AN UPDOWN CONTROL

Some Windows programs include an edit control with a small control to its right that has an arrow on top pointing upward and an arrow on the bottom pointing downward. The edit control contains a number within a range or a string in a list. When the user clicks the arrow buttons, the edit control moves through the numbers or the strings. You can easily add this functionality to your program using the UpDown control. The .NET framework has two types of UpDown controls: a DomainUpDown class for strings and a NumericUpDown class for numbers.

To use the control, you create a new instance and set its standard control properties, such as Location and BorderStyle. For a NumericUpDown control, you set the

range of numbers by setting its Minimum and Maximum properties, and set the starting point by setting its Value property. For the DomainUpDown class, you supply a list of strings by calling the item property Add method for each string.

With each type of UpDown control, the user can optionally enter any number of strings into the edit control. If you prefer to force the user to select from an item in the list, then set the ReadOnly property to true. For the DomainUpDown control, when ReadOnly is true, typing a letter moves the list to the next item in the list that begins with that letter.

ADD AN UPDOWN CONTROL

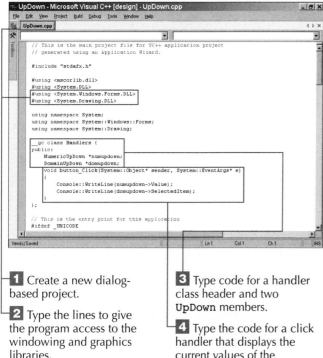

1 Create a new dialog-based project.

2 Type the lines to give the program access to the windowing and graphics libraries.

3 Type code for a handler class header and two UpDown members.

4 Type the code for a click handler that displays the current values of the UpDown controls.

5 Type a line to create a new form.

6 Type code to suspend the form's layout.

7 Type code to create a numeric UpDown control and set its location and border style.

8 Type code to set the minimum, maximum, and initial value of the numeric UpDown control.

Extra

The `UpDown` class includes an event handler for when the user chooses a different value. By using this, you can easily respond to the particular choice the user made. For example, if one `UpDown` control contains a list of months, and another contains a list of numbered days in the month, you can easily adjust the second control to have the correct number of days whenever the first control changes. To do this, you need to set a property to attach the event handler.

Example:

```
__gc class Handlers {
public:
    NumericUpDown *numupdown;
    DomainUpDown *domupdown;
    void domupdown_Change(System::Object *sender, System::EventArgs* e) {
        GregorianCalendar *cal = new System::Globalization:GregorianCalendar();
        numupdown->Maximum = cal->GetDaysInMonth(2002, domupdown->SelectedIndex + 1);
    }
};
```

You then attach the event handler to the `SelectedItemChanged` event using this code:

```
Handlers *handler = new Handlers();
handler->numupdown = numupdown;
handler->domupdown = domupdown;
domupdown->SelectedItemChanged += new System::EventHandler(
    handler, Handlers::domupdown_Change);
```

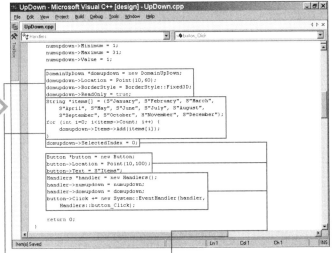

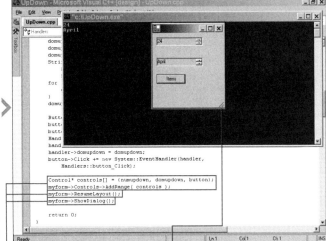

9 Type code to create a domain `UpDown` control, to set its location and border style, and to set its `ReadOnly` to `true`.

10 Type code to create a list of strings and insert them into the domain `UpDown` control.

11 Type code to initialize the index of the `UpDown` control.

12 Type code to create a button and set its caption.

13 Type code to create a handler and insert the handler into the `Click` event of the button control.

14 Type code to add the controls to the form.

15 Type code to resume the form layout.

16 Type code to show the form as a dialog box.

17 Compile and run the program.

■ The window appears showing the two `UpDown` controls. You can display their contents by clicking the button.

ADD AN IMAGELIST CONTROL

I f your program deals with several bitmap or icon images, such as the icons found on a toolbar, you can easily manage the icons using an ImageList object. As you load images, you place them in an ImageList and make the list available to other controls such as a toolbar or a Listview.

Each icon or bitmap within a single ImageList control must have the same width and the same height, but the images themselves do not have to be perfect squares. Their widths can be different from their heights. If you have one set of images with certain dimensions, they can all go in a single ImageList. Images of another dimension must go in another ImageList. Controls that use ImageLists are built with this understanding. For example, a ListView control, which is the control used by Windows Explorer for displaying files within folders, has two associated ImageLists, one for the large icons and one for the small icons.

To use an ImageList, create an instance and set the image dimensions with its ImageSize property. Load the images by calling its Image property Add method, passing an Icon instance or a Bitmap instance. If you are loading the image from a file, the easiest way is to pass Image::FromFile(filename) where filename is a string representing the name of the file.

The ImageList control also has the ability to read in a single image that contains multiple icons arranged side by side. For example, if you have a toolbar with 15 icons, each with a width of 22 pixels and a height of 20 pixels, you might have all 15 images saved in a single bitmap 330 pixels wide and 20 pixels high. To load these images into an ImageList object, you call its Image property AddStrip method.

ADD AN IMAGELIST CONTROL

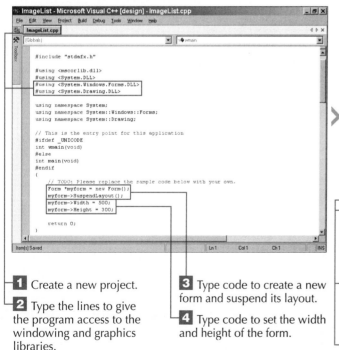

1 Create a new project.

2 Type the lines to give the program access to the windowing and graphics libraries.

3 Type code to create a new form and suspend its layout.

4 Type code to set the width and height of the form.

5 Type code to create a new **ImageList** object and set the size of the images it will hold.

6 Type code to choose the color of the images that will show transparent when the images are displayed.

7 Type code to add a strip of images to the **ImageList** object.

Extra

By using a `PictureBox`, you can view the images in the `ImageList` by cycling through the Images property of the `ImageList`, and displaying them in the `PictureBox`.

Example:
```
__gc class Handlers {
public:
    ImageList *imageList1;
    PictureBox *picturebox;
    int current;
    void next(System::Object* sender, EventArgs* e) {
        if (current < imageList1->Images->Count - 1) {
            current++;
            picturebox->Image = imageList1->Images-
>Item[current];
        }
    }
    void prev(System::Object* sender, EventArgs* e) {
        if (current > 0) {
            current-;
            picturebox->Image = imageList1->Images-
>Item[current];
        }
    }
};
```

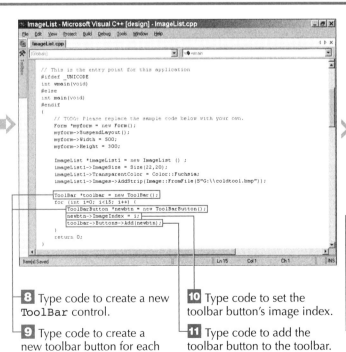

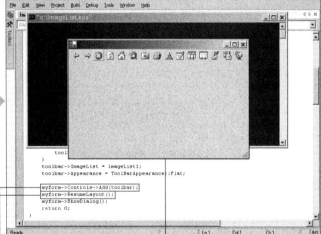

8 Type code to create a new **ToolBar** control.

9 Type code to create a new toolbar button for each image.

10 Type code to set the toolbar button's image index.

11 Type code to add the toolbar button to the toolbar.

12 Type code to add the **ToolBar** control to the form.

13 Type code to resume the form's layout.

14 Compile and run the program.

■ The window appears with a toolbar displaying the images from the **ImageList** object.

ADD A LISTVIEW CONTROL

Microsoft Windows makes extensive use of the `ListView` control, and you can include it in your programs to give them a standard Windows look. The `ListView` holds a set of items that display as icons with titles under them, as a set of small icons with titles beside them, as a list of names and icons, or as a detailed report listing with column headers. You see this control in Windows Explorer when you view a folder with icons representing files. The control allows you to add event handlers that respond to clicks or double-clicks on particular icons.

To use the control, create an instance of it and add its items. Each item includes a string representing the title of the icon, a tag property through which you can store an object such as a full path and filename if the icon represents a file and a

list of subitems that are the strings appearing in columns when the `ListView` is in detail mode.

To use the control, you also include a list of large and small icons by using two `ImageList` objects, one for the large icons and one for the small icons. Each icon in the `ImageList` objects has an index number associated with it.

To add an item to the `ListView` control, create an instance of `ListViewItem`, passing the icon title to the constructor. You then set the `ImageIndex` property, which is the index into the `ImageList` objects. Because there is only one `ImageIndex` property, the same index serves both the small icon and the large icon `ImageLists`.

ADD A LISTVIEW CONTROL

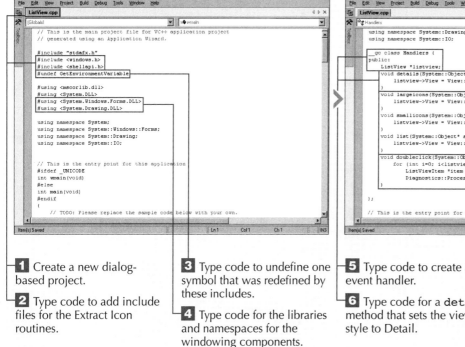

■1 Create a new dialog-based project.

■2 Type code to add include files for the Extract Icon routines.

■3 Type code to undefine one symbol that was redefined by these includes.

■4 Type code for the libraries and namespaces for the windowing components.

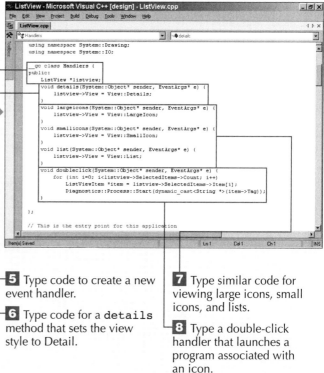

■5 Type code to create a new event handler.

■6 Type code for a **details** method that sets the view style to Detail.

■7 Type similar code for viewing large icons, small icons, and lists.

■8 Type a double-click handler that launches a program associated with an icon.

Extra

The `ListView` control includes a `DoubleClick` event handler that runs when the user double-clicks one of the icons. You can add your own code by specifying an event handler for the `DoubleClick` event. Inside this event handler, you can obtain the item that was double-clicked by the `Listview` `SelectedItems` array. This array contains a list of all the selected items. In the case of a double-click, this array will contain only one item. However, if you are responding to another event such as a menu click, the user could select multiple items, in which case all the items appear in the `SelectedItems` array. However, for the user to be able to select multiple items, the `ListView` `MultiSelect` property must be set to `true`.

If your icons represent programs and you want users to be able to start the programs by double-clicking the icons, you can respond to the `DoubleClick` event and call `Diagnostics::Process::Start` passing the name of the program to run. If you show filenames in the `ListView` items, you can store the full path and filename in the `Tag` item by using the following code.

Example:
```
ListViewItem *item = listview->SelectedItems->Item[0];
Diagnostics::Process::Start(dynamic_cast<String *>(item->Tag));
```

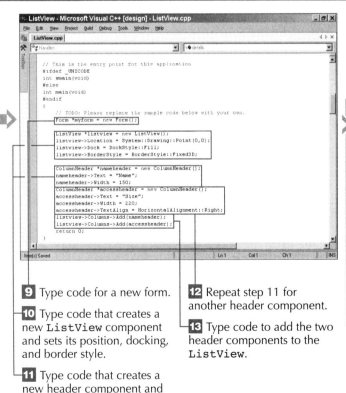

9 Type code for a new form.

10 Type code that creates a new `ListView` component and sets its position, docking, and border style.

11 Type code that creates a new header component and sets its text and width.

12 Repeat step 11 for another header component.

13 Type code to add the two header components to the `ListView`.

14 Type code to create a new `DoubleClick` handler.

15 Type code that creates a new context menu and menu items, and add the context menu to the `Listview`.

16 Type code to obtain the files in the Windows directory that end with .exe.

17 Type code that creates two image lists and suspends the `ListView` drawing.

CONTINUED ▶ 233

ADD A LISTVIEW CONTROL (CONTINUED)

After the Listview is on-screen, you can change its mode of appearance by setting its View property. The four choices are View::Details, View::LargeIcon, View::SmallIcon, and View::List. When you set the property at runtime, the control immediately redraws itself in the appropriate mode.

To add columns to a ListView that appear in the Detail view mode, create a ColumnHeader instance for each column you want in the control. Set the Text property of the instance to the text you want to appear in the column header, and set the Width property to a number representing the initial column of the width. This number is the initial value for the width, and users can adjust the width. However, you will probably want to test various numbers for the width and run the program to make sure they are a reasonable starting point. You can adjust whether

the column header text appears on the left, center, or right of the column by setting the ColumnHeader instance TextAlign property to HorizontalAlignment::Right, HorizontalAlignment::Left, or HorizontalAlignment::Center. After you create each ColumnHeader instance, you add it to the ListView control by calling the Column property Add method.

To specify the information that will appear with each item in the different columns, create a subitem for each column beside the first. The first column is always the same text that appears with the icons in the views other than the detailed report. The text for the remaining columns comes from the subitems. To create a subitem for the item, use the SubItem property for the item and call the SubItem property Add method, passing a string. The string is the text that appears in the column.

ADD A LISTVIEW CONTROL (CONTINUED)

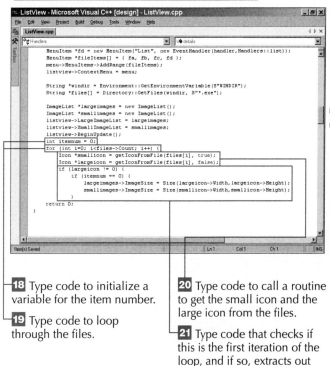

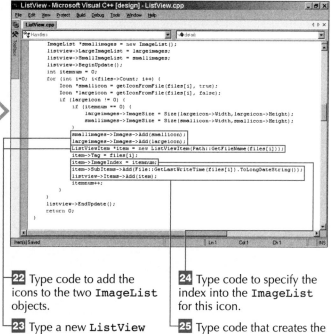

18 Type code to initialize a variable for the item number.

19 Type code to loop through the files.

20 Type code to call a routine to get the small icon and the large icon from the files.

21 Type code that checks if this is the first iteration of the loop, and if so, extracts out the icon sizes and saves them in the ImageLists.

22 Type code to add the icons to the two ImageList objects.

23 Type a new ListView and set its properties.

24 Type code to specify the index into the ImageList for this icon.

25 Type code that creates the subitem and adds the item to the ListView.

Extra

If you need to load icons from a file in the same manner that Windows Explorer uses, you can call the `SHFileInfo` function.

Example:
```
#include <windows.h>
#include <shellapi.h>
SHFILEINFO info;
SHGetFileInfo(charfilename, 0, &info, sizeof( SHFILEINFO ), flags);
```

For flags you either pass `SHGFI_ICON | SHGFI_SMALLICON` to obtain the small icon for the file, or `SHGFI_ICON | SHGFI_LARGEICON` to obtain the large icon for the file. This function returns a handle to an icon resource, from which you can build an `Icon` instance with the following call:

```
Icon *icon = Icon::FromHandle(info.hIcon);
```

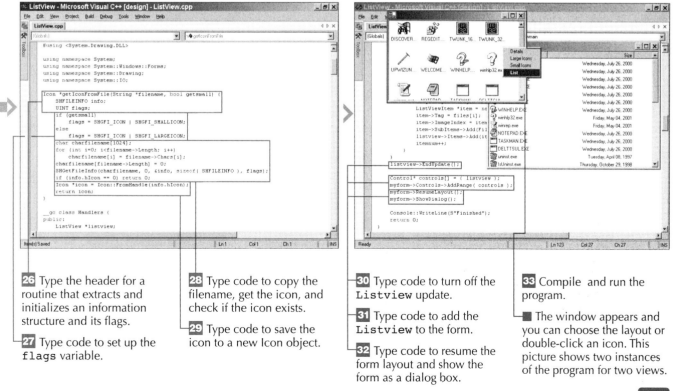

26 Type the header for a routine that extracts and initializes an information structure and its flags.

27 Type code to set up the `flags` variable.

28 Type code to copy the filename, get the icon, and check if the icon exists.

29 Type code to save the icon to a new Icon object.

30 Type code to turn off the `Listview` update.

31 Type code to add the `Listview` to the form.

32 Type code to resume the form layout and show the form as a dialog box.

33 Compile and run the program.

■ The window appears and you can choose the layout or double-click an icon. This picture shows two instances of the program for two views.

ADD A TREEVIEW CONTROL

Windows includes a standard control called a *TreeView*. You see this control on the left column of Windows Explorer. The control is a list of items arranged hierarchically. Each item in the list is called a *node*. A node can have child nodes underneath it, and clicking on a small minus sign beside the parent node can hide these child nodes. When the child nodes are hidden, the minus sign changes to a plus sign. If you click the plus sign, the nodes reappear, and the plus sign changes back to a minus sign.

You create a `TreeView` control by creating an instance of the `TreeView` class. You can set its size and position by setting its `Width`, `Height`, `Left,` and `Top` properties. You then add nodes to the `TreeView` control by calling the `Add` method of the control's `Nodes` property. This will add top-level nodes that have no parent nodes. To add child nodes,

find the node you wish to add children to, and call the `Add` method of its `Nodes` property.

You can determine which node the user selects by inspecting the `SelectedNode` property of the `TreeView`. This contains the node that the user selected, and you can look at the node's `TextProperty` to determine the text on the selected node.

A `TreeView` has vertical and horizontal lines that connect the parent nodes to the child nodes. If you prefer to hide these lines, you can set the `ShowLines` property of the `TreeView` to false. The + and - symbols will still be present. If you prefer to hide the + and - symbols, you can do so by setting the `ShowPlusMinus` property to false. When this is the case, to expand and contract the nodes you must double-click them.

ADD A TREEVIEW CONTROL

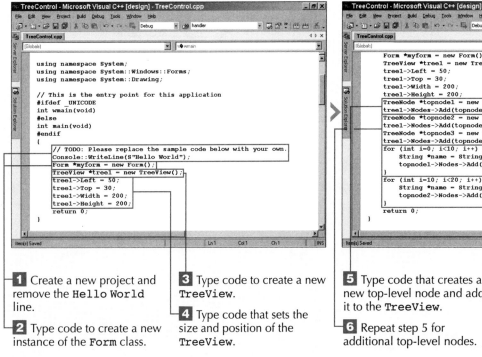

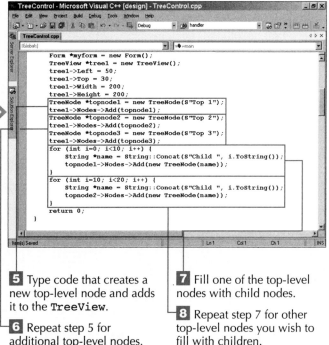

1 Create a new project and remove the `Hello World` line.

2 Type code to create a new instance of the `Form` class.

3 Type code to create a new `TreeView`.

4 Type code that sets the size and position of the `TreeView`.

5 Type code that creates a new top-level node and adds it to the `TreeView`.

6 Repeat step 5 for additional top-level nodes.

7 Fill one of the top-level nodes with child nodes.

8 Repeat step 7 for other top-level nodes you wish to fill with children.

1

Extra

You can add a feature called *hot tracking* to a `TreeView` control. When this feature is turned on, as you move the mouse over a node, the text of the node appears with an underline showing that you can click the node much like a Web page. To turn this feature on, simply set the `HotTracking` property of the `TreeView` control to true.

Nodes in a `TreeView` can have check boxes to the left of them. This allows the users of your program to check off multiple items inside the `TreeView`. To turn on this feature, set the `CheckBoxes` property to true. You can then determine if a node is checked or unchecked by inspecting its `Checked` property. Because the users can check multiple nodes, you will need to go through each node in the `TreeView` and inspect the `Checked` property of each node separately.

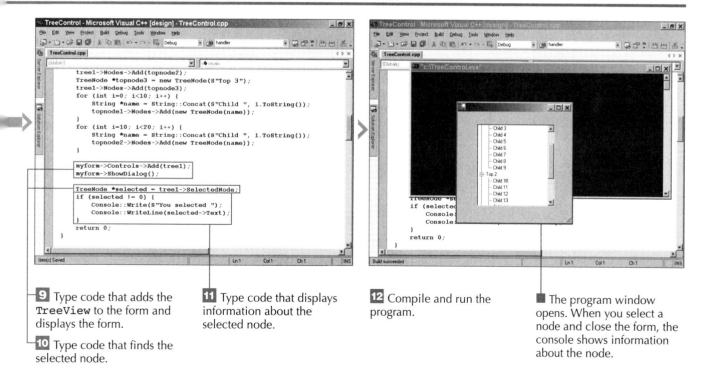

■9 Type code that adds the **TreeView** to the form and displays the form.

■10 Type code that finds the selected node.

■11 Type code that displays information about the selected node.

■12 Compile and run the program.

■ The program window opens. When you select a node and close the form, the console shows information about the node.

ADD A RICHTEXTBOX CONTROL

You can give your users the ability to enter high-quality text with formatting such as font size and colors, and to save and load the text using a file format known as *Rich Text Format*, or RTF. To do this, you use the RichTextBox control. This control is a text editor that includes the formatting functionality.

The RichTextBox includes methods and properties for setting the styles of the text either for the whole control or for only portions of it. It includes events for responding to various user actions, such as when the text control changes.

To use the control, create a new instance of RichTextBox with no parameters in the constructor. Without any further setup, the control is a basic text editor. You will set most additional properties in response to user actions. For example, if the user chooses a Font button on your form, you would open the FontDialog window, obtain the new

font, and set the font either for the whole control, or, more likely, for the selected text. You can set the font for the selected text with the SelectionFont property by calling:

```
MyRichEdit->SelectionFont =
        MyFontDialog->Font; .
```

You can load text into the RichEditBox using the LoadFile method of the control. You have the choice of loading plain text without any formatting or rich text with formatting. When you call LoadFile, you specify the filename as RichTextBoxStreamType::PlainText if the file contains plain text or RichTextBoxStreamType::RichText for rich-text with formatting. Similarly, you can save the text in the file using the SaveFile method. The parameters are the same as for the LoadFile method.

ADD A RICHTEXTBOX CONTROL

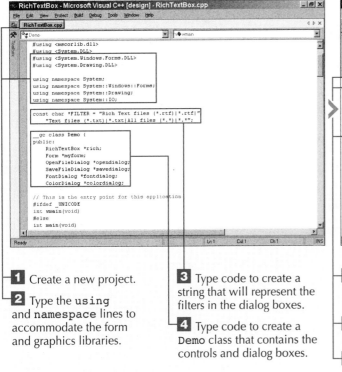

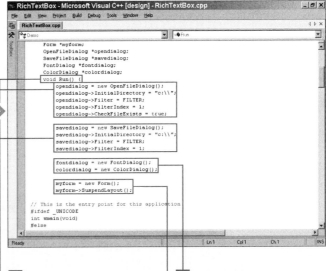

1 Create a new project.

2 Type the using and namespace lines to accommodate the form and graphics libraries.

3 Type code to create a string that will represent the filters in the dialog boxes.

4 Type code to create a Demo class that contains the controls and dialog boxes.

5 Type a Run method to the class that will contain the primary code.

6 Type code to initialize the OpenFileDialog object.

7 Type code to initialize the SaveFileDialog object.

8 Type code to initialize the Font dialog and Color dialog objects.

9 Type code to create a form and suspend the layout.

Extra

The `RichTextBox` has the ability to automatically highlight Web links found in the text if you set its `DetectUrls` property to `true`. The `RichTextBox` identifies links that start with http://, www., mailto://, news://, or ftp://. It colors the Web links blue and adds an underscore. The user can click these links. By default, nothing happens when the user clicks, but you can add an event handler using the `LinkClicked` event. The following code launches this link in a Web browser, mail program, or news program.

Example:
```
void linkClicked(System::Object* sender, LinkClickedEventArgs* e) {
    Diagnostics::Process::Start(e->LinkText);
}
```

You can set the margins of the edit control using the `RightMargin` and `SelectionIndent` properties. Both take an integer specifying a number of pixels. This allows your users to have greater control over the layout of the text. You can also set a viewable zoom by setting the `ZoomFactor` property. This property is a floating-point value between 0.64 and 64.0, representing a fraction of the original size.

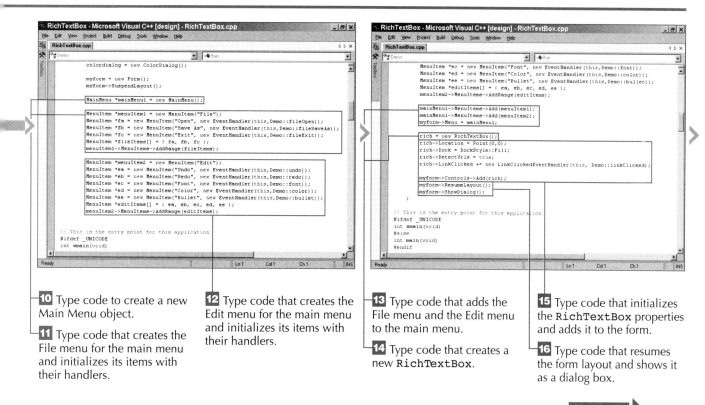

■ **10** Type code to create a new Main Menu object.

■ **11** Type code that creates the File menu for the main menu and initializes its items with their handlers.

■ **12** Type code that creates the Edit menu for the main menu and initializes its items with their handlers.

■ **13** Type code that adds the File menu and the Edit menu to the main menu.

■ **14** Type code that creates a new `RichTextBox`.

■ **15** Type code that initializes the `RichTextBox` properties and adds it to the form.

■ **16** Type code that resumes the form layout and shows it as a dialog box.

CONTINUED ▶

ADD A RICHTEXTBOX CONTROL (CONTINUED)

You generally set up the `RichTextBox` control to almost exclusively respond to user interface commands with little or no setting of the properties up front. For example, you might have a menu item called Open from which you open a `FileOpenDialog` window and then call the `RichTextBox LoadFile` method. You would probably also have a Save menu item from which you open a `SaveAsDialog` window and call the `SaveFile` method.

Similarly, you might have various buttons or menu items for formatting the text, such as Font and Color. These settings would most likely operate on selected text only, rather than the entire document.

The `RichTextBox` contains numerous other features. For example, it is easy to add Undo and Redo menu items. These simply call the `RichTextBox Undo` and `Redo` methods. You can find out the name of the next undo or

redo item by inspecting the `UndoActionName` and `RedoActionName` properties. A good use for these is to place them alongside the titles in the Redo and Undo menu items so the user can view the next redo or undo item.

The control also supports bulleted text. You can toggle the bullets among selected text by setting the `SelectionBullet` property to `true` or `false` by typing:

```
myRichEdit->SelectionBullet =
     !myRichEdit->SelectionBullet; .
```

You can search for text using the `Find` method and supplying a string to search for. Optionally, a `RichTextBoxFinds` enumeration specifies whether the search should be case-sensitive and whether to search for the whole word only. These are both common Find options in most word-processing programs. To search, call the `Find` method, passing the string to search and the optional `RichTextBoxFinds` enums.

ADD A RICHTEXTBOX CONTROL (CONTINUED)

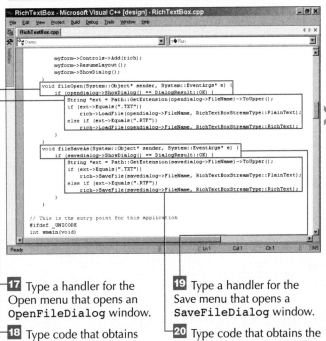

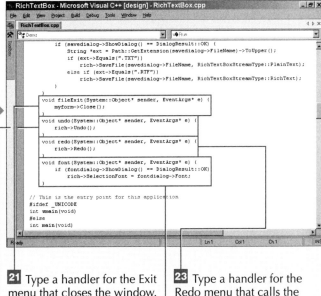

17 Type a handler for the Open menu that opens an **OpenFileDialog** window.

18 Type code that obtains the filename from the Open dialog box and opens the file based on its extension.

19 Type a handler for the Save menu that opens a **SaveFileDialog** window.

20 Type code that obtains the filename from the Save dialog box and saves the file based on its extension.

21 Type a handler for the Exit menu that closes the window.

22 Type a handler for the Undo menu that calls the **RichEditBox** Undo method.

23 Type a handler for the Redo menu that calls the **RichEditBox** Redo method.

24 Type a handler for the Font menu that opens a Font dialog box and sets the font of the selected text.

Extra

You can determine if the text in the RichTextBox has changed. For example, if your user chooses to close the program, you might want to first check to determine if the text has changed since the last save and prompt the user to ask whether to save the file before exiting. To do this, add code setting the Modified property of the RichTextBox to false when you save the file. The RichTextBox automatically changes this property to true as soon as the user types anything in the control. Next, add a handler for the Closing event of the form. In this event, check whether the Modified property of the RichTextBox is true. If so, the user made changes since the last save. You can then pop up a MessageBox class instance asking the user whether to save the file before closing.

Most programs have both a Save and a Save As feature. You can add this feature to your programs that use the RichTextBox control by keeping track of the filename and the state of the control. If the user chooses Save As, you open a Save As dialog box, save the file, and then store the filename in a variable. If the user chooses Save, you first check to determine if the filename variable contains a string. If not, you open the Save As dialog box and perform the same operations as a Save As. If the filename variable contains a string, you do not open the Save As dialog box; instead, you simply save the file using the name in the filename variable.

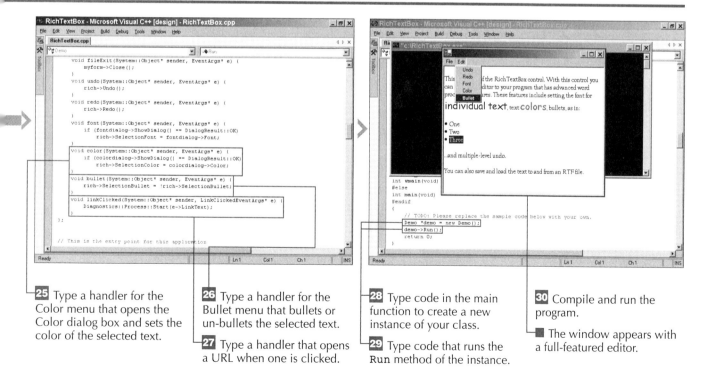

■25 Type a handler for the Color menu that opens the Color dialog box and sets the color of the selected text.

■26 Type a handler for the Bullet menu that bullets or un-bullets the selected text.

■27 Type a handler that opens a URL when one is clicked.

■28 Type code in the main function to create a new instance of your class.

■29 Type code that runs the Run method of the instance.

■30 Compile and run the program.

■ The window appears with a full-featured editor.

DISPLAY A COLORDIALOG DIALOG BOX

You can give your users the ability to changes colors in your program. For example, you might have a preferences window, where you allow the users to set the colors of the text in your program. Or, if you are writing a graphics program, you would probably want to give your users the ability to change the colors of the graphics. To do this, you can display a ColorDialog dialog box, allowing the users to choose a color. This is a standard dialog box that you have likely seen in other programs. The .NET framework makes it easy for you to display this dialog box using the ColorDialog class.

To use the ColorDialog class, you create a new instance of ColorDialog, and call the ShowDialog method. If you put this code inside an if statement, you can check the result of the call to ShowDialog. If the result is equal to

DialogResult::OK, then it means the user pressed OK. Otherwise, the user pressed Cancel.

If the user pressed Cancel, you should not make any color changes. But if the user pressed OK, then you can retrieve the color the user chose by checking the Color property of the ColorDialog instance. This property will contain the red, green, and blue components of the color chosen, as well as a color name. The components will be a number in the range of 0 to 255. The system knows approximately 300 names of colors, and if the red, green, and blue components match one of the predefined names, then the Name member of the Color property will contain this name. For example, if the red component is 0, the green component is 255, and the blue component is 0, the Name member will be lime.

DISPLAY A COLORDIALOG DIALOG BOX

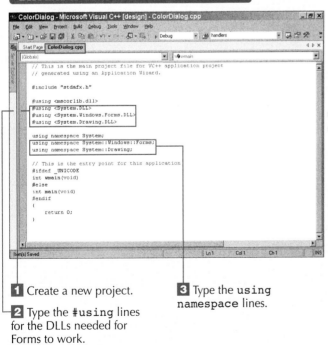

1 Create a new project.

2 Type the #using lines for the DLLs needed for Forms to work.

3 Type the using namespace lines.

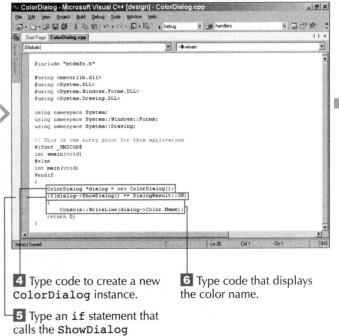

4 Type code to create a new ColorDialog instance.

5 Type an if statement that calls the ShowDialog method.

6 Type code that displays the color name.

Extra

After you display a `ColorDialog`, you can use the color in a user interface. To set the color of the form or a control, simply set the `Color` or `BackColor` property of the form or control to the `Color` property of the `ColorDialog` instance.

Example:
```cpp
#include "stdafx.h"
#using <mscorlib.dll>
#using <System.DLL>
#using <System.Windows.Forms.DLL>
#using <System.Drawing.DLL>
using namespace System;
using namespace System::Windows::Forms;
using namespace System::Drawing;
void main(void) {
    ColorDialog *dialog = new ColorDialog();
    if(dialog->ShowDialog() == DialogResult::OK)
    {
        Form *form = new Form();

        form->BackColor = dialog->Color;

        form->ShowDialog();
    }
}
```

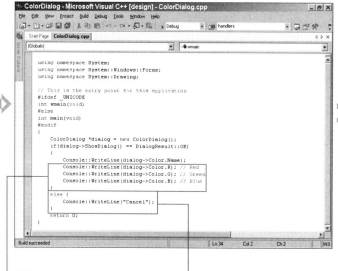

-7 Type code that displays the components of the color.

-8 Type code that runs if the user presses Cancel in the dialog box.

-9 Compile and run the program.

■ The program starts and the Color dialog box opens. If you choose OK, the color information appears in the console.

Visual C++ .NET

DISPLAY AN OPENFILEDIALOG DIALOG BOX

Windows provides a standard Open dialog box that most applications use. With the .NET framework, you can easily create an Open dialog box using the OpenFileDialog class found in the System.Windows.Forms namespace. To use the class, create a new instance of it and call its ShowDialog method. This method returns a value of either DialogResult::OK or DialogResult::Cancel. If you receive DialogResult::OK, you can obtain the filename chosen by inspecting the FileName member of the OpenFileDialog instance.

As with all the Forms classes, before you can use them in a C++ program, you need to include the following lines:

```
#using <System.DLL>
#using <System.Windows.Forms.DLL>
using namespace System::IO;
```

The OpenFileDialog window includes a filter where the user can choose to view only files of a certain type having a certain extension. You can set up a filter by setting the Filter property of the OpenFileDialog instance. This property is a string. For example, if you set this property to "Text files (*.txt)|*.txt|All files (*.*)|*.*", the filter contains two entries, one for text files with a .txt extension and one for all files with any extension. You list the filter types in the string separated by a vertical bar symbol (|). For each filter type, you type the name of the filter, followed by the actual file filter using the * wildcard in parentheses.

You can also specify the starting directory that appears in the Open dialog box by setting the InitialDirectory property. If you want to ensure that the user chooses a file that exists, rather than typing in a file that does not exist, set the CheckFileExists property to true. Finally, if you want to easily open the chosen file, the OpenFileDialog includes a method called OpenFile that allows you to open the file directly without having to call the File::Open method.

DISPLAY AN OPENFILEDIALOG DIALOG BOX

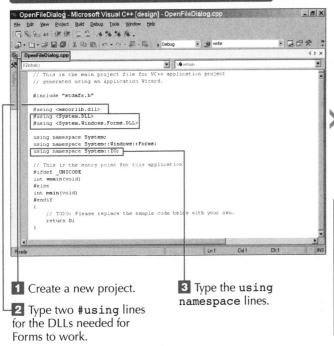

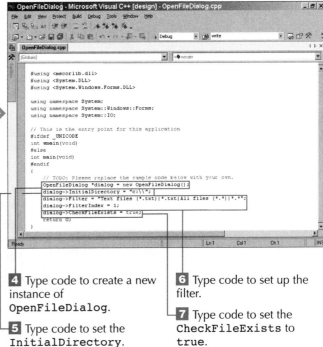

1 Create a new project.

2 Type two #using lines for the DLLs needed for Forms to work.

3 Type the using namespace lines.

4 Type code to create a new instance of OpenFileDialog.

5 Type code to set the InitialDirectory.

6 Type code to set up the filter.

7 Type code to set the CheckFileExists to true.

■ Setting the value to true ensures that the user chooses a file that exists.

244

Extra

You can also use the `OpenFileDialog` to allow the user to choose multiple files to open using the Shift and Control keys, provided the files are all within the same folder. To do this, set the `Multiselect` to true, and after the user clicks OK, inspect the `FileNames` member.

Example:
```
OpenFileDialog *dialog = new OpenFileDialog();
dialog->InitialDirectory = "c:\\";
dialog->Filter = "Text files (*.txt)|*.txt|All files (*.*)|*.*";
dialog->FilterIndex = 1;
dialog->CheckFileExists = true;
dialog->Multiselect = true;
if(dialog->ShowDialog() == DialogResult::OK)
{
    for (int i=0; i<dialog->FileNames->Count; i++) {
        Console::WriteLine(dialog->FileNames[i]);
    }
}
else {
    Console::WriteLine("Cancel");
}
return 0;
```

If you need to display the Open dialog box multiple times in your code, you need to create only one instance of the `OpenFileDialog` class and simply call `ShowDialog()` each time you need to display it. Having one instance not only saves memory space, but offers the added benefit that the dialog box remembers the last directory from which the user opened a file, provided you set the `RestoreDirectory` property to true. However, if you prefer to delete the instance after each use and re-create it when you need it, you can achieve the same result by not setting the `InitialDirectory` property.

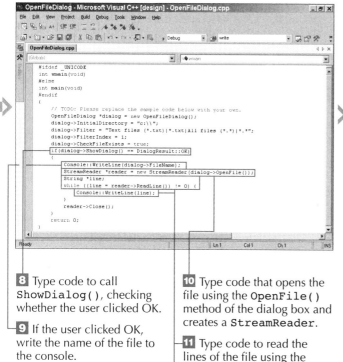

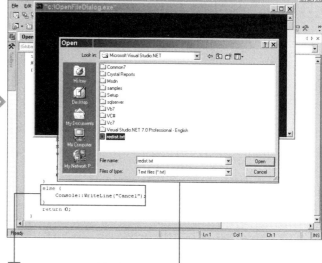

8 Type code to call `ShowDialog()`, checking whether the user clicked OK.

9 If the user clicked OK, write the name of the file to the console.

10 Type code that opens the file using the `OpenFile()` method of the dialog box and creates a `StreamReader`.

11 Type code to read the lines of the file using the `ReadLine` method.

12 Type code to print each line to the console.

13 Type an `else` block that runs when the user clicks Cancel to display a message to the console.

14 Compile and run the program.

■ The standard Windows Open dialog box appears. If you choose a text file, its contents appear in the console.

DISPLAY A SAVEFILEDIALOG DIALOG BOX

The .NET framework provides access to the common dialog boxes found in Windows, including the Save As dialog box. Using the `SaveFileDialog` class found in the `System::Windows::Forms` namespace, you can easily open a Save As dialog box, allowing your users to enter a filename to save data to.

To use the `SaveFileDialog` class, you create an instance of it and call its `ShowDialog()` method. `ShowDialog()` returns either `DialogResult::OK` or `DialogResult::Cancel` if the user clicks OK or Cancel, respectively. After the user clicks OK, you can obtain the name of the file by checking the `FileName` property.

Before you can use the `SaveFileDialog` class, you need to include the following lines in your program:

```
#using <System.DLL>
#using <System.Windows.Forms.DLL>
using namespace System::IO;
```

The `SaveFileDialog` class includes a property called `OverwritePrompt` that lets you tell the dialog box whether to warn the user if the user chooses a file that already exists. When set to `true`, if the user chooses a file that already exists, the dialog box prompts the user with a message box that shows the name of the file, a message that it exists, and a question, `Do you want to replace it?` The user can then click Yes or No. If the user clicks Yes, the dialog box closes, and you can obtain the filename through the `FileName` property. If the user clicks No, the user returns to the dialog box to enter a different file.

The `SaveFileDialog` class supports filtering, allowing you to specify that only certain files appear based on their extensions. You specify these extensions using the `Filter` property, such as `dialog->Filter = "Text files (*.txt)|*.txt|All files (*.*)|*.*";`.

DISPLAY A SAVEFILEDIALOG DIALOG BOX

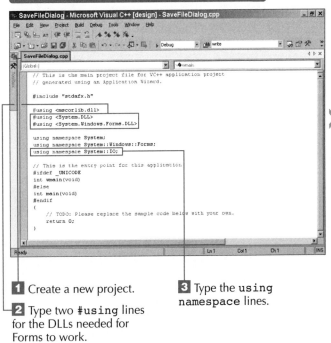

1 Create a new project.

2 Type two **#using** lines for the DLLs needed for Forms to work.

3 Type the **using namespace** lines.

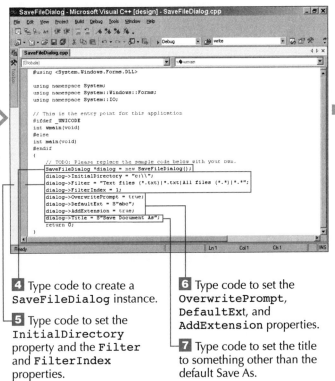

4 Type code to create a `SaveFileDialog` instance.

5 Type code to set the `InitialDirectory` property and the **Filter** and **FilterIndex** properties.

6 Type code to set the `OverwritePrompt`, `DefaultExt`, and `AddExtension` properties.

7 Type code to set the title to something other than the default Save As.

■ This title will appear at the top of the dialog box when it opens in your program.

Extra

You can set up the `SaveFileDialog` to automatically append a file extension if the user fails to specify one. For example, if you are saving text documents with a .txt extension and the user simply enters `MyFile`, you can set up the dialog box to automatically append .txt to the filename. When you retrieve the name through the `FileName` property, it has a .txt extension. Set the `AddExtension` property to true and set the extension in the `DefaultExt` member without the dot.

Example:
```
dialog->DefaultExt = S"txt";
dialog->AddExtension = true;
```

Be careful using the `SaveFileDialog::OpenFile` method. If the file already exists, it is replaced by the data you write to it. If you prefer to append to the existing data, do not use `SaveFileDialog::OpenFile`. Instead, call `File::Open(dialog->FileName, FileMode::Append)`.

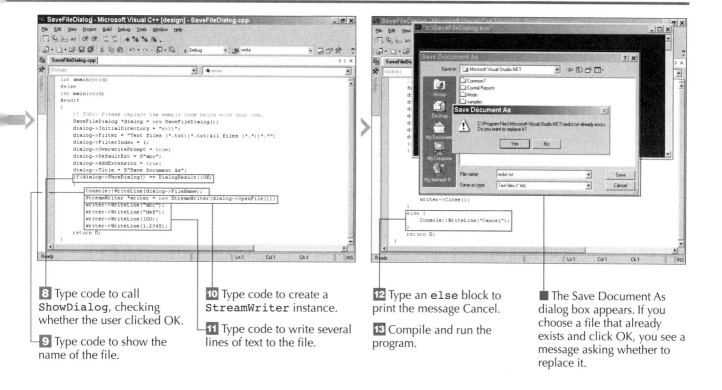

8 Type code to call `ShowDialog`, checking whether the user clicked OK.

9 Type code to show the name of the file.

10 Type code to create a `StreamWriter` instance.

11 Type code to write several lines of text to the file.

12 Type an **else** block to print the message Cancel.

13 Compile and run the program.

■ The Save Document As dialog box appears. If you choose a file that already exists and click OK, you see a message asking whether to replace it.

DISPLAY A FONTDIALOG DIALOG BOX

I f you are writing a program that involves displaying text, you can give your users the ability to set the font, size, and style of the text. For example, if you are writing a word processing program, you might want to allow your users to choose the font used for displaying the text. Or, you might want to give your users the ability to choose the font that appears on the buttons and in the controls in your window.

The .NET framework makes it easy for you to show the FontDialog dialog box, which is one of the standard dialog boxes found in the Windows system. You have likely seen this dialog box in many programs; it lets you choose a font name such as Arial or Times New Roman, and a font size, and a style such as bold or italic.

To display the FontDialog dialog box, you create a new instance of FontDialog, and call its ShowDialog method.

You then check the result of the ShowDialog call. If the result is DialogResult::OK, then the user pressed the OK button. Otherwise, the user pressed the Cancel button.

If the user pressed the Cancel button, you should not make any changes to the fonts. But if the user pressed the OK button, you can determine the font the user chose by inspecting the Font property of the FontDialog instance. This is an instance of class Font, and it contains the necessary information to define a font. One such member is the SizeInPoints member, which is the size the user chose, such as 12 point or 10 point. Other members include Bold, Italic, and Underline, which are Boolean values, and Name which is a string representing the face name, such as Arial or Times New Roman.

DISPLAY A FONTDIALOG DIALOG BOX

1 Create a new project.

2 Type the #using lines for the DLLs needed for Forms to work.

3 Type the using namespace lines.

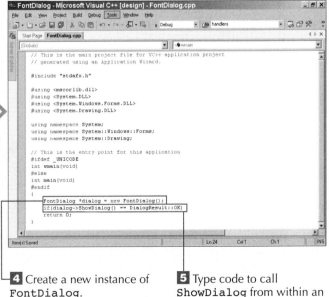

4 Create a new instance of FontDialog.

5 Type code to call ShowDialog from within an if statement.

Extra

When you display a `FontDialog`, you can use the font information that the user selected in a user interface. To do this, simply set the `Font` property of the form or control to the `Font` property of the `FontDialog` instance.

Example:
```cpp
#include "stdafx.h"
#using <mscorlib.dll>
#using <System.DLL>
#using <System.Windows.Forms.DLL>
#using <System.Drawing.DLL>
using namespace System;
using namespace System::Windows::Forms;
using namespace System::Drawing;
void main(void) {
    FontDialog *dialog = new FontDialog();
    if(dialog->ShowDialog() == DialogResult::OK) {
        Form *form = new Form();
        Button *button1 = new Button();
        button1->Text = "Click";

        button1->Font = dialog->Font;

        form->Controls->Add(button1);
        form->ShowDialog();
    }
}
```

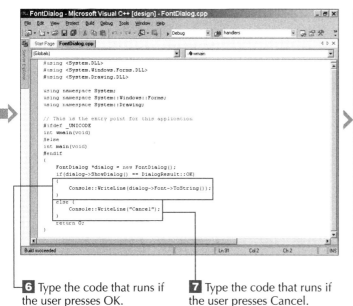

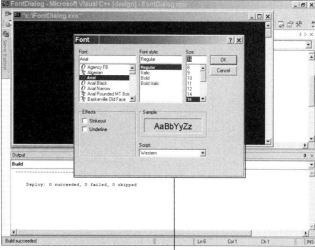

■ **6** Type the code that runs if the user presses OK.

■ **7** Type the code that runs if the user presses Cancel.

■ **8** Compile and run your program.

■ The program starts and the Font dialog box opens. If you choose a font, its information appears in the console.

DISPLAY A PRINTDIALOG DIALOG BOX

If you are writing a program that includes printing features, you can easily display a dialog box that allows the user to select printing attributes, such as which printer to use, and how many pages to print. This dialog box is called the PrintDialog dialog box, and it is a standard part of the Windows system. You have likely seen this dialog box many times when you have used the print features of other programs. The .NET framework includes a PrintDialog class that makes it easy to display this dialog box.

To use the PrintDialog class, first create an instance of PrintDialog, and then initialize its Document member. The PrintDialog object will save the printer settings in the Document member.

To display the dialog box, call the ShowDialog method of the PrintDialog instance. This causes the dialog box to open, displaying the information about the default printer.

The dialog box understands the Windows printer settings; thus, the user can choose other printers and configure them. Your code does not have to do any such configuration; the dialog box does it for you. After the user configures the printers and clicks OK, then the ShowDialog method will return DialogResult::OK. If the user instead clicks Cancel, the ShowDialog method will return DialogResult::Cancel.

With most dialog boxes other than PrintDialog, such as FontDialog, after the call to ShowDialog returns DialogResult::OK, it is up to you to make changes to your program such as changing the font or color. But with PrintDialog, you do not need to make any changes. The PrintDialog class stores all the changes to the printer settings in the Document member for you. Thus, after the call to ShowDialog returns DialogResult::OK, you can begin printing without manually changing any printer settings.

DISPLAY A PRINTDIALOG DIALOG BOX

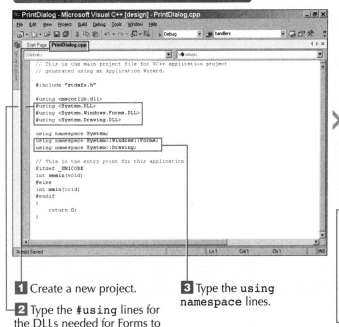

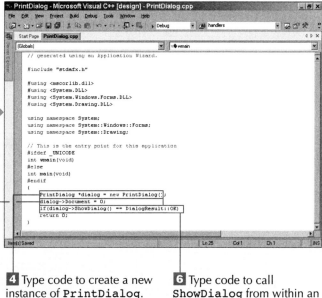

1 Create a new project.

2 Type the #using lines for the DLLs needed for Forms to work.

3 Type the using namespace lines.

4 Type code to create a new instance of PrintDialog.

5 Initialize the members of PrintDialog.

6 Type code to call ShowDialog from within an if statement.

Extra

After you have displayed the Print dialog box, you can easily use the Printing classes to print a document. To print a document, create a new `PrintDocument` object, and save it in the `PrintDialog::Document` member before calling `PrintDialog::ShowDialog`. Create an event handler of type `PrintPage` event, and call `PrintDialog::Document::Print()`. The `PrintPage` event handler does the printing with a `Graphics` object that is passed to it by the .NET framework.

Example:

```
__gc class Handler {
public:
    void PrintPage(Object *sender, Printing::PrintPageEventArgs *ev) {
        ev->Graphics->DrawImage(Image::FromFile
            ("c:\\temp\\picture.jpg"),ev->Graphics->VisibleClipBounds);
        ev->HasMorePages = false;
    }
};
void main(void) {
    PrintDialog *dialog = new PrintDialog();
    dialog->Document = new Printing::PrintDocument();
    if(dialog->ShowDialog() == DialogResult::OK) {
        dialog->Document->PrintPage += new
            Printing::PrintPageEventHandler(new Handler(), Handler::PrintPage);
        dialog->Document->Print();
    }
}
```

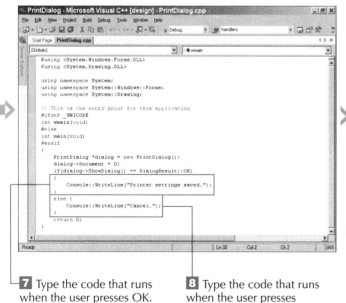

7 Type the code that runs when the user presses OK.

8 Type the code that runs when the user presses Cancel.

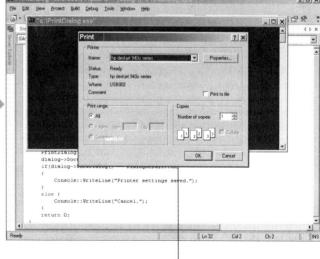

9 Compile and run your program.

■ The program starts and the Print dialog box opens. If you choose a font, its information prints in the console.

DISPLAY A CUSTOM MODAL DIALOG BOX

The .NET framework includes several classes for manipulating standard dialog boxes such as the Font dialog box. However, the framework also allows you to create your own custom dialog boxes. When you create your own dialog boxes, you create the window as well as its controls such as buttons and TextBoxes.

To create such as dialog box, first create a new instance of the Form class. This class represents a window. Next you create the instances of the control classes that you want to include in the dialog box. You then call the ShowDialog method of the Form class to show the window as a dialog box.

To make this window function as a dialog box when you create your controls, you can create an OK and a Cancel button. You create these two buttons as you would any other button and specify the text of the buttons as OK and

Cancel. You can make these two buttons work closely with the ShowDialog method by setting the DialogResult property of the two buttons. If you set this property to DialogResult::OK for the OK button and DialogResult::Cancel for the Cancel button, when the user clicks OK or Cancel, the call to ShowDialog will return DialogResult::OK or DialogResult::Cancel, respectively.

Your program can check the result of ShowDialog. If the result is DialogResult::OK, then your program can read the values of the control instances to determine the information the user entered into the dialog box. If the call to ShowDialog returns DialogResult::Cancel, you should neither check the values of the controls nor make any changes. This way, if the user clicks Cancel, the dialog box should close and no changes should occur.

DISPLAY A CUSTOM MODAL DIALOG BOX

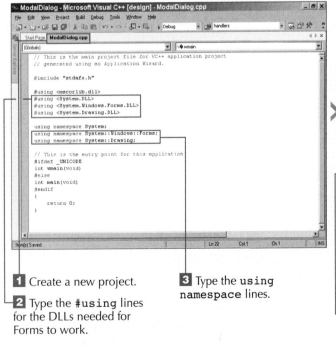

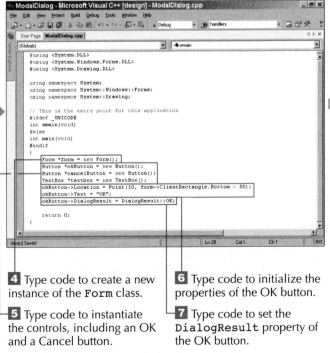

1 Create a new project.

2 Type the #using lines for the DLLs needed for Forms to work.

3 Type the using namespace lines.

4 Type code to create a new instance of the Form class.

5 Type code to instantiate the controls, including an OK and a Cancel button.

6 Type code to initialize the properties of the OK button.

7 Type code to set the DialogResult property of the OK button.

Extra

You can create dialog boxes that have other standard buttons besides OK and Cancel. You can have any combination of buttons in the `DialogResult` class. These choices are Abort, Cancel, Ignore, No, None, OK, Retry, and Yes.

Example:
```cpp
void main(void) {
    Form *form = new Form();
    Button *yesButton = new Button();
    Button *noButton = new Button();
    yesButton->Location = Point(10, form->ClientRectangle.Bottom - 50);
    yesButton->Text = "Yes";
    yesButton->DialogResult = DialogResult::Yes;
    noButton->Location = Point(100, form->ClientRectangle.Bottom - 50);
    noButton->Text = "No";
    noButton->DialogResult = DialogResult::No;
    Control* controls[] = { yesButton, noButton };
    form->Controls->AddRange( controls );
    if (form->ShowDialog() == DialogResult::Yes) {
        Console::WriteLine("Yes");
    }
    else {
        Console::WriteLine("No");
    }
}
```

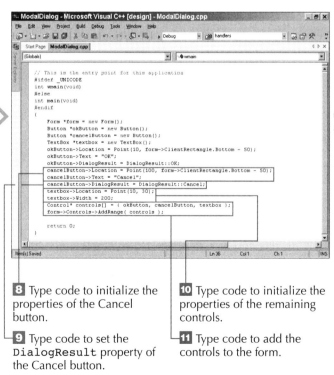

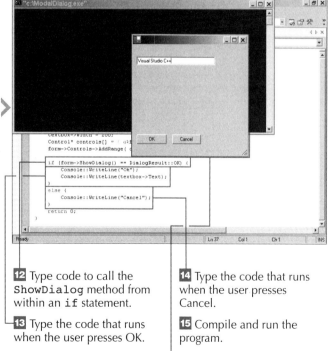

8 Type code to initialize the properties of the Cancel button.

9 Type code to set the `DialogResult` property of the Cancel button.

10 Type code to initialize the properties of the remaining controls.

11 Type code to add the controls to the form.

12 Type code to call the `ShowDialog` method from within an `if` statement.

13 Type the code that runs when the user presses OK.

14 Type the code that runs when the user presses Cancel.

15 Compile and run the program.

■ The program starts and the custom modal dialog box opens.

UNDERSTAND EVENTS

When you use a computer program on Windows, you interact with the program through a window and the controls inside the window. When you run a word processor, for example, the program will start and the main window will open. The program will then remain idle, doing nothing, as it waits for you to interact with it. You might then open a document or create a new document. Or you might begin typing. The program responds to your interactions. When you select the File ➪ Open menu, the word processor program asks you to select a document and it then opens it. When you type a letter, the program draws the letter inside the window. When you click the mouse somewhere in the document, the program moves the caret to the new position. Nearly everything the program does is in response to your interactions.

EVENTS

When you interact with a program, you are sending it events. When you click the mouse, you are sending a single event. When you click a button, you are sending a single event. When you click a menu item you are sending a single event. And when you type a key, you are sending a single event.

CATEGORIES OF EVENTS

You can divide the types of interactions into major categories. Some of these categories are listed in the following table.

EVENT	DESCRIPTION
Menu events	This refers to the way you interact with a program through its menus.
Mouse events	This refers to the way you interact with a program by clicking the mouse. You can press a button down, called a mouse-down event. You can move a mouse, called a mouse-move event. And you can let go of a mouse button that has been pressed, called a mouse-up event. You can single-click and you can double-click. You can click with either the right or the left button.
Control events	This refers to the way you interact through various controls such as buttons and listboxes. You can click a button or you can make a selection in a listbox.
Keyboard events	This refers to the way you interact using the keyboard. For example, you can type a letter, and you can include keys such as Shift, Ctrl, and Alt. Or you can press arrow keys or the Enter key.

PROGRAM FOR EVENTS

The programmers who created the word processor set up the program so it recognizes events. The code for the program included functions that execute in response to various events. For each menu item, there is likely a separate function that performs the work for the menu. For example, if you click the File ⇨ Open menu of the word processor, there is a function that opens up the File Open dialog, and waits for you to work with the File Open dialog. When you close the dialog, the function checks if you clicked OK or Cancel. If you clicked OK, it then opens the file in the word processor.

If you clicked Cancel, it does nothing. The programmers carefully wrote a separate function for each event.

When you write your programs, you can write for events. You can make a list of all the events that your program can respond to, and carefully write a function for each event. The function that handles the event is called an event handler. A common mistake in programs is to forget to write an event handler for one or two events. The result is a menu item that does nothing, or a mouse click that causes nothing to happen.

WRITE EVENT HANDLERS

You can write event handlers using .NET by putting all your event handlers functions into a single class. However, for a member function to run, you need an instance of the class. You can create a single instance of the class that will supply your event handlers.

You must create your class as a .NET managed class. A *managed class* is simply a class that the .NET framework carefully controls. To declare a managed class, you preceding the class definition with the __gc keyword. This tells the compiler to make the class a managed class, as in the following example.

```
__gc class MyHandlers {
};
```

You then fill the class with your event handler functions. You can tell the .NET framework about your event handlers by registering them with the events you want to handle. For example, if you create a button, you specify your event handler in the Click property for the Button. Since your event handler is a method within a particular instance, you supply both the name of the instance and the name of the method. You combine these two items into a single class instance. You then store this instance in the Click property.

DISCOVER EVENT HANDLERS

Most of the classes in the .NET framework that deal with forms, such as the Button class, include event handlers. The online help for the class includes a page called *All Members*. This page includes a heading in a table called *Public Instance Events*, which lists the

events. For example, inside the online help for the Button class, the All Members page includes the event Click. When you are creating classes for forms and controls, you can determine the events the class supports by checking this list on the All Members page.

WRITE AN EVENT HANDLER

Y ou can write code that responds to various events by writing an event handler. You write your event handler as a member function of a class.

To write an event handler, you first create a class with the __gc keyword. This tells the compiler that the class is a managed class, which means .NET carefully controls it.

Next, you write the event handler method. This method must have a definition that matches the event you are writing. You can determine this definition by opening the online help for the class containing the event. For example, if you are writing an event handler for the Click event in the Click class, you can find this event in the All Members page for the Button class. If you open the link for the Click event, you will see the event type. If you then click this type, you will see the function definition.

For example, the page for the Click event shows the following definition:

```
public __gc __delegate void EventHandler(
Object* sender,  EventArgs* e );
```

You will not include the __gc or __delegate keywords in your function definition. However, the return type and parameters of your function must match the definition shown.

After you declare your handler class, you must create an instance of it. Next, you create a new instance of the class shown at the top of the same online help page as that containing the function definition. To create this instance, you pass the name of your handler class instance, and the name of the member function for the handler.

Finally, this event instance represents the handler. You add this event instance to the event property for the control using the += notation.

WRITE AN EVENT HANDLER

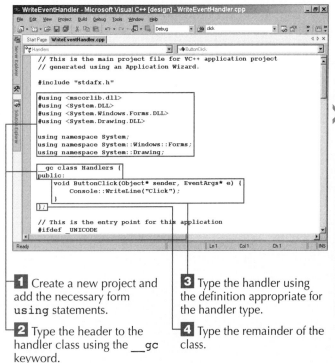

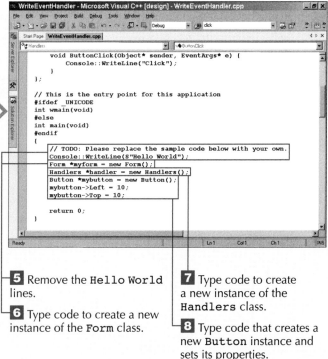

1 Create a new project and add the necessary form using statements.

2 Type the header to the handler class using the __gc keyword.

3 Type the handler using the definition appropriate for the handler type.

4 Type the remainder of the class.

5 Remove the Hello World lines.

6 Type code to create a new instance of the Form class.

7 Type code to create a new instance of the Handlers class.

8 Type code that creates a new Button instance and sets its properties.

Extra If you have similar controls, you can share a handler function, giving each control their own instance of the handler class. You can do this if the controls have similar behavior and require only slight differences.

Example:
```
__gc class Handlers {
public:
    Object *Info;
    Handlers(Object *aInfo) {Info = aInfo;}
    void ButtonClick(Object* sender, EventArgs* e) {
        Console::WriteLine(String::Concat(
            "Click ", Info->ToString()));
    }
};
// In the main function
Handlers *handler1 = new Handlers(S"Button1");
Button *button1 = new Button();
button1->Click +=
    new EventHandler(handler1, Handlers::ButtonClick);
Handlers *handler2 = new Handlers(S"Button2");
Button *button2 = new Button();
button2->Click +=
    new EventHandler(handler2, Handlers::ButtonClick);
```

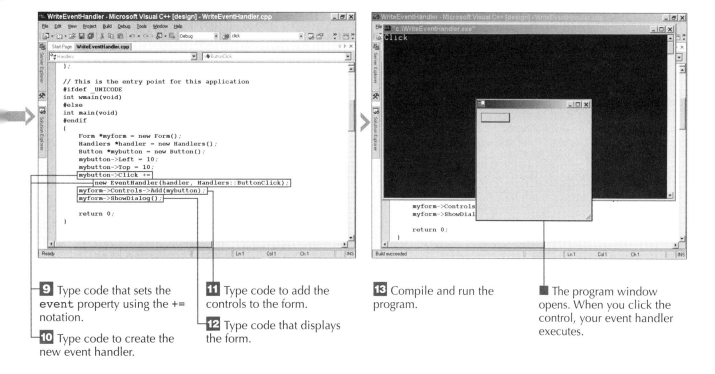

-9- Type code that sets the **event** property using the += notation.

-10- Type code to create the new event handler.

-11- Type code to add the controls to the form.

-12- Type code that displays the form.

-13- Compile and run the program.

■ The program window opens. When you click the control, your event handler executes.

RESPOND TO MOUSE EVENTS

When you work with a form, you can respond directly to mouse events. For example, if you are building a program that lets the users of the program draw lines and shapes on the form, you can respond to the clicks and moves of the mouse, drawing lines and shapes where the user clicks.

There are several kinds of mouse events that you can handle. You can handle an event when the user pushes the mouse button, and when the user lets go of the mouse button. These are called *mouse-down* and *mouse-up* events, and are associated with the MouseDown and MouseUp event properties. You can also handle an event when the mouse moves using the MouseMove event property.

The combination of a mouse-down and a mouse-up is called a *mouse-click*. Instead of responding to the mouse-down and mouse-up individually, you can respond to a mouse-click through the Click event property. You can also respond to a double-click through the DoubleClick event property.

To respond to these events, you create a MouseEventHandler. You put your handler inside a class designated as __gc. The handler must have the following definition:

```
void MouseEvent(Object*
sender,MouseEventArgs* e)
```

You can call the function whatever you want. However, your function must match this definition in return type and parameter types.

The MouseEventArgs parameter allows you to inspect information about the mouse event itself. The MouseEventArgs::Button property tells you which button was pressed, and its possible values include MouseButtons::Left, MouseButtons::Middle, and MouseButtons::Right. The MouseEventArgs parameter also has an X and Y property. These tell you the position of the mouse event. For example, if the user of your program clicks somewhere on the form, you can determine the position by inspecting the X and Y properties of the MouseEventArgs parameter.

RESPOND TO MOUSE EVENTS

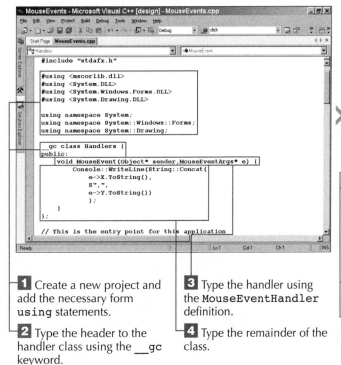

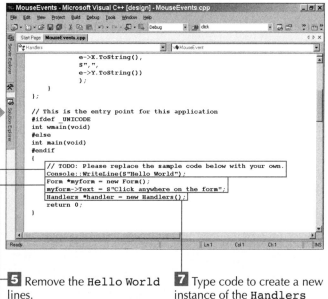

1 Create a new project and add the necessary form using statements.

2 Type the header to the handler class using the __gc keyword.

3 Type the handler using the MouseEventHandler definition.

4 Type the remainder of the class.

5 Remove the Hello World lines.

6 Type code that creates a new Form instance and sets its properties.

7 Type code to create a new instance of the Handlers class.

Extra

If you need to respond to the mouse-down, mouse-move, and mouse-up events together, you can ensure that you will receive the mouse-up event even if the mouse moves off your form. To do this, you set the `Capture` property of the form to true during `MouseDown`. You set the `Capture` property back to false during `MouseUp`.

Example:
```
void MouseDown(Object* sender,MouseEventArgs* e) {
    Down = true;
    form->Capture = true;
}
void MouseMove(Object* sender,MouseEventArgs* e) {
    if (Down) {
        // Handle the MouseMove event
    }
}
void MouseUp(Object* sender,MouseEventArgs* e) {
    Down = false;
    form->Capture = false;
}
```

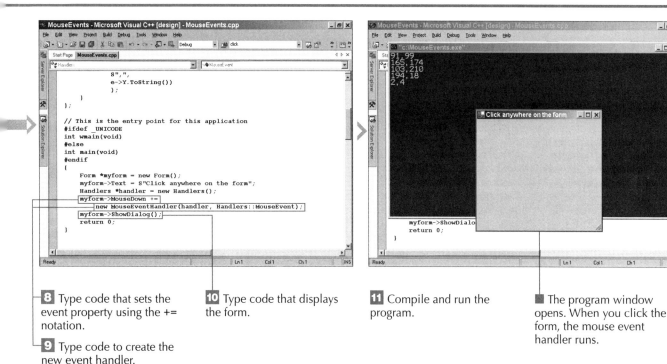

8 Type code that sets the event property using the += notation.

9 Type code to create the new event handler.

10 Type code that displays the form.

11 Compile and run the program.

■ The program window opens. When you click the form, the mouse event handler runs.

259

RESPOND TO MENU EVENTS

You can include menus in your windows. To use the menus, you can write menu handlers for them. You will write a separate handler function for each menu word that you wish to handle.

First, you create the handlers. As with other handlers, you put the handler functions in a managed class. The menu handlers must have the following function definition:

```
void ExitClick(System::Object* s,
System::EventArgs* e);
```

This function handles the File ⇨ Exit menu. You can choose your own name for the function. For example, if you are writing a handler for the File ⇨ Open menu, you can call the function OpenClick or perhaps FileOpen. However, you cannot change the return type and parameter types.

Next, you can create the menus. First, create an instance of MainMenu. This will hold the entire menu bar for the window. Next, create an instance of the MenuItem class for each word on the main menu. If you are adding multiple words to the menu bar, add the instances to the MainMenu by calling its AddRange method. If you are adding only one word to the MainMenu, call the Add method. Because the words on the menu bar open drop-down menus, you will not have handlers for these words.

For each menu item underneath the words on the menu bar, create a MenuItem instance. This is where you specify the event handlers. Create an instance of EventHandler, passing the name of the handler instance and the name of the handler function. Pass this instance of EventHandler to the MenuItem constructor. You will do this for each word on the drop-down menu. Finally, call the AddRange or Add method for the MenuItem associated with the word on the menu.

RESPOND TO MENU EVENTS

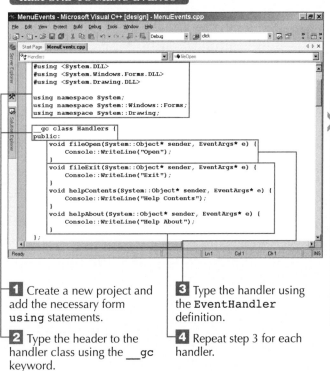

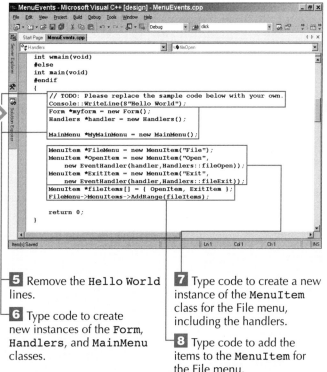

1 Create a new project and add the necessary form **using** statements.

2 Type the header to the handler class using the **__gc** keyword.

3 Type the handler using the **EventHandler** definition.

4 Repeat step 3 for each handler.

5 Remove the **Hello World** lines.

6 Type code to create new instances of the **Form**, **Handlers**, and **MainMenu** classes.

7 Type code to create a new instance of the **MenuItem** class for the File menu, including the handlers.

8 Type code to add the items to the **MenuItem** for the File menu.

Extra

You can enable and disable menu items. If you have certain menu items that only apply during certain times, you can gray out the menu items by disabling them. To enable or disable a menu item, set the `Enabled` property to `false`. To re-enable the menu, set the `Enabled` property back to `true`.

You can give a menu a shortcut key so that you can press a keystroke as a substitute for clicking the menu. To do this, set the `Shortcut` property. For example, `ExitMenu->Shortcut = Shortcut::CtrlX;` will assign Ctrl+X as the shortcut for the `ExitMenu MenuItem`. The name of the shortcut will appear on the menu to the right of the menu name.

You can add a check mark to a menu if you want the user of your program to be aware of a setting that the menu item represents. For example, if you have a menu item called Bold Text, you can add a check mark to this menu item when the text is bold. To turn on the check mark, set the `Checked` property to `true`. To turn the check off, set the `Checked` property to `false`.

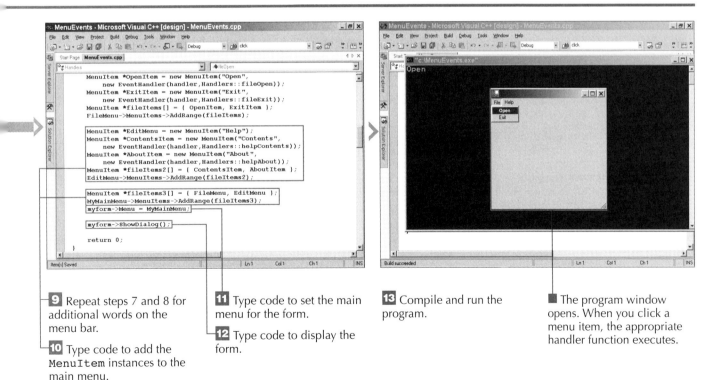

-◄ **9** Repeat steps 7 and 8 for additional words on the menu bar.

-◄ **10** Type code to add the `MenuItem` instances to the main menu.

◄ **11** Type code to set the main menu for the form.

◄ **12** Type code to display the form.

13 Compile and run the program.

■ The program window opens. When you click a menu item, the appropriate handler function executes.

RESPOND TO KEYBOARD EVENTS

You can write your programs to respond to keyboard events. For example, if you are writing a drawing program, you may want to display letters and characters on the form when the user presses a key. The Form class includes an event called KeyPress, which responds to keyboard events. When you write a handler for this event, you receive an event each time the user of your program presses a key. Additionally, if the user holds down a key, the key will repeat and you will receive several events for the same key.

To use the KeyPress event, create a new Handlers class and use the KeyPressEventHandler definition as follows:

```
void KeyPress(object sender,
KeyPressEventArgs e)
```

You can use whatever name you like for the function name. However, your function must match the return type and parameter types of this definition. Inside your event handler, you can determine the key by inspecting the

KeyPressEventArgs parameter. This parameter includes a KeyChar property. For example, if the user of your program presses the a key, KeyChar will be the character a. If the user holds down shift and presses the a key yielding an uppercase A, KeyChar will be the character A.

Next, you add your event handler to the KeyPress event for the form. The following shows how you do this using the += notation:

```
myform->KeyPress +=  new
KeyPressEventHandler(handler,
Handlers::KeyPress);
```

The KeyPressEventHandler constructor includes the instance of the handler class, and the name of the handler function.

The KeyPress event only handles printable characters, meaning keys that can be printed on a page. Thus, if you press the arrow keys or the keys such as Page Up and Page Down, you will not receive a KeyPress event.

RESPOND TO KEYBOARD EVENTS

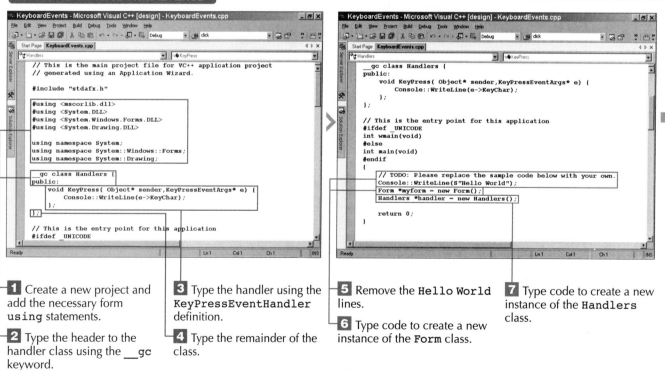

1 Create a new project and add the necessary form using statements.

2 Type the header to the handler class using the __gc keyword.

3 Type the handler using the KeyPressEventHandler definition.

4 Type the remainder of the class.

5 Remove the Hello World lines.

6 Type code to create a new instance of the Form class.

7 Type code to create a new instance of the Handlers class.

Extra

When you use the `KeyPress` event, you will not receive events for the Ctrl, Shift, and Alt keys and the cursor movement keys. If you need events for individual keys including the Ctrl, Shift, and Alt keys, you can use the `KeyDown` event. The `KeyDown` event tells exactly what keys are pressed and does not convert between uppercase and lowercase.

Example:
```
__gc class Handlers {
public:
    void KeyDown( Object* sender,KeyEventArgs* e) {
        if (e->Shift) {
            Console::Write("Shift ");
        }
        if (e->Control) {
            Console::Write("Control ");
        }
        if (e->Alt) {
            Console::Write("Alt ");
        }
        Console::WriteLine(
            Enum::GetName(__typeof(Keys), __box(e->KeyCode)));
    };
};
```

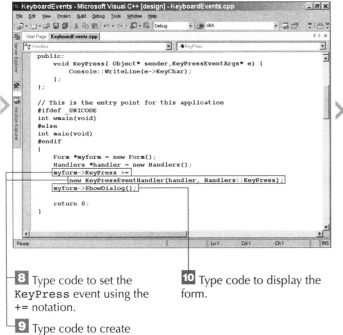

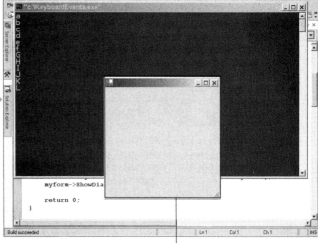

8 Type code to set the `KeyPress` event using the += notation.

9 Type code to create a new instance of the `KeyPressEventHandler` class.

10 Type code to display the form.

11 Compile and run the program.

■ The program window opens. When you type on the keyboard, the console window displays the keys.

INTRODUCTION TO MANAGED EXTENSIONS

The Visual Studio .NET environment provides you with a new tool for developing programs called *managed extensions*. Managed extensions are built into the environment through extensions to the C++ programming language. These extensions enhance the language by adding features such as garbage collection, which is a system that automatically deletes objects that are no longer needed, alleviating the need to delete your objects. Further, the managed extensions allow your programs to take advantage of the particular classes in the .NET framework that were written in other languages such as Visual Basic.

ACCESSING MANAGED EXTENSIONS

You access the managed extensions through the use of keywords that provide special commands to the compiler. For example, to define a managed class that includes garbage collection, you precede the `class` keyword with the `__gc` keyword, which is a new keyword for the managed extensions.

UNMANAGED CODE

When you develop a program that uses managed extensions, you have the option of mixing managed code with unmanaged code. For example, if you wrote the program using an earlier version of Visual Studio, your code would not have any managed extensions. But if you write new code for it using Visual Studio .NET, then you can freely take advantage of the managed extensions, while retaining the previous unmanaged code. Visual Studio .NET lets the two portions of the program work together as one.

CROSS LANGUAGE DEVELOPMENT

One primary advantage of the managed extensions is cross-language development. This means you can write parts of your program in various languages besides C++, including C# and Visual Basic. With the help of managed extensions, the C++ portion of the program can easily access classes, objects, and routines in the C# and Visual Basic portions of the program. With previous versions of Visual Studio, it was very difficult to access classes written in Visual Basic from C++.

Similarly, you can work the other way. You can develop code in C++ that can be used by other languages. This was always possible in the past and not very difficult, but now with .NET it is even easier. The extensions to C++ let you create enhanced classes that take advantage of features not normally found in C++, but found in other languages. For example, you can deem a class as *sealed*, meaning you cannot derive new classes from it. This is a feature found in other languages, but previously was not part of C++.

PROPERTIES

Another new feature of managed extensions is the `property` feature. This is a feature that has been available to other languages for some time, such as Visual Basic and Delphi. A property is similar to a member variable, except you define a function that gets called when the property is read, or a function that gets called when the property is set, or both. Using these functions, you can process the data before storing it or returning it. For example, if you have a class that includes a Units member and an Amount member, you can make the Amount member a property, and store the amount in a fixed unit type. Then you would use the `property get` method to convert the amount to the

unit specified in the Units variable. Similarly, you would use the `property set` method to convert the amount to the fixed unit type.

The property feature is particularly useful in cross-language development, since other languages might provide classes and objects that use properties. Without a property feature in C++, as it was in the past, you would simply have to call the property accessor methods directly. But with the new managed extensions, you can simply read and write the property as you would in the other languages, and the accessor methods would get called automatically.

EVENTS

Another feature found in other languages but not previously found in C++ is the `event` mechanism. Languages such as Visual Basic, Delphi, and Borland's C++ Builder, which is also an extended version of C++, allow for event handling code that gets called in response to user interactions with a window or control on the screen. For example, in other languages it is very easy to write a function that gets called automatically

when the user of the program clicks a button. In C++, this was not always so easy. But managed extensions now provide a mechanism making this possible. When you use the mechanism in conjunction with the .NET class framework, you can easily write event handling code and attach it to a control on your window. For more information on how to do this, see Chapter 14.

USING MANAGED EXTENSIONS

You can easily create a new project that takes advantage of the managed extensions features of C++.NET. To use the managed extensions in C++, you create a new C++ project and choose one of the managed extensions options. If you choose Managed C++ Application, you can create a standalone application with its own console. That is the one used throughout this book, and it gives you a simple console by default. This option also gives you several starting files including a source file with a main function.

After you create the project, you do not need to do any other preparatory work to use managed extensions. The compiler options will be set up automatically for you to include the managed extensions. You can then begin using the managed extensions in your code. For example, if you want to create a class that uses the garbage collection features, you can create it using the __gc keyword.

If you add additional source files to your project, in order for them to have access to the managed extensions, you

should type the following lines at the beginning of the source file:

```
#include "stdafx.h"
#using <mscorlib.dll>
using namespace System;
```

The first line is needed by the Visual C++ environment so the precompiled header files work properly, and is not part of the managed extensions. The second line is required in order to use the managed extensions. The third line is not required, but it simplifies the use of the classes in the .NET framework. If you include it, you can access the classes simply by name. For example, if you do not include the using namespace System line, you need to type

```
System::Console::WriteLine(S"Hello World");
```

to write to the console. But with the using namespace line, you do not need the System::.

USING MANAGED EXTENSIONS

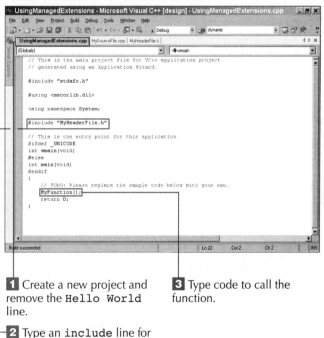

1 Create a new project and remove the Hello World line.

2 Type an include line for the header file containing the function.

3 Type code to call the function.

4 Click File ⇨ Add New Item.

■ The Add New Item dialog box opens.

5 Click C++ File (.cpp).

6 Type the name of the source file.

7 Click Open.

■ The source file opens.

Extra

You can also create managed libraries for use in other applications. These libraries are classes and functions that you want to make available to applications written in either C++ or any .NET language. The term for such a library is an assembly. To create a managed library, when you create the project, choose Managed C++ Class Library for the project type. The .NET environment will create a set of starter files for you, including a source file and a header file. The header file contains the beginnings for your class. You then fill it in with your own code.

Example:
```
namespace ManagedLibrary
{
    public __gc class Class1
    {
        void MyFunction();
    };
}
```

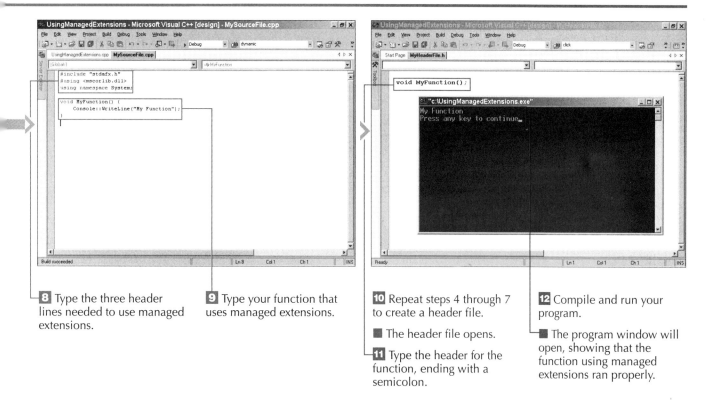

8 Type the three header lines needed to use managed extensions.

9 Type your function that uses managed extensions.

10 Repeat steps 4 through 7 to create a header file.

■ The header file opens.

11 Type the header for the function, ending with a semicolon.

12 Compile and run your program.

■ The program window will open, showing that the function using managed extensions ran properly.

ADD MANAGED EXTENSIONS TO AN EXISTING PROJECT

I f you have a program that you developed with a previous version of Visual C++, you can update it in Visual Studio .NET to take advantage of the managed extension features.

Visual Studio .NET will open a project built with a previous version of Visual Studio, such as version 6.0. When you do so, you can compile the project as is, but you will not have access to the managed extensions. In order to take advantage of the managed extensions, there are four options you must set for the project settings.

First, you must tell Visual Studio that you want this project to use managed extensions. You will find this in the General page in the project settings. Set `Use Managed Extensions` to `Yes`.

For the next three project settings, it is possible they will already be set correctly, depending on the options you chose when you first created the project with an earlier version of Visual Studio.

Second, you need to tell Visual Studio that you want to use basic runtime checks. You will find this setting in the C/C++ Code Generation page of the project settings. Set the `Basic Runtime Checks` option to `Default`.

Third, you need to tell Visual Studio the type of debug information you want to use. This setting is on the C/C++ General settings page. Set `Debug Information Format` to `Program Database (/Zi)`. Visual Studio also includes an option called Edit & Continue, but this option is not compatible with the Managed Extensions.

Finally, you need to tell Visual Studio the type of runtime library. You may use any of the Multi-threaded options, but not any of the Single-threaded options. This setting is on the C/C++ Code Generation settings page. Set `Runtime Library` to `Multi-threaded Debug (/MTd)` or any of the Multi-threaded options.

ADD MANAGED EXTENSIONS TO AN EXISTING PROJECT

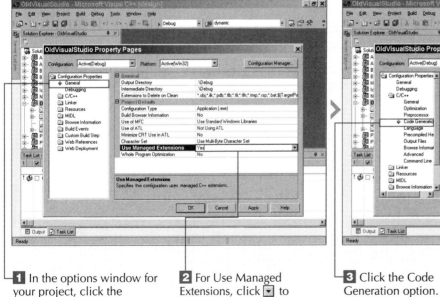

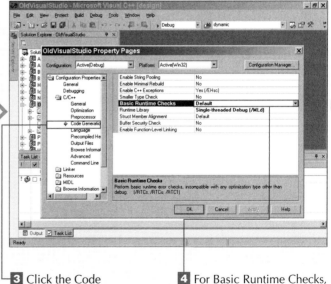

1 In the options window for your project, click the General item.

2 For Use Managed Extensions, click ▾ to select Yes.

3 Click the Code Generation option.

4 For Basic Runtime Checks, click ▾ to select Default.

Extra

You can use Visual Studio .NET to continue building and maintaining older software without having to add the managed extensions. If you prefer not to work with managed extensions for an older project, you can simply open the project within the Visual Studio .NET environment. The environment will convert the project to a new project file format. From there, you do not need to change any of the project options if you do not want managed extensions. You can then continue developing the project as you did in the previous versions of Visual Studio. All the same features will be present; plus, you will get to take advantage of the new environment features such as the integrated online help.

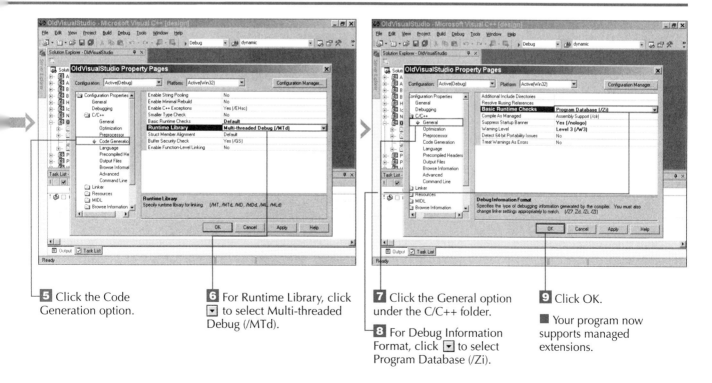

5 Click the Code Generation option.

6 For Runtime Library, click ⬇ to select Multi-threaded Debug (/MTd).

7 Click the General option under the C/C++ folder.

8 For Debug Information Format, click ⬇ to select Program Database (/Zi).

9 Click OK.

■ Your program now supports managed extensions.

USING AUTOMATIC CLEANUP

You can use the automatic cleanup features of the .NET framework, also known as garbage collection, by using the __gc keyword. This will allow you to worry less about the allocation and deallocation of resources and focus more on the high-level development of your program.

Variables of types declared as __gc are created inside the framework space called the *heap*. The framework carefully watches items declared inside the heap, and when they are no longer needed, the framework automatically deletes them. This function alleviates the need for calling delete. The framework deletes the objects for you when the object is no longer needed. It keeps track of how many times an object is referenced and within what scope, such as a function. When the scope is finished, the reference count is decreased. When a new variable is declared, the system scans the heap space and if it finds an object that no scope

needs any longer, it clears the space to make room for more variables.

You can declare a class as __gc by preceding the class definition with the __gc keyword, as in __gc class MyClass {};, so that each instance of this class you declare has automatic cleanup. When you derive a new class from a __gc class, you must declare the derived class as __gc.

You must allocate instances of classes declared as __gc as pointers. For example, if you have a __gc class called MyClass, you must declare variables of this class using a pointer as in MyClass *myinst = new MyClass();. You cannot declare it as MyClass mysint;. The reason is that the new keyword allocates space inside the heap, whereas a direct instantiation declares it on the stack, outside the space of the .NET framework.

USING AUTOMATIC CLEANUP

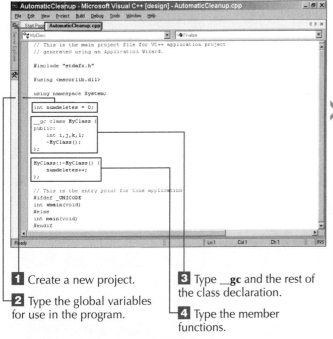

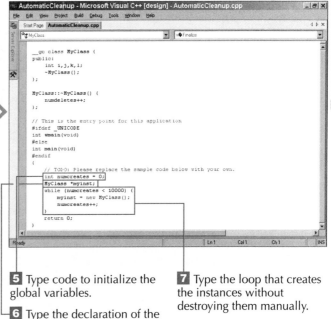

1 Create a new project.

2 Type the global variables for use in the program.

3 Type __**gc** and the rest of the class declaration.

4 Type the member functions.

5 Type code to initialize the global variables.

6 Type the declaration of the instance of the class.

7 Type the loop that creates the instances without destroying them manually.

Extra

You can declare arrays to have automatic cleanup. This will let you create large amounts of data and still take advantage of automatic cleanup.

Example:
```
int myarray __gc[] = new int __gc[50];
```

You can use any managed class in an array if you use the __gc keyword before the brackets of the array.

Example:
```
String *myarray2 __gc[] = new String *
__gc[10];
```

You can use your own structures in the managed array classes. If you have your own structure and you want to put it in an array, you must either make it a managed class or tag it as a __value class to make it known to the Managed Extensions library but not declare it in the .NET heap and not give it garbage collection.

Example:
```
__value struct MyStruct { int i; };
```
```
MyStruct myarray3 __gc[] = new MyStruct
__gc[10];
```

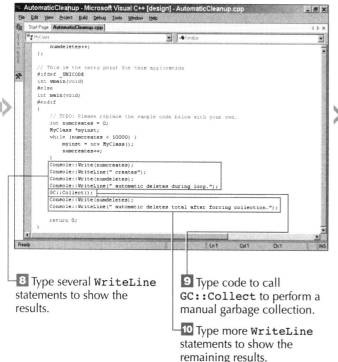

8 Type several `WriteLine` statements to show the results.

9 Type code to call `GC::Collect` to perform a manual garbage collection.

10 Type more `WriteLine` statements to show the remaining results.

11 Compile and run the program.

■ The program window appears. Because the pointer still referenced the final item, the final item was not deleted during the program output.

AVOID AUTOMATIC CLEANUP

Sometimes you might want to have more control over the automatic cleanup, if you have your own destructors that you want to run manually. To declare a class that does not have the automatic cleanup, you simply leave off the __gc. By omitting the __gc, you can create standard C++ classes that do not take advantage of the .NET garbage collection if you want to handle the deletes manually.

If you want other programmers who are reading your code to immediately recognize that the class is not a __gc class, you can optionally include the __nogc keyword, as in __nogc class MyNoGCClass { int x; };

Inside the computer, variables declared from __nogc types are not allocated inside the .NET storage space called the

.NET heap. Instead, they are declared in the standard C++ heap that is not maintained by the .NET framework.

Because __nogc classes are treated as standard C++ classes, you can declare variables of __nogc classes as either pointers or standard variables, as in MyNoGCClass *pointervariable; and MyNoGCClass stackvariable;.

An example of a __nogc class would be a class that you convert from a previous C++ program that was not written for the .NET platform. Although you do not need to specify __nogc, you might want to as a reminder that this is not managed with garbage collection. Then, later on in your development, you will have the reminder and can, if you prefer, change it to a __gc class.

AVOID AUTOMATIC CLEANUP

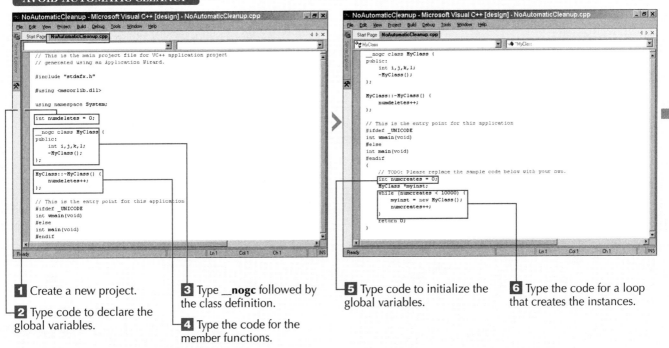

1 Create a new project.

2 Type code to declare the global variables.

3 Type **__nogc** followed by the class definition.

4 Type the code for the member functions.

5 Type code to initialize the global variables.

6 Type the code for a loop that creates the instances.

Extra

If you create instances of __nogc classes, then you must make sure that you manually clean up the objects that you create. This will help ensure that your programs do not use up memory without freeing it. A typical rule is that for every create there should be a delete. Sometimes the application of this rule can be elusive. For example, if a function creates an object and returns a pointer to the object, you still have to clean up the object even though the creation took place in the function. However, if the object was created in the method of another object, you need to find out whether that object will delete the new object or if you are expected to do so. You can make this determination by checking the documentation for the class of the other object or by inspecting the code manually.

If you create a class that is __nogc and later change your mind and decide to make it a __gc class, you will have to change any non-pointer variables into pointer variables. Because you cannot declare __gc class instances on the stack, meaning they are not pointers, any __gc class instances declared on the stack must be converted to pointers using the new keyword. Fortunately, the compiler will tell you when this needs to be done, as it will generate an error.

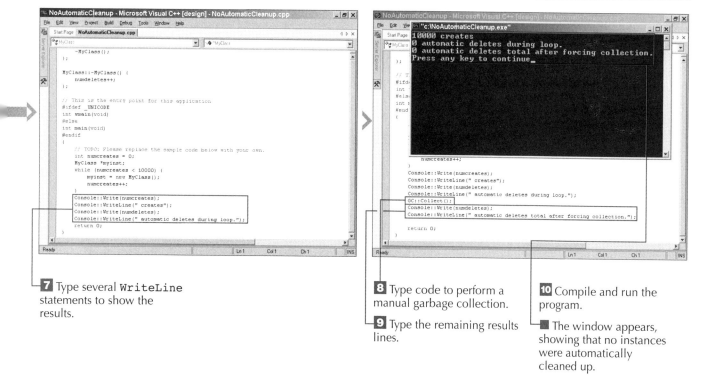

7 Type several `WriteLine` statements to show the results.

8 Type code to perform a manual garbage collection.

9 Type the remaining results lines.

10 Compile and run the program.

■ The window appears, showing that no instances were automatically cleaned up.

ENSURE THAT A VARIABLE DOES NOT MOVE

When the .NET framework performs its automatic garbage collection and cleans out the objects that are no longer used, it may move the remaining objects around inside its storage space, called its heap. One reason for this action is to bring all the free space into one contiguous piece of memory so that multiple chunks of free space are not scattered about the heap. Otherwise, if your program needs a particularly large allocation, there might not be room for it — even if enough total free space is available.

When an object moves in this manner within the heap, normally the .NET framework makes sure to update any pointers to the objects in the heap with the new location. However, if you pass the pointer of a managed object to a

routine that is not part of the .NET framework, your pointer may become invalid. An example of such a function would be a method within an unmanaged or __nogc class.

The way to prevent this from happening is to *pin* the object down so it does not move by using the __pin keyword. To use the __pin keyword, declare your object pointer, following the class name with the keyword __pin, as in MyClass __pin * inst = new MyClass();, where MyClass is a managed class declared with the __gc keyword.

A class itself is not declared as __pin. Only pointers to objects can be declared as pinned.

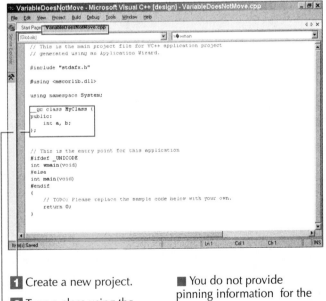

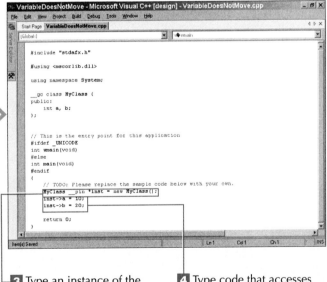

1 Create a new project.

2 Type a class using the __gc keyword.

■ You do not provide pinning information for the class.

3 Type an instance of the class, using the __pin keyword to show that this instance cannot move.

4 Type code that accesses the members of the class.

Extra

If you have two or more pointers pointing to the same managed object in memory, the object remains pinned if at least one of the pointers is declared as pinned. If that pointer goes out of scope and only non-pinned pointers remain, the object is no longer pinned by the framework.

In general, you should be careful with pinned pointers. Only use them when necessary, because otherwise the .NET heap could be filled with non-moveable objects, potentially leaving no room for large allocations when necessary.

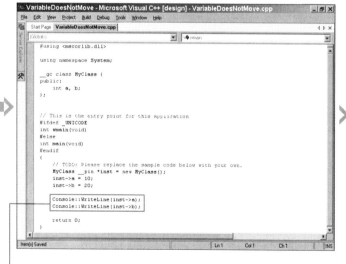

5 Type several `WriteLine` statements to show the members.

6 Compile and run the program.

■ The program window appears, showing the pinned instance's members.

REFERENCE A FUNCTION WITH A DELEGATE

In C++ without managed extensions, you can take the address of a function, save it in a pointer variable, and call the function through the pointer. However, it is difficult to take the address of a class member function for a particular object.

Suppose you have several classes, and each has at least one member function. Each class serves a different purpose, and their member functions each do something different. You then have a program that checks the current day, and it executes a member function of a particular object based on the day. Before managed extensions, the way to do this would involve creating a base class from which all the other classes are derived, and then naming the member function the same.

Implementing this with managed extensions is easy using delegates. You can think of a delegate as a pointer to a member function for a particular object. To use a delegate, you declare a type by specifying the keyword __delegate,

followed by the type that the function returns, then a name for the variable, and finally a parameter list that is the same as the function, for example __delegate void MyDelegate(). This example declares a delegate type called MyDelegate. This type has a constructor much like a class. To create a variable of this delegate type, you then call a new constructor, passing the object and the class method that you want the variable to point to, as in

```
MyDelegate *pointer = new MyDelegate(myobj,
MyClass::MyFunction);
```

The first parameter is a pointer to the object. The second parameter is the class method specified by class name, two colons, and the function name.

Finally, to call the function, you call the Invoke method on the pointer object, as in pointer->Invoke().

REFERENCE A FUNCTION WITH A DELEGATE

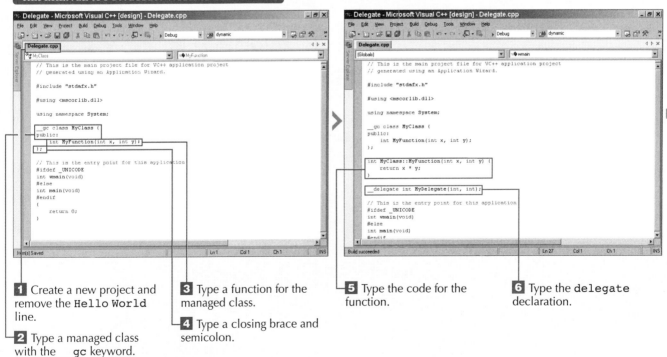

1 Create a new project and remove the Hello World line.

2 Type a managed class with the __gc keyword.

3 Type a function for the managed class.

4 Type a closing brace and semicolon.

5 Type the code for the function.

6 Type the delegate declaration.

Extra

You can use delegates to respond to user events. Delegates are the mechanism through which the event handling system works. When you create window controls such as buttons and ListBox, and you want to respond to events such as a button click or a selection of a ListBox item, you can do so by creating a delegate and passing it into the .NET library. Because a delegate is a combination of an object and a class function, together these items represent a single instance method that can handle the processing of the GUI event.

Although delegate types are typically defined globally outside of a function, they can be defined inside member functions of classes, provided the classes are managed classes defined with the __gc keyword.

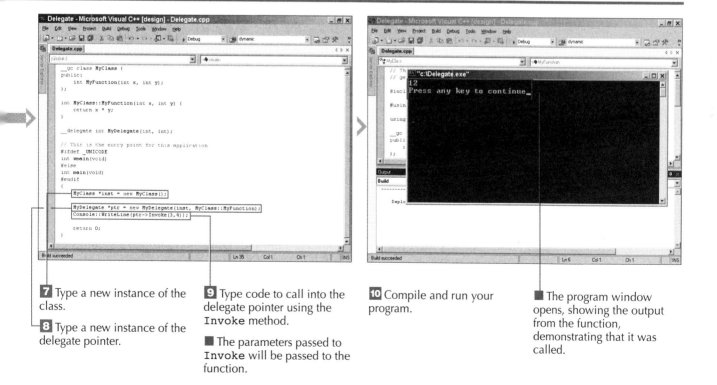

7 Type a new instance of the class.

8 Type a new instance of the delegate pointer.

9 Type code to call into the delegate pointer using the **Invoke** method.

■ The parameters passed to **Invoke** will be passed to the function.

10 Compile and run your program.

■ The program window opens, showing the output from the function, demonstrating that it was called.

CREATE PROPERTIES FOR MANAGED CLASSES

Y ou can give your managed classes properties with the use of the __property keyword. Using properties, you can have data members that include special code that gets executed when you read or write them. A property is similar to a member data item, except you can supply functions that get called in response to setting the property value or retrieving it. For example, if you have a class with a standard data member Name and you create an instance of this class and set the value of Name, nothing happens beyond that action. However, if you want to check the name against a list of existing names and automatically determine a last name based on the first name, you can put such code in a property function. When you use the class, you set the property in the same way you set the value of a standard member. Instead of simply setting the value, the property function executes.

You can access a class property by writing code such as the following:

```
MyPropertyClass *inst = new MyPropertyClass();
inst->Name = "John";
Console::WriteLine(inst->Name);
```

The final line would include both the first and last names: John Smith.

To use a property, you create the property get method by typing a standard function but preceding it with the keyword __property. The function name must be get_ followed by the name of the property as in this example: __property String *get_Name() {return myname; }.

To create the property set function, you again create a function starting with __property, but instead precede the name with set_, as in __property void set_Name(String *newname) { myname = newname}.

CREATE PROPERTIES FOR MANAGED CLASSES

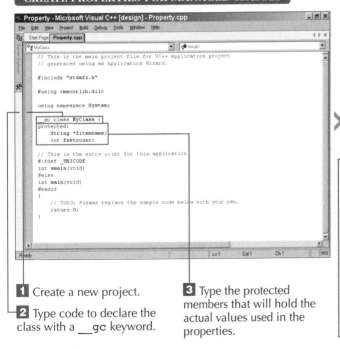

1 Create a new project.

2 Type code to declare the class with a __gc keyword.

3 Type the protected members that will hold the actual values used in the properties.

4 Type the initialization of the protected members through the constructor.

5 Type code to create the get method for the first property.

■ The first property is read-only so it does not have a set method.

6 Type code for the get method for the second property.

7 Type code for the set method for the second property.

Extra

You can put logic in either the set or the get method. In this way you can have more control over whether your code functions before the data is set, or after. If you have a class that models a window component and includes a property Width that changes the width of the window component, you might include the property calls in the property set_ function to actually set the width of the component. If you have a property called Text, on the other hand, that retrieves the text a user types into the component, you would likely have logic in the property get_ method that retrieves the text from the actual component and returns it as the value of the property.

You can supply a property set function, a property get function, or both. This lets you decide whether the property is read-only or write-only. If you supply only a property get function, the property is read-only and cannot be set by the code outside of the class. If you supply only a property set function, the code using the class can only set it but not inspect the value. If you provide both, the code using the class can set or get the value of the property.

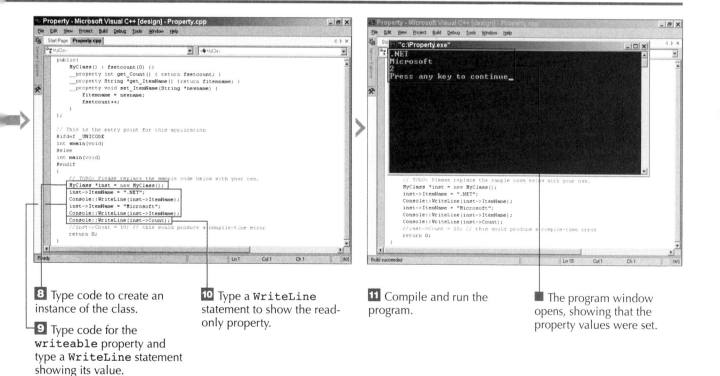

8 Type code to create an instance of the class.

9 Type code for the **writeable** property and type a **WriteLine** statement showing its value.

10 Type a **WriteLine** statement to show the read-only property.

11 Compile and run the program.

■ The program window opens, showing that the property values were set.

PREVENT CLASS INHERITANCE

Sometimes when you design a class you might want to ensure that others cannot create new classes derived from your class or make modified versions of your class by deriving from it. In C++ outside of .NET, you would generally give the class no virtual functions to prevent others from deriving from your class. Regardless, any class could derive from it; the class simply could not override the functions. Also, if your class itself is derived from another providing virtual functions, those functions can always be overridden in C++ outside of .NET.

In C++ for .NET, you can use the __sealed keyword to prevent a class from being inherited. Put the __sealed keyword before the class definition as in the following example:

```
__sealed __gc class MyClass : public
    AnotherClass {
public:
    virtual void f() {
Console::WriteLine(S"This class is sealed");
    }
};
```

If you attempt to derive a new class from a sealed class, you receive a compile-time error message: cannot inherit from 'MyClass' as it has been declared as '__sealed'.

You can only seal __gc classes. You must either declare the class you are sealing as __gc or derive it from a class that is __gc. Attempting to seal a non-gc class returns a compile time error.

PREVENT CLASS INHERITANCE

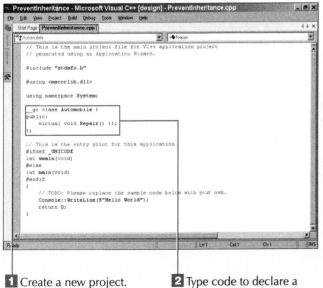

1 Create a new project.

2 Type code to declare a __gc class with a virtual function.

3 Type a __sealed class.

Extra

You can allow classes to be derived from your class while disallowing certain virtual functions from being overridden. You would only want to seal a virtual function because non-virtual functions are sealed by default. You might have virtual functions that you want sealed if your class is derived from another class providing virtual functions. To ensure that no class derived from your class overrides one of the virtual functions, you seal the function in your class, but do not put the __sealed keyword in the class definition. Instead, you seal a function by specifying the __sealed keyword before the function definition and before the virtual keyword, as in the following example.

Example:
```
__gc class MyClass : public AnotherClass {
   __sealed virtual void f() {
Console::WriteLine("This function is
sealed."); }
};
```

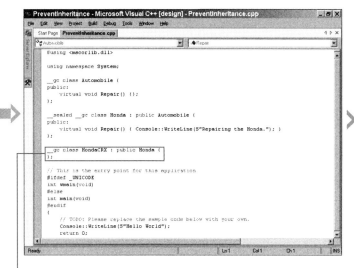

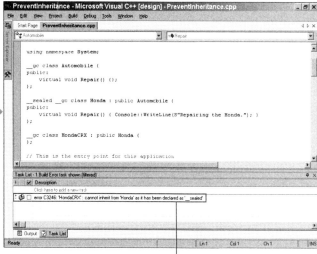

4 Type code that attempts to derive a class from the __sealed class.

5 Compile the program.

■ The compile-time errors show that you cannot derive from the __sealed class.

CREATE VALUE CLASSES

When you create a managed class, you normally declare it as __gc. All instances of this class must be declared as pointers because the managed objects are allocated inside the .NET storage space known as the heap. Objects inside the heap must have pointers to them. At times, however, you may want to create a managed class that can be accessed directly rather than through a pointer and not in the heap. You can allocate such objects on the stack. Objects of this type are called value types and are declared with the __value keyword.

The purpose for using value types is that you can create small short-lived data types that include all the benefits of managed objects without the overhead of garbage

collection. One of the benefits of managed objects is language interoperability. For example, you might need to create a library of code containing a small data type that you are making available to other programs. Those programs might be written in C++, C#, or Visual Basic. To make the type available, you need to use a managed class. Value classes are ideal for such types when they are not created on the heap and do not need garbage collection.

You can declare a structure or a class as __value. Classes and structures declared as __value cannot be inherited from other classes or structures except for __gc interfaces that are used in COM programming. You cannot derive classes from value classes.

CREATE VALUE CLASSES

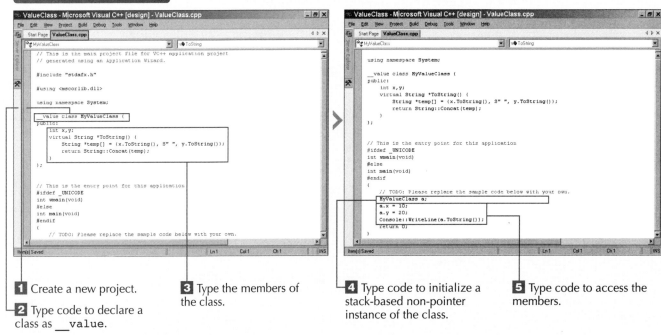

1 Create a new project.

2 Type code to declare a class as __value.

3 Type the members of the class.

4 Type code to initialize a stack-based non-pointer instance of the class.

5 Type code to access the members.

Extra

Most of the primitive types available to C++ such as `int` and `float` have a .NET value class associated with them, allowing you to use the primitive types with many of the managed extension benefits. For example, `int` has class `Int32`, and `float` has class `Single`. When you create a variable of the primitive types, you can treat them as objects of the associated value classes and access their members. For example, normally an integer does not have members. But with .NET you can access `Int32` members of an integer as in the following example.

Example:

```
int i = 100;
Console::WriteLine(String::Concat(S"The
initial value is ", i.ToString()));
```

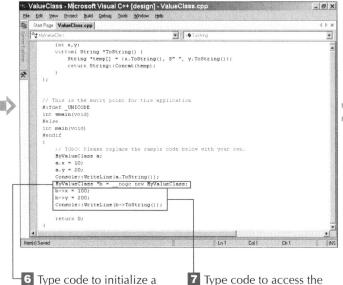

6 Type code to initialize a pointer-based instance of the class.

7 Type code to access the members.

8 Compile and run the program.

■ The program compiles successfully and the members are shown in the window.

BOX A VALUE CLASS

Although value classes are managed types, .NET treats them separately from __gc classes. For example, if you want to use some of the powerful data structures found in the .NET framework, such as the stack class in the `System::Collections` namespace, you would normally be unable to use the value types because the Collections classes can only hold __gc objects.

The way around this restriction is to box a value class. When you box a value class, you put the value into a collection and can then use it in any way that you use a __gc object. To box a value, you call the __box function, passing the value object, as in `mystack->Push(__box(value1));`, where `mystack` is a stack of type `Collections::Stack` having method `Push` that accepts a __gc object. The boxed value is of type `Object *`.

To get the value out, you take the `Object *` variable and do a dynamic cast back to the original:

```
Object *storedvalue = mystack->Pop();
MyValue value2 =
    *dynamic_cast<MyValue*>(storedvalue);
```

This code extracts the stored value, which is a pointer, and casts it to a `MyValue*`, which is also a pointer. It then dereferences the pointer and saves it in `value2`. This technique is called unboxing. If you box a value, obtain an `Object *`, and then modify the original value, the value in the `Object *` remains unchanged because it is a copy of the original value.

BOX A VALUE CLASS

1 Create a new project.

2 Type code to declare a **__value** class and its members.

3 Type code to create an instance of a class that requires a **__gc** class.

4 Type code to create an instance of the **__value** class and initialize its members.

5 Type code to add the members to the container by using the **__box** keyword.

Extra

You can box enums if the enum is a `__value` enum. For example, if you have an enum type declared as `__value enum MyEnum { ENUMA, ENUMB, ENUMC, ENUMD };`, you can box the enum as the following example shows.

Example:
```
Collections::Stack* mystack = new
Collections::Stack();

MyEnum enumvalue = ENUMA;

mystack->Push(__box(enumvalue));
```

To get the most out of your boxed values, remember that the boxing creates a copy of the original value. Thus, if you change the boxed value, the original variable will not change and vice versa.

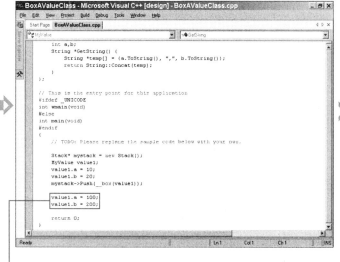

6 Type code to change the original value classes for comparison purposes.

7 Extract the values by using the `dynamic_cast` keyword.

8 Compile and run the program.

■ The window appears, showing that the boxed value was successfully retrieved and that it holds the original values.

USE A KEYWORD AS AN IDENTIFIER

The .NET framework is intended to allow multiple computer languages to work together, and you can prepare your programs by using the __identifier tag. The __identifier tag allows your programs to use libraries containing variables that happen to be C++ keywords. The other libraries could be written in other languages, and they may allow words that are not allowed in the C++ language. Thus, when you access the library, those words would cause a compiler error. For example, a library might include a function called float. Because float is a C++ identifier, you would not be able to access the function. If you attempt to call it, the compiler will generate an error at compile time. The solution is, therefore, to call it, but use the __identifier tag.

To use a C++ keyword as an identifier, you type the word __identifier and follow it with the keyword inside parentheses, as in __identifier(template).

You can use this construct any place that an identifier would go. It can be the name of a type, class, or variable. However, each time you use the identifier, you must use the __identifier keyword and parentheses. For example, you might have a class called float:

```
class __identifier(float) {
public:
        int num;
};
```

When you use the class, you would again include the __identifier keyword as __identifier(float) x;.

USE A KEYWORD AS AN IDENTIFIER

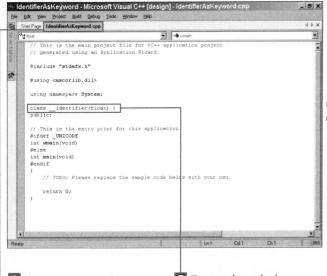

1 Create a new project.

2 Type code to declare a class using a keyword preceded by __identifier and surrounded with parentheses.

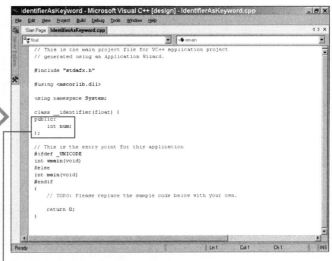

3 Type code to declare the remainder of the class.

Extra

Exercise great care when using the __identifier keyword. It is not intended for general use just so you can use an identifier as a keyword. The reason is that if you use it simply because it is there, you will end up with code that is often unreadable and confusing. The main intent is to allow your software to work with libraries written in other languages that supply types matching a C++ keyword.

If you are going to be using Visual Studio .NET to develop applications in other languages such as Visual Basic or the C# programming language, you can use your C++ knowledge to make sure you do not use names that are keywords in C++. For example, you know that float is a keyword in C++, and therefore should avoid using the name float in Visual Basic, even though it is allowed. This way, if you share your code with others and they will be using C++, you will not force them to use the __identifier keyword.

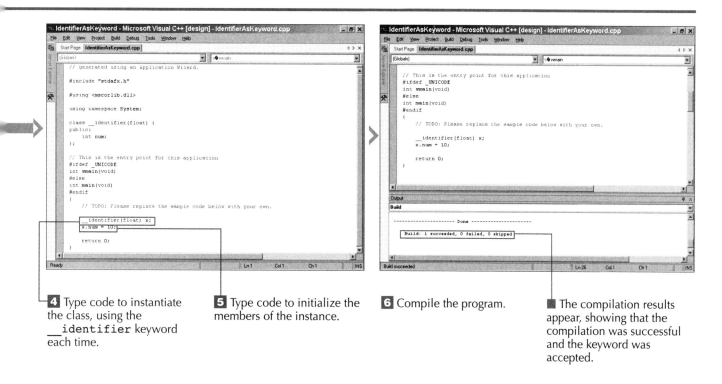

4 Type code to instantiate the class, using the __identifier keyword each time.

5 Type code to initialize the members of the instance.

6 Compile the program.

■ The compilation results appear, showing that the compilation was successful and the keyword was accepted.

DECLARE AN ABSTRACT CLASS

When you build classes, you can get the most out of object-oriented design by supplying a root class from which other classes are derived. Typically, you do not want to create instances of the root class. Instead you want it to be abstract, which means it is not intended to be instantiated. The purpose of such a root class is to define the standard methods, data members, and properties present in all of its derived classes.

To declare an abstract class and guarantee that it cannot be instantiated, precede the class definition with the __abstract keyword, as follows:

```
__abstract class MyRootClass {
      int a;
};
```

You must type the word **class**.

Abstract classes can be either managed or unmanaged classes. To make a managed abstract class, include the __gc

keyword after the __abstract keyword. Otherwise, the class will be unmanaged by default.

If you attempt to instantiate an abstract class using code such as MyRootClass inst;, you will get the error message error C3622: 'MyRootClass': a class declared as '__abstract' cannot be instantiated.

When you are creating your classes, you will often group them together by common traits, and then you will discover that the common traits can typically be put into a single class that provides the code and members for those traits. Generally, then, you will not want to create instances of this class. It would be abstract. For example, if you are writing classes for types of cars, you might have a root class called car that has members common to all types of cars. But you would not actually create an instance of a car. This parallels real life, as any car you see on the road is a type of car; it is not simply a car with no further type of description.

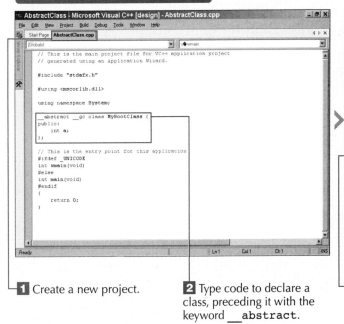

1 Create a new project.

2 Type code to declare a class, preceding it with the keyword **__abstract**.

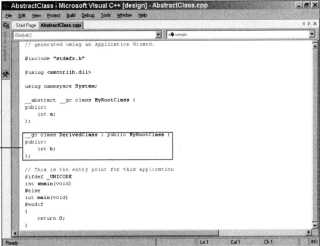

3 Type code to declare a class derived from the **abstract** class.

Extra

Another way to declare an abstract class is to create a pure virtual function. You create a pure virtual function by declaring the function in the class header and following it with =0; as in `virtual void MyFunction() = 0;`. You then supply no code for the function. When you declare a class in this manner, the compiler does not allow you to create an instance of this class. You do not need the `__abstract` keyword in this case. This approach does not use the .NET features, but uses the standard C++ features instead. The advantage of using the `__abstract` keyword instead of creating a pure virtual function is that with the `__abstract` keyword you can supply code for all the functions in your root class. You do not need to leave at least one as a virtual abstract function with no code.

Carefully planning the design of your classes allows you to see that similar classes tend to have similar characteristics. When you see these similarities, you can create a common abstract class from which you derive all the other classes. When you do so, you take advantage of the power of object-oriented design by sharing code and putting it in a common place.

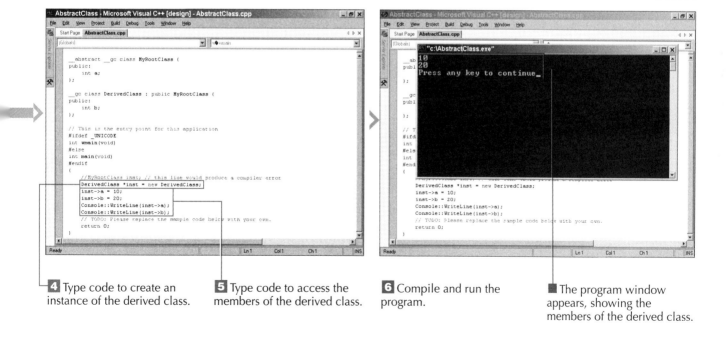

4 Type code to create an instance of the derived class.

5 Type code to access the members of the derived class.

6 Compile and run the program.

■ The program window appears, showing the members of the derived class.

HANDLE UNSUCCESSFUL CASTS

When you attempt to cast from one type to another, you can use the .NET __try_cast keyword to allow for exception handling in your casting. If the cast does not work, the dynamic_cast keyword returns a null-pointer, but __try_cast throws an exception. The __try_cast keyword lets you add an exception handler in which you place error-handling code and you might also inform the user of the error.

When casting between classes, you can generally only cast between a base type and a derived type or vice versa. If you cast outside of the base and derived types, the cast fails. If you use the __try_cast keyword to attempt this cast and the cast fails, it throws an exception. Otherwise the cast proceeds as expected.

The exception to watch for in your catch block is InvalidCastException. This exception class is declared

in the System namespace and derived from Exception, the root class for all .NET exceptions.

To use the __try_cast keyword, you type the variable you want to receive the cast, an equals sign, the __try_cast keyword, the type in angle brackets, and the variable you are casting, as in receivevariable = __try_cast<RecieveType*>(castvariable); .

You put this line in a try block and follow it with a catch block.

Finally, to use the __try_cast keyword, you must turn on RTTI, or run-time type info. Right-click the project in Solutions Explorer and click Properties. In the Properties window, open the C/C++ folder and click Language. Set Enable Run-Time Type Info to true. You must turn on RTTI before compiling your program.

HANDLE UNSUCCESSFUL CASTS

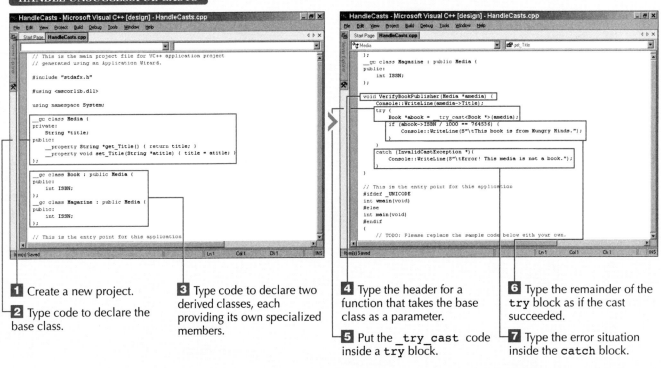

1 Create a new project.

2 Type code to declare the base class.

3 Type code to declare two derived classes, each providing its own specialized members.

4 Type the header for a function that takes the base class as a parameter.

5 Put the __try_cast code inside a try block.

6 Type the remainder of the try block as if the cast succeeded.

7 Type the error situation inside the catch block.

Extra

If you are doing extensive casting, the `__try_cast` keyword provides a good way to check whether the casts succeed. It is always good programming practice to include the proper exception handlers in your code and to anticipate the problems that could occur. In your handler code, you would either notify the user of the problem or fix the problem automatically.

As with any `try/catch` block, you can have multiple `catch` blocks for different exceptions that may be thrown. Although the `__try_cast` keyword will only throw the `InvalidCastException`, you can have other code in the `try` block that may throw other exceptions. For example, you might have code that performs some file input/output. You might also have a `catch` block, then, for a file exception error.

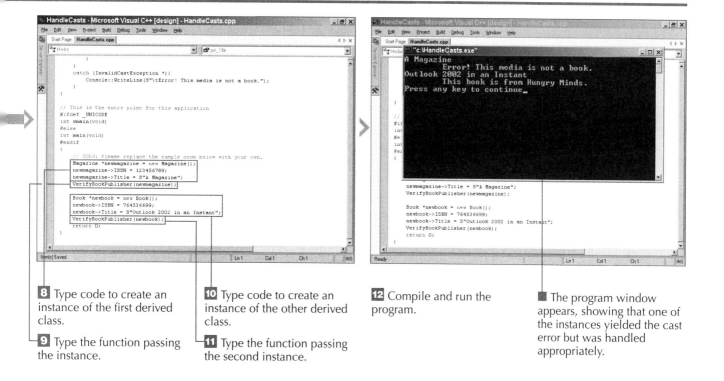

8 Type code to create an instance of the first derived class.

9 Type the function passing the instance.

10 Type code to create an instance of the other derived class.

11 Type the function passing the second instance.

12 Compile and run the program.

■ The program window appears, showing that one of the instances yielded the cast error but was handled appropriately.

.NET PROGRAMMING ENVIRONMENT

The Visual Studio .NET programming environment includes many features for developing programs. Finding your way around is important. Here are what some of the different windows do.

FEATURE	DESCRIPTION
Dragging and Moving Windows	You can drag and drop most windows within the environment . If you drop a window over an existing window, the existing window moves to make room for the window you are moving. However, you can force the window you are moving to occupy a tab within the existing window by carefully dropping it beside the existing tabs at the bottom of the existing window. If the existing window does not have a tab, try dragging the window over the title bar of the existing window.
Solutions Explorer	A solution is a set of projects that can be compiled together. Solutions Explorer is the main window in which you can view and manipulate all the projects within a solution. To create a new project within the same solution, click File ⇨ Add Project ⇨ New Project. To rename a project, right-click the project name within Solutions Explorer and click Rename. To remove a project from the solution but not delete it from the hard drive, right-click the project name within Solutions Explorer and click Remove. If you want to add a project back into the solution or add a project from another solution, click File ⇨ Add Project ⇨ Existing Project.
Output Window	This window contains the output from your compilations and builds. You can click an error line and the source file opens in the source window.
Task List	The Task List is similar to the one in Microsoft Outlook. It contains the errors from your compilations and represents fixes that you must perform. You can add your own tasks to the list to serve as reminders of things you need to do.
Index Window	The Index Window is the main index of the online help system.
Contents Window	The Contents Window provides a table-of-contents view of the online help system.
Search Window	The Search Window is the search view of the online help system, allowing you to search for individual words within the help documents.
Browser Window	The Browser window is actually Internet Explorer embedded in the environment. The online help files are internet HTML files embedded within the help system. The Web toolbar accompanies the browser window. You can perform most of the same tasks here that you do in Internet Explorer. If you type www.yahoo.com in the edit control of this toolbar, the Yahoo! Web site opens inside the Visual Studio .NET. Similarly, when you open an online help page, you can right-click it and click Add to Favorites. From there, if you are running Internet Explorer separately, you can open the online help entry in Internet Explorer by clicking this entry in the Favorites list.
Favorites List	You can also open the same Internet Explorer Favorites list from within the .NET environment by clicking View ⇨ Other Windows ⇨ Favorites.
Object Browser	The object browser is a powerful mechanism through which you can browse all the classes, functions, and variables of your solution. Double-clicking an entry in it takes you to the position in the source code where that entry is defined. You can single-click a class to see its members in the right pane of the window.

NAMESPACES

Several namespaces are available in the .NET platform, each containing numerous classes. To use the classes in the namespace, you either fully-qualify the name, as in `System::IO::File`, or you include a `using namespace` prior to actually using the class name, as in `using namespace System::IO::File;`.

The following list includes the most common namespaces available in the C++ environment, along with some of the classes found in them.

MICROSOFT.WIN32

This namespace includes classes for working with the Registry.

CLASS	DESCRIPTION
Registry	This class allows for traversing the Registry hierarchy.
Registry Key	This class lets you obtain and set individual keys within the system Registry.

SYSTEM

This namespace contains the basic classes, types, and event handlers used throughout the language. It includes many sub-namespaces.

CLASS	DESCRIPTION
Array	This class provides the basic functionality for system arrays, such as sorting and obtaining the size of the array.
Boolean	This is a `__value` structure that supports the use of Boolean values. It mirrors the built-in `bool` type.
Console	This class provides reading and writing to the console window. Its members include `ReadLine` for reading a line of text from the user and `WriteLine` for writing a line of text to the window.
Convert	This class includes the standard functions for converting between different basic types such as between an integer stored as `Int32` and a float stored as `Single`.
DateTime	This is a `__value` structure that allows for the manipulation of dates and times. It includes a `Now` property for obtaining the current date and time and also includes various methods for manipulating the obtained date and time.
Decimal	This class stores large integers for extended arithmetic. The integers can be used in scientific and business applications and can range from an extremely large negative number (such as -79,228,162,514,264,337,593,543,950,335) to an extremely large positive number (such as +79,228,162,514,264,337,593,543,950,335).
Delegate	This class allows a program to reference a method that is in a particular class. This class allows for the use of event processing.
Environment	This class lets you obtain various information about the environment in which the program is running. Examples include the command-line arguments, the username, and the current working directory.

Continued

NAMESPACES (CONTINUED)

CLASS	DESCRIPTION
EventArgs	This is the base class for the arguments passed to an event.
Exception	This is the base class from which all .NET exceptions are derived.
GC	This class controls the .NET garbage collector. For example, a program can force the garbage collector to run by calling the static Collect() method of this class.
Int16, Int32, Int64	These are __value classes that mirror the basic integer types. The number in the name represents the number of bits in the integer. Normally a standard int type corresponds to Int32.
Math	This class contains mathematical functions. Examples include the trig functions Sin, Cos, and Tan, as well as Pow, Min, and Max.
Object	This is the root of every managed __gc class in the system. Almost every class in this chapter derives from Object. The exceptions are the __value classes.
Operating System	This class lets your program determine which platform and version it is running. The platform is one of three values: *WinNT* for Windows NT, Windows 2000, and Windows XP; *Win32S* for early 16-bit Windows operating systems; and *Win32Windows* for Windows 9x versions.
Random	This class provides for random-number generation. Advanced programmers will also find a hash code generator here that they can use for advanced random-number generation.
Single	This is a __value type for mirroring the float type for single-precision floating-point numbers.
String	This is the basic type for string manipulation. See page 297 for more information on string reference.
Timezone	This class includes methods for determining the local time zone of the current computer and whether daylight savings time is in effect.
UInt16, UInt32, UInt64	These classes provide unsigned versions of the Integer classes Int16, Int32, and Int64. Numbers represented by these classes are always positive.

This namespace includes standard data structures for dealing with collections of objects.

CLASS	DESCRIPTION
BitArray	This class allows for sets of true/false bits.
DictionaryBase	This is the base class for data that exists in paired combinations of keys and values. Items are obtained based on the keys.
Queue	This is a standard data structure that allows items to be placed in a list. Items are accessed in a first-in-first-out manner much like a line of people at a ticket booth.
Stack	This is a standard data structure that allows items to be placed in a list. Items are accessed in a last-in-first-out manner, much like a stack of mail sitting on a desk, where mail is added to the stack and letters are taken from the top of the stack.

This namespace contains the basis for the ADO.NET database system. It includes classes `DataSet`, `DataTable`, and `DataView` that allow for managing and viewing data.

This namespace contains the basic classes for manipulating graphics under Windows.

CLASS	DESCRIPTION
Bitmap	This class manages a bitmap image. It includes methods for reading bitmap files of many different formats.
Brush	This class represents a style of filling a geometric figure.
Font	This class represents a font. You can set font name, size, and style, such as italic or bold.
FontFamily	This class is used for obtaining a list of the available fonts installed on the system.
Graphics	This class provides a drawing surface on which you can draw various geometric shapes or a bitmap image.
Icon	This class is for loading an icon from a file.
Pen	This class describes how lines and the perimeters of geometric shapes are drawn.

This namespace includes classes primarily for dealing with time and geography. It includes various calendar classes such as `GregorianCalendar` and `HebrewCalendar`. It also includes a class called `RegionInfo` that provides static data about the region in which the program is currently running. Data includes the currency symbol for the region, a two-letter country code identifier, and whether the region uses the metric system as a standard.

This namespace handles the file operations.

CLASS	DESCRIPTION
BinaryReader and Binary Writer classes	These two classes allow for access to binary data stored in a file.
Directory	This class contains methods for reading the names of files and subdirectories in a directory. It also includes methods for creating, removing, and moving directories, as well as obtaining information about a directory such as its creation time.

Continued

NAMESPACES (CONTINUED)

CLASS	DESCRIPTION
File	This class contains methods for opening, reading, writing, and closing files. It also includes methods for creating FileStream, BinaryReader, BinaryWriter, TextReader, and TextWriter instances for easy access to the information in a file.
FileStream	Instances of this class are generally created by the operations in the File class. It allows data to be read in as a stream of bytes.
Path	This class includes methods for manipulating the names of files, their paths, and their extensions. It does not actually modify any files.
StreamReader	This is a class derived from TextReader that implements the functionality of TextReader. TextReader is an abstract class, so you work with StreamReader instances to access the features of a TextReader.
StreamWriter	This is a class derived from TextWriter that implements the functionality of TextWriter. TextWriter is an abstract class, so you work with StreamWriter instances to access the features of a TextWriter.
TextReader	This class provides the base functionality for the StreamReader class and provides operations such as ReadLine for reading a line of text into a String instance.
TextWriter	This class provides the base functionality for the StreamWriter class and provides operations such as WriteLine for writing a line of text to a file.

This namespace provides a large set of classes for dealing with Internet functionality.

CLASS	DESCRIPTION
Cookie, CookieCollection, CookieContainer	These classes allow a program to manipulate the system cookies. A cookie is a small piece of information that a Web site may store on the computer of a user.
DNS	This class allows for converting host names such as www.microsoft.com to an IP address and vice versa. It does so by attaching to a DNS server and looking up the information.
FileWebRequest	This class allows for accessing files through URLs that start with file://. Typically, Web browsers use this method to read files on a local machine in the local computer zone, outside of the Internet.
HttpWebRequest	This class allows for accessing files remotely using the HTTP protocol, the protocol commonly used by Web browsers. The files are typically on computers elsewhere on the Internet.
WebProxy	A proxy server accepts a request for Web pages, and the server attaches to the remote Web site to obtain the page, passing it down to the local computer. Often large corporations use proxy servers to manage the flow of Web pages through the company. The WebProxy class allows a program to work with the proxy server.

STRING REFERENCE

Strings are a fundamental part of programming, and .NET has introduced a powerful string mechanism that has never been present in C++. The following notes highlight how to perform string-handling features.

DECLARING A STRING CONSTANT

To declare a `String` constant, place the string in quotes and precede it with a capital S, as in `S"This is a String"`. The constant is automatically an instance of the `String` class, and you can perform methods on it just as with any other `String` instance, such as `S"abc"->ToUpper()`.

CONCATENATING STRINGS

If you have multiple `String` instances to combine into a single `String`, the easiest way is to use this trick:

```
String *temp[] = {S"abc", S"def", S"ghi", S"123", S"456"};
```

```
String *mystring = String::Concat(temp);
```

The `String` instance `mystring` will contain the single string `"abcdefghi123456"`.

STRING FUNCTIONS

These functions operate on `String` instances. The functions that modify a string actually do not modify the `String` instance itself. Instead, they return a new `String` instance that has the specified modifications. For example, although `ToUpper()` converts a `String` instance to uppercase, the original `String` instance remains intact, and this function returns a new `String` instance in all uppercase. Generally, you immediately assign the results back to the same pointer you are attempting to modify, as in `mystring = mystring->ToUpper()`.

STRING	DESCRIPTION
CompareTo	Use this method to compare two strings. If the string matches, this method returns 0.
EndsWith	You can test whether a string ends with a certain substring by calling `EndsWith` and passing the substring.
Equals	This method is easier to use than `CompareTo` for a quick test of whether two strings are equal. It returns a Boolean true or false value.
IndexOf	Use this method to find the first position of a character in a string, either from the start or from some place within the string.
PadLeft and PadRight	Use these methods to right- or left-align a string, padding it with spaces or a character.
Remove	Use this method to remove characters from a string. The string itself does not actually change. Instead, this method returns a new `String` instance with the removed characters.
Replace	This method replaces a character within the string with a new character or string.
Split	This method splits a string based on a character that you specify, and it returns an array of `String` instances.
SubString	Use this method to determine a substring that begins at a position you specify and runs for the number of characters that you specify.
ToLower and ToUpper	Use these methods to convert a string to uppercase or lowercase.

WHAT'S ON THE CD-ROM

The CD-ROM disc included in this book contains many useful files that can be used when programming on the .NET platform. You will find files that contain all the sample code used in this book. Before installing any program from a disc, make sure a newer version of the program is not already installed on your computer. For information on installing different versions of the same program, contact the program's manufacturer.

SYSTEM REQUIREMENTS

To use the contents of the CD-ROM, your computer must be equipped with the following hardware and software:

- A PC with a 450-MHz Pentium II or faster processor.
- Microsoft Windows NT 4.0 or Windows 2000.
- At least 128MB of total RAM installed on your computer.
- At least 3 GB of hard drive space for OS and related software for the .NET Platform.
- A CD-ROM drive.
- A monitor capable of displaying at least 800 by 600 pixels (super VGA resolution) with 256 colors.
- A modem with a speed of at least 14,400 bps.

AUTHOR'S SOURCE CODE

For Windows 2000. The CD provides files that contain all the sample code used throughout this book. You can browse these files directly from the CD-ROM, or you can copy them to your hard drive and use them as the basis for your own projects. You should open the files in Visual Studio .NET. To find the files on the CD-ROM, open the D:\SAMPLE folder. To copy the files to your hard drive, just run the installation program D:\SAMPLES.EXE. The files will be placed on your hard drive at C:\C++.NetVB. You will need to have the .NET framework installed on the machine in order to run the samples.

ACROBAT VERSION

This CD-ROM contains an e-version of this book that you can view and search using Adobe Acrobat Reader. You cannot print the pages or copy text from the Acrobat files. If you do not currently have Adobe Acrobat Reader 5 installed, the computer will prompt you to install the software. An evaluation version of Adobe Acrobat Reader is also included on the disc.

INSTALLING AND USING THE SOFTWARE

This CD-ROM disc contains Acrobat Reader. Before installing a program from the CD, you should exit all other programs. In order to use most of the programs, you must accept the license agreement provided with the program. Make sure you read any ReadMe files provided with each program.

Program Versions

Shareware programs are fully functional, free trial versions of copyrighted programs. If you like a particular program, you can register with its author for a nominal fee and receive licenses, enhanced versions, and technical support.

Visual C++ .NET:
Your visual blueprint for
programming on the .NET platform

Freeware programs are free copyrighted games, applications, and utilities. You can copy them to as many computers as you like, but they have no technical support.

GNU software is governed by its own license, which is included inside the folder of the GNU software. There are no restrictions on distribution of this software. See the GNU license for more details.

Trial, demo, or evaluation versions are usually limited either by time or functionality. For example, you may not be able to save projects using these versions.

For your convenience, the software titles on the CD are listed in alphabetic order.

Acrobat Reader
Freeware. For Windows. Acrobat Reader lets you view the online version of this book. For more information on using Adobe Acrobat Reader, see page 300. From Adobe Systems, Inc., .

TROUBLESHOOTING

We tried our best to compile programs that work on most computers with the minimum system requirements. Your computer, however, may differ and some programs may not work properly for some reason.

The two most likely problems are that you do not have enough memory (RAM) for the programs you want to use, or you have other programs running that are affecting installation or running of a program. If you get error messages like Not enough memory or Setup cannot continue, try one or more of these methods and then try using the software again:

- Turn off any anti-virus software.
- Close all running programs.
- In Windows, close the CD-ROM interface and run demos or installations directly from Windows Explorer.
- Have your local computer store add more RAM to your computer.

If you still have trouble installing the items from the CD-ROM, please call the Hungry Minds Customer Service phone number: 800-762-2974 (outside the U.S.: 317-572-3994).

APPENDIX

USING THE E-VERSION OF THE BOOK

You can view C++: Your visual blueprint for programming on the .NET framework on your screen using the CD-ROM included at the back of this book. The CD-ROM allows you to search the contents of each chapter of the book for a specific word or phrase. The CD-ROM also provides a convenient way of keeping the book handy while traveling.

You must install Adobe Acrobat Reader on your computer before you can view the book on the CD-ROM. This program is provided on the disc. Acrobat Reader allows you to view Portable Document Format (PDF) files, which can display

books and magazines on your screen exactly as they appear in printed form.

To view the contents of the book using Acrobat Reader, insert the CD-ROM into your drive. The autorun interface will appear. Navigate to the eBook, and open the book.pdf file. You may be required to install Acrobat Reader 5.0 on your computer, which you can do by following the simple intallation instructions. If you choose to disable the autorun interface, you can open the CD root menu and open the Resources folder, then open the eBook folder. In the window that appears, double-click the eBook.pdf icon.

USING THE E-VERSION OF THE BOOK

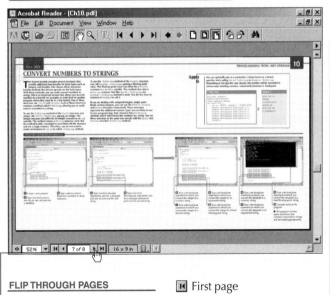

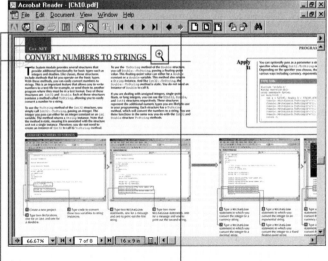

FLIP THROUGH PAGES

■1 Click one of these options to flip through the pages of a section.

⏮ First page
◀ Previous page
▶ Next page
⏭ Last page

ZOOM IN

■1 Click 🔍 to magnify an area of the page.

■2 Click the area of the page you want to magnify.

■ Click one of these options to display the page at 100% magnification (🗔) or to fit the entire page inside the window (🗔).

Visual C++ .NET:
Your visual blueprint for
programming on the .NET platform

Extra

To install Acrobat Reader, insert the CD-ROM disc into a drive. In the screen that appears, click Software. Click Acrobat Reader and then click Install at the bottom of the screen. Then follow the instructions on your screen to install the program.

You can make searching the book more convenient by copying the .pdf files to your own computer. Display the contents of the CD-ROM disc and then copy the PDFs folder from the CD to your hard drive. This allows you to easily access the contents of the book at any time.

Acrobat Reader is a popular and useful program. There are many files available on the Web that are designed to be viewed using Acrobat Reader. Look for files with the .pdf extension. For more information about Acrobat Reader, visit the Web site at www.adobe.com/products/acrobat/readermain.html.

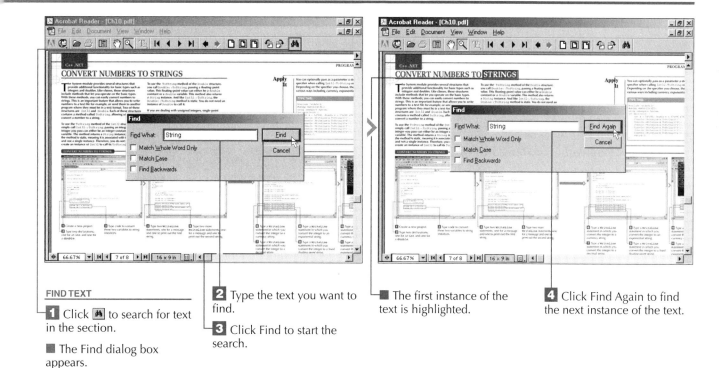

FIND TEXT

■1 Click 🔍 to search for text in the section.

■ The Find dialog box appears.

■2 Type the text you want to find.

■3 Click Find to start the search.

■ The first instance of the text is highlighted.

■4 Click Find Again to find the next instance of the text.

APPENDIX

HUNGRY MINDS, INC.
END-USER LICENSE AGREEMENT

READ THIS. You should carefully read these terms and conditions before opening the software packet(s) included with this book ("Book"). This is a license agreement ("Agreement") between you and Hungry Minds, Inc. ("HMI"). By opening the accompanying software packet(s), you acknowledge that you have read and accept the following terms and conditions. If you do not agree and do not want to be bound by such terms and conditions, promptly return the Book and the unopened software packet(s) to the place you obtained them for a full refund.

1. License Grant. HMI grants to you (either an individual or entity) a nonexclusive license to use one copy of the enclosed software program(s) (collectively, the "Software") solely for your own personal or business purposes on a single computer (whether a standard computer or a workstation component of a multi-user network). The Software is in use on a computer when it is loaded into temporary memory (RAM) or installed into permanent memory (hard disk, CD-ROM, or other storage device). HMI reserves all rights not expressly granted herein.

2. Ownership. HMI is the owner of all right, title, and interest, including copyright, in and to the compilation of the Software recorded on the disk(s) or CD-ROM ("Software Media"). Copyright to the individual programs recorded on the Software Media is owned by the author or other authorized copyright owner of each program. Ownership of the Software and all proprietary rights relating thereto remain with HMI and its licensers.

3. Restrictions On Use and Transfer.

(a) You may only (i) make one copy of the Software for backup or archival purposes, or (ii) transfer the Software to a single hard disk, provided that you keep the original for backup or archival purposes. You may not (i) rent or lease the Software, (ii) copy or reproduce the Software through a LAN or other network system or through any computer subscriber system or bulletin-board system, or (iii) modify, adapt, or create derivative works based on the Software.

(b) You may not reverse engineer, decompile, or disassemble the Software. You may transfer the Software and user documentation on a permanent basis, provided that the transferee agrees to accept the terms and conditions of this Agreement and you retain no copies. If the Software is an update or has been updated, any transfer must include the most recent update and all prior versions.

4. Restrictions on Use of Individual Programs. You must follow the individual requirements and restrictions detailed for each individual program in the What's on the CD-ROM appendix of this Book. These limitations are also contained in the individual license agreements recorded on the Software Media. These limitations may include a requirement that after using the program for a specified period of time, the user must pay a registration fee or discontinue use. By opening the Software packet(s), you will be agreeing to abide by the licenses and restrictions for these individual programs that are detailed in the What's on the CD-ROM appendix and on the Software Media. None of the material on this Software Media or listed in this Book may ever be redistributed, in original or modified form, for commercial purposes.

5. Limited Warranty.

(a) HMI warrants that the Software and Software Media are free from defects in materials and workmanship under normal use for a period of sixty (60) days from the date of purchase of this Book. If HMI receives notification within the warranty period of defects in materials or workmanship, HMI will replace the defective Software Media.

Visual C++ .NET:
Your visual blueprint for
programming on the .NET platform

(b) HMI AND THE AUTHOR OF THE BOOK DISCLAIM ALL OTHER WARRANTIES, EXPRESS OR IMPLIED, INCLUDING WITHOUT LIMITATION IMPLIED WARRANTIES OF MERCHANTABILITY AND FITNESS FOR A PARTICULAR PURPOSE, WITH RESPECT TO THE SOFTWARE, THE PROGRAMS, THE SOURCE CODE CONTAINED THEREIN, AND/OR THE TECHNIQUES DESCRIBED IN THIS BOOK. HMI DOES NOT WARRANT THAT THE FUNCTIONS CONTAINED IN THE SOFTWARE WILL MEET YOUR REQUIREMENTS OR THAT THE OPERATION OF THE SOFTWARE WILL BE ERROR FREE.

(c) This limited warranty gives you specific legal rights, and you may have other rights that vary from jurisdiction to jurisdiction.

6. Remedies.

(a) HMI's entire liability and your exclusive remedy for defects in materials and workmanship shall be limited to replacement of the Software Media, which may be returned to HMI with a copy of your receipt at the following address: Software Media Fulfillment Department, Attn.: *Visual C++ .NET: Your visual blueprint for programming on the .NET platform*, Hungry Minds, Inc., 10475 Crosspoint Blvd., Indianapolis, IN 46256, or call 1-800-762-2974. Please allow four to six weeks for delivery. This Limited Warranty is void if failure of the Software Media has resulted from accident, abuse, or misapplication. Any replacement Software Media will be warranted for the remainder of the original warranty period or thirty (30) days, whichever is longer.

(b) In no event shall HMI or the author be liable for any damages whatsoever (including without limitation damages for loss of business profits, business interruption, loss of business information, or any other pecuniary loss) arising from the use of or inability to use the Book or the Software, even if HMI has been advised of the possibility of such damages.

(c) Because some jurisdictions do not allow the exclusion or limitation of liability for consequential or incidental damages, the above limitation or exclusion may not apply to you.

7. U.S. Government Restricted Rights. Use, duplication, or disclosure of the Software for or on behalf of the United States of America, its agencies and/or instrumentalities (the "U.S. Government") is subject to restrictions as stated in paragraph (c)(1)(ii) of the Rights in Technical Data and Computer Software clause of DFARS 252.227-7013, or subparagraphs (c) (1) and (2) of the Commercial Computer Software - Restricted Rights clause at FAR 52.227-19, and in similar clauses in the NASA FAR supplement, as applicable.

8. General. This Agreement constitutes the entire understanding of the parties and revokes and supersedes all prior agreements, oral or written, between them and may not be modified or amended except in a writing signed by both parties hereto that specifically refers to this Agreement. This Agreement shall take precedence over any other documents that may be in conflict herewith. If any one or more provisions contained in this Agreement are held by any court or tribunal to be invalid, illegal, or otherwise unenforceable, each and every other provision shall remain in full force and effect.

APPENDIX

GNU GENERAL PUBLIC LICENSE

Version 2, June 1991

PREAMBLE

The licenses for most software are designed to take away your freedom to share and change it. By contrast, the GNU General Public License is intended to guarantee your freedom to share and change free software—to make sure the software is free for all its users. This General Public License applies to most of the Free Software Foundation's software and to any other program whose authors commit to using it. (Some other Free Software Foundation software is covered by the GNU Library General Public License instead.) You can apply it to your programs, too.

When we speak of free software, we are referring to freedom, not price. Our General Public Licenses are designed to make sure that you have the freedom to distribute copies of free software (and charge for this service if you wish), that you receive source code or can get it if you want it, that you can change the software or use pieces of it in new free programs; and that you know you can do these things.

To protect your rights, we need to make restrictions that forbid anyone to deny you these rights or to ask you to surrender the rights. These restrictions translate to certain responsibilities for you if you distribute copies of the software, or if you modify it.

For example, if you distribute copies of such a program, whether gratis or for a fee, you must give the recipients all the rights that you have. You must make sure that they, too, receive or can get the source code. And you must show them these terms so they know their rights.

We protect your rights with two steps: (1) copyright the software, and (2) offer you this license which gives you legal permission to copy, distribute and/or modify the software.

Also, for each author's protection and ours, we want to make certain that everyone understands that there is no warranty for this free software. If the software is modified by someone else and passed on, we want its recipients to know that what they have is not the original, so that any problems introduced by others will not reflect on the original authors' reputations.

Finally, any free program is threatened constantly by software patents. We wish to avoid the danger that redistributors of a free program will individually obtain patent licenses, in effect making the program proprietary. To prevent this, we have made it clear that any patent must be licensed for everyone's free use or not licensed at all.

The precise terms and conditions for copying, distribution and modification follow.

TERMS AND CONDITIONS FOR COPYING, DISTRIBUTION AND MODIFICATION

0. This License applies to any program or other work which contains a notice placed by the copyright holder saying it may be distributed under the terms of this General Public License. The "Program", below, refers to any such program or work, and a "work based on the Program" means either the Program or any derivative work under copyright law: that is to say, a work containing the Program or a portion of it, either verbatim or with modifications and/or translated into another language. (Hereinafter, translation is included without limitation in the term "modification".) Each licensee is addressed as "you".

    Activities other than copying, distribution and modification are not covered by this License; they are outside its scope. The act of running the Program is not restricted, and the output from the Program is covered only if its contents constitute a work based on the Program (independent of having been made by running the Program). Whether that is true depends on what the Program does.

1. You may copy and distribute verbatim copies of the Program's source code as you receive it, in any medium, provided that you conspicuously and appropriately publish on each copy an appropriate

VISUAL C++.NET:
Your visual blueprint for
programming on the .NET platform

copyright notice and disclaimer of warranty; keep intact all the notices that refer to this License and to the absence of any warranty; and give any other recipients of the Program a copy of this License along with the Program.

You may charge a fee for the physical act of transferring a copy, and you may at your option offer warranty protection in exchange for a fee.

2. You may modify your copy or copies of the Program or any portion of it, thus forming a work based on the Program, and copy and distribute such modifications or work under the terms of Section 1 above, provided that you also meet all of these conditions:

a) You must cause the modified files to carry prominent notices stating that you changed the files and the date of any change.

b) You must cause any work that you distribute or publish, that in whole or in part contains or is derived from the Program or any part thereof, to be licensed as a whole at no charge to all third parties under the terms of this License.

c) If the modified program normally reads commands interactively when run, you must cause it, when started running for such interactive use in the most ordinary way, to print or display an announcement including an appropriate copyright notice and a notice that there is no warranty (or else, saying that you provide a warranty) and that users may redistribute the program under these conditions, and telling the user how to view a copy of this License. (Exception: if the Program itself is interactive but does not normally print such an announcement, your work based on the Program is not required to print an announcement.)

These requirements apply to the modified work as a whole. If identifiable sections of that work are not derived from the Program, and can be reasonably considered independent and separate works in themselves, then this License, and its terms, do not apply to those sections when you distribute them as separate works. But when you distribute the same sections as part of a whole which is a work based on the Program, the distribution of the whole must be

on the terms of this License, whose permissions for other licensees extend to the entire whole, and thus to each and every part regardless of who wrote it.

Thus, it is not the intent of this section to claim rights or contest your rights to work written entirely by you; rather, the intent is to exercise the right to control the distribution of derivative or collective works based on the Program. In addition, mere aggregation of another work not based on the Program with the Program (or with a work based on the Program) on a volume of a storage or distribution medium does not bring the other work under the scope of this License.

3. You may copy and distribute the Program (or a work based on it, under Section 2) in object code or executable form under the terms of Sections 1 and 2 above provided that you also do one of the following:

a) Accompany it with the complete corresponding machine-readable source code, which must be distributed under the terms of Sections 1 and 2 above on a medium customarily used for software interchange; or,

b) Accompany it with a written offer, valid for at least three years, to give any third party, for a charge no more than your cost of physically performing source distribution, a complete machine-readable copy of the corresponding source code, to be distributed under the terms of Sections 1 and 2 above on a medium customarily used for software interchange; or,

c) Accompany it with the information you received as to the offer to distribute corresponding source code. (This alternative is allowed only for noncommercial distribution and only if you received the program in object code or executable form with such an offer, in accord with Subsection b above.)

The source code for a work means the preferred form of the work for making modifications to it. For an executable work, complete source code means all the source code for all modules it contains, plus any associated interface definition files, plus the scripts used to control compilation and installation of the executable. However, as a special exception, the source code distributed need not include anything that is normally distributed (in either source or binary form) with the major components (compiler, kernel, and so on) of the operating system on which the executable runs, unless that component itself accompanies the executable.

If distribution of executable or object code is made by offering access to copy from a designated place, then offering equivalent access to copy the source code from the same place counts as distribution of the source code, even though third parties are not compelled to copy the source along with the object code.

4. You may not copy, modify, sublicense, or distribute the Program except as expressly provided under this License. Any attempt otherwise to copy, modify, sublicense or distribute the Program is void, and will automatically terminate your rights under this License. However, parties who have received copies, or rights, from you under this License will not have their licenses terminated so long as such parties remain in full compliance.

5. You are not required to accept this License, since you have not signed it. However, nothing else grants you permission to modify or distribute the Program or its derivative works. These actions are prohibited by law if you do not accept this License. Therefore, by modifying or distributing the Program (or any work based on the Program), you indicate your acceptance of this License to do so, and all its terms and conditions for copying, distributing or modifying the Program or works based on it.

6. Each time you redistribute the Program (or any work based on the Program), the recipient automatically receives a license from the original licensor to copy, distribute or modify the Program subject to these terms and conditions. You may not impose any further restrictions on the recipients' exercise of the rights granted herein. You are not responsible for enforcing compliance by third parties to this License.

7. If, as a consequence of a court judgment or allegation of patent infringement or for any other reason (not limited to patent issues), conditions are imposed on you (whether by court order, agreement or otherwise) that contradict the conditions of this License, they do not excuse you from the conditions of this License. If

you cannot distribute so as to satisfy simultaneously your obligations under this License and any other pertinent obligations, then as a consequence you may not distribute the Program at all. For example, if a patent license would not permit royalty-free redistribution of the Program by all those who receive copies directly or indirectly through you, then the only way you could satisfy both it and this License would be to refrain entirely from distribution of the Program.

If any portion of this section is held invalid or unenforceable under any particular circumstance, the balance of the section is intended to apply and the section as a whole is intended to apply in other circumstances.

It is not the purpose of this section to induce you to infringe any patents or other property right claims or to contest validity of any such claims; this section has the sole purpose of protecting the integrity of the free software distribution system, which is implemented by public license practices. Many people have made generous contributions to the wide range of software distributed through that system in reliance on consistent application of that system; it is up to the author/donor to decide if he or she is willing to distribute software through any other system and a licensee cannot impose that choice.

This section is intended to make thoroughly clear what is believed to be a consequence of the rest of this License.

8. If the distribution and/or use of the Program is restricted in certain countries either by patents or by copyrighted interfaces, the original copyright holder who places the Program under this License may add an explicit geographical distribution limitation excluding those countries, so that distribution is permitted only in or among countries not thus excluded. In such case, this License incorporates the limitation as if written in the body of this License.

9. The Free Software Foundation may publish revised and/or new versions of the General Public License from time to time. Such new versions will be similar in spirit to the present version, but may differ in detail to address new problems or concerns.

VISUAL C++.NET:™
Your visual blueprint for
programming on the .NET platform

Each version is given a distinguishing version number. If the Program specifies a version number of this License which applies to it and "any later version", you have the option of following the terms and conditions either of that version or of any later version published by the Free Software Foundation. If the Program does not specify a version number of this License, you may choose any version ever published by the Free Software Foundation.

10. If you wish to incorporate parts of the Program into other free programs whose distribution conditions are different, write to the author to ask for permission. For software which is copyrighted by the Free Software Foundation, write to the Free Software Foundation; we sometimes make exceptions for this. Our decision will be guided by the two goals of preserving the free status of all derivatives of our free software and of promoting the sharing and reuse of software generally.

NO WARRANTY

11. BECAUSE THE PROGRAM IS LICENSED FREE OF CHARGE, THERE IS NO WARRANTY FOR THE PROGRAM, TO THE EXTENT PERMITTED BY APPLICABLE LAW. EXCEPT WHEN OTHERWISE STATED IN WRITING THE COPYRIGHT HOLDERS AND/OR OTHER PARTIES PROVIDE THE PROGRAM "AS IS" WITHOUT WARRANTY OF ANY KIND, EITHER EXPRESSED OR IMPLIED, INCLUDING, BUT NOT LIMITED TO, THE IMPLIED WARRANTIES OF MERCHANTABILITY AND FITNESS FOR A PARTICULAR PURPOSE. THE ENTIRE RISK AS TO THE QUALITY AND PERFORMANCE OF THE PROGRAM IS WITH YOU. SHOULD THE PROGRAM PROVE DEFECTIVE, YOU ASSUME THE COST OF ALL NECESSARY SERVICING, REPAIR OR CORRECTION.

12. IN NO EVENT UNLESS REQUIRED BY APPLICABLE LAW OR AGREED TO IN WRITING WILL ANY COPYRIGHT HOLDER, OR ANY OTHER PARTY WHO MAY MODIFY AND/OR REDISTRIBUTE THE PROGRAM AS PERMITTED ABOVE, BE LIABLE TO YOU FOR DAMAGES, INCLUDING ANY GENERAL, SPECIAL, INCIDENTAL OR CONSEQUENTIAL DAMAGES ARISING OUT OF THE USE OR INABILITY TO USE THE PROGRAM (INCLUDING BUT NOT LIMITED TO LOSS OF DATA OR DATA BEING RENDERED INACCURATE OR LOSSES SUSTAINED BY YOU OR THIRD PARTIES OR A FAILURE OF THE PROGRAM TO OPERATE WITH ANY OTHER PROGRAMS), EVEN IF SUCH HOLDER OR OTHER PARTY HAS BEEN ADVISED OF THE POSSIBILITY OF SUCH DAMAGES.

END OF TERMS AND CONDITIONS

INDEX

Visual C++ .NET
Your visual blueprint for
programming on the .NET platform

Visual C++ .NET
Your visual blueprint for
programming on the .NET platform

INDEX

Visual C++ .NET
Your visual blueprint for
programming on the .NET platform

INDEX

G

H

I

Visual C++ .NET
Your visual blueprint for
programming on the .NET platform

INDEX

Visual C++ .NET
Your visual blueprint for
programming on the .NET platform

INDEX

strings and, 148
structures and, 46, 51, 52
working with, 80–81
polymorphism, 60, 126–127
Pop method, 172
popping items, from stacks, 172
PrintDialog class, 250–251
PrintDialog dialog box, 250–251
printing
  dialog boxes for, 250–251
  nested classes and, 116–117
PrintPage event, 251
printStatus method, 126
private interfaces
  compiler errors and, 113
  creating classes and, 96–97
  derived classes and, 120
  functions and, 119
  member variables and, 102–103
  methods and, 107
  structures and, 55
private keyword, 97
ProcessInventory function, 48
programs traces, 10
ProgressBar class, 226
ProgressBar control, 226–227
Project Properties dialog box, 60
projects
  adding files to, 11
  build process for, 9–10
  described, 3
  files for, location of, 4
  opening, 5
  starting, 6, 9–10
Properties command, 67
Properties Window, 190
_property keyword, 278–279
Property Pages dialog box, 63, 67
protected interface, 119, 122–123
protected keyword, 122
prototypes, 30–31
public interfaces
  creating classes and, 96–97
  described, 112, 119
  derived classes and, 120
  initializing base classes and, 122–123
  member variables and, 102

methods and, 107
  polymorphism and, 126
  static variables and, 104
public keyword, 97
pure abstract functions, 128
Push method, 172

Q

question mark (?), 196
Queue class, 173, 294
Quick Watch command, 141
QuickWatch dialog box, 141
QuickWatch window, 141, 143
quit command, 197

R

RadioButton, 216–217
RadioButton controls, 216
Random class, 294
random-access memory (RAM). *See* memory
Read method, 202
ReadLine method, 188, 196–198
ReadOnly property, 228
ReadToEnd method, 188
Rectangle class, 96
redirection operator, 191
Redo menu item, 240
RedoActionName property, 240
references
  casts and, 79
  const_cast keyword and, 72
  conversion of, 65
  dynamic_cast operator and, 69
  passing parameters by, 85–86
reinterpret_cast operator, 58–59
Release build process, 10
Remove method, 145
RemoveAt method, 222
rename method, 199
Replace command, 6
Replace method, 145, 297
RestoreDirectory property, 245
Retry button, 253
return keyword, 88
return statement, 29, 88
Rich Text Format (RTF), 238–241
RichEditBoxRedo method, 240

Visual C++ .NET
Your visual blueprint for
programming on the .NET platform

INDEX

Visual C++ .NET
Your visual blueprint for
programming on the .NET platform

Read Less – Learn More™

Visual

The visual alternative to learning complex computer topics

New Series!

For experienced computer users, developers, network professionals who learn best visually.

Extra

Apply It

"Apply It" and "Extra" provide ready-to-run code and useful tips.

Title	ISBN	Price
Active Server™ Pages 3.0: Your visual blueprint for developing interactive Web sites	0-7645-3472-6	$26.99
ASP.NET: Your visual blueprint for creating Web applications on the .NET Framework	0-7645-3617-6	$26.99
C#: Your visual blueprint for building .NETapplications	0-7645-3601-X	$26.99
Excel Programming: Your visual blueprint for building interactive spreadsheets	0-7645-3646-X	$26.99
Flash™ ActionScript: Your visual blueprint for creating Flash™-enhanced Web sites	0-7645-3657-5	$26.99
HTML: Your visual blueprint for designing effective Web pages	0-7645-3471-8	$26.99
Java™: Your visual blueprint for building portable Java programs	0-7645-3543-9	$26.99
Java™ and XML: Your visual blueprint for creating Java™ enhanced Web programs	0-765-36830-4	$26.99
JavaScript™: Your visual blueprint for building dynamic Web pages	0-7645-4730-5	$26.99
JavaServer™ Pages: Your visual blueprint for designing dynamic content with JSP	0-7645-3542-0	$26.99
Linux®: Your visual blueprint to the Linux platform	0-7645-3481-5	$26.99
Perl: Your visual blueprint for building Perl scripts	0-7645-3478-5	$26.99
PHP: Your visual blueprint for creating open source, server-side content	0-7645-3561-7	$26.99
Unix®: Your visual blueprint to the universe of Unix	0-7645-3480-7	$26.99
Visual Basic® .NET: Your visual blueprint for building versatile programs on the .NET Framework	0-7645-3649-4	$26.99
Visual C++® .NET: Your visual blueprint for programming on the .NET platform	0-7645-3664-3	$26.99
XML: Your visual blueprint for building expert Web pages	0-7645-3477-7	$26.99

Over 10 million *Visual* books in print!

with these two-color Visual™ guides

The Complete Visual Reference

"Master It" tips provide additional topic coverage.

Title	ISBN	Price
Master Active Directory™ VISUALLY™	0-7645-3425-4	$39.99
Master Microsoft® Access 2000 VISUALLY™	0-7645-6048-4	$39.99
Master Microsoft® Office 2000 VISUALLY™	0-7645-6050-6	$39.99
Master Microsoft® Word 2000 VISUALLY™	0-7645-6046-8	$39.99
Master Office 97 VISUALLY™	0-7645-6036-0	$39.99
Master Photoshop® 5.5 VISUALLY™	0-7645-6045-X	$39.99
Master Red Hat® Linux® VISUALLY™	0-7645-3436-X	$39.99
Master VISUALLY™ Adobe® Photoshop®, Illustrator®, Premiere®, and After Effects®	0-7645-3668-0	$39.99
Master VISUALLY™ Dreamweaver® 4 and Flash™ 5	0-7645-0855-5	$39.99
Master VISUALLY™ FrontPage® 2002	0-7645-3580-3	$39.99
Master VISUALLY™ HTML 4 & XHTML™ 1	0-7645-3454-8	$39.99
Master VISUALLY™ Microsoft® Windows® Me Millennium Edition	0-7645-3496-3	$39.99
Master VISUALLY™ Office XP	0-7645-3599-4	$39.99
Master VISUALLY™ Photoshop® 6	0-7645-3541-2	$39.99
Master VISUALLY™ Web Design	0-7645-3610-9	$39.99
Master VISUALLY™ Windows® 2000 Server	0-7645-3426-2	$39.99
Master VISUALLY™ Windows® XP	0-7645-3621-4	$39.99
Master Windows® 95 VISUALLY™	0-7645-6024-7	$39.99
Master Windows® 98 VISUALLY™	0-7645-6034-4	$39.99
Master Windows® 2000 Professional VISUALLY™	0-7645-3421-1	$39.99

ORDER FORM

TRADE & INDIVIDUAL ORDERS

Phone: **(800) 762-2974**
or **(317) 572-3993**
FAX : **(800) 550-2747**
or **(317) 572-4002**

EDUCATIONAL ORDERS & DISCOUNTS

Phone: **(800) 434-2086**
FAX : **(317) 572-4005**

CORPORATE ORDERS FOR VISUAL™ SERIES

Phone: **(800) 469-6616**
FAX : **(905) 890-9434**

Qty	ISBN	Title	Price	Total

Shipping & Handling Charges

	Description	First book	Each add'l. book	Total
Domestic	Normal	$4.50	$1.50	$
	Two Day Air	$8.50	$2.50	$
	Overnight	$18.00	$3.00	$
International	Surface	$8.00	$8.00	$
	Airmail	$16.00	$16.00	$
	DHL Air	$17.00	$17.00	$

Subtotal _____

CA residents add
applicable sales tax _____

IN, MA and MD
residents add
5% sales tax _____

IL residents add
6.25% sales tax _____

RI residents add
7% sales tax _____

TX residents add
8.25% sales tax _____

Shipping _____

Total _____

Ship to:

Name _____

Address _____

Company _____

City/State/Zip _____

Daytime Phone _____

Payment: ☐ Check to Hungry Minds (US Funds Only)
☐ Visa ☐ MasterCard ☐ American Express

Card # _____ Exp. _____ Signature _____

Hungry Minds™

maranGraphics®